DATE DUE

NIETZSCHE
Critical Assessments

Routledge Critical Assessments of Leading Philosophers

Already published

SOCRATES
JOHN LOCKE
FRIEDRICH A. HAYEK
NOAM CHOMSKY
RENÉ DESCARTES
JEREMY BENTHAM
J.S. MILL
THOMAS HOBBES
IMMANUEL KANT
JOHN DEWEY
KARL MARX'S SOCIAL AND POLITICAL THOUGHT
GEORGE BERKELEY
MARTIN HEIDEGGER
G.W.F. HEGEL
G.W. LEIBNIZ
DAVID HUME
PLATO

NIETZSCHE
Critical Assessments

**Edited by Daniel W. Conway
with Peter S. Groff**

**VOLUME III
ON MORALITY AND THE ORDER OF RANK**

London and New York

First published 1998
by Routledge
11 New Fetter Lane, London EC4P 4EE

Simultaneously published in the USA and Canada
by Routledge
29 West 35th Street, New York, NY 10001

© 1998 Daniel W. Conway: introduction and selection of editorial matter
Individual chapters © 1998 the respective authors

Typeset in Times by RefineCatch Limited, Bungay, Suffolk
Printed and bound in Great Britain by
TJ International Ltd, Padstow, Cornwall

British Library Cataloguing in Publication Data
A catalogue record for this book is available from the British Library

Library of Congress Cataloging in Publication Data
Nietzsche : critical assessments / edited by Daniel W. Conway.
        p.   cm.
     Includes bibliographical references.
     Contents: v. 1. Incipit Zarathustra / Incipit tragoedia: art, music,
representation, and style – v. 2. The world as will to power – and
nothing else?: metaphysics and epistemology – v. 3. On morality –
v. 4. The last man and the overman: Nietzsche's politics.
     1. Nietzsche, Friedrich Wilhelm, 1844–1900.   I. Conway, Daniel W.
B3317.N492   1998
193—dc21   97–29031
                                                                CIP

ISBN 0–415–13561–3 (set)
Volume I: 0–415–13562–1
Volume II: 0–415–13563–X
Volume III: 0–415–13564–8
Volume IV: 0–415–13565–6

Contents

Introduction

Morality – no longer the expression of the conditions for the life and growth of a people, no longer its most basic instinct of life, but become abstract, become the antithesis of life – morality as the systematic degradation of the imagination, as the 'evil eye' for all things.

(*The Antichrist(ian)*, Section 25)

I negate a type of morality that has become prevalent and predominant as morality itself – the morality of decadence or, more concretely, Christian morality. . . . Morality – the idiosyncrasy of decadents, with the ulterior motive of revenging oneself against life – successfully.

(*Ecce Homo*, 'Why I am a Destiny,' Section 7)

Nietzsche is perhaps best known to his popular audiences for his destructive, iconoclastic contributions to the Western moral tradition. Alternately describing himself as an 'immoralist,' an 'anti-moralist,' and a willing émigré 'beyond good and evil,' he reserves his greatest enmity for the dominant teachings and institutions of Christian morality. In various formulations throughout his philosophical career, he angrily vows to destroy the 'herd' morality of Christianity and to dismantle the supporting apparatus of the metaphysics of morals.

But Nietzsche's full contribution to the Western moral tradition is in fact more complicated, and difficult to reckon, than this popular interpretation would suggest. In addition to his widely influential exposé of the calumnies perpetrated by Christian morality, he also formulates a positive, constructive agenda. As he famously remarks, the logical relation that binds destruction and creation is simply irresistible:

If a temple is to be erected *a temple must be destroyed*: that is the law – let anyone who can show me a case in which it is not fulfilled![1]

As this passage suggests, Nietzsche's unrelenting attack on sundry permutations of 'slave' or 'herd' morality is intended to serve the greater goal of contributing to the founding and renewal of alternative moralities. Although he wavers with respect to the extent of his own direct participation in erecting these new 'temples,' his indirect contributions are nevertheless impressive. One prominent contribution to this constructive goal is his attempt to restore to morality a misplaced element of multiplicity and variety, such that there might flourish as many moralities as there exist types of human beings. In fact, he regularly reminds his readers that the type of morality that he opposes is only one among several possible moralities:

> *Morality in Europe today is herd animal morality* – in other words, as we understand it, merely *one* type of human morality beside which, before which, and after which many other types, above all *higher* moralities, are or ought to be possible. But this morality resists such a 'possibility,' such an 'ought' with all its power: it says stubbornly and inexorably, 'I am morality itself, and nothing besides is morality.'[2]

Included among these '*higher* moralities' are those that Nietzsche reserves for exemplary human beings, those who, by dint of their *übermenschlich* regimen of self-experimentation, might contribute to the extant complement of human virtues. These 'higher moralities' actually aim at their own self-overcoming, in order that their adherents might eventually 'return to nature,' i.e., live without the constraints of any morality whatsoever.

Toward this end of acknowledging viable alternatives to the 'herd animal morality,' Nietzsche marshals his creative energies to promote a moral pluralism, which would be best articulated, he believes, in the hierarchical organization of an aristocratic society. The greatest danger of Christian morality, as of all forms of 'herd' morality, lies in its nihilistic insistence that all (or most) human beings must prostrate themselves before a single, universally binding moral law. This sort of moral monism, Nietzsche believes, merely reduces humankind to its lowest common denominator, forcing all human types to lie in a Procrustean bed of homogeneous design. The logical outcome of moral monism is succinctly captured in Zarathustra's cautionary tale of the nodding, blinking 'last man,' who has altogether lost the will to improve and perfect himself.

But Nietzsche is not interested in promoting moral pluralism simply to honor diversity for its own sake. As we have seen, he also believes that this plurality should foster the emergence of specific kinds of morality, especially those moralities that will most likely enable the nurture and development of the highest human exemplars. Indeed, another of Nietzsche's constructive contributions to the Western moral tradition is his campaign to create the cultural conditions under which there might transpire a renascence of the 'noble' morality, i.e., a morality that originates in an immediate, pre-reflective proclamation of one's own native 'goodness.' According to Nietzsche, this originary proclamation subsequently emanates outward, to bestow 'goodness' on everything that one is, owns, covets, and esteems. This originary act of 'noble' self-valorization would stand in sharp contrast to the originary self-hatred that motivates all forms of 'slave' morality. Unable to confer non-derivative 'goodness' upon their broken, empty souls, the 'slaves' must first locate originary 'evil' in an external world that they perceive to be hostile toward them; only then can they deem themselves 'good,' in contradistinction to the 'evil' that surrounds them. Their 'goodness' is confirmed, moreover, by the suffering and injustice inflicted upon them by the hostile external world. This necromantic transformation of their besetting weaknesses into beatific virtues thus fuels what Nietzsche calls the 'slave revolt in morality,' whereby the 'slaves' fashion a counter-morality from the abundant raw materials of their own suffering, resentment, and dispossession. The 'slaves' thereby gain their (psychological) revenge on the 'nobles,' claiming for themselves a final, definitive victory to be transacted in a metaphysical afterworld.

While it would be both anachronistic and fatuous for Nietzsche to attempt to renew the 'noble' lineage depicted in *On the Genealogy of Morals* (1887), he nevertheless believes that specific 'noble' modifications of the dominant 'slave' morality are possible. Indeed, since the renascence of a genuinely 'noble' form of morality would very likely outstrip the depleted resources of modernity, he turns in his post-Zarathustran writings to the more modest task of experimenting with quasi-noble permutations of the dominant slave morality. The successful implementation of these 'noble' modifications to the 'slave' morality might signal, for example, the overcoming (or weakening) of the pathogenic guilt that continues to sap humankind of its native vitality.

Although it clearly lies beyond his creative and recuperative faculties to heal souls sundered by guilt, it may be possible for him to contribute to the development of mutant strains of slave morality, which effectively would turn their corrosive power against its own source and preconditions. One such experiment might involve educating individuals to direct their copious resentment against their own prevailing sense of guilt. In a passage pregnant with political promise, Nietzsche allows that

> Man has all too long had an 'evil eye' for his natural inclinations, so that they have finally become inseparable from his 'bad conscience.' An attempt at the reverse would *in itself* be possible – but who is strong enough for it? – that is, to wed the bad conscience to all the *unnatural* inclinations, all those aspirations to the beyond, to that which runs counter to sense, instinct, nature, animal, in short all ideals hitherto, which are one and all hostile to life and ideals that slander the world.[3]

Although such experiments are unlikely to redeem the sense of indebtedness that haunts most human beings and drains their creative energies, they may nevertheless enable humankind to survive the twilight of the idols, until such time as a 'transvaluation of all values' becomes truly possible.

Nietzsche's diverse contributions to the Western moral tradition are captured by the slogan that he selects for the title of his first post-Zarathustran book: *beyond good and evil*. This slogan evokes multiple meanings and resonances, which collectively convey the range and daring of Nietzsche's moral project. In its most straightforward sense, this slogan publicly announces his intention to move beyond the stultifying moral monism that prevails in the West, toward a moral pluralism that both reflects and nurtures the (potentially) rich diversity of human types. He consequently insists that

> Moralities must be forced to bow first of all before the *order of rank*; their presumption must be brought home to their conscience – until they finally reach agreement that it is *immoral* to say: 'what is right for one is fair for the other.'[4]

Nietzsche's endorsement of this provocative slogan furthermore announces his intention to challenge and subvert the guiding dualism of 'slave' morality. While the 'slave' is physiologically constituted to divide the world into the polar categories of *good* (*gut*) and *evil* (*böse*), the 'noble' morality operates under the guiding dichotomy between *good* (*gut*) and *bad* (*schlecht*). To move beyond good and evil would therefore involve the transcendence of slave morality, especially in its dominant Christianized dispositions, but not necessarily the transcendence of morality itself. To abandon altogether the enterprise of morality would be to confirm the legitimacy of the 'slave' morality, which gains its peculiar authority only as a *faute de mieux*, only by crowding out and suffocating all competing forms of morality. Rather than concede the enterprise of morality to the monopolistic sprawl of the 'slave' morality, Nietzsche vows instead to cultivate a cultural space within which other, more 'noble' forms of morality might be allowed to take root and flourish. Moving 'beyond good and evil,' that is, would not necessarily require us also to move 'beyond good and bad.'

By documenting the extent of the damage wrought by the 'slave' morality – especially through its perverse reliance on the self-destructive power of guilt – Nietzsche thus hopes to inaugurate a reversal of the 'slave revolt in morality.' With respect to his plan to engineer the *self*-overcoming of Christian morality, he is both uncharacteristically optimistic and suspiciously dialectical:

> All great things bring about their own destruction through an act of self-overcoming [*Selbstaufhebung*]: thus the law of Life will have it, the law of the necessity of 'self-overcoming' [*,Selbstüberwindung'*] in the nature of Life – the lawgiver himself eventually receives the call: '*patere legem, quam*

ipse tulisti.' In this way Christianity *as a dogma* was destroyed by its own morality; in the same way Christianity *as morality* must now perish, too: we stand on the threshold of *this* event. After Christian truthfulness has drawn one inference after another, it must end by drawing its *most striking inference*, its inference *against* itself; this will happen, however, when it poses the question '*what is the meaning of all will to truth?*'[5]

A third, and equally important, resonance of the slogan *beyond good and evil* is suggested by the following passage from *Twilight of the Idols*:

> My demand upon the philosopher is known, that he take his stand *beyond* good and evil and leave the illusion of moral judgment *beneath* himself. This demand follows from an insight which I was the first to formulate: that *there are altogether no moral facts.* . . . Morality is mere sign language, mere symptomatology: one must know what it is all about to be able to profit from it.[6]

As this passage suggests, Nietzsche hopes to replace the folk metaphysics of morality – complete with its naive belief in 'will,' 'agency,' 'causality,' 'responsibility,' 'guilt,' and other such spectral atavisms of the nonage of humankind – with the superior, post-moral ontology that he associates with his teaching of the will to power. Toward this end, he attempts to replace the conventional vocabulary of morality with the revolutionary vocabulary of *symptomatology*. According to the linguistic transformation that he pioneers, moral 'facts' are summarily reduced to physiological signs and symptoms. That a sinner bears witness to the terrors of 'hell' or 'eternal damnation' tells us nothing about the existence or nature of an afterworld, but it tells us a great deal about the nature of the sinner's besetting physiological afflictions.

As this last resonance suggests, the slogan *beyond good and evil* ultimately connects Nietzsche's contributions to morality to his pioneering work in ontology. To transport oneself beyond the metaphysical confections that sustain the distinction between good and evil is to position oneself to behold the world *as it is*, in its painfully brute, amoral immanence. The real world boasts no moral order that guarantees the triumph of good over evil; no consummatory wisdom that will heal broken souls and restore humankind to a 'second innocence'; no salvific regimen of penance and purgation; no anthropocentric entelechy that ensures the continued progress and prosperity of featherless bipeds; no cognizant deity (or daimon) who invisibly guides us toward prudent (or disastrous) choices; and no promise whatsoever of an afterlife, afterworld, or aftersoul.

While the stark naturalism of Nietzsche's post-metaphysical ontology is likely to frighten away most prospective adherents, he envisions its influence on some select readers as salutary and inspiring. To stand beyond good and evil is not only to confront the real world in its radical indifference to human design, but also to appreciate its immeasurable plenitude as a transient shelter for the pursuit and realization of human goals. Having asked himself, 'What alone can be *our* doctrine?', he responds with a summary ontological gloss on his most provocative slogan:

> No one is responsible for man's being there at all, for his being such-and-such, or for his being in these circumstances or in this environment. The fatality of his essence is not to be disentangled from the fatality of all that has been and will be. Man is not the effect of some special purpose, of a will, an end; nor is he the object of an attempt to attain an 'ideal of humanity' or an 'ideal of happiness' or an 'ideal of morality'. . . . That nobody is held responsible any longer, that the mode of being may not be traced back to a *causa prima*, that the world does not form a unity either as a sensorium or as 'spirit' – that alone is the great liberation; with this alone is the innocence of becoming restored.[7]

Notes

1. *On the Genealogy of Morals*, Essay III, Section 24. With the exception of occasional emendations, I rely throughout this Introduction on Walter Kaufmann's translations/editions of Nietzsche's books for Viking Press/Random House, and on R. J. Hollingdale's translations for Cambridge University Press. My occasional references to the original German text rely on *Friedrich Nietzsche: Sämtliche Werke, Kritische Studienausgabe in 15 Bänden*, ed. G. Colli and M. Montinari (Berlin: Walter de Gruyter/Deutscher Taschenbuch Verlag, 1980).
2. *Beyond Good and Evil*, Section 202.
3. *On the Genealogy of Morals*, Essay II, Section 24.
4. *Beyond Good and Evil*, Section 221.
5. *On the Genealogy of Morals*, Essay III, Section 27.
6. *Twilight of the Idols*, 'The "Improvers" of Mankind,' Section 1.
7. *Twilight of the Idols*, 'The Four Great Errors,' Section 8.

On Nietzsche: Preface*

Georges Bataille

*Source: Georges Bataille, *On Nietzsche*, trans. Bruce Boone, Paragon House, 1992, pp. xix–xxxiv.

1

> Do you seek warmth of me? Come not too close, I counsel, or your hands may burn. For look! My ardor exceeds the limit, and I barely restrain the flames from leaping from my body!
>
> $(1881–86)^1$

Motivating this writing – as I see it – is fear of going crazy.

I'm on fire with painful longings, persisting in me like unsatisfied desire.

In one sense, my tension is a crazy urge to laugh, not so different in its way from the ravaging passions of Sade's heroes but close, too, to the tensions of the martyrs and saints . . .

On this score, I have few doubts – my delirium brings out human qualities. Though by implication an imbalance is there as well – and distressingly I'm deprived of all rest. I'm ablaze, disoriented – and finally empty. Whatever great or necessary actions come to mind, none answers to this feverishness. I'm speaking of moral concerns – of discovering some object that surpasses all others in value!

Compared to the moral ends normally advanced, the object I refer to is incommensurable. Moral ends seem deceptive and lusterless. Still, only moral ends translate to acts (aren't they determined as a demand for definite acts?).

The truth is, concern about this or that limited good can sometimes lead to the summit I am approaching. But this occurs in a roundabout way. And moral ends, in this case, are distinct from any excesses they occasion. States of glory and moments of sacredness (which reveal incommensurability) surpass results intentionally sought. Ordinary morality puts these results on the same footing as sacrificial ends. Sacrifice explores the grounding of worlds, and the destruction realized discloses a sacrificial laceration. All the same, it's for the most banal reasons that sacrifice is celebrated. Morality addresses our good.

(Things changed in appearance when God was represented as a unique and veritable end. Now, some will say the incommensurability of which I speak is simply God's transcendence. But for me transcendence is avoiding my object. Nothing radically changes when instead of human satisfaction, we think of the satisfaction of some heavenly being! God's person displaces the problem and does not abolish it. It simply introduces confusions. When so moved or when circumstances require – in regard to God – being will grant itself an incommensurable essence. *By serving God and acting on his behalf* we reduce him to ordinary ends that exist in action. *If he were situated beyond, there would be nothing to be done on his behalf.*)

2

An extreme, unconditional human yearning was expressed for the first time by Nietzsche *independently of moral goals or of serving God.*

Nietzsche can't really define it, but it motivates him and it's what he unreservedly makes his own. Of course, ardor that doesn't address a dramatically articulated moral obligation is a paradox. In this context there is no preaching or action that is possible. The result from this is something disturbing. If we stop looking at states of ardor as simply preliminary to other and subsequent conditions grasped as beneficial, the state I propose seems a pure play of lightning, merely an empty consummation. Lacking any relation to material benefits such as power or the growth of the state (or of God or a Church or a party), this consuming can't even be comprehended. *It appears that the positive value of loss can only be given as gain.*

Nietzsche wasn't entirely clear on this difficulty. He must have known he failed, and in the end knew he was a voice crying out in the wilderness. To be done with obligation and *good*, to expose the lying emptiness of morality, he destroyed the effective value of language. Fame came late to him, and as it did, he thwarted it. His expectations went unanswered.

Today it appears that I ought to say his readers and his admirers show him scant respect (he knew this and said so).[2] *Except for me?* (I am oversimplifying). Still ... to try, as he asked, to follow him is to be vulnerable to trials and tribulations similar to his.

This total liberation of human possibility as he defined it, of all possibilities is, of course, the only one to remain untried (I repeat by way of simplification, except perhaps by me?). At the current historical juncture, I suppose each conceivable teaching preached has had its effect. Nietzsche in turn conceived and preached a new doctrine, he gathered disciples, aspired to found an order. He had contempt for what he received – vulgar praise!

I think it is appropriate today to state my confusion. Within myself I tried to draw out consequences of a lucid doctrine impelling and attracting me to it as if to the light. I've reaped a harvest of anguish and, most often, a feeling of going under.

3

Going under, I don't abandon the yearnings I spoke of. Or rather they don't abandon me. And I die. Even dying doesn't silence me: at least that's my belief. And I want those I love also to undergo – to go under also.

In the essence of humanness a fierce impulse seeks autonomy, the freedom to be. Naturally freedom can be understood in many different ways – but is it any wonder that people today are dying for it? On my own, I'll have to face the same difficulties as Nietzsche – putting God and the good behind him, though all ablaze with the ardor possessed by those who lay down their lives for God or the good. The discouraging loneliness he described oppresses me. But breaking away from moral entities gives such truth to the air I breathe, I'd rather live as a cripple or die than fall back into slavery!

4

As I write, I'll admit that moral investigations that aim to surpass the good lead first of all to disorder. There's no guarantee yet I'll pass the test. Founded on painful experience, this admission allows me to dismiss those who, in attacks on or exploitations of Nietzsche, confuse his position with that of Hitler.

> '*In what height is my abode? Ascending, I've never counted the steps leading to myself – and where the steps cease, that is where I have my roof and my abode.*'[3]

Thus a demand is expressed, one not directed at some comprehensible good – but all the more consuming to the degree that it's experienced.

I lose patience with crude equivocations. It's frightening to see thought reduced to the propaganda level – thought that remains comically unemployable, opening to those whom the void inspires. According to some critics, Nietzsche exercised a great influence on his times. I doubt it: No one expected him to dismiss moral laws. But above all he took no political stance and, when pressed to, refused to choose a party, disturbed at the possibility of either a right- or left-wing identification. The idea of a person's subordinating his or her thinking to a cause appalled him.

His strong feelings on politics date from his falling out with Wagner and from his disillusionment with Wagner's German grossness – Wagner the socialist, the Francophobe, the anti-Semite . . . The spirit of the Second Reich, especially in its pre-Hitlerite tendencies – the emblem of which is anti-Semitism – is what he most despised. Pan-German propaganda made him sick.

'I like creating from *tabula rasa*,' he wrote. 'It is in fact one of my ambitions to be imputed a great scorner of the Germans. Even at the age of twenty-six, I expressed the suspicions that their nature had aroused in me' (*Third Jeremiad*). 'To me, there is something impossible about the Germans, and if I try to imagine a type repellent to all my instincts, it's always a German who comes to mind' (*Ecce Homo*). For the clear-sighted, at a political level Nietzsche was a prophet, foretelling the crude German fate. He was the first to give it in detail. He loathed the impervious, vengeful, self-satisfied foolishness that took hold of the German mind after 1870, which today is being spent in Hitlerite madness. No more deadly error has ever led a whole people astray and so terribly ordained it for destruction. But taking leave of the (by now) dedicated crowd, he went his way, refusing to be part of orgies of 'self-satisfaction. ' His strictness had its consequences. Germany chose to ignore a genius so unwilling to flatter her. It was only Nietzsche's notoriety abroad that belatedly secured the attention of his people ... I know of no better example of the wall of incomprehension existing between one person and his or her country: for fifteen years a whole nation remaining deaf to that voice – isn't this a serious matter? As witnesses to that destruction, we ought to look in admiration at the fact that while Germany took the path leading to the worst developments, one of the best and most passionate Germans turned away from his country with feelings of horror and uncontrollable disgust. Taken all round in any case, in their attempts to evade him as much as in their aberrations, doesn't hindsight let us see something vulnerable in this inconclusiveness?

In their opposition to each other, at last both Nietzsche and Germany will probably experience the same fate: both equally, aroused by demented hopes, though not to any purpose. Beyond this tragically pointless confusion, lacerations, and hatreds governed their relations. The resemblances are insignificant. If the habit of not taking Nietzsche seriously did not exist, the habit of doing what most annoyed him, giving him a cursory reading to exploit him, *without even putting aside positions which he saw as being incompatible with his*, his teaching would be seen for what it is – the most violent of solvents. To view this teaching as supporting causes it actually discredits not only insults it but rides roughshod over it – showing that his readers know nothing at all about what they claim to like. To try, as I have, to push the possibilities of his teaching to the limit is to become, like Nietzsche, a field of infinite contradictions. Following his paradoxical doctrines, you are forced to see yourself as excluded from partcipating in current causes. You'll eventually see that solitude is your only lot.

5

In the helter-skelter of this book, I didn't develop my views as theory. In fact, I even believe that efforts of that kind are tainted with ponderousness.

Nietzsche wrote 'with his blood,' and criticizing or, better, *experiencing* him means pouring out one's lifeblood.

I wrote hoping my book would appear in time for the centenary of his birth (October 15, 1844). I wrote from February through August, counting on the German retreat to make publication possible. I began with a theoretical statement of the problem (this is part 2, p. 29), but that short section is essentially only the account of a personal experience, an experience which continued for twenty years and came to be weighted in fear. It might prove useful here to dispel an ambiguity. There exists an idea of Nietzsche as the philosopher of a 'will to power,' the idea that this is how he saw himself and how he was accepted. I think of him more as a philosopher of *evil*. For him the attraction and *value* of evil, it seems to me, gave significance to what he intended when he spoke of power. Otherwise, how can passages like this be explained? 'WET BLANKET. A: You're a wet blanket, and everybody knows it! B: Obviously! I'm dampening an enthusiasm that encourages belonging to some party, which is what parties won't forgive' (*Gay Science*).

That observation, among many others, doesn't in any way square with the type of practical conduct or politics derived from the 'will to power' principle. In his lifetime Nietzsche had a distinct dislike for anything the expression of that will produced. If he was drawn, felt it necessary, even, to trample on received morality it's equally certain that methods of oppression (the police) aroused his disgust too. He justified his hatred of the good as a condition for freedom itself. Personally, and with no illusions concerning the impact of this attitude, I am opposed to all forms of coercion – but this doesn't keep me from seeing *evil* as an object of moral exploration. Because evil is the opposite of a constraint that on principle is practiced with a view toward good. Of course evil isn't what a hypocritical series of misunderstandings makes it out to be: isn't it essentially a concrete *freedom*, the uneasy breaking of a taboo?

Anarchy bothers me, particularly run-of-the-mill doctrines apologizing for those commonly taken to be criminals. *Gestapo* practices now coming to light show how deep the affinities are that unite the underworld and the police. It is people who hold nothing sacred who're the ones most likely to torture people and cruelly carry out the orders of a coercive apparatus. I can only feel intense dislike for muddled thinkers who confusedly demand all rights for the individual. An individual's limit is not represented simply by the rights of another individual but even more by rights of the *masses*. We are all inextricably bound up with the masses, participating in their innermost sufferings and their victories. And in our innermost being, we form part of a living group – though we are no less alone, for all that, when things go wrong.

As a means to triumph over significant difficulties of this kind and over the opposition between individual and collective or good and evil, over the exasperating contradictions from which, generally speaking, we are able to disentangle ourselves mostly through denial – it seems to me that only certain chance movements, or the audacity that comes from taking chances, will freely prevail. Chance represents a way of going beyond when life reaches the outer limits of the possible and gives up. Refusing to pull back, never looking behind, our uninhibited boldness discovers that solutions develop where cautious logic is baffled. So that it was only *with my life* that I wrote the Nietzsche book that I had planned – a book in which I intended to pose and resolve intimate problems of morality.

Only my life, only its ludicrous resources, only these made a quest for the grail of chance possible for me. Chance, as it turned out, corresponded to Nietzsche's intentions more accurately than power could. Only 'play' gave me the possibility of exploring the far reaches of possibility and not prejudicing the results, of giving to the future alone and its free occurrence the power usually assigned to choosing sides (which is only a form of the past). In a sense my book is the day-to-day record of what turned up as the dice were thrown – without, I hasten to say, there being a lot by way of resources. I apologize for the truly comical year of personal interests chronicled in my diary entries. They are not a source of pain, and I'm glad to make fun of myself, knowing no better way to lose myself in immanence.

6

Nonetheless, I don't want my inclination to make fun of myself or act comic to lead readers astray. The basic problem tackled in this chaotic book (chaotic because it has to be) is the same one Nietzsche experienced and attempted to resolve in his work – the problem of the whole human being.

'The majority of people,' he wrote, 'are a fragmentary, exclusive image of what humanity is; you have to add them up to get humanity. In this sense, whole eras and whole peoples have something fragmentary about them; and it may be necessary for humanity's growth for it to develop only in parts. It is a crucial matter therefore to see that what is at stake is always the idea of producing a synthetic humanity and that the inferior humans who make up a majority of us are only preliminaries, or preparatory attempts whose concerted play allows a *whole human being* to appear here and there like a military boundary marker showing the extent of humanity's advance' (*The Will to Power*).

But what does that fragmentation mean? Or better, what causes it if not a need to *act* that specializes us and limits us to the horizon of a particular activity? Even if it turns out to be for the general interest (which normally isn't true), the activity that subordinates each of our aspects to a specific result suppresses our being as an entirety. Whoever acts, substitutes a particular end for what he or she is, as a total being: in the least specialized cases it is the glory of the state or the triumph of a party. Every action specializes insofar as it is limited as action. A plant usually doesn't act, and isn't specialized; it's specialised when gobbling up flies!

I cannot exist *entirely* except when somehow I go beyond the stage of action. Otherwise I'm a soldier, a professional, a man of learning, not a 'total human being.' The fragmentary state of humanity is basically the same as the choice of an object. When you limit your desires to possessing political power, for instance, you act and know what you have to do. The possibility of failure isn't important – and right from the start, you insert your existence advantageously into time. Each of your moments becomes *useful*. With each moment, the possibility is given you to advance to some chosen goal, and your time becomes a march toward that goal – what's normally called living. Similarly, if salvation is the goal. Every action makes you a fragmentary existence. I hold onto my nature as an entirety only by refusing to act – or at least by denying the superiority of time, which is reserved for action.

Life is whole only when it isn't subordinate to a specific object that exceeds it. In this way, the essence of entirety is freedom. Still, I can't choose to become an entire human being by simply fighting for freedom, even if the struggle for freedom is an appropriate activity for me – because within me I can't confuse the state of entirety with my struggle. It's the positive practice of freedom, not the negative struggle against a particular oppression, that has lifted me above a mutilated existence. Each of us learns with bitterness that to struggle for freedom is first of all to alienate ourselves.

I've already said it: the practice of freedom lies within evil, not beyond it, while the struggle for freedom is a struggle to conquer a *good*. To the extent that life is entire within me, I can't distribute it or let it serve the interests of a good belonging to someone else, to God or myself. I can't acquire anything at all: I can only give and give unstintingly, without the gift ever having as its object anyone's interest. (In this respect, I look at the other's good as deceptive, since if I will that good it's to find my own, unless I identify it as my own. Entirety exists within me as exuberance. Only in empty longing, only in an unlucky desire to be consumed simply by the desire to burn with desire, *is entirety wholly what it is*. In this respect, entirety is also longing for laughter, longing for pleasure, holiness, or death. Entirety lacks further tasks to fulfill.)

7

You have to experience a problem like this to understand how strange it really is. It's easy to argue its meaning by saying, Infinite tasks are imposed on us. Precisely in the present. That much is obvious and undeniable. Still, it is at least equally true that human entirety or totality (the inevitable term) is making its initial appearance now. For two reasons. The first, negative, is that specialization is everywhere, and emphasized alarmingly. The second is that in our time overwhelming tasks nonetheless appear *within their exact limits*.

In earlier times the horizon couldn't be discerned. The object of serious-ness was first defined as the good of the city, although the city was confused with the gods. The object thereafter became the salvation of the soul. In both cases the goal of action, on the one hand, was some limited and comprehen-sible end, and on the other, a totality defined as inaccessible in this world (transcendent). Action in modern conditions has precise ends that are com-pletely adequate to the possible, and human totality no longer has a mythic aspect. Seen as accessible in all that surrounds us, totality becomes the ful-fillment of tasks as they are defined materially. So that totality is remote, and the tasks that subordinate our minds also fragment them. Totality, however, is still discernible.

A totality like this, necessarily aborted by our work, is nonetheless offered by that very work. Not as a goal, since the goal is to change the world and give it human dimensions. But as the inevitable result. As change comes about, humanity-attached-to-the-task-of-changing-the-world, which is only a single and fragmentary aspect of humanity, will itself be changed to humanity-as-entirety. For humanity this result seems remote, but *defined* tasks describe it: It doesn't transcend us like the gods (the sacred city), nor is it like the soul's afterlife; it is in the immanence of 'humanity-attached . . .' We can put off thinking about it till later, though it's still contiguous to us. If human beings can't yet be consciously aware of it in their common exist-ence, what separates them from this notion isn't that they are human instead of divine, nor the fact of not being dead: It's the duties of a particular moment.

Similarly, a man in combat must only think (provisionally) of driving back the enemy. To be sure, situations of calm during even the most violent wars give rise to peacetime interests. Still, such matters immediately appear minor. The toughest minds will join in these moments of relaxation as they seek a way to put aside their seriousness. In some sense they're wrong to do so. Since isn't seriousness essentially *why* blood flows? And that's inevitable. For how could seriousness *not* be the same as blood? How could a free life, a life unconstrained by combat, a life disengaged from the necessities of action and no longer fragmented – how could such a life *not* appear frivolous? In a world released from the gods and from any interest in salvation, even 'tragedy' seems a distraction, a moment of relaxation within the context of goals shaped by activity alone.

More than one advantage accrues when human 'reason for being' comes in *the back way*. So the total person is first disclosed in immanence in areas of life that are lived frivolously. A life like this – a frivolous life – can't be taken seriously. Even if it is deeply tragic. And that is its liberating prospect – it acquires the worst simplicity and nakedness. Without any guile I'm saying, I feel grateful to those whose serious attitudes and life lived at the edge of death define me as an empty human being and dreamer (there are moments when I'm on their side). Fundamentally an entire human being is simply a being in whom transcendence is abolished, from whom there's no separating anything now. An entire human being is partly a clown, partly God, partly crazy . . . and is transparence.

8

If I want to realize totality in my consciousness, I have to relate myself to an immense, ludicrous, and painful convulsion of all of humanity. This impulse moves toward *all* meanings. It's true: sensible action (action proceeding toward some single meaning) goes beyond such incoherence, but that is exactly what gives humanity in my time (as well as in the past) its fragmentary aspect. If for a single moment I forget that meaning, will I see Shakespeare's tragical/ridiculous sum total of eccentricities, his lies, pain, and laughter; the awareness of an immanent totality becomes clear to me – but as laceration. Existence as entirety remains beyond any one meaning – and it is the conscious presence of humanness in the world inasmuch as this is nonmeaning, having nothing to do other than be what it is, no longer able to go beyond itself or give itself some kind of meaning through action.

This consciousness of totality relates to two opposed ways of using that expression. *Nonmeaning* normally is a simple negation and is said of an object to be canceled. An intention that rejects what has no meaning in fact is a rejection of the entirety of being – and it's by reason of this rejection that we're conscious of the totality of being within us. But if I say *nonmeaning* with the opposite intention, in the sense of *nonsense*, with the intention of searching for an object free of meaning, I don't deny anything. But I make an affirmation in which *all life* is clarified in consciousness.

Whatever moves toward this consciousness of totality, toward this total friendship of humanness and humanity for itself, is quite correctly held to be lacking a basic seriousness. Following this path I become ridiculous. I acquire the inconsistency of all humans (humanness taken as a whole, and overlooking whatever leads to important changes). I'm not suggesting that I'm accounting for Nietzsche's illness this way (from what we know, it had some somatic basis), though it must be said, all the same, that the main impulse that leads to human entirety is tantamount to madness. I let go of good. I let go of reason (meaning). And under my feet, I open an abyss which my activity and my binding judgments once kept from me. At least the awareness of totality is first of all within me as a despair and a crisis. If I give up the viewpoint of action, my perfect nakedness is revealed to me. I have no recourse in the world, there's nothing to help me – and I collapse. No other outcome is possible, except endless incoherence, in which only chance is my guide.

9

Now clearly, such an experience of helplessness can't be effected till all other experiences have been attempted and accomplished – till all other possibilities have been exhausted. So it can't become the fact of human entirety until the last minute. Only an extremely isolated individual can attempt it in our day, as a consequence of mental confusion and at the same time an undeniable vigor. If chance is on such a person's side, the individual can determine an unforeseen balance in this incoherence. Since this audaciously easy and divine state of balance again and again translates into a profound discordancy that remains a tightrope act, I don't imagine that the 'will to power' can attain such a condition in any other way. Given this, the 'will to power' considered as an end is regressive. Taking such a course would return me to slavish fragmentation. I'd assign myself another duty, and the good that chooses power would control me. The divine exuberance and lightheartedness expressed in Zarathustra's laughter and dancing would be reabsorbed. And instead of happiness at the brink of the abyss, I'd be tied to weightiness, the slavishness of *Kraft durch Freude.* If we put aside the equivocations of the 'will to power,' the destiny Nietzsche gave humankind places him beyond laceration. There is no return, hence the profound nonviability of this doctrine. In the notes compiled in *The Will to Power*, proposals for activity and the temptation to work out a goal or politics end up as a maze. His last completed work, *Ecce Homo*, affirms absence of goals as well as the author's complete lack of a plan.[4] Considered from the standpoint of action, Nietzsche's work amounts to failure (one of the most indefensible!) and his life amounts to nothing – like the life of anyone who tries to put these writings into practice.

10

I want to be very clear on this: not a word of Nietzsche's work can be understood without *experiencing* that dazzling dissolution into totality, without living it out. Beyond that, this philosophy is just a maze of contradictions. Or worse, the pretext for lies of omission (if, as with the Fascists, certain passages are isolated for ends disavowed by the rest of the work). I now must ask that closer attention be paid. It must have been clear how the preceding criticism masks an approval. It justifies the following definition of the entire human – *human existence as the life of 'unmotivated' celebration*, celebration in all meanings of the word: laughter, dancing, orgy, the rejection of subordination, and sacrifice that scornfully puts aside any consideration of ends, property, and morality.

The preceding introduces a necessity to make distinctions. Extreme states, either individual or collective, once were motivated by ends. Some of these have lost their meaning (expiation and salvation). The search for the good of collectivities today no longer is pursued via recourse to dubious means, but directly through action. In previous conditions, extreme states came under the jurisdiction of the arts, though certain drawbacks existed. People substituted writing (fiction) for what was once spiritual life, poetry (chaotic words) for actual ecstasies. Art constitutes a minor free zone outside action, paying for its freedom by giving up the real world. A heavy price! Rare is the writer who doesn't yearn for the rediscovery of a vanished reality; but the payment required is relinquishing his or her freedom and serving propaganda. Artists who limit themselves to fiction know they aren't human entireties, though the situation isn't any different for literary propagandists. The province of the arts in a sense encompasses totality, though just the same, totality escapes it in all aspects.

Nietzsche is far from having resolved the difficulty, since Zarathustra is himself a poet, in fact a literary fiction. Only he never accepted this. Praise exasperated him. He frantically looked for a way out – in every direction. He never abandoned the watchword of *not having any end*, not serving a cause, because, as he knew, causes *pluck off the wings we fly with*. Although the absence of causes, on the other hand, pushes us into solitude, which is the sickness of a desert, the shout lost in the silence . . .

The understanding I encourage involves a similar absence of outcome and takes a similar enthusiasm for torment for granted. In this sense I think the idea of the eternal return should be reversed. It's not a promise of infinite and lacerating repetitions: It's what makes moments caught up in the immanence of return suddenly appear as ends. In every system, don't forget, these moments are viewed and given as means: Every moral system proclaims that 'each moment of life ought to be *motivated.*' Return *unmotivates* the moment and frees life of ends – thus first of all destroys it. Return is the mode of drama, the mask of human entirety, a human desert wherein each moment is unmotivated.

There are no two ways about it, and a choice has to be made. On one side is the desert, on the other, mutilation. Misfortune can't just be left behind like a package. Suspended in the void, extreme moments are followed by depressions that no hope can alleviate. If, however, I come to a clear awareness of what's experienced along such a path, I can give up my search for a way out where none is to be found (for that reason I've retained my criticism). Can we believe that the absence of a goal inherent in Nietzsche's outlook wouldn't have certain consequences? Inevitably, chance and the search for chance represent the single applicable recourse (to the vicissitudes he described in his book). But to proceed rigorously in such a fashion necessarily implies dissociation in the impulse itself.

Even if it's true that, as it is usually understood, a man of action can't be a human entirety, human entirety nonetheless retains the possibility of acting. Provided, however, that such action is reduced to appropriately human (or reasonable) principles and ends. Human entirety can't be transcended (that is, subdued) by action, since it would lose its totality. Nor can it transcend action (submit it to its ends), since in this way it would define itself as a motive and would enter into and be annihilated by the mechanism of motivation. It's important to distinguish between the world of motives on the one hand, that is, things making sense (rational), and the (senseless) world of non-sense on the other. Each of us sometimes belongs to one, sometimes to the other. We can consciously and clearly distinguish what is connected only in ignorance. Reason for me is limited only by itself. If we act, we stray outside the motivation of equity and a rational order of acts. Between the two worlds only a single relationship is possible: action has to be *rationally* limited by a principle of freedom.[5]

The rest is silence.

Notes

1. Quotation from Nietzsche are given without the author's name, and the dates mentioned refer to posthumous notes.

2. See [Georges Bataille, *On Nietzsche* (Paragon House, 1992)] p. 7.

3. *The Will to Power*.

4. See [Bataille, 1992], p. 86.

5. Since the accursed fiery or mad share, or the *part maudite*, of human entireness is meted out (sponsored from outside) by reason following liberal and reasonable norms, capitalism is condemned as an irrational mode of activity. As soon as human entirety (that is, its irrationality) is able to recognize itself as outside action, or sees in every transcendent possibility a trap and loss of its totality, we will give up irrational (feudal, capitalist) dominations in the sphere of activity. Nietzsche certainly foresaw the necessity for this relinquishment without noting its cause. Human entirety can only be what it is when giving up the addiction to others' *ends*; it enslaves itself in going beyond, in limiting itself to the feudal or bourgeois spheres this side of freedom. True, Nietzsche still believed in social transcendence or hierarchy. To say that 'there is nothing sacred in immanence' signifies that what once was sacred can no longer serve. The time derived from freedom is the time for laughter: 'To see tragic natures go under and be able to laugh . . .' (Do we dare apply that proposition to present events – instead of involving ourselves in new moral transcendencies?) In freedom, abandon, and the immanence of laughter, Nietzsche was among the first to eliminate what still linked him (still linked his adolescent immoralism) to vulgar forms of transcendence, which remain freedoms still in chains. To choose evil is to choose freedoms – freedom, emancipation from all constraint.'

41

The Uses and Disadvantages of Morality for Life*

Daniel W. Conway

*Source: Daniel W. Conway, *Nietzsche and the Political*, Routledge, 1997, pp. 28–42, 146–9.

> The genius, in work and deed, is necessarily a squanderer: that he squanders himself, that is his greatness ... Yet, because much is owed to such explosives, much has also been given them in return: for example, a kind of higher morality. After all, that is the way of human gratitude: it *misunderstands* its benefactors.
>
> (*Twilight of the Idols*, IX:44)

The ethical core of Nietzsche's perfectionism is often eclipsed by his scathing attack on the Western moral tradition. But his critique of morality is not inhospitable to all forms of morality, and it in fact clears a space for the 'morality of breeding' that motivates his perfectionism. He actually intends his perfectionism to shelter a moral pluralism, informed by an order of rank, which yields a hierarchical organization of ethical communities.

Nietzsche's Defense of Moral Pluralism

Although Nietzsche's perfectionism lies at the very heart of his political thinking, it remains one of the most obscure elements of his philosophy. His critics routinely dismiss his perfectionism, often assuming that he proposes a crude eugenics project, which will culminate in the savage, unprincipled rule of some blond beast or barbarian caste. John Rawls, for example, attributes to Nietzsche a version of 'teleological perfectionism' that is not even worthy of consideration in the 'original position.'[1] The closest Rawls comes to a critical assessment of this 'teleological perfectionism' is his terse observation that '[t]he absolute weight that Nietzsche sometimes gives the lives of great men such as Socrates and Goethe is unusual.'[2] Rather than elaborate, Rawls moves on to consider the merits of a 'more moderate doctrine' of perfectionism, which 'has far stronger claims,' but which he rejects nonetheless as a source of viable principles of justice.[3]

Rawls's response is typical in its summary rejection of the ethical claims of Nietzsche's perfectionism. Like Rawls, many readers conclude that Nietzsche's political thinking shelters virtually no ethical content whatsoever. Nietzsche himself is certainly responsible for much of the misunderstanding surrounding his perfectionism, for he often presents himself as an uncompromising opponent of morality *simpliciter*. He proudly describes himself as an 'immoralist,' and he congratulates himself for being the 'first' of this noble breed (EH XIV:6). Fully representative of his rhetorical excesses is the following 'definition of morality':

> Morality – the idiosyncrasy of decadents, with the ulterior motive of revenging oneself against life – successfully.
>
> (EH XIV:7)

Continuing this telegraphic line of argumentation, he submits the following summary epigram: 'Morality as vampirism' (EH XIV:8).

Especially when viewed from the broadly historical perspective that Nietzsche favors, however, the enterprise of morality encompasses far more than the universal prescriptions and metaphysical fictions that he so famously debunks. In fact, he regularly reminds his readers that the type of morality he opposes is only one among several possible moralities:

> *Morality in Europe today is herd animal morality* – in other words, as we understand it, merely *one* type of human morality beside which, before which, and after which many other types, above all *higher* moralities, are or ought to be, possible. But this morality resists such a 'possibility,' such an 'ought' with all its power: it says stubbornly and inexorably, 'I am morality itself, and nothing besides is morality.'
>
> (BGE 202)

Continuing this critique of moral monism in his next book, *On the Genealogy of Morals*, he declares that contemporary morality, despite its claims to universality, is in fact descended from a 'slave' morality, which in turn emerged only in response to the hegemony of a logically and historically prior 'noble' morality. The history of morality, encrypted in the 'long hieroglyphic record' that Nietzsche aims to decipher (GM P:7), thus contradicts the claim of *any* morality, including the ubiquitous 'herd animal morality,' to a privileged, monistic prerogative as the arbiter of ethical life. In his 'review' of the *Genealogy*, he explicitly identifies the 'slave revolt in morality' with 'the birth of Christianity out of the spirit of *ressentiment*' (EH XI).

Rather than reject the enterprise of morality itself, Nietzsche instead rejects the claim of any single morality to universal scope and application. A universally binding morality would necessarily erect a monolithic moral ideal, thereby reducing a plurality of human types and kinds to a lowest common denominator. Ethical laws should (and do) bind collectively, but only across a limited number of individuals, such as constitute a people, race, tribe, or community. As Zarathustra puts it, 'I am a law only for my kind [*die Meinen*], I am no law for all' (Z IV:12). The dream of an ethical community comprising all human beings, or all sentient beings, thus spells political nightmare. The laws of an omni-inclusive ethical community would express only the commonalities and banalities of the individuals involved, rather than their unique strengths and virtues. Morality should always serve the enhancement of the ethical life of a particular people, and not the other way around:

> *Morality* – no longer the expression of the conditions for the life and growth of a people, no longer its most basic instinct of life, but become abstract, become the antithesis of life – morality as the systematic degradation of the imagination, as the 'evil eye' for all things.
>
> (AC 25)

Nietzsche's critique of Christian morality is best understood within the context of his political opposition to moral monism. He has no quarrel, for example, with Christian morality in its 'pure' forms, which he applauds for providing comfort and solace to the demotic strata of hierarchically organized societies. He goes so far as to praise the contributions of Christian morality to the 'hygienic' maintenance of intramural political boundaries, readily acknowledging the value of moralities that serve the inwardly destroyed (BGE 62). As his commitment to moral pluralism would suggest, he objects to Christian morality only in its most virulent political form, insofar as it arrogates to itself a universal application across all of humankind; as we have seen, this objection is sustained strictly on political, rather than epistemological or theological, grounds. He consequently aims to disabuse his readers of the belief that Christian morality is coextensive with morality itself: 'I negate a type of morality that has become prevalent and predominant as morality itself – the morality of decadence or, more concretely, *Christian* morality' (EH XIV:4). He thus explains that his self-awarded title, 'the immoralist,' designates an opposition specifically to *Christian* morality, which in his day held (or so he believed) a virtual monopoly over ethical life throughout the diverse cultures of Western civilization (EH XIV:6).

As an alternative to the moral monism he detects at the rotten core of Christianity, Nietzsche espouses a moral pluralism that reflects the rich diversity of human types, while reminding us that these moralities vary in worth as widely as the individuals whose needs and perfections they express:

> Moralities must be forced to bow first of all before the *order of rank*; their presumption must be brought home to their conscience – until they finally

reach agreement that it is *immoral* to say: 'what is right for one is fair for the other.'

(BGE 221)

Indeed, a primary aim of Nietzsche's perfectionism is to promote the design of hierarchically organized political regimes, each of which would simultaneously sustain several grades of morality. The aristocratic regimes he favors would shelter a pyramidal hierarchy of ethical communities, each equipped with a distinctive morality that reflects its unique needs and strengths.[4] At the pinnacle of this pyramidal structure would stand the community of agonistic 'friends' founded by the *Übermensch*.

As modernity nears exhaustion, the pyramidal structure of this hierarchy of moral communities becomes deformed accordingly, flattened by the glacial advance of decadence. In times such as these, Nietzsche recommends a renewed vigilance to the order of rank that separates human types:

> The more normal sickliness becomes among men . . . the higher should be the honor accorded the rare cases of great power of soul and body, humankind's *lucky strikes*; the more we should protect the well-constituted from the worst kind of air, the air of the sickroom.

(GM III:14)

In order to resist collectively the decadence of late modernity, he urges his 'friends' to band together, seeking strength in numbers and prophylaxis in seclusion:

> And therefore let us have good company, *our* company! . . . So that we may, at least for a while yet, guard ourselves, my friends, against the two worst contagions that may be reserved just for us – against the *great nausea at man*! against *great pity for man*!

(GM III:14)

While it is not entirely inaccurate to portray Nietzsche as an amoral champion of autarkic individualism, we might think of him more precisely as a moral pluralist, who eschews the claims of any morality to a universal compass across the (potentially) wide expanse of human types:

> what is fair for one *cannot* by any means for that reason alone also be fair for others; . . . the demand of one morality for all is detrimental for the higher men; in short, . . . there is an order of rank between man and man, hence also between morality and morality.

(BGE 228)

The most exacting moralities, those which assign the greatest privileges *and* responsibilities, are operative in the lives of the rarest and most exotic human beings. As evidence of his own exemplary standing relative to most of his contemporaries, Nietzsche reserves a 'stricter' morality for himself and his unknown 'friends' (BGE 219, 226).

Just as he opposes the moral monism of Christianity, so he refuses to prescribe his own 'stricter' morality to those who are not of his kind. While he would clearly welcome the renascence of some descendant strain of the recessive 'noble' morality, he just as clearly understands that any such morality would appeal only to a limited number of human beings. Indeed, although the ethical dimension of his perfectionism is not intended to serve demotic interests, it *is* fully compatible with a demotic morality that is properly bounded in scope and application. He consequently prefers those aristocratic political regimes that shelter multiple moralities simultaneously, including a demotic morality designed to alleviate the suffering of the incurably sick and infirm.

Nietzsche's love of solitude is well known. The specific form of solitude he praises, however, derives its appeal from its dependence on a logically prior ethical community. As Zarathustra discovers only after repeated *Untergänge*, solitude independent of community is indistinguishable from loneliness. Nietzsche speaks fondly and repeatedly of his unknown 'friends,' precisely because they represent a community from which his self-imposed exile involves only a temporary respite. These 'friends,' many of whom he draws from the pages of history or from the nether reaches of his febrile imagination, inspire him to persevere in his solitary task. The imaginary 'free spirits,' for example, were summoned in order that their 'brave companionship' might 'keep [him] in good spirits while surrounded by ills' (H I:P:2).

These communitarian and pluralist currents in Nietzsche's political thinking furthermore reflect his lifelong yearning for a community in which he might realize his destiny as a philosopher and lawgiver. Here we recall his founding membership in Germania and the Leipzig Philological Society; his complicated Oedipal alliance with the Wagners in Tribschen; his fantasies (including Peter Gast, his friend and amanuensis) of a Knightly Brotherhood of the *gaya scienza*; his proposal to Lou Salomé and Paul Rée of an intellectual *ménage à trois*; and his imagination in 1887–88 of a 'subterranean' Nietzsche cult growing among 'radical parties' in Europe (excepting Germany) and North America.[5]

As these examples indicate, however, Nietzsche's impulse toward community is characteristically deflected by his tendency to identify only with imaginary communities, including those of the mythical past and future. Availing himself freely of his prodigious powers of imagination, he regularly identifies himself as party to a contrived or fictitious collective: 'we scholars,' 'we free spirits,' 'we Hyperboreans,' 'we Europeans of the day after tomorrow,' 'we philologists,' 'we psychologists,' 'we revaluers,' and so on. He readily admits, for example, that he invented the 'free spirits' to whom he dedicated *Human, All Too Human*, explaining that 'these brave companions and familiars' served 'as compensation for the friends [he] lacked' (H I:P2).

Since he never specifies an existing audience with which he identifies his most basic hopes and desires (a luxury unavailable to his rival, the phonocentric Socrates), his ethical thinking operates at a level of generality and abstraction that is inimical to the creation of new communities and the cultivation of existing ones. Like (Groucho) Marx, Nietzsche would never deign to join a community that would have him as a member. Rather than identify his aims and aspirations with those of any existing community, he saves himself for a transhistorical community that is worthy of the allegiance of his beautiful soul.

While this strategy of endless deferral surely involves a romantic flight from the present and the concrete, it also illuminates some of the perils of community, which Nietzsche's critics occasionally neglect to reckon accurately. His prolonged solitude clearly exacts a heavy toll, but it also enables him to resist the (decadent) impulse to seek recognition from those 'beneath' himself. Since he cannot rely on the hygienic stratification of a hierarchical society to insulate him from the resentment of the weak and bedraggled, he must protect his pursuit of self-perfection by imposing his own regimen of prophylactic solitude. He thus identifies the refusal of community as a prerequisite of his own moral growth (EH II:8), and he observes that the preference for solitude over unworthy company often constitutes a sign of health (EH I:2).

Rather than treat solitude as necessarily a privation, to be recuperated by the flowering of community, Nietzsche views community as an accidental, outward extension of one's ownmost self, which, under the best of conditions, honors and commemorates the self-sufficiency of the noble soul. Healthy individuals thus value community not as the precondition of their redemption and becoming whole, but as an opportunity to revel in the externalized emanations of their own virtue and character. Hence only weak, corrupt souls, whose constitutive misery leads them to crave the distractions and diversions of facile companionship, need be alone in solitude: 'a well-turned-out person . . . is always in his own company, whether he associates with books, human beings, or landscapes: he honors by *choosing*, by *admitting*, by *trusting*' (EH I:2). A thriving moral community that requires no other living human members: perhaps no image conveys more accurately than this the peculiar ethical content of Nietzsche's perfectionism. As we shall see later on in more detail, he defends this principled aversion to unworthy community as a corollary to his highest (and sole) moral obligation.

There is no prima facie warrant, then, for excluding Nietzsche's perfectionism from consideration as the source of a bona fide ethical position. The point of his perfectionism is to shelter the delicate resources of ethical life and to preserve the possibility of the sort of moral development that constitutes an enhancement of humankind as a whole. The ethical content of his perfectionism may be objectionable to liberal critics, but these objections are themselves open to philosophical scrutiny and evaluation. Nietzsche himself would maintain that all such objections bespeak the pre-philosophical prejudices of his critics; as such, they would reveal much more about these critics than they do about his perfectionism.

Nietzsche and Manu: Moralities of Breeding

Nietzsche's discussion of a kindred political thinker sheds clarifying light on the ethical content of his perfectionism. Both in *Twilight of the Idols* and *The Antichrist(ian)*, he expresses his admiration for Manu, the legendary Hindu lawgiver. Nietzsche recommends the law of Manu not as a blueprint for political reform in late modernity, but as evidence of the importance 'noble' cultures have traditionally attached to the morality of breeding. While the restoration of political aristocracy is simply out of the question for late modernity, a (modified) morality of breeding, as established by Nietzsche's perfectionism, is not.

On Nietzsche's reconstruction, Manu successfully enforced a political regime that enabled several distinct social classes to flourish simultaneously. Manu understood that the enhancement of Hindu culture would require the prophylaxis supplied by a fairly rigid social stratification. His regime effectively quarantined the relatively 'sick' from the relatively 'healthy,' while providing for the relative well-being of all social classes. The ethical motivation behind Manu's system is the perfectionism that Nietzsche too advocates: 'To set up a code of laws after the manner of Manu means to give a people the chance henceforth to become master, to become perfect – to aspire to the highest art of life' (AC 57).

Nietzsche consequently credits Manu with designing a political organization and social structure that reflect the order of Nature itself:

> The *order of castes*, the supreme, the dominant law, is merely the sanction of a *natural order*, a natural lawfulness of the first rank, over which no arbitrariness, no 'modern idea' has any power . . . The order of castes . . . is necessary for the preservation of society, to make possible the higher and the highest types.
>
> (AC 57)

Following Manu (and Nature), Nietzsche endorses the pyramidal caste system, or 'natural aristocracy,' as the supreme form of political regime. His characterization of the three 'castes' of Nature – distinguished, respectively, by pre-eminent spirituality, pre-eminent strength 'in muscle and temperament,' and by mediocrity (AC 57) – bears a remarkable resemblance to

Socrates' sketch of his pyramidal 'city in speech' in the *Republic*.[6] As we shall soon see, Nietzsche also follows Socrates (and Manu) in furnishing a 'noble lie' about the origins and justification of the political regime he recommends.

Nietzsche admires Manu for his commitment to *the morality of breeding*, wherein the lawgiver establishes the social preconditions of a plurality of types, from which in turn rare and exotic specimens are most likely to emerge (TI VII:3). Like Manu, Nietzsche tracks the enhancement of humankind to the proliferation of unanticipated, unimagined human types, and he endorses the political project of 'breeding' these exemplary human beings. He contrasts this approach to political legislation with the *morality of taming*, of which he cites Western Christianity as representative. Whereas 'breeding' encourages the simultaneous flourishing of a plurality of forms of life, 'taming' imposes upon all forms of life a single ideal, with respect to which the higher, more exotic types must be broken down:

> Physiologically speaking: in the struggle with beasts, to make them sick *may* be the only means for making them weak. This the church understood: it *ruined* man, it weakened him – but it claimed to have 'improved' him.
>
> (TI VII:2)

These competing approaches to political legislation are predicated on diametrically opposed ethical principles. A morality of taming structures society in accordance with a predetermined ideal, while a morality of breeding establishes a political order in which a plurality of forms of life is pursued – including, for the highest types, a form of life that is unfettered by all known ideals. He dismisses 'idealism' in any guise as 'cowardice' as a 'flight from reality' (EH XIV:3), for ideals invariably place preordained constraints on the range of human types that a society might produce. Like Manu, Nietzsche is an 'immoralist.' He refrains from proposing a single ideal in accordance with which all types must be domesticated; instead he encourages an untamed proliferation of rare and exotic individuals.[7]

If a morality of breeding is to succeed in producing exemplary specimens, then the lawgiver must eventually exclude those types that pose an immediate threat to the flourishing of the society as a whole. Hence the ethical archprinciple that engenders Nietzsche's admiration for hierarchically organized political regimes: 'That the sick should *not* make the healthy sick . . . should surely be our supreme concern on earth' (GM III:14). The implementation of this hygienic principle thus affords each stratum of society the prophylactic luxury of *not* associating with lower, pathogenic strata (GM I:10).

Manu understood, as few since have, that only structure and stratification beget the fecund plurality from which rare specimens spring forth; the more exacting the discipline, the more exotic the emergent fruits and blossoms.[8] Unlike Nature, which can afford to be a 'bad economist' (SE 7), the lawgiver must legislate the terms of exclusion and expenditure.[9] As a means of ensuring the success of the morality of breeding he implemented, Manu legislated the exclusion of the impure chandalas, whom his political regime simply could not accommodate. Manu understood the need both to exclude the chandalas *and* to render them politically impotent, lest their exclusion strengthen and embolden them (TI VII:3).

The cruelty of Manu's exclusionary legislations is palpable, for the chandalas are in no way responsible for falling outside the arbitrary class designations that he enforces; nor do they deserve the harsh, inhuman treatment they receive.[10] Yet some such cruelty is necessary if the morality of breeding is to succeed, and Manu's appeal to the purity of social caste furnishes his political regime with the sustaining myth it needs in order to 'justify' the cruelty it inflicts. While it may be possible for modern lawgivers to temper the cruelty of Manu's legislations – through improvements in technology and distributive justice, or through the invention of more humane forms of exclusion – the practice of exclusion is itself unavoidable.

Nietzsche does not personally advocate the caste system developed by Manu, but he fully endorses the willed practice of political exclusion, which Manu's system was designed to convey. With respect to this precise point, he does not mince his words:

> The essential characteristic of a good and healthy aristocracy, however, is that it . . . accepts with a good conscience the sacrifice of untold human beings who, *for its sake*, must be reduced and lowered to incomplete human beings, to slaves, to instruments.
>
> (BGE 258)[11]

Nietzsche thus presents slavery as a necessary, indispensable practice in those hierarchically organized societies that contribute to the permanent enhancement of humankind (BGE 44), a practice he associates with spiritual husbandry: 'Slavery is, as it seems, both in the cruder and in the more subtle sense, the indispensable means of spiritual discipline and cultivation, too' (BGE 188).

Although it turns out that he is more interested in the sort of 'slavery' that one imposes on oneself in the cultivation of one's soul, his peculiar, metaphorical use of the term 'slavery' is itself a concession to the besetting decadence of his epoch. If *real* slavery were possible in late modernity – that is, if the establishment of an aristocratic political regime were a viable option in the twilight of the idols – then he would surely, and unabashedly, endorse it as a precondition of the perfectionism he advocates. And although he might prefer the practice of slavery in its 'more subtle sense,' allowing the 'slaves,' for example, an (illusory) feeling of their freedom and self-determination, he also justifies the institution of slavery by appealing to the 'moral imperative of Nature,' which is directed, he insists, at humankind itself (BGE 188).

Nietzsche thus views the practice of exclusion as an inescapable element – a 'necessary evil' as it were – of political legislation in any regime. In order for a society to produce a few whole human beings, it must legislate and enforce the fragmentation of countless others. Only by virtue of this exclusion is culture – an artificial subsystem sheltered within the indifferent economy of Nature – possible at all. He thus insists that 'the greatest of all tasks, the attempt to raise humanity higher, includ[es] the relentless destruction of everything that [is] degenerating and parasitical' (EH IV:4). It is simply the nature of politics, he believes, that all regimes must practice exclusion, whether or not they do so knowingly and resolutely. Despite their visceral aversion to Manu's grisly decrees, modern lawgivers are no more at liberty to dispense with political exclusion than to reprise his specific practice of it. The morality of taming too practices a form of exclusion, insofar as it forces all higher, singular types to lie in a Procrustean bed of its own mediocre design (TI IX:43); it too justifies its exclusionary practices by appealing to a sustaining myth, that of '*equal* rights for all' (CW 7).

While Manu is by no means alone in practicing exclusion, he distinguishes himself – at least in Nietzsche's mind – by subjecting this practice to willful legislation. Manu does not require the implementation of exclusionary strati- fications – Nature does (AC 57). But Manu *wills* the practice of exclusion, furnishing it with a particular aspect and *modus operandi* within the caste system he designs; he unflinchingly inscribes the canon of Nature into the constitution of his political regime. Rather than consign to chance the regula- tion of his political regime, Manu legislates the exclusionary practices that will best promote his morality of breeding. Nietzsche consequently admires Manu not for practicing exclusion *per se* (which all lawgivers must do), nor for the specific practices he implements, but for doing so as a matter of design.

Nietzsche is no champion of democracy, but he believes that demotic inter- ests are best served in hierarchical political regimes devoted to the breeding and production of exemplary human beings. All members of a thriving community are, and should be, elevated by the 'immoral' exploits of its highest exemplars. While this elevation is least visible (and least appreciated) within the demotic stratum of a hierarchical society, he nevertheless insists, like J. S. Mill, that some attenuated benefits of perfectionism trickle down to everyone.[12] Unlike the 'flathead' Mill, however, Nietzsche does not propose the benefits of involuntary cultural elevation as a justification for the perfec- tionism he legislates. With reference to the 'higher' human types, he declares that

> Their right to exist, the privilege of the full-toned bell over the false and cracked, is a thousand times greater: they alone are our *warranty* for the future, they alone are *liable* for the future of humankind.
>
> (GM III:14)

A utilitarian defense of perfectionism, such as the one Mill concocts, would not only yoke political legislation to the tyrannical whims of ochlocratic taste – a problem Mill never adequately solved – but would also presuppose that the *demos* can in fact recognize and pursue its own best interests, which Nietzsche expressly denies.[13] It is an unalterable fact of political life that most individuals fail to discern, much less appreciate, the spiritual and material elevation they derive from their involuntary contributions to the production of exemplary human beings. This fact is not sufficient, however, to deter Nietzsche from his promotion and defense of perfectionism.

In order to obviate the disaffection of the demotic stratum of a hierarchical society, and thereby attend to its genuine (as opposed to its perceived) self-interest, the lawgiver must always reinforce the perfectionist aims of the regime with a sustaining myth. Toward this end, Nietzsche recommends the use of state-sponsored religions to elevate the *demos* against its will:

> To ordinary human beings, finally – the vast majority who exist for service and the general advantage, and who *may* exist only for that – religion gives an inestimable contentment with their situation and type, manifold peace of the heart, an ennobling of obedience, one further happiness and sorrow with their peers and something transfiguring and beautifying, something of a justification for the whole everyday character, the whole lowliness, the whole half-brutish poverty of their souls. Religion and religious significance spread the splendor of the sun over such ever-toiling human beings and make their own sight tolerable to them.
>
> (BGE 61)

State-sponsored religions thus furnish and perpetuate the sustaining myths of a hierarchically organized society, which in turn supply 'ordinary human beings' with the solace and comfort they need. It should be noted, moreover, that state-sponsored religions also function to co-opt the disaffections that invariably suffuse the barren souls of 'ordinary human beings,' thereby preventing, or at least dampening, explosive outbreaks of resentment within the lowest strata of society.

Nietzsche often associates the perfectionism he advocates with aristocratic political regimes, which, as his critics observe, are incompatible with the depleted vitality he attributes to late modernity. If his perfectionism required the structure and discipline that aristocratic regimes alone can supply, then his ethical and political thinking would be hopelessly anachronistic; his vision of the future of humankind would be incompatible with his critique of modernity. He may yearn for the halcyon days of the Roman Empire and the Florentine Republics, but he is not so foolish as to confuse those days with his own. He unabashedly admires Manu as a lawgiver, but he neither recommends nor advocates Manu's aristocratic regime as a viable solution to the unique political problems of modernity. The institutions of modernity are simply too corrupt to impress into service as he would have us believe Manu did, and he is too decadent to supply the requisite nomothesis in any event. The 'philosophers of the future' may someday successfully emulate Manu, Caesar or Napoleon in their political lawgiving, but Nietzsche cannot.[14]

The *Pathos* of Distance

In order to account for the legislative predilections that he shares with Manu and other 'noble' souls, Nietzsche occasionally alludes to a '*pathos* of distance' resident within himself. Although he usually associates this *pathos* of distance with the aristocratic regimes he expressly admires, its existence is not dependent on any particular form of political regime. Indeed, his own *pathos* of distance not only suggests the viability of his perfectionism in the twilight of the idols, but also secures his claim to the hyperopic perspective of the 'immoral' lawgiver.

Nietzsche introduces the *pathos* of distance as definitive of the 'noble' mode of evaluation, describing it as

> the protracted and domineering fundamental total feeling on the part of a higher ruling order in relation to a lower order, to a 'below' – *that* is the origin of the antithesis 'good' and 'bad.'

(GM I:2)

This *pathos* of distance, he later explains, is 'characteristic of every strong age,' for it expresses 'the cleavage between man and man, status and status, the plurality of types, the will to be oneself, to stand out' (TI IX:37). As we shall see, a diminished '*pathos* of distance' not only is possible in decadent epochs like late modernity, but also may sustain in these twilight epochs a modest morality of breeding.

The *pathos* of distance signifies an enhanced sensibility for, or attunement to, the order of rank that 'naturally' informs the rich plurality of human types. According to Nietzsche, the *pathos* of distance animates those aristocratic regimes that he most admires:

> Every enhancement of the type 'man' has so far been the work of an aristocratic society . . . that believes in the long ladder of an order of rank and differences in value between man and man, and that needs slavery in some sense or another.

(BGE 257)

He furthermore associates the absence or diminution of this *pathos* of distance with decadence and decline: 'Today nobody has the courage any longer for privileges, for masters' rights, for a sense of respect for oneself and one's peers – for a *pathos of distance*' (AC 43).

While Nietzsche usually discusses the *pathos* of distance in the context of his praise for aristocratic political regimes, the motivation for his celebration of this *pathos* of distance – and of aristocracy itself, for that matter – is distinctly ethical. His perfectionism, which shelters the ethical core of his thought, not only is separable from the particular structure provided by political aristocracy, but also operates independently of this and any other particular form of political regime. As he explains, it is not the aristocratic political regime itself that stimulates human flourishing, but the *pathos* of distance sustained therein:

> Without that *pathos of distance* which grows out of the ingrained difference between strata . . . that other, more mysterious *pathos* could not have grown up either – the craving for an ever new widening of distances within the soul itself, the development of ever higher, rarer, more remote, further-stretching, more comprehensive states – in brief, simply the enhancement of the type 'man,' the continual 'self-overcoming of man,' to use a moral formula in a supra-moral sense.
>
> (BGE 257)

In this passage, Nietzsche discloses the ethical core of his perfectionism. The permanent enhancement of humankind is attributable to the attainment of ever rarer states of the soul. This 'aristocracy of the soul' is in turn the product of an internal *pathos* of distance, a 'mysterious' craving for multiplicity and stratification within the soul itself. Nietzsche thus believes that the internal *pathos* of distance is itself instilled (or nourished) by the external *pathos* of distance evoked by any stable political aristocracy. As we shall see later on, this mysterious craving for internal distance either is, or is related to, *erōs*.

The attraction for Nietzsche of aristocratic regimes thus lies in their capacity to accommodate and implement human design. The rigid hierarchical stratification that he generally recommends is maximally effective at insulating political legislation from accident and chance. Aristocratic political regimes enable the lawgiver to intervene in Nature, to correct for Nature's indifference, and to assume (limited) dominion over the continued enhancement of the species. He consequently favors aristocratic political regimes, but only because they preserve and embellish the *pathos* of distance, which he in turn reveres for its evocation of a craving for 'self-overcoming.' As we shall see, 'self-overcoming' is Nietzsche's preferred term for the moral content of his perfectionism.

Our attention to the *pathos* of distance thus reveals the ethical basis of Nietzsche's perfectionism. Natural aristocracy is the best form of political regime *not* in the sense that all peoples and epochs ought to aspire to its grandeur, but in the sense that it expresses the highest degree of strength and vitality known to humankind. With few exceptions, political regimes will accurately reflect the vitality of the peoples and ages they serve; for the most part, human beings establish the best political regimes they can also afford to sustain. While aristocracy is grander than democracy as an expression of an epoch's vitality, it is not a better regime for those epochs that can afford only democracy. Nature always requires the pyramidal organization that aristocracy attains most perfectly, but it does not always supply the lawgiver with the tools and materials to fashion an aristocratic political regime. In that event, lacking the macropolitical resources needed to reprise the law of Manu, the lawgiver must aspire instead to reproduce Nature's pyramid in diminished miniature.

Nietzsche consequently defends aristocratic regimes, but only insofar as they nurture (or preserve) the *pathos* of distance that alone enables moral development. His notorious fascination with the morality of breeding is similarly grounded in ethical concerns: by preserving the stratification of types – and the *pathos* of distance it evokes – the morality of breeding sustains the possibility of moral progress. The morality of taming, on the other hand, elides the difference between types, thus threatening to extinguish the *pathos* of distance that genuine moral progress necessarily presupposes.

As a political thinker, then, Nietzsche is a consequentialist, for he aims to impress politics into the service of ethics. Political regimes are valuable only insofar as they enable psychic regimes, rather than the other way around. He favors political aristocracy as the form of institutional organization that is most conducive to the 'aristocracy of soul' that he associates with nobility, but it is by no means a necessary condition of self-perfection.[15] The essential element of his political thinking lies not in his yearning for an institutionally reinforced hierarchy, but in his perfectionism. While the former requires a degree of strength and vitality unknown to late modernity, the latter is in principle compatible even with the depleted resources of Nietzsche's own epoch.

We need not conclude, then, that his political thinking is either hopelessly anachronistic or irrelevant to the peculiar conditions of late modernity, for his perfectionism *can* operate independently of his romantic yearnings for political aristocracy. So long as a culture preserves some minimal *pathos* of distance, expressed however faintly in some trace of pyramidal structure, the permanent enhancement of humankind remains possible. Isolating the ethical content of his perfectionism is crucial to our understanding of his project, for in the event that an aristocratic regime were no longer possible (as is the case in late modernity), he could still advocate the perfectionism that lies at the heart of his political thinking.

Nietzsche offers no further defense of his preference for the morality of breeding, and the reason for his silence is simple: the *pathos* of distance does not admit of further, theoretical justification. Lawgivers are 'justified' not by virtue of some epistemic privilege, divine decree, natural right or Promethean insight, but simply by virtue of their audacious desire to subject to design what naturally falls to chance. The sole justification for a lawgiver's decrees resides exclusively in the vision of humankind that informs them. Nietzsche consequently does not pretend to offer any further justification for his morality of breeding than the products of such 'breeding' personally embody. One either shares his attunement to the *pathos* of distance that motivates his perfectionism, or one does not.

The perceived need to advance or receive a theoretical justification of political legislation is symptomatic, he believes, of the decadence of modernity. A healthy people or age neither demands nor requires a discursive justification for its legislations:

> What must first be proved is worth little. Wherever authority still forms part of good bearing, where one does not give reasons but commands, the dialectician is a kind of buffoon: one laughs at him, one does not take him seriously.

> (TI II:5)

Nobility is expressed simply in the attempt to create or preserve an order of rank in the face of the indifference of Nature; the noble soul consequently requires no prior or independent justification of its creations. A decadent people or age, on the other hand, which cannot afford to squander its dwindling resources, generally resolves to expend itself only if given good reason to do so, usually in the form of a discursive justification. Only decadent peoples need to justify the practices and policies whereby they express their signature virtues, and only decadent peoples bemoan the absence of such justifications. The conspicuous failure of Nietzsche's critics to satisfy the very conditions of justification to which they hold him suggests that he may have a point.

Notes

1. John Rawls, *A Theory of Justice* (Cambridge, MA: Harvard University Press, 1971), p. 325.
2. Ibid.
3. Ibid.
4. Nietzsche finds a 'natural' basis for the pyramidal structure he prefers for hierarchically organized societies in the 'powerful pyramidal rock' he spies near the lake at Silvaplana, at the time that the thought of eternal recurrence descends upon him (EH III:1).
5. Letter to Franz Overbeck on 24 March 1887. Friedrich Nietzsche, *Sämtliche Briefe: Kritische Studienausgabe*, ed G. Colli and M. Montinari (Berlin: de Gruyter/Deutscher Taschenbuch Verlag, 1986), vol. 8, #820, p. 48.
6. Nietzsche thus adds a third caste to the two-tiered system he proposed in H I:439.

7. Nietzsche distinguishes himself from the 'whole European and American species of *libres penseurs*,' who 'still believe in the "ideal."' Declaring himself 'the first *immoralist*,' he thus implies that immoralists no longer want 'to "improve" humankind in their own image' (EH V:2).

8. Nietzsche maintains that 'the claim for independence, for free development, for *laisser aller* is pressed most hotly by the very people for whom no reins would be too strict. This is true *in politics*, this is true in art' (TI IX:41).

9. As early as his *Untimely Meditation* on Schopenhauer, Nietzsche proposed that the task of culture is to correct for the profligacy of Nature: 'Nature propels the philosopher into humankind like an arrow; it takes no aim but hopes the arrow will stick somewhere. But countless times it misses and is depressed at the fact ... The artist and the philosopher are evidence against the purposiveness of nature as regards the means it employs, though they are also first-rate evidence as to the wisdom of its purpose' (SE 7).

10. Allowing that Manu 'found it necessary to be *terrible* [*furchtbar*]' in the struggle against 'the unbred man, the mish-mash man, the chandala,' Nietzsche recounts some of the more grisly edicts of Manu's law (TI VII:3).

11. While Nietzsche's endorsement of slavery may be irrecuperably offensive to contemporary liberal sensibilities, we should bear in mind the plethora of forms – many of them documented by Nietzsche himself – that slavery has assumed over the millennia. Surely the most efficient forms of slavery are those psychological forms embraced by the slaves themselves, such that their slavery becomes the precondition for their perceived happiness or freedom. Although Nietzsche's perfectionism expressly dismisses the political claim of demotic interests, it could nevertheless inspire a 'Grand Inquisitor' regime that rewards its 'slaves' with material comforts and spiritual anesthesia. In his notes, he speculates that 'European democracy must become ultimately' a 'new and sublime development of slavery.' A political regime that could 'make use of' democracy to further the enhancement of humankind would represent 'a kind of goal, redemption and justification for the democratic movement' (WP 954).

12. Mill argues that even those who do not benefit personally and directly from 'individuality' should nevertheless endorse its promotion, for they derive an indirect benefit from the 'individuality' of others. *On Liberty*, ed. Elizabeth Rapaport. (Indianapolis: Hackett, 1978), ch. 3: 'Of Individuality,' esp. pp. 61–68.

13. Nietzsche does argue that 'The philosopher and the artist ... strike home at only a few, while they ought to strike home at everybody' (SE 7), but his remarks on education later in that essay indicate that he does not intend a democratic justification of culture.

14. Nietzsche's shift in orientation to the political microsphere deflects many of the criticisms leveled against his political thinking. Keith Ansell-Pearson, for example, argues that '[Nietzsche] too demands a politics of transfiguration in which modern individuals are to elevate themselves through a process of "going-down" and "going-across" to higher tasks and to higher responsibilities (the *Übermensch*). But the conditions – namely, a tragic culture – which would serve to cultivate such individuals are absent in modern liberal societies.' *Nietzsche contra Rousseau* (Cambridge: Cambridge University Press, 1991), p. 224. If Nietzsche *were* invested in some such 'politics of transfiguration,' then it might be true that 'modern liberal societies' lack the resources 'to culitivate such individuals.' But Nietzsche does not rely on the macropolitical resources of modern liberal societies to produce the exemplary human beings he has in mind. He is well aware that the macropolitical ambitions of his youth are simply incompatible with his historical situation.

15. For a sympathetic treatment of Nietzsche's attempt to legislate an 'aristocracy of soul,' see Leslie Paul Thiele, *Friedrich Nietzsche and the Politics of the Soul* (Princeton: Princeton University Press, 1990), esp. chs. 3–4.

42

Some Remarks on *The Genealogy of Morals**

Arthur Danto

*Source: *International Studies in Philosophy*, vol. 18, no. 2, pp. 3–15.

The third essay of the three which compose *On the Genealogy of Morals* is, according to Nietzsche's preface to the work, a gloss on its prefixed aphorism, which reads: 'Unconcerned, mocking, violent – thus wisdom wants *us*: she is a woman, and always loves only a warrior.' What sort of warrior is unconcerned? One, I suppose, for whom the means is an end, for whom warmaking is not so much what you do but what you are, so that it is not a matter of warring for but as an end. There is, he tells us in the first essay, 'no "being" behind doing . . . "the doer" is merely a fiction added to the deed.' So the unconcerned warrior is perhaps best exemplified by the great archer Arjuna, in the *Bhagavad Gita*, instructed by Krishna that unconcern for consequences, hence disinterested participation in the battle, is the path to follow if release is sought from karma: it is not desisting from action, which is in any case impossible as much for the Gita as for Nietzsche, but a certain enlightened view of the metaphysics of action, which wisdom loves.

If this is the recommended morality, what does the warrior mock? Clearly those still locked in the world of goals and purposes, who subscribe to hypothetical imperatives, who fight for causes, rather than those who are categorical fighters, for whom warring is for its own sake. So violence too is not instrumental but the moral essence of the warrior, not something he especially uses to terrorize, but a secondary effect of the martial art. Why should wisdom then love only the anticonsequentialist? The author of the Gita would answer this out of a moral metaphysics in which karmic transmigration is a form of hell, a view finally negativistic and, as we shall see, predicated on a kind of *ressentiment*, since we blame our suffering on karmic pollutions we ourselves are responsible for. These considerations scarcely would have daunted the discoverer of eternal recurrence, hence of the certitude of unending repeated Mahabharatas, in each of which Arjuna fulfills himself by drawing bowstrings and steering chariots; nor would they faze the prophet of *amor fati* for whom the evil to be avoided consists in trying to be something other than what one is. Kant, the other dominant anticonsequentialist, has a metaphysics of morals, in which it is true that an effort is made to derive our duties from our being, *except* that it construes derivation itself to be our characteristic form of action and our essence itself to be reason, and so entraps an opponent as a confirmer, since denial too exemplifies rationality.

So, if you are Nietzsche, you don't deny, you *reject*. And that is what is to be expected from a warrior whose campaigns happen to be philosophical and who philosophizes with a hammer: who does not so much love wisdom as is, like a warrior, loved by wisdom. So not Nietzsche as a philosopher but Nietzsche as *sophiaphilos*, and whose weapons are words, sometimes used as hammers. (Erase the human-all-too-human fraudulence of 'the old artillery-man,' as he referred to himself on occasion with an affected gruffness.) As one does not argue with an idealist if one does not want to be enmeshed in his web – one instead kicks a rock; or, to cite the practice of one of our most influential contemporary philosophic critics, one does not refute the thinkers one opposes, but instead sneers at them. One puts metaphysics *on ice*, as Nietzsche says in another place: one *mocks*. Mockery is the violence of the metaphysician as warrior. And if one's writings are to be mocking and violent, hence meant to *hurt*, the aphorism is a natural, obvious form to use; for, piercing like a dart the defenses of reason, it lodges inextricably in the mind's flesh, where it sticks as a perpetual invasion: like a barbed arrow, it cannot be extricated without tearing its host.

This aphorism has a complex pragmatics, since it is at once used *and* used to demonstrate what it means to use language in this way, and the commentary, while it does not quite mitigate the pain to philosophical susceptibilities the aphorism may cause – wisdom does not love those who love wisdom – at least reduces the chance of such suffering as it may cause being smothered in *ressentiment* it is also the task of that commentary to dissolve. And in some way its use is meant to have an effect quite opposite to the instillation of an ascetic ideal, as he generalizes upon that concept in the third essay, and so is not meant to transform one into a philosopher, since philosophers are the first to be discussed in that essay as falling under the balefulness of asceticism.

The aphorism is a special use of the language it is also *about*, and it is the second time in two books that he has drawn a joke from the grammar of gender, feminizing wisdom and truth, and both times in order to emphasize a difference between the way he uses language and the ways 'philosophers' use it. In *Beyond Good and Evil* he observes that if truth has the attributes of femininity, then she is unlikely to yield her favors to the cloddish and clumsy idiom of philosophers who do not know how to seduce, as he, Nietzsche, does. But in the same way, the aphorism is the way to approach wisdom, epitomized as female in *this* aphorism: wisdom does not bestow herself upon writers who write as philosophers write, hence not from books that are read as philosophical books are read. Rather language must *implant* itself in the reader, and wisdom comes from an experience which is literary only in the sense that it is caused by a book. So it is language used in a way as to bypass the faculties used ordinarily in reading. 'An aphorism', he writes aphoristic-ally, 'when properly stamped and molded, has not been "deciphered" when it has simply been read.'

In my address to the American Philosophical Association, 'Philosophy as/ and/of Literature,' I argued that by treating philosophy in general as the sort of thing that can be expressed in articles of the sort through which we define ourselves professionally as readers and writers, we misperceive that vast diversity of literary forms the historical bibliography of our discipline dis-plays. Each kind of book has to be read in its kind of way, and just possibly each kind of reader is to be transformed into a different kind of person – the sort of person the philosopher requires the reader to be if the philosophy is to reach him. So we have to realize that in reading Nietzsche we are being attacked; we need some kind of shield or the aphorism will *land* and we lose to the words. One way of fighting back *is* of course to treat him as a phil-osopher himself: the net, too, is a gladiatorial weapon in the skilled left hand of the *retiarius*. So to cage him into a system of repressive categories, to put his toxin on ice, to slip the manacles of asceticism onto his wrists, to locate him in the history of thought, is like driving a stake through Nero's heart in order to keep his ghost stable.

There is a tendency to divide commentators on Nietzsche into those who portray a hard Nietzsche and those who portray a soft Nietzsche. But it is possible to acknowledge him as hard by treating him as though he were soft; so when Philippa Foot reviewed my book on him with a certain appreciation for the originality of treating him as a kind of linguistic epistemologist, and then raised the question of why, if this was what he was *au fond*, anyone would be especially interested in him any longer, I felt I had won a kind of victory – as though I had transformed him into a minotaur by devising a maze. But certainly there is a Nietzsche who genuinely stands against philosophy rather than illustrating it, and who is dangerous and even terrible: and in this paper I would like to acknowledge the virulent Nietzsche, not this time examining his views on language but his use of language, to see what he must have intended by this use and what his beliefs may have been for such intentions to have been coherent. This approach too is a way of standing aside and at a distance.

The psychology of metaphorical address, since metaphor is a rhetorician's device, is that the audience will itself supply the connection withheld by the metaphor, so that the rhetorician opens a kind of gap with the intention that the logical energies of his audience will arc it, with the consequence that having participated in the progression of argument, that audience convinces itself. There is another but comparable psychology for the aphorism, namely that once heard it is unlikely to pass from recollection, so its pointed terseness is a means to ensoul the message it carries, and to counteract the predictable deteriorations of memory. So it is a natural instrument for the moralist. The whole great second essay of the *Genealogy* is precisely addressed to the role of pain in the forging of a moral memory. *Forgetting* is a dimension of animal health, a requisite of mental hygiene – 'no mere *vis inertiae* as the superficial imagine.' Nietzsche writes: 'It is rather an active and in the strictest sense positive faculty of repression.' *Consciousness*, in which attention and memory or memorability coincide, is contrary to the animal nature and possibly even a sort of disease – one of the discontents of civilization – disturbance against which forgetfulness is a preserver of psychic order and peace: 'It will be immediately obvious how there could be no happiness, no cheerfulness, no hope, no pride, no present, without forgetfulness.'

Nietzsche is speaking of what we might call deep forgetfulness here, a complete metabolization of experience rather than the repressive forgetfulness that Freud's later concept of the Unconscious introduces into mental economy, where what is put there clamors to be made conscious and so is not *deeply* forgotten. In order, then, that this sustaining mental entropy should be arrested or reversed, some mnemotechnic is required. As he puts it, 'If something is to stay in the memory it must be burned in; only that which never ceases *hurting* stays in the memory.' This, he continues, 'is a main cause of the oldest (unhappily also the most enduring) psychology on earth.' And, a moment later, 'Man could never do without blood, torture, and sacrifices when he felt a need to create a memory for himself.' Then, after a catalog of medieval cruelties, he concludes, 'All this has its origin in the instinct that realizes that pain is the most powerful aid to mnemonics.' We still talk of teaching someone a lesson as a synonym for administering a beating; we still say 'this will learn you' as we land a punch. And we all admire Kafka's brilliant image in *The Penal Colony* where the inscription of the crime is the crime's punishment, since it is in the medium of the victim's agony. And, when one comes to it – as we shall in more detail – the entire office of religion has consisted in teaching us that our suffering has meaning, so that the chosen people spontaneously turns to its prophets to explain what lesson it is being taught through the suffering it has come to accept as the avenue of communication.

Nietzsche was too much the classicist not to know that aphorism and remembering are pragmatically complicated, or to be ignorant that the earliest collection of aphorisms was attributed to Hippocrates, and constituted a kind of *vade mecum* of medical praxiology, a body of maxims pointed and polished in order to stick in the intern's mind. Since aphoristic form is prophylactic against forgetfulness, and since pain is the prime reenforcer of retention, aphorism and pain are internally related, and so this form spontaneously presents itself to a writer whose warrior violence must be turned against those he appears to admire: the healthy forgetters, the innocent brutes. So when, in the second essay's discussion of the mnemonics of hurt, he writes, 'In a certain sense the whole of asceticism lies here,' he is being disingenuous when he inveighs against asceticism while using language specifically framed to scourge. Someone who uses ascetic practices to kill asceticism is engaged in a very complex communication, supposing he is coherent at all, and he would be right that we are missing what is taking place when we merely *read the words*. An apologist for paganism, for the happy instinctive unconscious life of the spontaneously unremembering beast, has no business creating a moral memory in the course of such apologetics, leaving a scar of consciousness against the easy viscosities of the mental life he celebrates: so the apology for paganism must itself be a moral stab, and self-conscious paganism is logically unlivable. So the remarks on paganism are *meant to hurt* in a way in which the memory of happiness becomes, in Dante's scale, the *maggiore dolore* in a general context of torment: it is as though the entirety of the *Genealogy* is a cell of inflictions and instrument of asectic transformation and a very rough book.

'Even those who suppose, erroneously, that *Beyond Good and Evil* is a collection of aphorisms that may be read in any order whatever,' Walter Kaufmann wrote, having in mind by 'those' specifically me, 'generally recognize that the *Genealogy* comprises three essays.' This in his view brings the book closest to what we Anglo-American philosophers expect philosophical writing to be, all the more so in that 'Nietzsche's manner is much more sober and single-minded than usual.' But the manner of the essayist is a marvelous camouflage for the sort of moral terrorist Nietzsche really was, as the essay itself is a kind of literary camouflage for the sharpened stakes of aphorism he has concealed for the unwary, making this in a deep sense the most treacherous book he ever compiled, one almost impossible to read without being cut to ribbons. Flaying alive – 'cutting straps' – is itemized in his inventory of ghastly interventions which at last instill 'the kind of memory by the aid of which one comes at last to reason!' For how precisely is one to forget what he writes about Jews, slaves, justice, seriousness; about barbarism, morality itself, sensuality, torture, cruelty; about war, women, and will? – even if the book also seems to provide passages of modulating analgesis, enabling him to say, soothingly, that he did not exactly mean what he said, enabling his commentators to reassure us that those who took him at his word had taken him out of context – as though he was after all just to be read. It is like saying the lace handkerchief is the context for the stiletto it hides, or the wine the context for the powdered glass, or the rose an attenuation of the thorn. A man cannot write this way and then stand back in mock innocence and point to the fine print, to the footnote, to the subtle conciliatory phrase written in all but invisible ink, or say that one had expected we were subtle enough to read between the lines!

This book was not written for Nietzsche scholars, capable of handling even deadly poison with the long forceps of *Wissenschaft*. And often Nietzsche tells us as much. At the very beginning, for example, he talks about the English moral psychologists whose interest for us in part lies in the fact that they have written uninteresting books, the question being what were they *doing* by writing such books – 'What do they really want?' – hoping we will be clever enough to ask that of this book, take the hint, raise the query as to why he wipes away with his left hand the blood he has drawn with his right, and not pretend that we are not bleeding or that it is our fault if we are. Just by printing on that package the warning against the contents, you have not provided prophylaxis. There is a passage in Wittgenstein in which he explains certain confusions about language as due to 'the uniform appearance of words when we hear them spoken or meet them in script or print.' 'It is like looking into the cabin of the locomotive,' he goes on to say; 'We see handles all looking more or less alike.' But what shows a greater uniformity of appearance than *books*? *The Genealogy of Morals* is of about the shape and heft of *Utilitarianism* or *Foundations of the Metapysics of Morals* – or for that matter the *Imitatio Christi*. But that does not mean that they are all to be treated the same way, or that reading is a uniform matter – 'especially,' as Wittgenstein writes, 'when we are doing philosophy.' To treat the *Genealogy* as though it were precocious analytical philosophy is to have swallowed a bait without having yet felt the hook. After all the subtitle is: *Eine Streitschrift.* So *à la guerre comme à la guerre*: one had better study one's defenses!

In fact the *Genealogy* is in some ways the least analytical of Nietzsche's books, for it contains one of the subtlest discussions of moral predicates I know. For the question must be raised as to who the readers were to be, what was to bring them to this book, and what particularly were they to get from it. And this returns me to the Hippocratic model of the aphoristic collection. Such collections, our sources claim, were regarded as suitable for dealing with subjects to which no scientific or methodical treatment has been as yet successfully applied, such as in particular medicine. I want to claim that the *Genealogy* is in this respect a medical book: etiological, diagnostic, therapeutic, prognostic. I want to underscore *therapeutic* here, for the book is not for other practitioners of the caring art so much as it is for those who suffer from the diseases it addresses. So the assumption must be that the intended reader is sick, if typically in ways unrecognized by him: one learns the nature of one's illness as one reads the book. And part of the reason the aphorism is so suitable a form is that the language has to get past the defenses we bring to the book since the defenses are in a way part of the disease, as in neurosis according to the classic analysis, where the repression of the pathogen is part of the pathogen. As in analysis, a task of the therapist is to bring to consciousness the mechanisms of disassociation and, if there is such a word, of disconsciation. So the reader is as it were being treated as he reads, and a condition of therapeutic success is that he be kept continuously conscious of the disorder the book means to drive out: as Hippocrates says, the practitioner is to be 'seconded by the patient.' And in a way the patient, or reader here, must be helped by the practitioner to cure himself. In a way, I suppose, there is an analogy to Socratic maieutic, here the point being that only the sufferer can solve the problem of his suffering, the doctor's role consisting in showing him that he is sick. So the book has to be painful. And arguably the cure more painful than the disease, with which, after all, we have grown comfortable.

It scarcely can pass notice how frequently and characteristically Nietztsche here employs the vocabularies of pathology (it would be an interesting scholarly enterprise to see the degree to which the same vocabularies occur in all the main books in this way, or whether each book has its paradigm lexicon, from which the mode of literary address can then be inferred). The period of Nietzsche's great productivity was the great age of German physiology – Johannes Müller, Justus von Liebig, Karl Ludwig, had made Germany the center for physiological investigation in the form it has had ever since, and though in no sense myself a historian of medicine, I am certain that a suitable scholarship would discover among their procedures certain which Nietzsche adapted, transforming them of course through his own special genius. It is still difficult, and it must in Nietzsche's time have been all but impossible, to draw a careful distinction between physiological and physiognomic differences, and to suppose that a certain blue-eyed blondness might not connote a physiological distinctiveness of some importance: or that shortness of stature might not be a physiological defect.

The physiologization of moral concepts, the proposal that in the end moral differences must be physiological differences, or that a certain physiognomical paradigm must be a paradigm of health, all other variants being sick, are among his most reckless and dangerous conjectures. But the shock of Darwinism was still being felt, and he was not immune to the moralization of natural selection that almost defines nineteenth-century thought, which can lead to the view, as we know, that those with different moral beliefs may be contagious, ought to be segregated at least, and at worst may have to be eliminated in the interests of moral sepsis. And they can lead, in the other direction, to the view that those who are physiologically distinctive, and for that matter different, must fall under a different moral order, and need not be treated in the way we treat one another. I imagine that the great movements toward equal rights, equal no matter what one's age, sex, color, competence, or creed, constitute an effort to make physiological differences irrelevant to moral considerations. And while we must not be dismissive since, as Hippocrates says, 'art is long, life is short,' and there will always be more to find out than we can possibly hope, and no one knows whether criminality is chromosomal – or for that matter generosity genetic – it remains unclear how such discoveries should be responded to morally. It is also doubtful that reading a book of *this* sort could be regarded a significant intervention if it turned out that a certain moral difference *were* a physiological one in that way. But neither would Nietzsche have supposed it were – so the question is what sort of disease could it have been for which he might have thought the book *was* significantly interventive? And here I can say perhaps most of what I have to say about this work.

I think the answer must lie in a distinction between what I shall term extensional suffering and intensional suffering, where the latter consists in an interpretation of the former. As I see Nietzsche's thesis, it is this: the main sufferings human beings have been subject to throughout history are due to certain interpretive responses to the fact of extensional suffering. It is not clear that Nietzsche believes he can deal with extensional suffering. But he can deal with intentional suffering, thus helping reduce, often by a significant factor, the total suffering in the world. For while extensional suffering is bad enough, often it is many times compounded by our interpretations of it, themselves often far worse than the disorder itself.

Consider the example of impotence in the human male, in certain cases genuinely a physiological symptom of an underlying sickness with no clinical identity of its own, due, say, to diabetes, prostate disorder, and the like. For most men, and doubtless for most women sexually involved with men, it is a pretty appalling symptom. But to explain why it is refers us to the complex of ideas connected with the male self-image of adequacy and power, and the extreme vulnerability in the male ego which sexual incapacity opens up. It can lead, it has led, to suicide, depression, despair, divorce. So if we subtracted all this suffering from the sum total of suffering, the actual symptom might not amount to very much in the scale of human agony. Compare it to the other symptoms of diabetes: polyuria, polydipsia, retinopathy, renal malfunction, circulatory problems, propensity to gangrene, susceptibility to fungus, to heart disease, acidosis, coma – and a merely flaccid penis seems pretty minor. But knowing the male temperament I am certain that this morally over-charged symptom would be singled out as the most intolerable effect of this disorder. Very few, I think, attach much significance to the mere fact of hyperglycemia, or would commit suicide over that, or regard themselves as flawed – or sick. It is a good example of moralized physiology, but in any case the disorders addressed by Nietzsche in this book, and which it is his enterprise to help us cure ourselves of, are interpretations of suffering which themselves generate suffering.

They are due, one and all, to bad philosophy, bad psychology, to religion – which in Nietzsche's scheme does not have a *good* form so as to make 'bad religion' nonredundant – and of course bad moral systems, such as the one which takes as its primary value-opposition the distinction between good and evil. All of these are in a way modalities of *schlechtes Gewissen*, which I shall persist in translating as 'bad consciousness.' Bad *conscience* – in English usage at least – is more or less the same as guilty conscience, but guilt is only one of the modalities of badness. Bad consciousness is consciousness of badness, which of course may be illusory, as when someone good falsely seems bad to himself. Any suffering due to false moral beliefs about ourselves is due to bad consciousness, when there is nothing bad about us *except* consciousness of being bad. And the book might then in part be addressed specifically to the cure of this sort of suffering.

Though at times Nietzsche speaks as though only the extensionally strong and healthy are subject to bad consciousness, in truth it is difficult to see how anyone in our civilization can have altogether escaped it: and even those who in his view really do suffer, really are in his sense 'bad' – that is, bad specimens of the species *human* – typically also suffer from misinterpretations of this disorder, and no less than the good may be for this reason subject to bad consciousness. It is possible, of course, that Nietzsche's psycho-historical account is correct, and the particular form bad consciousness takes may be traced back to the pathogens of what he terms *ressentiment*, to which the extensionally bad are subject; even so they themselves suffer from the epidemics of bad consciousness which define the subsequent history of our civilization, that is, not to be coy about it, from Christianity if he is right. So even the bad might profit from dissipation of this sort of intensional suffering, leaving extensional suffering to be treated by those whose speciality it is. After all, identification of the real disease is the first step in medicine.

Let us attend, for a moment, to the concept of *ressentiment*. Nietzsche more or less assumed that anyone in a state of *ressentiment* must also be in some state or other, in his scheme, of actual physiological suffering, for what *ressentiment* – which is only distantly connected to the English word *resentment* – amounts to is a certain sort of interpretive explanation of suffering in the mind of the sufferer. In actual fact it would not matter if the suffering in question were real, that is, physiological, or only believed to be real, as in cases of what used to be called hysteria. Nietzsche's point is put into what one might term an *a priori* of suffering:

> Every sufferer instinctively seeks a cause for his suffering; more exactly an agent . . . some living thing upon which he can, on some pretext or other vent his affects, actually or in effigy: for the venting of his affects represents the greatest attempt on the part of the sufferer to win relief, *anaesthesia* – the narcotic he cannot help desiring to deaden pain of every kind.

This, which Nietzsche glosses as 'the actual physiological cause off *ressentiment*, vengefulness, and the like,' could easily have formed a section in the Hippocratic collection. And the implication is clear: sufferers tend to *moralize* suffering by holding someone or something responsible for it: as though mere suffering, undeserved only in the sense that it makes no sense to speak of it as deserved, is simply unintelligible. 'Why me, Lord?' is the spontaneous response to sickness; 'What did I do to deserve this?' – as though there were no as it were unearned suffering, as though suffering were in every instance a *sentence* of some sort. 'Someone or other must be to blame for my feeling ill,' Nietzsche puts in the mind of the sufferer – a kind of reasoning 'held the more firmly the more the real cause of their feeling ill, the physiological cause, remains hidden.' And Nietzsche adds at this point a parade of medical opinion that reflects the state of knowledge of the time, or his state of know-ledge, as well as the intention of the text:

> It may perhaps lie in some disease of the *nervus sympathicus*, or in an excessive secretion of bile, or in a deficiency of potassium sulfate and phosphate in the blood, or in an obstruction in the abdomen which impedes blood circulation, or in degeneration of the ovaries, and the like.

Readers of Nietzsche's letters appreciate the degree to which he was a dietary crank; but in any case, amateur diagnostic notwithstanding, it is per-fectly plain that the disease he was addressing was not of the sort itemized here, but a metadisease which requires of the sufferer that his illness, as Susan Sontag has phrased it, be metaphorical. In any case *ressentiment* consists in re-feeling suffering as the *effect* of a *moral* cause one may also *resent* if one feels it is undeserved. As in the case of Job, whose classic posture is exactly that of resentment in this form, since he can see no *reason* why God should be causing him to suffer. But even if he did feel he deserved the boils and losses, this would still be a case of *ressentiment* because he moralized his suffering.

Religion, save the rather rare case of Job, abolishes all possibility of resentment; but it scarcely abolishes all possibility of *ressentiment*, since in fact it depends upon it for existence: for what does religion do except to teach us that the suffering we endure we also deserve? Religion redirects *ressenti-ment*, as Nietzsche puts it, by making the patient the very agent he seeks, informing us that we have brought it on ourselves. Consider the Black Death which swept Florence and Sienna in the fourteenth century. Of course it was physiological, but men alive at that time had no way of knowing how: *b. plagus* was not an available concept. But they immediately assumed they were at fault (as they doubtless were in matters of elementary hygiene), chiefly through their arrogance vis-à-vis God, as shown in their treatment of human subjects in painting after Giotto! So the most rational thing, under prevailing theory, was to change the styles of representation, which have been traced for us by Millard Miess. I don't say this was wholly silly, and the consequences could be benign, as when an outbreak of some epidemic in Venice moved the governing body to commission a church from Palladio. True, this did not help any sufferers, but nothing they knew how to do would have done that anyway, and *Il Redentore* still stands. Religion, then, makes suffering intelligible – but only in the framework of a scheme which makes search after its true causes unintelligible. And this is true even in those cases where we ourselves *have* brought on our own suffering, as in the case of gout or obesity, or venereal disease or cirrhosis of the liver or chronic drug addiction: these disorders are the consequences of, they are not *punishments* for, the excesses that led to them.

Interestingly, Nietzsche observes that 'this plant blooms best today among the anarchists and the Anti-Semites.' That is, blaming the Jews, or blaming the bourgeoisie, for all social ills, rather than looking more deeply into the social structure for proper etiology, parallels the classic forms of the *a priori* of affect. Admittedly, we may know about as much regarding what affects society as Florentines knew in the Cinquecento what affects the human body, and often in our ignorance we attack as cause what may only be another effect. I tend to think that certain accounts by feminists, in which men as men are blamed for the suffering of women as women, must ultimately yield to a finer analysis in which what coarsely is considered a cause of feminine agony is itself a symptom of the same sickness from which they doubtless suffer. I have often thought no better specimen of *schlechtes Gewissen* can be found than the sort of self-castigation shown by men, say in the weekly column 'For Men' in *The New York Times* magazine section, where men boast of their degree of feminization. I have no criticism of this, and nothing but criticism of its opposite, where men vaunt the paraphernalia of *machismo*: but it is a good case of self-despising to illustrate that term in Nietzsche's moral psychology. Nietzsche condenses his general insight in one of his profoundest aphorisms: 'What really arouses indignation against suffering is not suffering as such but the senselessness of suffering.' And if there is any single moral/metaphysical teaching I would ascribe to him, it would be this: suffering really is meaningless, there is no point to it, and the amount of suffering caused by *giving* it a meaning chills the blood to contemplate.

I of course am not talking about suffering we cause under the name of punishment, where some complex balance must be struck between the suffering caused by the culprit and the suffering the culprit must undergo in order to restore equilibrium. That is a model of justice that must be debated on grounds other than any I want to advance here. What Nietzsche objects to is not so much this model but its total generalization, making *every* suffering a punition and the entire *world* a court of justice with a penitentiary annex. If I am right that this is his view, the final aphorism of the *Genealogy*, 'man would rather will the *nothing* than *not* will,' does not so much heroize mankind, after all. What it does is restate the instinct of *ressentiment*: man would rather his suffering be meaningful, hence would rather will meaning onto it, than acquiesce in the meaninglessness of it. It goes against this instinct to believe what is essentially the most liberating thought imaginable, that life is without meaning. In a way, the deep affliction from which he seeks to relieve us is what today we think of as hermeneutics: the method of interpretation primarily of suffering. And when he says, in so many places and in so many ways, 'there are no facts, only interpretation,' he is, I believe, finally addressing the deep, perhaps ineradicable propensities of *ressentiment*. Meaning, *si je peux aphoriser moi-même*, is demeaning.

There is an obverse, which is that in order to accept the consolations of religion, the dubious gift of meaning, as it were, one must accept the anthropology which alone makes religion applicable in the first place, namely that we are weak, defective, and almost defined through our propensity to suffer. The limits of man are emphasized as such that we are unable to release ourselves save through the mediation of a being whose power is adequate to the salvation. Of course, with religions in general, the salvation is often from suffering we would not know we had were it not revealed, to a state abstractly defined through the absence of revealed suffering, by means we again would not understand but for revelation. Who would know we were contaminated by original sin, for instance, that we need to be saved from it, and that the means whereby this might be achieved is if God took on a form whereby he might purge our suffering through his? Leaving everything as it was so far as life itself is concerned, since the suffering we were told was ours was not felt, and the redemption we have been given does not connect with release from any felt suffering. And the limits are finally limits only relative to the scheme of suffering and relief erected alongside the actual schedule of human agonies and joys the scheme itself does not penetrate. Whatever the case, the picture of man as limited and weak, if believed, goes hand in hand exactly with *schlechtem Gewissen*. And to release us from that is to release us from the picture: and that is the therapeutic task of the *Genealogy*, and of Nietzsche's philosophical work as such.

Let me return to hermeneutics. I would concede to the continental theorists that it is the fundamental fact of human being, and hence must be the final datum for the human sciences, that men cannot experience without interpreting, and that we live in a world of intersignification. I am far from certain that the human sciences must themselves reflect the structure of their subject, that science itself is only a form of interpretation of a piece with the interpretations it is supposed to study: hence am far from certain that there is a hermeneutical circle which somehow invalidates such a science: for there may be ways of representing interpretations which are not at all of a piece with the interpretations represented. Even so, we may accept the hermeneutical picture that our *esse est interpretari*. But then the contrast must be perfect between ourselves and the *Bestie*, and it is less their cheerful innocent savagery that Nietzsche applauds in the blond beasts than their absolute freedom from meaning. They live, as he says in his early book on history, as beasts do, 'in a happy blindness between the walls of the past and the future.' Human existence, by deep contrast, is 'an imperfect tense that never becomes a present.' It is not so much history as the philosophy of history that robs life of happiness, since the latter seeks perennially the significance of events it would be happiness instead merely to forget or, next best, to take as they came, at a kind of absolute magnitude, without forming a kind of text. Nietzsche's doctrine of Eternal Recurrence, itself the topic of so much speculation and scholarship, must be perceived by everyone, however otherwise divided on its cognitive status, as deeply contrary to any philosophy of history: iteration dissolves meaning, and infinite iteration erases it totally. It is a rock against which history as significance must shatter, and in particular religious history, the history of fall, covenant, sin, redemption, trial, judgment, and hell, where it is an unrelieved anxiety as to where we stand and what we can hope.

When Zarathustra announces the death of God, he goes on to say he died of pity. The implication is that what he pitied us for was him: pitied us for the hopeless disproportion between a being of infinite value and his creatures who must in relationship to him be incalculably worthless. By his disappearing, the ratio is broken and the disvalue which depended upon the disproportion itself vanishes. It is a beautiful gift, that of disappearance: which of the parents among us is capable of it? By comparison sacrificing even only begotten sons is easy: our world is full of gold star mothers and fathers, proud of their distinction. With the death of God we are returned to what Kundera speaks of, alas as unbearable: a certain lightness of being.

It is plain that God did not die in order that something else should take his place: rather, he meant for the place to die with the occupant. The genius of the third essay of the *Genealogy* lies in its inventory of disguises the ascetic ideal takes, so that often positions which define themselves as contrary to asceticism only exemplify it. As a class, these occupants of the position vacated by God impose on their subscribers a network of interpretation of suffering, and project a kind of utopian redemption: science, politics, art, and certainly much that passes for psychological therapy only change the name of the game. There are even ways of understanding the notorious concept of the Superman which vest themselves in the same demeaning armature that Christianity did, another disguise of asceticism. But this could not be Nietzsche's Superman if he has the least consistency. The Superman does not reside in a kind of *beyond* since it is precisely that kind of beyond that Nietzsche is bent on stultifying. The man of the future, he writes at the end of the second essay is 'this bell-stroke of man and the great decision that liberates the will again and restores its goal to earth and his hope to man.'

I return to the aphorism I began by interpreting. The *unconcern* that wisdom is supposed to love clearly connects with the will. It is an unconcern with goals which impose a program of choices on life, where these depend on schemes of meaning it is the goal of Nietzsche's philosophy to demolish. It is not so much the extirpation of the will as its reeducation and redirection: its return to the goals of simply normal life. Nietzsche's philosophical mood is one of lightness, cheer, sunniness, which was also his personal mood, heroic in view of his familiar sufferings. He complains of terrible headaches, nausea, stomach ache: he was afflicted by the cold, the damp, bad food, and of course a sense of isolation and unrecognition. He sought like a cat for a comfortable corner of Europe, and the preposterous exultation of his discovery of the alleged salubrities of Turin are an index to his discomforts. He did not suffer, however, in the way in which, on his view, the bulk of mankind suffer: from meanings which truncate the lives they are supposed to redeem. When we contemplate the sufferings human beings have endured in the century since God made the supreme sacrifice, we wonder at the wisdom of that evacuation. If we were to subtract all the intensional suffering from the history of our century, we would subtract the history of the century.

But that is what Nietzsche would like to have achieved: to subtract all those schemes of disvaluation of the present by reference to an inflated valuation of a future; to make the world the place we live rather than pass through to some higher state; to restore the present to the present; to replace a morality of means with a morality of principle; to act in such a way as to be consistent with acting that way eternally; to stultify the instinct for significance. This is the posture of unconcern, and while it is unclear that it would make us altogether happy, it is perfectly plain that it erases most of what has made for human unhappiness through history: the martyrdoms, the crucifixions, the eggs cracked in the name of political omelettes, man as a means. Not surprisingly it is the only view consistent with human dignity, the only view of man as an end.

43

Nietzsche's Immoralism*

Philippa Foot

*Source: *New York Review of Books*, vol. 38 no. 11, 13 June 1991 (revised).

In this essay on Nietzsche's immoralism I am going to do something rather difficult, because I am going to ask a simple question about Nietzsche, and it is hard to ask a simple question about Nietzsche: it is hard to hold onto anything simple in the face of this determined joker, who loved masks and hidden things, and whose Protean style is sometimes of the most lapidary aphoristic simplicity but often lush and rhetorical. It has been said that *Thus Spake Zarathustra* should be read as opera, and it is surely a great shame that we never had a rendition by Anna Russell of those wild journeys between mountain, market place and cave.

Nietzsche thought he could discredit morality; and I want to ask 'Was he right?' I think the question should be asked. It is always respectful to ask of a great philosopher whether what he says is true, and hardly respectful not to ask it. Why do so many contemporary moral philosophers, particularly of the Anglo-American analytic school, ignore Nietzsche's attack on morality – just go on as if this extraordinary event in the history of thought had never occurred? It is true, of course, that, even apart from the difficulty of getting even a very modest competence in Nietzsche studies, it is hard for those of us who belong to the plain-speaking school of analytic philosophers to get our hands on his work. We are used to ferreting out entailments, and lines of argument, building up a theory from individual passages. And I do not think that one can work on Nietzsche quite like that. The unity of his writings – which is most remarkable in spite of their amazing richness and many superficial contradictions – comes from his attitudes, from his daring, his readiness to query *everything*, and from his special nose for vanity, for pretence, for timid evasion, and for that drive to domination which he finally supposed to be the principle of all life. One must take account of Nietzsche's attitudes; of the contempt he felt for modern European man, for the 'newspaper-reading' public,[1] for democracy, for nationalism, for Bismarck and all things German (excepting Goethe, 'the exception among Germans'[2]). And account too, of course, of his vituperative but none the less recognisant attitude to Christianity, which he saw as the religion of pity and weakness but also, at times, as the beneficially tyrannical source of spiritualisation in man.[3] One has to remember that Nietzsche was one who wanted to be an *affirmer*, not a caviller, who repeatedly praised lightness of spirit, and wrote much about dancing and laughter. When he put forward his strange theory of the eternal recurrence of all things – round and round again – this was most significantly a rejection of gloomy nihilism and a way of saying 'yes' even to his own physically painful and painfully lonely life.

All this, and much more, is needed to interpret Nietzsche. But what, then, can he have to offer to the descendants of Frege and Russell, of G. E. Moore and Wittgenstein? What can *we* take from the strange Nietzschean symphony of subjectively interrelated attitudes and beliefs? Even in those areas in which there is overlap between his interests and ours, can we assume that he is seriously concerned with the truth? Was it not Nietzsche who saw truth in terms of divergent 'perspectives', and who insisted on questioning the value of truth itself? He said all this, and meant it. Nevertheless he saw as a great sign of those things he so much celebrated, 'strength' and 'life', the ability to face reality as it is. Honesty (*Redlichkeit*) was, he wrote, the one virtue that he and other 'free spirits' must take from morality, that they could not leave behind:

> . . . let us work on it with all our malice and love and not weary of 'perfect-ing' ourselves in *our* virtue, the only one left us. . . . And if our honesty should nevertheless grow weary one day and sigh and stretch its limbs and find us too hard . . . let us dispatch to her assistance whatever we have in us of devilry . . .[4]

Nietzsche may have thought of even his own views as merely *his* truths (whatever exactly that means). But his love of truth was based on one of the strongest things in him: that is, on his contempt for evasive falsification.

So, in spite of all the discouraging omens, I want to ask what truth there could be in the doctrine that makes us name Nietzsche, as he sometimes named himself, 'immoralist'.

Nietzsche's immoralism. A host of problems and many interpretations live together under this roof. Was he perhaps preaching in favour of a new moral-ity rather than against morality as such? I think not. Nor was Nietzsche simply a run-of-the-mill moral relativist. He branded as 'childish' the idea that no morality can be binding because moral valuations are necessarily different among different nations.[5] So even his arguments for the subjectivity of moral judgement were idiosyncratic. He saw different moralities as deter-mined by the desires and needs of peoples and generations: at one time the need to control aggressive individuals when they were no longer useful in meeting external enemies; in the long reign of Christianity the desire of the weak and 'misbegotten' to brand themselves as 'good' and those stronger characters, whom they feared, as 'evil'; in modern Europe the longing of the mediocre 'to look nobler, more important, more respectable, "divine".'[6] Throughout all these changes morality was, Nietzsche insisted, fundamentally a subterfuge by which the weak – the members of the herd – tried to dress up their weakness and their fears as 'goodness', a device by which they produced self-doubt and a bad conscience in those who, as nobles, had once called *themselves* good. The 'nobles', the type of the original barbaric Greek and the Renaissance Man, had called 'inferior' men bad (*schlecht*) only by contrast to themselves. The 'inferiors', on the other hand, needed to see dangerous men as 'evil' (*böse*) in order to see themselves as good.

In suggesting that different moralities were rooted in the different needs, fears, and desires of different peoples Nietzsche was applying to valuations the characteristically Nietzschean 'perspectivism': the interpretation by historical genealogy and above all by underlying desires that he applied to all modes of thought. He applied it particularly to abstract philosophies, which he saw as expressing instincts, needs, and fears rather than that will-o'-the-wisp 'pure thought'. Thoughts he said, 'are the shadows of our feelings – darker, emptier, and simpler.'[7] But there is something more specific than this in Nietzsche's insistence that 'there are no moral facts'.[8]

> This problem of the *value* of pity and of the morality of pity [he says] . . . seems at first sight to be merely something detached, an isolated question mark; but whoever sticks with it and *learns* how to ask questions here will experience what I experienced – a tremendous new prospect opens up for him, a new possibility comes over him like a vertigo, . . . fear leaps up, his belief in morality, in all morality, falters – finally a new demand becomes audible . . . we need a *critique* of moral values, *the value of these values themselves must be called in question . . .*[9]

Nietzsche says that he is going to query the *value* of moral values, which suggests that he has some other value in play. And there is, indeed, a positive side to Nietzsche's ideology. He is affirming a special kind of aestheticism, and attacking morality partly on its own ground but partly in the interest of what he calls the 'ascending' type of man. What was to be seen as 'good' was the 'strong', 'fine', 'noble', 'subtle' type of human being. This free and joyous spirit, subjecting himself to the sternest discipline, but accepting no rule from others, was sometimes seen by Nietzsche as the 'overman', the superman of Nietzschean popular legend: that is, as one who belonged to the future. But actual human beings might be stepping-stones or bridges on the way to this future. The important question to ask about any man was whether he represented an ascending or descending type. This was the profound classification, and determined the worth *for the particular instance* of those elements of character and action that moralists wrongly thought significant in themselves. So egoism, for instance, should not be thought of as either bad or good in all individuals.

> The value of egoism depends on the physiological value of him who possesses it: it can be very valuable, it can be worthless and contemptible. Every individual may be regarded as representing the ascending or descending line of life. When one has decided which, one has thereby established a canon for the value of his egoism.[10]

Nietzsche thus, very characteristically, saw our common moral classifications as reflecting reality in a herd-based way that was deleterious to the exceptional man. What was worst about them, and was common to all morality, was the attempt to determine the value of any *kind* of conduct in the case of each and every individual agent. 'Good and evil the same for all!' he scoffed.[11] There could be no beneficial *rules* of conduct. 'A virtue has to be *our* invention, *our* most personal defence and necessity: in any other sense it is merely a danger.'[12] And again '"Good" is no longer good when one's neighbour mouths it.'[13] Thus Nietzsche thinks of value as belonging only to an individual who has created his own character in a pattern that cannot be prescribed for others, and it is here that his shift from a moral to an aesthetic form of evaluation becomes clear. Not surprisingly, he is writing of what he himself, as a genius of a style and image, knew best. Not for nothing does he say in one place '. . . we want to be the poets of our lives.'[14] The discipline that he so much stresses for the creation of a splendid individual human being is modelled on the discipline of the artist. For an artist, rules would indeed be problematic: the goodness of what he or she makes cannot be the same as the goodness of other artists' work, as if there could be a manual for producing what is good. This analogy seems to be an essential element in Nietzsche's aestheticism – in his shift from moral to aesthetic valuation. Theoretically, it is separate from his perspectivism, since, after all, the absence of rules for artistic creativity does not entail the subjectivity of aesthetic judgement. But when the individual himself is both artist and art-work they come together in the fact of his special 'interpretation' of the world, the interpretation that determines what he sees as good.

There have been many attempts to see all this as an inspiring call to a kind of joyous paganism that would leave us with all that is best in morals. Can this be sustained? I think not, just because of Nietzsche's attack on the universalism in morality. He insists that there are no kinds of actions that are good or bad in themselves, and this has, it seems, a fatal implication for the teaching of justice. It is justice, as understood in the traditional catalogue of the virtues, that forbids certain acts, as of murder, torture, and enslavement, and brands them as evil whosoever carries them out. Nietzsche, on the other hand, says that there is nothing good or evil 'the same for all' and tells us we must look to see what *kind of a person* is doing an action before we can determine its 'value'.

If this implies, as it seems, that not even the most flagrant acts of injustice can be called evil in themselves, then was Thomas Mann not perhaps right in saying that Nietzsche had not faced the reality of evil? Thomas Mann said in 1947:

> How bound in time, how theoretical too, how inexperienced does Nietzsche's romanticizing about wickedness appear . . . today! We have learned to know it in all its miserableness.[15]

Mann was writing, of course, soon after the facts about Belsen and Buchenwald, and their images, had come to haunt us. So however much the Nazis had had to distort Nietzsche in order to claim him as one of their prophets, Nazi actions and Nietzsche's reputation may be linked in this other way, as suggested by Mann; that is in the way his treatment of evil has come to look to us, in the light of what they did.

It may be argued that this is unfair to Nietzsche. It may be pointed out that neither Hitler nor Stalin were individuals of whom it *should* be thought for a moment that they embodied his ideals. J. P. Stern is surely mistaken when he writes 'No man came closer to the full realisation of self created "values" than . . . Hitler.'[16] Nietzsche is, after all, vituperative about merely cruel monsters, and while, to be sure, he praises the (as he says) 'pranksomely' ruthless 'nobles' above the resentful 'herd', Alexander Nehamas seems right to say that they do not need to be seen as his ideal for all times.

Nietzsche's defenders may also remind us of what he said about the need to discipline the passions, which is indeed a central element in his philosophy. For Nietzsche is not at all like Callicles, the immoralist in Plato's *Gorgias* whose ideal is that of the libertine. Nietzsche preaches hardness and self-mastery. The passions are not to be weakened or extirpated, but used in the creation (once more one thinks 'it's like the artist's creation') of the self. Moreover he has a doctrine of the sublimation of the passions, being one of the first actually to use the term *sublimieren*, and believing, for instance, that the 'drive' of cruelty could be be turned into a desire for truth. It will be said, therefore, that Nietzsche did not actually countenance acts of injustice in substituting his own prescription of self-creation for morality's canon against such things as murder and oppression. Did he perhaps believe that no one who truly embodied the Nietzschean ideal would ever find *himself* in such actions? Might the ideal of self-realization turn out to be unshocking in the end?

I am sure that *something* of all this is true, and that one side of Nietzsche would have welcomed such an accommodation. He speaks of gentleness in some convincing passages. And he was himself, I would suppose, for all his insistence on the beneficial effect of suffering, actually over-sensitive to it in others, really experiencing *pity* as he notoriously represented it: that is, as suffering's contagion. The character of the man himself shows too in his heroes and the books he loved. Caesare Borgia was not a hero of his, in spite of his preference 'even', as he notoriously said, for him over a mean-spirited member of 'the herd.' [17] True, he admired Napoleon, but said that he was 'half superman half monster'. Nietzsche's great hero was, it seems, Goethe, whom he praised especially for his moulding of sensuality and spirit into a harmonious self. And among the literary works Nietzsche most loved there were not only the novels of Stendhal and Dostoevsky but also two quiet-mannered books Eckerman's *Conversations with Goethe* and Emerson's *Essays*, a book he 'felt at home in' and seems to have kept by him for much of his life. (One gets interesting light on Nietzsche from both of these works.)

Nevertheless there was a side of Nietzsche's deeply pathological psyche that seems to have gloried in the fact that his immoralism allowed, if done by certain people, even terrible deeds. Unlike other proponents of self-realization Nietzsche does not say that these acts could never be a sign of health and of truly 'becoming what one is'. On the contrary he stresses the fearfulness of his 'revaluation of values'. He insists that he has set out on a journey over terrifying seas, and, from the time in the early eighties when he first started to attack morality to the end of his working life, one can find passages that stress the fearfulness of his thought, and seem to license injustice.

In *The Gay Science* of 1882 he writes

> Hatred, the mischievous delight in the misfortunes of others, the lust to rob and dominate, and whatever else is called evil belongs to the most amazing economy of the preservation of the species.[18]

And again in the same work:

> some kinds of hatred, jealousy, stubbornness, mistrust, hardness, avarice, and violence . . . belong among the *favorable* conditions without which any great growth even of virtue is scarcely possible. The poison of which weaker natures perish strengthens the strong – nor do they call it poison.[19]

Four years later, in *Beyond Good and Evil*, he writes that

> . . . everything evil, terrible, tyrannical in man, everything in him that is kin to beasts of prey and serpents, serves the enhancement of the species 'man' as much as its opposite does.[20]

And in a note from 1887 included in the *Nachlass* collection *The Will to Power*:

when one makes men more evil, one makes them better – . . . one cannot be one without being the other – At this point the curtain rises on the dreadful *forgery of the psychology of man hitherto.*[21]

Perhaps these passages are not absolutely decisive. Perhaps Nietzsche is talking about *'drives'* which might be 'enhanced' and 'strengthened' before being sublimated into harmless actions. But this does not seem at all plausible in the face of his insistence that his doctrine is vertiginously fearful.

In any case I do not think it should be argued that the virtue of justice can be accommodated within Nietzsche's picture of splendid individuals finding each *his own* values and 'his own way.' For there is something in Nietzsche's description of this 'higher type' of human being that positively tells against it. I mean the way in which the self-guiding person is described as seeing those whom he counts as 'inferiors'. One simply cannot ignore all that Nietzsche says, approvingly, of the experience, the feeling, the *'pathos'* as he likes to put it, 'of distance', of being not just apart from, but higher than, those who belong to 'the herd'. Nietzsche says at one point that contempt is better than hatred, and he thinks the idea of equality utterly despicable.

Now what I wonder is this: whether the practice of justice may not absolutely require a certain recognition of equality between human beings, not a pretence of equality of talents but the equality that is spoken of in a passage of Gertrude Stein's when she says (pretending to be Alice B. Toklas) that she herself had a sense of equality, and that that was why people would help her. 'The important thing . . . is that you must have deep down as the deepest thing in you a sense of equality.' This is particularly striking in Gertrude Stein, who was certainly not one to underestimate her own individuality, talent, or place in literary history. The sense of equality that she is thinking of must, surely, have to do with thinking that one is always, fundamentally, in the same boat as everybody else, and therefore that it is quite unsuitable for anyone to be grand.

Perhaps I am wrong in thinking of this sense of equality as necessary for the practice of justice. That the two are connected seems, however, to be supported in a certain passage I once came across in which G. K. Chesterton wrote about Charles Dickens.

Dickens, Chesterton said,

> . . . did not dislike this or that argument for oppression: he disliked oppression. He disliked a certain look on the face of a man when he looks down on another man. And the look on that face is the only thing in the world that we really have to fight between here and the fires of hell.[22]

Nietzsche's endless talk about inferiors and superiors, and the way he countenances some men looking down on others, together with his own readiness to sacrifice – to write off – the 'mediocre,' confirms the impression that justice gets short shrift in Nietzsche's scheme of things: that it is quite wrong to see his 'aesthetic' as taking nothing we think precious from the morality he attacks. Nietzsche's defenders will rise up, no doubt, to insist that the 'looking down' that he speaks of is nothing so crude as that of which G. K. Chesterton speaks. But the language of contempt is undeniably there. Nietzsche's defenders are like those who say of Wagner that he is better than he sounds.

To our objections on behalf of justice Nietzsche would, no doubt, reply that what should be in question is not whether we *want* to hold on to a moral mode of valuation, but whether we *can* do so with honesty. For his contention is that morality is tainted by certain pious falsehoods that are necessary to it; so that morality in praising honesty sowed the seeds of its own demise. Therefore we do have to ask ourselves not just what Nietzsche's own system of valuation amounts to but also if morality can, as we hope, withstand his attack.

What were these falsehoods – the 'errors' that Nietzsche saw as endemic to morality? I will list them in what I see as an ascending order of interest.

First there is the belief in free will, which he challenged on the ground that will itself, as required for either free or unfree will, is non-existent. What we call will is, he said, in truth nothing but a complex of sensations, as of power and resistance, and it is pure illusion to think of it as a basis for 'moral responsibility.' Our actions arise not primarily from conscious motivations but rather from physiological and psychological factors of which we are unaware.

It follows, Nietzsche thinks, that men are totally innocent, as innocent as anything else in the world, though this, he says, is something we hate to accept.

> Man's complete lack of responsibility for his behavior and for his nature, is the bitterest drop which the man of knowledge must swallow if he had been in the habit of seeing responsibility and duty as humanity's claim to nobility. All his judgments, distinctions, dislikes have thereby become worthless and wrong: the deepest feeling he had offered a victim or a hero was misdirected; he may no longer praise, no longer blame, for it is nonsensical to praise and blame nature and necessity. Just as he loves a good work of art, but does not praise it, because it can do nothing about itself, just as he regards a plant, so he must see the actions of men and his own actions.[23]

The topic of free will and moral responsibility is itself so large that one cannot quickly assess Nietzsche's idea that there is an error here on which morality is based. But it may be pointed out that the theory of the will that he attacks would find few defenders today; and few would now deny unconscious motivation. Nevertheless moral, as opposed to aesthetic, evaluation does require *some* distinction between actions for which we are, and actions for which we are not, responsible. For moral evaluation describes its subject in terms of virtues such as courage and justice and charity, and we cannot, of course, ascribe virtues to anyone without knowing first of all which of the things that he did were intended and which unintentional, and secondly which of the unintentional actions were due to lack of care, or to ignorance of that which he could and should have known. It is not, however, obvious that these distinctions rest on a doctrine of 'moral responsibility' that Nietzsche is in a position to deny. He is surely wrong in thinking that we might have to give up thinking in a *special* way about the goodness of men, that we should have to relinquish the concept of a virtue as it applies to human beings and not to plants or to the objects of aesthetic evaluation. The idea of a virtue might even be the correct starting point for a solution to the problem of moral responsibility. For the way in which moral responsibility exists can perhaps be traced precisely by asking how it enters into the concept of a virtue, as shown by the irrelevance to virtue of things done accidentally or in (most kinds of) ignorance. And as for unconscious motivation: we might say that this is relevant to moral evaluation (as when we count deep-hidden malice against his possession of the virtue of charity) without any implication that the subject is 'responsible' for being as he is. So far from destroying morality, Nietzsche's challenge to the possibility of distinctively moral evaluation may actually help us to see what it does and does not require.

Second among 'errors,' there is the moral classification of types of actions under the descriptions 'good' and 'bad.' For Nietzsche's objection to this we must go back once more to his scorn for the universality in moral judgement, his scorn for its branding of certain *kinds* of action as good or bad 'for all.' This was not the commonplace insistence on the relevance of circumstances to moral good and evil. It was not *that* objection to absolutism which Nietzsche had in mind; he meant rather that moral generalisation was impossible because the proper subject of valuation was, instead, the individual agent's individual act. We were to ask not what is done, but rather who it is done by. He even said that no two actions can be the same, meaning, again, that each individual action takes its character from the character of the one who does it.

His chief defence for this comes, I think, from the sceptical eye that he casts over the motives of the actions that moralists call good. Thus he points out the vanity that is behind many acts of 'kindness': the wish to create a good opinion in others by a kindly deed, so as to be able to buy this good opinion back from them. (As T. S. Eliot said, 'the eternal struggle to think well of ourselves'.) The wish to be a benefactor was, he said, impertinent, as claiming understanding, and jealous in the desire to possess the one to whom 'good' was done. Where moralists find altruism Nietzsche sees various kinds of egoism, self-mistrust, and fear: above all the desire to 'live abroad' with others rather than at home with oneself. Under the heading 'The elevating aspect of our neighbours' misfortune,' he says that we gather to bemoan the ill that has befallen him and 'spend an enjoyable afternoon.'[24] Nietzsche was a genius at finding hidden motivations, and it is not surprising that Freud found him so much of a kindred spirit that he deliberately avoided reading Nietzsche until his own work was well advanced.

It is surprising, however, that Nietzsche thought that the discovery of the possibility of dubious motivation behind, e.g., acts of 'kindness' counted against the moral mode of valuation itself. For it is traditional in moral philosophy that actions are to be judged not only for the type of actions that they are but also as each individual act done by a particular agent at a particular time. Aquinas, for instance, pointed out that a concrete act could be spoiled, morally speaking, either by what it was 'in its kind', as, e.g., murder or robbery, or by the motive from which it was done, using for this latter possibility the example of giving alms 'for the praise of men'. If Nietzsche extends the area of honesty about motives, moralists should not take this amiss.

So far, then, Nietzsche seems to be on strong ground in his psychology, even if mistaken about the *import* of his psychological observations. It is not, however, always so, and the next of the 'errors' he claims to find in morality sees him far out in a very doubtful field of psychological speculation. For he believed that he could discern the 'drives' (*Triebe*) that motivate all human action, and could map their dependence on each other. He thought he knew, for instance, that 'drives' such as cruelty, which were branded by moralists as 'evil,' were the condition of all 'good.'

Thus, in *Beyond Good and Evil* he speaks of 'the reciprocal dependence of the "good" and the "wicked" drives' and the derivation of good impulses from wicked ones; continuing, in a famous passage, that we

> should regard even the affects of hatred, envy, covetousness, and the lust to rule as conditions of life, as factors which, fundamentally and essentially, must be present in the general economy of life (and must therefore be further enhanced if life is to be further enhanced).[25]

This was a favourite thought of Nietzsche's: one that he several times illustrated with the image of a tree which to flourish had to have its roots in the mud.[26] He saw the thought about the 'evil' drives as inimical to morality, because morality has to set its face against certain desires; and he must surely be right about that. But whether there is the least warrant for the kind of psychological speculations that are needed for this part of Nietzsche's immoralism is quite another matter. In the theory of 'drives' that finally crystallised into the theory that all 'drives' are contained in the Will to Power, Nietzsche seems to have fallen into that philosopher-trap of working a modicum of psychological observation into an all-embracing theory which threatens to become cut off from facts that could possibly refute it. Nietzsche saw himself as a wonderful psychologist, but the truth is that he was partly a wonderful psychologist and partly a mere speculating philosopher far exceeding his brief.

Is no part of Nietzsche's attack on morality, then, convincing? Probably it is not. It would be wrong, however, to conclude that we analytic philosophers should leave him alone. On the contrary, I think that he should shake us up. For his deepest conviction was that the fact that 'God is dead' (so that nothing is guaranteed to us) could not leave our faith in morality unchanged.[27] He was particularly scornful of 'philosophers' – he singled out George Eliot – who were 'fanatics' for morality in spite of their atheism. Nietzsche believed, in effect, that as the facts of human psychology really were, there could be no such things as *human virtues*, dispositions good in any man; and even if he did not prove it, might he not alert us to the fact that that *could* be how it is? For if 'God is dead', what guarantees that there is a human aptitude for the virtue of justice, given that this requires *quite generally* that men and women can do certain things – as, e.g. pass up great advantage in refraining from murder or theft and moreover do this *in a certain way*: that is, without ulterior motive, false elevation, or bitterness? Wittgenstein has taught us to see the existence of some things we take for granted as being a remarkable fact. Should we, perhaps, see the capacity to acquire justice in this light, as depending on certain general human reactions to teaching, somewhat as it is with the capacity to learn to talk or to make calculations?

On grounds such as this one can well believe that analytic philosophers must lose something if they do not study a philosopher as surpassingly bold and original as Nietzsche, if only because of his capacity to stretch our philosophical imagination.

And of course if I am right there is also a job that must be done in criticising his theories from the point of view of philosophical argument and truth. This is what I have been just beginning to do in this lecture. In a way it is bound to be a somewhat comical proceeding, because it has to be carried out at a schematic level that leaves behind all the riches of Nietzsche's psychological insights and images. So one feels rather like a surveyor reducing a glorious countryside to contours: or like someone telling the Sirens they are singing out of tune. But that is not to say that this rather dry philosophical work can be left undone, especially if, as I think, Nietzschean teaching is inimical to justice. His teaching has been sadly seductive in the past. Who can promise that it will never be seductive again?

Notes

1. *Beyond Good and Evil*, section 263.
2. *Gay Science* 103.
3. BGE 188.
4. BGE 227.
5. GS 345.

6. GS 352.
7. GS 179.
8. *Twilight of the Idols*, VII, 1.
9. *Genealogy of Morals*, Preface 6.
10. TI 33.
11 *Zarathustra*, Part III, 'Of the spirit of Gravity,' Ch. 2.
12. *The Antichrist* 11.
13. BGE 43.
14. GS 299.
15. 'Nietzsche's Philosophy in the Light of Contemporary Events.'
16. J. P. Stern, *Friedrich Nietzsche*, p. 86.
17. *Ecce Homo* III, I.
18. GS 1.
19. GS 190.
20; BGE 44.
21. WP 786.
22. Introduction to the Everyman edition of *Oliver Twist*. [Initialled 'G.K.C.']
23. Human All Too Human 107.
24. D of D, Bk IV (section 224).
25. BGE 23.
26. See Z, Part I, 'Of the Tree on the Mountainside.'
27. GS 343.

44

Nietzsche, Genealogy, History*

Michel Foucault

*Source: *Michel Foucault, Language, Counter-Memory, Practice: Selected Essays and Interviews*, ed. Donald F. Bouchard, trans. Donald F. Bouchard and Sherry Simon, Cornell University Press, 1977, pp. 139–64.

1. Genealogy is gray, meticulous, and patiently documentary. It operates on a field of entangled and confused parchments, on documents that have been scratched over and recopied many times.

On this basis, it is obvious that Paul Rée[1] was wrong to follow the English tendency in describing the history of morality in terms of a linear development – in reducing its entire history and genesis to an exclusive concern for utility. He assumed that words had kept their meaning, that desires still pointed in a single direction, and that ideas retained their logic; and he ignored the fact that the world of speech and desires has known invasions, struggles, plundering, disguises, ploys. From these elements, however, genealogy retrieves an indispensable restraint: it must record the singularity of events outside of any monotonous finality; it must seek them in the most unpromising places, in what we tend to feel is without history – in sentiments, love, conscience, instincts; it must be sensitive to their recurrence, not in order to trace the gradual curve of their evolution, but to isolate the different scenes where they engaged in different roles. Finally, genealogy must define even those instances where they are absent, the moment when they remained unrealized (Plato, at Syracuse, did not become Mohammed).

Genealogy, consequently, requires patience and a knowledge of details and it depends on a vast accumulation of source material. Its 'cyclopean monuments'[2] are constructed from 'discreet and apparently insignificant truths and according to a rigorous method'; they cannot be the product of 'large and well-meaning errors.'[3] In short, genealogy demands relentless erudition. Genealogy does not oppose itself to history as the lofty and profound gaze of the philosopher might compare to the molelike perspective of the scholar; on the contrary, it rejects the meta-historical deployment of ideal significations and indefinite teleologies. It opposes itself to the search for 'origins.'

2. In Nietzsche, we find two uses of the word *Ursprung*. The first is unstressed, and it is found alternately with other terms such as *Entstehung*,

Herkunft, Abkunft, Geburt. In *The Genealogy of Morals*, for example, *Entstehung* or *Ursprung* serve equally well to denote the origin of duty or guilty conscience;[4] and in the discussion of logic or knowledge in *The Gay Science*, their origin is indiscriminately referred to as *Ursprung, Entstehung*, or *Herkunft*.[5]

The other use of the word is stressed. On occasion, Nietzsche places the term in opposition to another: in the first paragraph of *Human, All Too Human* the miraculous origin (*Wunderursprung*) sought by metaphysics is set against the analyses of historical philosophy, which poses questions *über Herkunft und Anfang. Ursprung* is also used in an ironic and deceptive manner. In what, for instance, do we find the original basis (*Ursprung*) of morality, a foundation sought after since Plato? 'In detestable, narrowminded conclusions. *Pudenda origo.*'[6] Or in a related context, where should we seek the origin of religion (*Ursprung*), which Schopenhauer located in a particular metaphysical sentiment of the hereafter? It belongs, very simply, to an invention (*Erfindung*), a sleight-of-hand, an artifice (*Kunststück*), a secret formula, in the rituals of black magic, in the work of the *Schwarzkünstler.*[7]

One of the most significant texts with respect to the use of all these terms and to the variations in the use of *Ursprung* is the preface to the *Genealogy*. At the beginning of the text, its objective is defined as an examination of the origin of moral preconceptions and the term used is *Herkunft*. Then, Nietzsche proceeds by retracing his personal involvement with this question: he recalls the period when he 'calligraphied' philosophy, when he questioned if God must be held responsible for the origin of evil. He now finds this question amusing and properly characterizes it as a search for *Ursprung* (he will shortly use the same term to summarize Paul Rée's activity).[8] Further on, he evokes the analyses that are characteristically Nietzschean and that began with *Human, All Too Human*. Here, he speaks of *Herkunfthypothesen*. This use of the word *Herkunft* cannot be arbitrary, since it serves to designate a number of texts, beginning with *Human, All Too Human*, which deal with the origin of morality, asceticism, justice, and punishment. And yet, the word used in all these works had been *Ursprung*.[9] It would seem that at this point in the *Genealogy* Nietzsche wished to validate an opposition between *Herkunft* and *Ursprung* that did not exist ten years earlier. But immediately following the use of the two terms in a specific sense, Nietzsche reverts, in the final paragraphs of the preface, to a usage that is neutral and equivalent.[10]

Why does Nietzsche challenge the pursuit of the origin (*Ursprung*), at least on those occasions when he is truly a genealogist? First, because it is an attempt to capture the exact essence of things, their purest possibilities, and their carefully protected identities, because this search assumes the existence of immobile forms that precede the external world of accident and succession. This search is directed to 'that which was already there,' the image of a primordial truth fully adequate to its nature, and it necessitates the removal of every mask to ultimately disclose an original identity. However, if the genealogist refuses to extend his faith in metaphysics, if he listens to history, he finds that there is 'something altogether different' behind things: not a timeless and essential secret, but the secret that they have no essence or that their essence was fabricated in a piecemeal fashion from alien forms. Examining the history of reason, he learns that it was born in an altogether 'reasonable' fashion – from chance;[11] devotion to truth and the precision of scientific methods arose from the passion of scholars, their reciprocal hatred, their fanatical and unending discussions, and their spirit of competition – the personal conflicts that slowly forged the weapons of reason.[12] Further genealogical analysis shows that the concept of liberty is an 'invention of the ruling classes'[13] and not fundamental to man's nature or at the root of his attachment to being and truth. What is found at the historical beginning of things is not the inviolable identity of their origin; it is the dissension of other things. It is disparity.[14]

History also teaches how to laugh at the solemnities of the origin. The lofty origin is no more than 'a metaphysical extension which arises from the belief that things are most precious and essential at the moment of birth.'[15] We tend to think that this is the moment of their greatest perfection, when they emerged dazzling from the hands of a creator or in the shadowless light of a first morning. The origin always precedes the Fall. It comes before the body, before the world and time; it is associated with the gods, and its story is always sung as a theogony. But historical beginnings are lowly: not in the sense of modest or discreet like the steps of a dove, but derisive and ironic, capable of undoing every infatuation. 'We wished to awaken the feeling of man's sovereignty by showing his divine birth: this path is now forbidden, since a monkey stands at the entrance.'[16] Man originated with a grimace over his future development; and Zarathustra himself is plagued by a monkey who jumps along behind him, pulling on his coattails.

The final postulate of the origin is linked to the first two in being the site of truth. From the vantage point of an absolute distance, free from the restraints of positive knowledge, the origin makes possible a field of knowledge whose function is to recover it, but always in a false recognition due to the excesses of its own speech. The origin lies at a place of inevitable loss, the point where the truth of things corresponded to a truthful discourse, the site of a fleeting articulation that discourse has obscured and finally lost. It is a new cruelty of history that compels a reversal of this relationship and the abandonment of 'adolescent' quests: behind the always recent, avaricious, and measured truth, it posits the ancient proliferation of errors. It is now impossible to believe that 'in the rending of the veil, truth remains truthful; we have lived long enough not to be taken in.'[17] Truth is undoubtedly the sort of error that cannot be refuted because it was hardened into an unalterable form in the long baking process of history.[18] Moreover, the very question of truth, the right it appropriates to refute error and oppose itself to appearance,[19] the manner in which it developed (initially made available to the wise, then withdrawn by men of piety to an unattainable world where it was given the double role of consolation and imperative, finally rejected as a useless notion, superfluous, and contradicted on all sides) – does this not form a history, the history of an error we call truth? Truth, and its original reign, has had a history within history from which we are barely emerging 'in the time of the shortest shadow,' when light no longer seems to flow from the depths of the sky or to arise from the first moments of the day.[20]

A genealogy of values, morality, asceticism, and knowledge will never confuse itself with a quest for their 'origins,' will never neglect as inaccessible the vicissitudes of history. On the contrary, it will cultivate the details and accidents that accompany every beginning; it will be scrupulously attentive to their petty malice; it will await their emergence, once unmasked, as the face of the other. Wherever it is made to go, it will not be reticent – in 'excavating the depths,' in allowing time for these elements to escape from a labyrinth where no truth had ever detained them. The genealogist needs history to dispel the chimeras of the origin, somewhat in the manner of the pious philosopher who needs a doctor to exorcise the shadow of his soul. He must be able to recognize the events of history, its jolts, its surprises, its unsteady victories and unpalatable defeats – the basis of all beginnings, atavisms, and heredities. Similarly, he must be able to diagnose the illnesses of the body, its conditions of weakness and strength, its breakdown and resistances, to be in a position to judge philosophical discourse. History is the concrete body of a development, with its moments of intensity, its lapses, its extended periods of feverish agitation, its fainting spells; and only a metaphysician would seek its soul in the distant ideality of the origin.

3. *Entstehung* and *Herkunft* are more exact than *Ursprung* in recording the true objective of genealogy; and, while they are ordinarily translated as 'origin,' we must attempt to reestablish their proper use.

Herkunft is the equivalent of stock or *descent*; it is the ancient affiliation to a group, sustained by the bonds of blood, tradition, or social class. The analysis of *Herkunft* often involves a consideration of race[21] or social type.[22] But the traits it attempts to identify are not the exclusive generic characteristics of an individual, a sentiment, or an idea, which permit us to qualify them as 'Greek' or 'English'; rather, it seeks the subtle, singular, and subindividual marks that might possibly intersect in them to form a network that is difficult to unravel. Far from being a category of resemblance, this origin allows the sorting out of different traits: the Germans imagined that they had finally accounted for their complexity by saying they possessed a double soul; they were fooled by a simple computation, or rather, they were simply trying to master the racial disorder from which they had formed themselves.[23] Where the soul pretends unification or the self fabricates a coherent identity, the genealogist sets out to study the beginning – numberless beginnings whose faint traces and hints of color are readily seen by an historical eye. The analysis of descent permits the dissociation of the self, its recognition and displacement as an empty synthesis, in liberating a profusion of lost events.[24]

An examination of descent also permits the discovery, under the unique aspect of a trait or a concept, of the myriad events through which – thanks to which, against which – they were formed. Genealogy does not pretend to go back in time to restore an unbroken continuity that operates beyond the dispersion of forgotten things; its duty is not to demonstrate that the past actively exists in the present, that it continues secretly to animate the present, having imposed a predetermined form to all its vicissitudes. Genealogy does not resemble the evolution of a species and does not map the destiny of a people. On the contrary, to follow the complex course of descent is to maintain passing events in their proper dispersion; it is to identify the accidents, the minute deviations – or conversely, the complete reversals – the errors, the false appraisals, and the faulty calculations that gave birth to those things that continue to exist and have value for us; it is to discover that truth or being do not lie at the root of what we know and what we are, but the exteriority of accidents.[25] This is undoubtedly why every origin of morality from the moment it stops being pious – and *Herkunft* can never be – has value as a critique.[26]

Deriving from such a source is a dangerous legacy. In numerous instances, Nietzsche associates the terms *Herkunft* and *Erbschaft*. Nevertheless, we should not be deceived into thinking that this heritage is an acquisition, a possession that grows and solidifies; rather, it is an unstable assemblage of faults, fissures, and heterogeneous layers that threaten the fragile inheritor from within or from underneath: 'injustice or instability in the minds of certain men, their disorder and lack of decorum, are the final consequences of their ancestors' numberless logical inaccuracies, hasty conclusions, and superficiality.'[27] The search for descent is not the erecting of foundations: on the contrary, it disturbs what was previously considered immobile; it fragments what was thought unified; it shows the heterogeneity of what was imagined consistent with itself. What convictions and, far more decisively, what knowledge can resist it? If a genealogical analysis of a scholar were made – of one who collects facts and carefully accounts for them – his *Herkunft* would quickly divulge the official papers of the scribe and the pleadings of the lawyer – their father[28] – in their apparently disinterested attention, in the 'pure' devotion to objectivity.

Finally, descent attaches itself to the body.[29] It inscribes itself in the nervous system, in temperament, in the digestive apparatus; it appears in faulty respiration, in improper diets, in the debilitated and prostrate body of those whose ancestors committed errors. Fathers have only to mistake effects for causes, believe in the reality of an 'afterlife,' or maintain the value of eternal truths, and the bodies of their children will suffer. Cowardice and hypocrisy, for their part, are the simple offshoots of error: not in a Socratic sense, not that evil is the result of a mistake, not because of a turning away from an original truth, but because the body maintains, in life as in death, through its strength or weakness, the sanction of every truth and error, as it sustains, in an inverse manner, the origin – descent. Why did men invent the contemplative life? Why give a supreme value to this form of existence? Why maintain the absolute truth of those fictions which sustain it? 'During barbarous ages . . . if the strength of an individual declined, if he felt himself tired or sick, melancholy or satiated and, as a consequence, without desire or appetite for a short time, he became relatively a better man, that is, less dangerous. His pessimistic ideas could only take form as words or reflections. In this frame of mind, he either became a thinker and prophet or used his imagination to feed his superstitions.'[30] The body – and everything that touches it: diet, climate, and soil – is the domain of the *Herkunft*. The body manifests the stigmata of past experience and also gives rise to desires, failings, and errors. These elements may join in a body where they achieve a sudden expression, but as often, their encounter is an engagement in which they efface each other, where the body becomes the pretext of their insurmountable conflict.

The body is the inscribed surface of events (traced by language and dissolved by ideas), the locus of a dissociated Self (adopting the illusion of a substantial unity), and a volume in perpetual disintegration. Genealogy, as an analysis of descent, is thus situated within the articulation of the body and history. Its task is to expose a body totally imprinted by history and the process of history's destruction of the body.

4. *Entstehung* designates *emergence*, the moment of arising. It stands as the principle and the singular law of an apparition. As it is wrong to search for descent in an uninterrupted continuity, we should avoid thinking of emergence as the final term of an historical development; the eye was not always intended for contemplation, and punishment has had other purposes than setting an example. These developments may appear as a culmination, but they are merely the current episodes in a series of subjugations: the eye initially responded to the requirements of hunting and warfare; and punishment has been subjected, throughout its history, to a variety of needs – revenge, excluding an aggressor, compensating a victim, creating fear. In placing present needs at the origin, the metaphysician would convince us of an obscure purpose that seeks its realization at the moment it arises. Genealogy, however, seeks to reestablish the various systems of subjection: not the anticipatory power of meaning, but the hazardous play of dominations.

Emergence is always produced through a particular stage of forces. The analysis of the *Entstehung* must delineate this interaction, the struggle these forces wage against each other or against adverse circumstances, and the attempt to avoid degeneration and regain strength by dividing these forces against themselves. It is in this sense that the emergence of a species (animal or human) and its solidification are secured 'in an extended battle against conditions which are essentially and constantly unfavorable.' In fact, 'the species must realize itself as a species, as something – characterized by the durability, uniformity, and simplicity of its form – which can prevail in the perpetual struggle against outsiders or the uprising of those it oppresses from within.' On the other hand, individual differences emerge at another stage of the relationship of forces, when the species has become victorious and when it is no longer threatened from outside. In this condition, we find a struggle 'of egoisms turned against each other, each bursting forth in a splintering of forces and a general striving for the sun and for the light.'[31] There are also times when force contends against itself, and not only in the intoxication of an abundance, which allows it to divide itself, but at the moment when it weakens. Force reacts against its growing lassitude and gains strength; it imposes limits, inflicts torments and mortifications; it masks these actions as a higher morality, and, in exchange, regains its strength. In this manner, the ascetic ideal was born, 'in the instinct of a decadent life which . . . struggles for its own existence.'[32] This also describes the movement in which the Reformation arose, precisely where the church was least corrupt;[33] German Catholicism, in the sixteenth century, retained enough strength to turn against itself, to mortify its own body and history, and to spiritualize itself into a pure religion of conscience.

Emergence is thus the entry of forces; it is their eruption, the leap from the wings to center stage, each in its youthful strength. What Nietzsche calls the *Entstehungsherd*[34] of the concept of goodness is not specifically the energy of the strong or the reaction of the weak, but precisely this scene where they are displayed superimposed or face-to-face. It is nothing but the space that divides them, the void through which they exchange their threatening gestures and speeches. As descent qualifies the strength or weakness of an instinct and its inscription on a body, emergence designates a place of confrontation but not as a closed field offering the spectacle of a struggle among equals. Rather, as Nietzsche demonstrates in his analysis of good and evil, it is a 'non-place,' a pure distance, which indicates that the adversaries do not belong to a common space. Consequently, no one is responsible for an emergence; no one can glory in it, since it always occurs in the interstice.

In a sense, only a single drama is ever staged in this 'non-place,' the endlessly repeated play of dominations. The domination of certain men over others leads to the differentiation of values;[35] class domination generates the idea of liberty;[36] and the forceful appropriation of things necessary to survival and the imposition of a duration not intrinsic to them account for the origin of logic.[37] This relationship of domination is no more a 'relationship' than the place where it occurs is a place; and, precisely for this reason, it is fixed, throughout its history, in rituals, in meticulous procedures that impose rights and obligations. It establishes marks of its power and engraves memories on things and even within bodies. It makes itself accountable for debts and gives rise to the universe of rules, which is by no means designed to temper violence, but rather to satisfy it. Following traditional beliefs, it would be false to think that total war exhausts itself in its own contradictions and ends by renouncing violence and submitting to civil laws. On the contrary, the law is a calculated and relentless pleasure, delight in the promised blood, which permits the perpetual instigation of new dominations and the staging of meticulously repeated scenes of violence. The desire for peace, the serenity of compromise, and the tacit acceptance of the law, far from representing a major moral conversion or a utilitarian calculation that gave rise to the law, are but its result and, in point of fact, its perversion: 'guilt, conscience, and duty had their threshold of emergence in the right to secure obligations; and their inception, like that of any major event on earth, was saturated in blood.'[38] Humanity does not gradually progress from combat to combat until it arrives at universal reciprocity, where the rule of law finally replaces warfare; humanity installs each of its violences in a system of rules and thus proceeds from domination to domination.

The nature of these rules allows violence to be inflicted on violence and the resurgence of new forces that are sufficiently strong to dominate those in power. Rules are empty in themselves, violent and unfinalized; they are impersonal and can be bent to any purpose. The successes of history belong to those who are capable of seizing these rules, to replace those who had used them, to disguise themselves so as to pervert them, invert their meaning, and redirect them against those who had initially imposed them; controlling this complex mechanism, they will make it function so as to overcome the rulers through their own rules.

The isolation of different points of emergence does not conform to the successive configurations of an identical meaning; rather, they result from substitutions, displacements, disguised conquests, and systematic reversals. If interpretation were the slow exposure of the meaning hidden in an origin, then only metaphysics could interpret the development of humanity. But if interpretation is the violent or surreptitious appropriation of a system of rules, which in itself has no essential meaning, in order to impose a direction, to bend it to a new will, to force its participation in a different game, and to subject it to secondary rules, then the development of humanity is a series of interpretations. The role of genealogy is to record its history: the history of morals, ideals, and metaphysical concepts, the history of the concept of liberty or of the ascetic life; as they stand for the emergence of different interpretations, they must be made to appear as events on the stage of historical process.

5. How can we define the relationship between genealogy, seen as the examination of *Herkunft* and *Entstehung*, and history in the traditional sense? We could, of course, examine Nietzsche's celebrated apostrophes against history, but we will put these aside for the moment and consider those instances when he conceives of genealogy as '*wirkliche Historie*,' or its more frequent characterization as historical 'spirit' or 'sense.'[39] In fact, Nietzsche's criticism, beginning with the second of the *Untimely Meditations*, always questioned the form of history that reintroduces (and always assumes) a suprahistorical perspective: a history whose function is to compose the finally

reduced diversity of time into a totality fully closed upon itself; a history that always encourages subjective recognitions and attributes a form of reconciliation to all the displacements of the past; a history whose perspective on all that precedes it implies the end of time, a completed development. The historian's history finds its support outside of time and pretends to base its judgments on an apocalyptic objectivity. This is only possible, however, because of its belief in eternal truth, the immortality of the soul, and the nature of consciousness as always identical to itself. Once the historical sense is mastered by a suprahistorical perspective, metaphysics can bend it to its own purpose and, by aligning it to the demands of objective science, it can impose its own 'Egyptianism.' On the other hand, the historical sense can evade metaphysics and become a privileged instrument of genealogy if it refuses the certainty of absolutes. Given this, it corresponds to the acuity of a glance that distinguishes, separates, and disperses, that is capable of liberating divergence and marginal elements – the kind of dissociating view that is capable of decomposing itself, capable of shattering the unity of man's being through which it was thought that he could extend his sovereignty to the events of his past.

Historical meaning becomes a dimension of '*wirkliche Historie*' to the extent that it places within a process of development everything considered immortal in man. We believe that feelings are immutable, but every sentiment, particularly the noblest and most disinterested, has a history. We believe in the dull constancy of instinctual life and imagine that it continues to exert its force indiscriminately in the present as it did in the past. But a knowledge of history easily disintegrates this unity, depicts its wavering course, locates its moments of strength and weakness, and defines its oscillating reign. It easily seizes the slow elaboration of instincts and those movements where, in turning upon themselves, they relentlessly set about their self-destruction.[40] We believe, in any event, that the body obeys the exclusive laws of physiology and that it escapes the influence of history, but this too is false. The body is molded by a great many distinct regimes; it is broken down by the rhythms of work, rest, and holidays; it is poisoned by food or values, through eating habits or moral laws; it constructs resistances.[41] 'Effective' history differs from traditional history in being without constants. Nothing in man – not even his body – is sufficiently stable to serve as the basis for self-recognition or for understanding other men. The traditional devices for constructing a comprehensive view of history and for retracing the past as a patient and continuous development must be systematically dismantled. Necessarily, we must dismiss those tendencies that encourage the consoling play of recognitions. Knowledge, even under the banner of history, does not depend on 'rediscovery,' and it emphatically excludes the 'rediscovery of ourselves.'[42] History becomes 'effective' to the degree that it introduces discontinuity into our very being – as it divides our emotions, dramatizes our instincts, multiplies our body and sets it against itself. 'Effective' history deprives the self of the reassuring stability of life and nature, and it will not permit itself to be transported by a voiceless obstinacy toward a millennial ending. It will uproot its traditional foundations and relentlessly disrupt its pretended continuity. This is because knowledge is not made for understanding; it is made for cutting.[43]

From these observations, we can grasp the particular traits of historical meaning as Nietzsche understood it – the sense which opposes '*wirkliche Historie*' to traditional history. The former transposes the relationship ordinarily established between the eruption of an event and necessary continuity. An entire historical tradition (theological or rationalistic) aims at dissolving the singular event into an ideal continuity – as a teleological movement or a natural process. 'Effective' history, however, deals with events in terms of their most unique characteristics, their most acute manifestations. An event, consequently, is not a decision, a treaty, a reign, or a battle, but the reversal of a relationship of forces, the usurpation of power, the appropriation of a vocabulary turned against those who had once used it, a feeble domination that poisons itself as it grows lax, the entry of a masked 'other.' The forces operating in history are not controlled by destiny or regulative mechanisms, but respond to haphazard conflicts.[44] They do not manifest the successive forms of a primordial intention and their attraction is not that of a conclusion, for they always appear through the singular randomness of events. The inverse of the Christian world, spun entirely by a divine spider, and different from the world of the Greeks, divided between the realm of will and the great cosmic folly, the world of effective history knows only one kingdom, without providence or final cause, where there is only 'the iron hand of necessity shaking the dice-box of chance.'[45] Chance is not simply the drawing of lots, but raising the stakes in every attempt to master chance through the will to power, and giving rise to the risk of an even greater chance.[46] The world we know is not this ultimately simple configuration where events are reduced to accentuate their essential traits, their final meaning, or their initial and final value. On the contrary, it is a profusion of entangled events. If it appears as a 'marvelous motley, profound and totally meaningful,' this is because it began and continues its secret existence through a 'host of errors and phantasms.'[47] We want historians to confirm our belief that the present rests upon profound intentions and immutable necessities. But the true historical sense confirms our existence among countless lost events, without a landmark or a point of reference.

Effective history can also invert the relationship that traditional history, in its dependence on metaphysics, establishes between proximity and distance. The latter is given to a contemplation of distances and heights: the noblest periods, the highest forms, the most abstract ideas, the purest individualities. It accomplishes this by getting as near as possible, placing itself at the foot of its mountain peaks, at the risk of adopting the famous perspective of frogs. Effective history, on the other hand, shortens its vision to those things nearest to it – the body, the nervous system, nutrition, digestion, and energies; it unearths the periods of decadence and if it chances upon lofty epochs, it is with the suspicion – not vindictive but joyous – of finding a barbarous and shameful confusion. It has no fear of looking down, so long as it is understood that it looks from above and descends to seize the various perspectives, to disclose dispersions and differences, to leave things undisturbed in their own dimension and intensity.[48] It reverses the surreptitious practice of historians, their pretension to examine things furthest from themselves, the grovelling manner in which they approach this promising distance (like the metaphysicians who proclaim the existence of an afterlife, situated at a distance from this world, as a promise of their reward). Effective history studies what is closest, but in an abrupt dispossession, so as to seize it at a distance (an approach similar to that of a doctor who looks closely, who plunges to make a diagnosis and to state its difference). Historical sense has more in common with medicine than philosophy; and it should not surprise us that Nietzsche occasionally employs the phrase 'historically and physiologically,'[49] since among the philosopher's idiosyncrasies is a complete denial of the body. This includes, as well, 'the absence of historical sense, a hatred for the idea of development, Egyptianism,' the obstinate 'placing of conclusions at the beginning,' of 'making last things first.'[50] History has a more important task than to be a handmaiden to philosophy, to recount the necessary birth of truth and values; it should become a differential knowledge of energies and failings, heights and degenerations, poisons and antidotes. Its task is to become a curative science.[51]

The final trait of effective history is its affirmation of knowledge as perspective. Historians take unusual pains to erase the elements in their work which reveal their grounding in a particular time and place, their preferences in a controversy – the unavoidable obstacles of their passion. Nietzsche's version of historical sense is explicit in its perspective and acknowledges its system of injustice. Its perception is slanted, being a deliberate appraisal, affirmation, or negation; it reaches the lingering and poisonous traces in order to prescribe the best antidote. It is not given to a discreet effacement before the objects it observes and does not submit itself to their processes; nor does it seek laws, since it gives equal weight to its own sight and to its objects. Through this historical sense, knowledge is allowed to create its own genealogy in the act of cognition; and '*wirkliche Historie*' composes a genealogy of history as the vertical projection of its position.

6. In this context, Nietzsche links historical sense to the historian's history. They share a beginning that is similarly impure and confused, share the same sign in which the symptoms of sickness can be recognized as well as the seed of an exquisite flower.[52] They arose simultaneously to follow their separate ways, but our task is to trace their common genealogy.

The descent (*Herkunft*) of the historian is unequivocal: he is of humble birth. A characteristic of history is to be without choice: it encourages thorough understanding and excludes qualitative judgments – a sensitivity to all things without distinction, a comprehensive view excluding differences. Nothing must escape it and, more importantly, nothing must be excluded. Historians argue that this proves their tact and discretion. After all, what right have they to impose their tastes and preferences when they seek to determine what actually occurred in the past? Their mistake is to exhibit a total lack of taste, the kind of crudeness that becomes smug in the presence of the loftiest elements and finds satisfaction in reducing them to size. The historian is insensitive to the most disgusting things; or rather, he especially enjoys those things that should be repugnant to him. His apparent serenity follows from his concerted avoidance of the exceptional and his reduction of all things to the lowest common denominator. Nothing is allowed to stand above him; and underlying his desire for total knowledge is his search for the secrets that belittle everything: 'base curiosity.' What is the source of history? It comes from the plebs. To whom is it addressed? To the plebs. And its discourse strongly resembles the demagogue's refrain: 'No one is greater than you and anyone who presumes to get the better of you – you who are good – is evil.' The historian, who functions as his double, can be heard to echo: 'No past is greater than your present, and, through my meticulous erudition, I will rid you of your infatuations and transform the grandeur of history into pettiness, evil, and misfortune.' The historian's ancestry goes back to Socrates.

This demagogy, of course, must be masked. It must hide its singular malice under the cloak of universals. As the demagogue is obliged to invoke truth, laws of essences, and eternal necessity, the historian must invoke objectivity, the accuracy of facts, and the permanence of the past. The demagogue denies the body to secure the sovereignty of a timeless idea and the historian effaces his proper individuality so that others may enter the stage and reclaim their own speech.[53] He is divided against himself: forced to silence his preferences and overcome his distaste, to blur his own perspective and replace it with the fiction of a universal geometry, to mimic death in order to enter the kingdom of the dead, to adopt a faceless anonymity. In this world where he has conquered his individual will, he becomes a guide to the inevitable law of a superior will. Having curbed the demands of his individual will in his knowledge, he will disclose the form of an eternal will in his object of study. The objectivity of historians inverts the relationships of will and knowledge and it is, in the same stroke, a necessary belief in Providence, in final causes and teleology – the beliefs that place the historian in the family of ascetics. 'I can't stand these lustful eunuchs of history, all the seductions of an ascetic ideal; I can't stand these blanched tombs producing life or those tired and indifferent beings who dress up in the part of wisdom and adopt an objective point of view.[54]

The *Entstehung* of history is found in nineteenth-century Europe: the land of interminglings and bastardy, the period of the 'man-of-mixture.' We have become barbarians with respect to those rare moments of high civilization:

cities in ruin and enigmatic monuments are spread out before us; we stop before gaping walls; we ask what gods inhabited these empty temples. Great epochs lacked this curiosity, lacked our excessive deference; they ignored their predecessors: the classical period ignored Shakespeare. The decadence of Europe presents an immense spectacle (while stronger periods refrained from such exhibitions), and the nature of this scene is to represent a theater; lacking monuments of our own making, which properly belong to us, we live among crowded scenes. But there is more. Europeans no longer know themselves; they ignore their mixed ancestries and seek a proper role. They lack individuality. We can begin to understand the spontaneous historical bent of the nineteenth century: the anemia of its forces and those mixtures that effaced all its individual traits produced the same results as the mortifications of asceticism; its inability to create, its absence of artistic works, and its need to rely on past achievements forced it to adopt the base curiosity of plebs.

If this fully represents the genealogy of history, how could it become, in its own right, a genealogical analysis? Why did it not continue as a form of demagogic or religious knowledge? How could it change roles on the same stage? Only by being seized, dominated, and turned against its birth. And it is this movement which properly describes the specific nature of the *Entstehung*: it is not the unavoidable conclusion of a long preparation, but a scene where forces are risked in the chance of confrontations, where they emerge triumphant, where they can also be confiscated. The locus of emergence for metaphysics was surely Athenian demagogy, the vulgar spite of Socrates and his belief in immortality, and Plato could have seized this Socratic philosophy to turn it against itself. Undoubtedly, he was often tempted to do so, but his defeat lies in its consecration. The problem was similar in the nineteenth century: to avoid doing for the popular asceticism of historians what Plato did for Socrates. This historical trait should not be founded upon a philosophy of history, but dismantled beginning with the things it produced; it is necessary to master history so as to turn it to genealogical uses, that is, strictly anti-Platonic purposes. Only then will the historical sense free itself from the demands of a suprahistorical history.

7. The historical sense gives rise to three uses that oppose and correspond to the three Platonic modalities of history. The first is parodic, directed against reality, and opposes the theme of history as reminiscence or recognition; the second is dissociative, directed against identity, and opposes history given as continuity or representative of a tradition; the third is sacrificial, directed against truth, and opposes history as knowledge. They imply a use of history that severs its connection to memory, its metaphysical and anthropological model, and constructs a counter-memory – a transformation of history into a totally different form of time.

First, the parodic and farcical use. The historian offers this confused and anonymous European, who no longer knows himself or what name he should adopt, the possibility of alternate identities, more individualized and substantial than his own. But the man with historical sense will see that this substitution is simply a disguise. Historians supplied the Revolution with Roman prototypes, romanticism with knight's armor, and the Wagnerian era was given the sword of a German hero – ephemeral props that point to our own unreality. No one kept them from venerating these religions, from going to Bayreuth to commemorate a new afterlife; they were free, as well, to be transformed into street-vendors of empty identities. The new historian, the genealogist, will know what to make of this masquerade. He will not be too serious to enjoy it; on the contrary, he will push the masquerade to its limit and prepare the great carnival of time where masks are constantly reappearing. No longer the identification of our faint individuality with the solid identities of the past, but our 'unrealization' through the excessive choice of identities – Frederick of Hohenstaufen, Caesar, Jesus, Dionysus, and possibly Zarathustra. Taking up these masks, revitalizing the buffoonery of history, we adopt an identity whose unreality surpasses that of God who started the charade. 'Perhaps, we can discover a realm where originality is again possible as parodists of history and buffoons of God.'[55] In this, we recognize the parodic double of what the second of the *Untimely Meditations* called 'monumental history': a history given to reestablishing the high points of historical development and their maintenance in a perpetual presence, given to the recovery of works, actions, and creations through the monogram of their personal essence. But in 1874, Nietzsche accused this history, one totally devoted to veneration, of barring access to the actual intensities and creations of life. The parody of his last texts serves to emphasize that 'monumental history' is itself a parody. Genealogy is history in the form of a concerted carnival.

The second use of history is the systematic dissociation of identity. This is necessary because this rather weak identity, which we attempt to support and to unify under a mask, is in itself only a parody: it is plural; countless spirits dispute its possession; numerous systems intersect and compete. The study of history makes one 'happy, unlike the metaphysicians, to possess in oneself not an immortal soul but many mortal ones.'[56] And in each of these souls, history will not discover a forgotten identity, eager to be reborn, but a complex system of distinct and multiple elements, unable to be mastered by the powers of synthesis: 'it is a sign of superior culture to maintain, in a fully conscious way, certain phases of its evolution which lesser men pass through without thought. The initial result is that we can understand those who resemble us as completely determined systems and as representative of diverse cultures, that is to say, as necessary and capable of modification. And in return, we are able to separate the phases of our own evolution and consider them individually.'[57] The purpose of history, guided by genealogy, is not to discover the roots of our identity but to commit itself to its dissipation. It does not seek to define our unique threshold of emergence, the homeland to which metaphysicians promise a return; it seeks to make visible all of those discontinuities that cross us. 'Antiquarian history,' according to the *Untimely Meditations*, pursues opposite goals. It seeks the continuities of soil, language, and urban life in which our present is rooted and, 'by cultivating in a delicate manner that which existed for all time, it tries to conserve for posterity the conditions under which we were born.'[58] This type of history was objected to in the *Meditations* because it tended to block creativity in support of the laws of fidelity. Somewhat later – and already in *Human, All Too Human* – Nietzsche reconsiders the task of the antiquarian, but with an altogether different emphasis. If genealogy in its own right gives rise to questions concerning our native land, native language, or the laws that govern us, its intention is to reveal the heterogeneous systems which, masked by the self, inhibit the formation of any form of identity.

The third use of history is the sacrifice of the subject of knowledge. In appearance, or rather, according to the mask it bears, historical consciousness is neutral, devoid of passions, and committed solely to truth. But if it examines itself and if, more generally, it interrogates the various forms of scientific consciousness in its history, it finds that all these forms and transformations are aspects of the will to knowledge: instinct, passion, the inquisitor's devotion, cruel subtlety, and malice. It discovers the violence of a position that sides against those who are happy in their ignorance, against the effective illusions by which humanity protects itself, a position that encourages the dangers of research and delights in disturbing discoveries.[59] The historical analysis of this rancorous will to knowledge[60] reveals that all knowledge rests upon injustice (that there is no right, not even in the act of knowing, to truth or a foundation for truth) and that the instinct for knowledge is malicious (sometimes murderous, opposed to the happiness of mankind). Even in the greatly expanded form it assumes today, the will to knowledge does not achieve a universal truth; man is not given an exact and serene mastery of nature. On the contrary, it ceaselessly multiplies the risks, creates dangers in every area; it breaks down illusory defences; it dissolves the unity of the subject; it releases those elements of itself that are devoted to its subversion and destruction. Knowledge does not slowly detach itself from its empirical roots, the initial needs from which it arose, to become pure speculation subject only to the demands of reason; its development is not tied to the constitution and affirmation of a free subject; rather, it creates a progressive enslavement to its instinctive violence. Where religions once demanded the sacrifice of bodies, knowledge now calls for experimentation on ourselves,[61] calls us to the sacrifice of the subject of knowledge. 'The desire for knowledge has been transformed among us into a passion which fears no sacrifice, which fears nothing but its own extinction. It may be that mankind will eventually perish from this passion for knowledge. If not through passion, then through weakness. We must be prepared to state our choice: do we wish humanity to end in fire and light or to end on the sands?[62] We should now replace the two great problems of nineteenth-century philosophy, passed on by Fichte and

Hegel (the reciprocal basis of truth and liberty and the possibility of absolute knowledge), with the theme that 'to perish through absolute knowledge may well form a part of the basis of being.'[63] This does not mean, in terms of a critical procedure, that the will to truth is limited by the intrinsic finitude of cognition, but that it loses all sense of limitations and all claim to truth in its unavoidable sacrifice of the subject of knowledge. 'It may be that there remains one prodigious idea which might be made to prevail over every other aspiration, which might overcome the most victorious: the idea of humanity sacrificing itself. It seems indisputable that if this new constellation appeared on the horizon, only the desire for truth, with its enormous prerogatives, could direct and sustain such a sacrifice. For to knowledge, no sacrifice is too great. Of course, this problem has never been posed.'[64]

The *Untimely Meditations* discussed the critical use of history: its just treatment of the past, its decisive cutting of the roots, its rejection of traditional attitudes of reverence, its liberation of man by presenting him with other origins than those in which he prefers to see himself. Nietzsche, however, reproached critical history for detaching us from every real source and for sacrificing the very movement of life to the exclusive concern for truth. Somewhat later, as we have seen, Nietzsche reconsiders this line of thought he had at first refused, but directs it to altogether different ends. It is no longer a question of judging the past in the name of a truth that only we can possess in the present; but risking the destruction of the subject who seeks knowledge in the endless deployment of the will to knowledge.

In a sense, genealogy returns to the three modalities of history that Nietzsche recognized in 1874. It returns to them in spite of the objections that Nietzsche raised in the name of the affirmative and creative powers of life. But they are metamorphosed; the veneration of monuments becomes parody; the respect for ancient continuities becomes systematic dissociation; the critique of the injustices of the past by a truth held by men in the present becomes the destruction of the man who maintains knowledge by the injustice proper to the will to knowledge.

Notes

This essay first appeared in *Hommage à Jean Hyppolite* (Paris: Presses Universitaires de France, 1971), pp. 145–172. Along with 'Réponse au cercle d'épistémologie,' which became the introductory chapter of *The Archaeology of Knowledge*, this essay represents Foucault's attempt to explain his relationship to those sources which are fundamental to his development. Its importance, in terms of understanding Foucault's objectives, cannot be exaggerated.

1. See Nietzsche's Preface to *The Genealogy of Morals*, 4, 7 – ED.
2. *The Gay Science*, 7.
3. *Human, All Too Human*, 3.

4. *The Genealogy*, II, 6, 8.

5. *The Gay Science*, 110, 111, 300.

6. *The Dawn*, 102 ('Shameful origin' – ED.).

7. *The Gay Science*, 151, 353; and also *The Dawn*, 62; *The Genealogy*, I, 14; *Twilight of the Idols*, 'The Great Errors', 7. (*Schwarzkünstler* is a black magician – ED.)

8. Paul Rée's text was entitled *Ursprung der Moralischen Empfindungen*.

9. In *Human, All Too Human*, aphorism 92 was entitled *Ursprung der Gerechtigkeit*.

10. In the main body of *The Genealogy*, *Ursprung* and *Herkunft* are used interchangeably in numerous instances (I, 2; II, 8, 11, 12, 16, 17).

11. *The Dawn*, 123.

12. *Human, All Too Human*, 34.

13. *The Wanderer and his Shadow*, 9.

14. A wide range of key terms, found in *The Archaeology of Knowledge*, are related to this theme of 'disparity': the concepts of series, discontinuity, division, and difference. If the *same* is found in the realm and movement of dialectics, the *disparate* presents itself as an 'event' in the world of chance. For a more detailed discussion, see below, 'Theatrum Philosophicum,' pp. 180, 193–196 – ED.

15. *The Wanderer and his Shadow*, 3.

16. *The Dawn*, 49.

17. *Nietzsche contra Wagner*, p. 99.

18. *The Gay Science*, 265 and 110.

19. See 'Theatrum Philosophicum' below, pp. 167–168, for a discussion of the development of truth; and also 'History of Systems of Thought: Summary of a Course at the Collège de France – 1970–1971,' pp. 202–204 – ED.

20. *Twilight of the Idols*, 'How the world of truth becomes a fable.'

21. For example, *The Gay Science*, 135; *Beyond Good and Evil*, 200, 242, 244; *The Genealogy*, I, 5.

22. *The Gay Science*, 348–349; *Beyond Good and Evil*, 260.

23. *Beyond Good and Evil*, 244.

24. See below, 'Theatrum Philosophicum,' pp. 172–176 – ED.

25. *The Genealogy*, III, 17. The *Abkunft* of feelings of depression.

26. *Twilight*, 'Reasons for philosophy.'

27. *The Dawn*, 247.

28. *The Gay Science*, 348–349.

29. Ibid., 200.

30. *The Dawn*, 42.

31. *Beyond Good and Evil*, 262.

32. *The Genealogy*, III, 13.

33. *The Gay Science*, 148. It is also to an anemia of the will that one must attribute the *Entstehung* of Buddhism and Christianity, 347.

34. *The Genealogy*, I, 2.

35. *Beyond Good and Evil*, 260; cf. also *The Genealogy*, II, 12.

36. *The Wanderer*, 9.

37. *The Gay Science*, 111.

38. *The Genealogy*, II, 6.

39. *The Genealogy*, Preface, 7; and I, 2. *Beyond Good and Evil*, 224.

40. *The Gay Science*, 7.

41. Ibid.

42. See 'What is an Author?' above, p. 134, on rediscoveries – ED.

43. This statement is echoed in Foucault's discussion of 'differentiations' in *The Archaeology of Knowledge*, pp. 130–131, 206; or the use of the word 'division' above in 'A Preface to Transgression,' p. 36 – ED.

44. *The Genealogy*, II, 12.

45. *The Dawn*, 130.

46. *The Genealogy*, II, 12.

47. *Human, All Too Human*, 16.

48. See 'Theatrum Philosophicum' below, p. 183, for an analysis of Deleuze's thought as intensity of difference – ED.

49. *Twilight*, 44.

50. *Twilight*, 'Reason within philosophy,' 1 and 4.

51. *The Wanderer*, 188. (This conception underlies the task of *Madness and Civilization* and *The Birth of the Clinic* even though it is not found as a conscious formulation until *The Archaeology of Knowledge*; for a discussion of archaeology as 'diagnosis,' see especially p. 131 – ED.)

52. *The Gay Science*, 337.

53. See below, 'Intellectuals and Power,' p. 211 – ED.

54 *The Genealogy*, III, 26.

55. *Beyond Good and Evil*, 223.

56. *The Wanderer*, (Opinions and Mixed Statements), 17.

57. *Human, All Too Human*, 274.

58. *Untimely Meditations*, II, 3.

59. Cf. *The Dawn*, 429 and 432; *The Gay Science*, 333; *Beyond Good and Evil*, 229–230.

60. 'Vouloir-savoir': the phrase in French means both the will to knowledge and knowledge as revenge – ED.

61. *The Dawn*, 501.

62. Ibid., 429.

63. *Beyond Good and Evil*, 39.

64. *The Dawn*, 45.

45

'Experimental Philosophy': An Attempt at a Reconstruction*

Volker Gerhardt

Translated by Peter S. Groff and Herbert Möller

*Source: Volker Gerhardt, 'Experimental-Philosophie': Versuch einer Rekonstruktion', in *Pathos und Distanz: Studien zur Philosophie Friedrich Nietzsches*, Philipp Reclam, 1988, pp. 163–87.

Nietzsche's thinking moves in contradictions and seeks the extreme in everything. To reconstruct such a thinking may seem like a bad joke to reconstructionists and Nietzscheans alike: those who have confidence in reconstructions will regard Nietzsche as an unsuitable object, and those who are sympathetic to Nietzsche will not want to see him handed over to a technical-rational method. However, although the term rarely occurs in recent Nietzsche scholarship, the reconstruction of Nietzsche is in fact already under way,[1] despite the fact that formulated plans towards the reconstruction of our scientific wealth of experience, having only just emerged, are already being forgotten. Reconstruction [*Rekonstruktivismus*], in the narrow sense, e.g., in the sense employed by the Erlangener school, has long been out of fashion.

If I nevertheless consider reconstruction to be meaningful, one should remember not only Rudolf Carnap, who – based on the preliminary work of Paul Natorp[2] and Bertrand Russell[3] – raised '*rational Nachkonstruction*'[4] to a program, but also John Dewey, who in 1919, under the impact of the destructive force of the First World War, declared reconstruction to be the most important task of philosophy. Dewey's lectures on the philosophy of the new millennium, given for the first time in Japan in the winter of 1919, were published that same year under the title *Reconstruction in Philosophy*. In the new edition, published in 1948, he stressed that the horrifying experience of the preceding years made the task even more urgent. And he added a statement which brings us directly into the domain of Nietzsche: 'Today Reconstruction *of* Philosophy is a more suitable title than Reconstruction *in* Philosophy.'[5]

According to Dewey, philosophical theories have not been able to keep up with the rapid development of modern knowledge. Philosophy since Francis Bacon had reacted with essentially inadequate means to the unprecedented release of natural forces by science and technology, because it failed to question the unifying function of 'universal Reason,' which it inherited from classical metaphysics. Even Kant, who, according to Dewey, succeeded in transforming a metaphysical and cosmological idealism into an epistemological and ethical idealism, offered no essential progress, because he failed to provide a consistent conceptual orientation of that power, which, with the help of knowledge, would be able to lead the forces of nature in a new direction. This 'power' is nothing other than self-conscious human action: 'purposeful, experimental action acting to reshape beliefs and institutions' (ibid., p. 61). All classical theory aims ultimately at the securing of finite goods, a function which made sense up until the threshold of modernity. After that, however, metaphysical conservatism becomes a danger for the free development of the human being, and it therefore becomes crucial to liberate philosophical thinking from traditional restrictions, so that it can be transformed into an adequate expression of the new world-power [*Weltmacht*] – a power which is, for Dewey, the goal-oriented, *experimental* action of human beings.

Reconstruction, 'essential philosophic reconstruction,' is what Dewey calls that effort to liberate the 'really modern powers and demands' from all inherited burdens. Through a reconstruction of the factors at work in nature and society, philosophy itself becomes a creative force (ibid.). It goes without saying that philosophy should be based on scientific experience. Even logical means should be used as long as they don't serve to establish an autonomous reason and isolate understanding from the senses (pp. 113ff.)

This short comment should make it sufficiently clear that reconstruction is in no way limited to the improved comprehension of arguments – that it touches immediately upon the *matter of philosophy*. I don't want to pursue the question of what of Dewey's program remains in the thinking of the reconstructionists who followed him; his influence on analytic philosophy is surely greater than is usually believed. It also remains an open question what in Dewey's hopefully declared new beginning points back to Nietzsche. Anyone who is aware of the influence of Emerson upon Nietzsche, and who knows how both of them, independently of one another, influenced American pragmatism – and thus Dewey as well – shouldn't be surprised by the obvious points of contact.[6] Nor is it surprising that in this context the *experiment* plays a role, because it is Emerson who said of himself that he is 'only an experimenter': 'I unsettle all things. No facts are to me sacred, none are profane; I simply experiment, an endless seeker with no Past at my back.'[7]

Interesting historical connections become visible here, connections which can be traced back through German Romanticism to Kant and the philosophy of the Enlightenment.[8] It is not possible at this point to consider the historical and systematic relations between reconstruction, experiment, and philosophy any more than it is possible to consider all the dependencies in which Nietzsche is caught up. I limit myself to the question of how to understand and judge Nietzsche's outline of an experimental philosophy. What are the concepts of experimental philosophy that Nietzsche programmatically calls for from the beginning of the eighties? The question seems important to me, because the crucial provocation that Nietzsche poses is this: how is it possible to philosophize after him?

Nietzsche is known for having judged philosophy so harshly that one must ask oneself how he could concede a future for it at all. For it is not only the 'embarrassing object' of academic philosophy – the dilapidated 'dream- and thought-business' of professors living off the state – with which he tries to settle up (SE 8); it is philosophy in general which becomes the target of his devastating invectives.[9] Philosophy has something 'diseased,' something 'pandering' [*Kupplerisches*], something 'violent' in it. It shows 'symptoms of degenerated instincts' (N 1879, 40 [18], [21]), and in its antisensuality lies the 'biggest absurdity of the human being' (N 1884, 25 [438]). It has created a superabundance of 'failures' [*Missrathenen*] who, out of a fanaticism based on their herd instinct, try to take 'revenge on reality': 'how much *rabble and petty bourgeois* is in all this hatred' of the sensuality and Becoming [*Werden*] of the world! Here arises 'the great *school of slandering*' (N 1888, 14 [134]). With their 'mummified concepts,' their continual 'counterfeiting,' their systematic misunderstanding of life and the body, this species of philosophers 'corrupted by theologians' blood' is nothing but an *'impediment [Hemmschuh] in the wheel of time'* (AC 10; N 1872–73, 19 [17]). And if it is true that for Nietzsche philosophizing is 'always a kind of vampirism,' then we must ask ourselves what he still seeks in philosophy – assuming that he does not understand himself as a vampire and does not want to write primarily for vampires.

Nietzsche does not give a justified answer to the question of why he still practices philosophy. That is a point in his favor, because there cannot be any logically necessary justification for philosophy. This would be a philosopher's self-justification that always presupposes what is to be proven. It is simply a fact that we philosophize, and so it is a fact that we still expect something from philosophy. The most we can do is to imagine conditions under which philosophy is not objectively possible anymore, or not subjectively necessary anymore, and then ask ourselves if we want to live under such circumstances – assuming that we still know who we are and what 'wanting to live' really means.

So the fact remains that Nietzsche, despite all of this, doesn't want to do without philosophy. For him it is a necessity of life, to which he refers over and over again as a great task not restricted to himself alone. He is indeed possessed by the *'furor philosophicus'* (SE 7), which seduces him to talk more about philosophy than he himself thinks proper. In his countless programmatic remarks about what a philosopher of the future should do – and even more, what he should not do – we find good intentions, maybe even a few too many good intentions. It is always suspicious when one talks too much about a matter that has to be done. It also causes some uneasiness that the theoretician of the present moment [*Augenblick*] so often conjures up the future. One cannot avoid the conclusion that Nietzsche has an *ideal* which he himself knows he does not fulfill. This is also a reason, I believe, why there are some tragic aspects to his philosophizing.

When Nietzsche's program for a philosophy of the future is outlined in what follows, it may remain open how much of it was fulfilled by Nietzsche himself. I will therefore reconstruct a *model* that certainly was not only developed for others. Nietzsche understood *himself* first and foremost as an experimental philosopher.

'We are experiments: let us also want to be them!' – so it says in the fifth book of *Daybreak* (D 453; cf. also D 187 and D 501), and to dispel all doubts about the legitimacy of this intention, Nietzsche exclaims a bit later: 'We are permitted to experiment with ourselves! Yes, mankind is permitted to do that!' Approximately around the same time, he jots down the sentence: 'We experiment with our virtues and good deeds, and are never sure whether they are the necessary ones with regard to our goal' (N 1880, 6 [32]). The 'more common breed of humans' especially can lose sight of this goal; they lose all 'fear,' they don't believe in any 'authority,' they have most trust in what is most opposed to the earlier goals': 'an attempting and experimenting, a feeling of irresponsibility, the lust for anarchy!' (N 1880, 6 [31]).[10] The human being is at the same time not only the subject, but also the object of its own lust: 'our attitude towards *ourselves* is *hubris*, for we experiment with ourselves in a way we would never permit ourselves to experiment with animals, and carried away by curiosity, we cheerfully slice open our living souls . . .' (GM III.9).

In the human being's grand experiment with itself, which is already underway, the *philosopher* occupies an exposed position. As a 'free spirit,' as he is now explicitly called, he is an 'experimental laboratory [*Versuchs-station*] of humanity' (N 1880, 1 [38]). Already in the seventies, Nietzsche ascribes to the 'free spirits' the task of showing the educated humans 'paths to and goals of culture' (HATH, 282). For this reason, he sends them on 'a highly perilous wandering on glaciers and polar seas' (AOM 2, 21), into deserts, thunderstorms and loneliness even amongst human beings – thus in any case into extreme situations. In the eighties, the motive of these risky wanderings is stated more precisely through the goals of expedition and self-exploration – obviously under the influence of the great life crisis [*Lebenskrise*] in 1881. The overcoming of the most extreme despair through the monstrous thought of the eternal return of the same becomes the paradigm of the free spirit's self-liberation to tasks undreamt of: after 'morbid isolation,' which already banishes him to a 'desert' of self-experiments, the free spirit is overcome by a 'great liberation' [*grosse Loslösung*], which leads him to the 'great health' and to an 'overflowing confidence.' The great liberation leads him finally 'to that superfluity of formative, curative, molding and restorative forces which is precisely the sign of *great* health, that superfluity which grants to the free spirit the dangerous privilege of living *experimentally* and of being allowed to offer itself to adventure: the master's privilege of the free spirit!' (HATH, P 4).

As a result of the 'great liberation' towards an experimental freedom with respect to oneself and the world, Nietzsche sees finally 'a new species of philosophers' arise: 'I venture,' as it says in *Beyond Good and Evil*, 'to baptize them with a name that is not free of danger. As I unriddle them, insofar as they allow themselves to be unriddled . . . these philosophers of the future may have a right – it may also be a wrong – to be called *attempters* [*Versucher*]. This name itself is in the end a mere attempt [*Versuch*] and, if you will, a temptation [*Versuchung*]' (BGE 42).

Experimental philosophy does not acknowledge any limitations with regard to the human being, as the word-play above suggests. It leads us into temptation even where we think we are most secure, which means self-confident, free, and dignified. It doesn't acknowledge any kind of moral limitation – nothing is sacred to it, as Emerson had already said. And this way of thinking and living is certainly not only typical of the 'common species of human beings'. The exceptional characters especially are subject to the epochal imperative to the experiment: 'The age of the experiment! The assumptions of Darwin have to be tested – through the experiment!' – so it says in 1881. 'Likewise the genesis [*Entstehung*] of higher organisms out of the lowest ones. Experiments must be performed for thousands of years! Apes must be brought up [*erziehen*] to be human beings!' [N 1881, 11 [177]].

The range of experimental philosophy becomes recognizable above all in a passage from the notebooks of Spring/Summer 1888, in which Nietzsche clearly expresses its relation to the great themes of the later works, as well as to himself: 'Philosophy as I have understood and lived it so far is the free-willed visitation of even the accursed and loathsome aspects of existence. Out of the long experience acquired by these wanderings through ice and desert, I learned to look differently at everyone who has hitherto philosophized: the *concealed* history of philosophy; the psychology of its great names, came to light for me. "How much truth can a spirit *endure*, how much truth can it *risk*?" – This became the real yardstick for me . . . Such an experimental philosophy, as I live it, anticipates the possibilities of fundamental nihilism in an experimental way without saying that it would stop at a No, at a negation, at a will to negate. It wants to get through to the opposite – to a *Dionysian affirmation* of the world as it is, without withdrawal, exception or discrimination – it wants the eternal cycle, the same things, the same logic and unlogic of the knot. The highest state which a philosopher can reach: to be Dionysian towards existence – my formula for this is *amor fati* . . .' (N 1888, 16 [32]).

After this reminder about the program of experimental philosophy, I can only hope that the following ten points, towards which my reconstruction attempt leads, are intelligible despite their brevity.

The *first* point, simply put, stays true to Nietzsche's claim to practice

philosophy. It goes without saying that not everything in Nietzsche is philosophically significant, and it may be that his contribution to literature – or the
example of his self-consuming existence – is of greater importance than his
philosophical fragments. Be that as it may, his experimental thinking is conceived of *as philosophy*. It is not called experimental poetics or experimental
art; it is intended as a philosophy, however new it may be. With that,
Nietzsche places himself – in spite of all his developed objections – in a great
tradition. He has confidence in the power of concepts to nail things down, he
still aims at knowledge, still wants to comprehend life, still wants to comprehend himself, in spite of all the deception and groundlessness of the world.
And more: he wants to be guided by these concepts [*will sich nach diesen
Begriffen richten*]. 'We knowers' is the rubric under which he prefers to place
himself. His 'fundamental will' aims at knowledge; he is a 'tree of knowledge.'
And if the fruit of this tree isn't tasty? 'But what is that to the trees! What is
that to *us*, to us philosophers! . . .' (GM, P 2).

It is, besides other things, a peculiarity of this philosophy that it orients
itself according to the model of *modern science*. Experimental philosophy
expressly follows the success of experimental science.[11] It is no coincidence
that the experimental method becomes a model for Nietzsche during that
part of his life in which he increasingly supplies himself with literature on the
natural sciences, and again begins plans for a corresponding course of study
dedicated to science and philosophy.

With that my *second* point is introduced: experimental philosophy understands itself as a *scientific* philosophy, because it attempts to start from modern discoveries [*Erkenntnissen*]. The 'view through the portals of science,' as it
says in connection with the first mentioning of the experimental method,
seems 'like the magic of all magic.' The 'sweet allurement,' the 'glad tidings'
of science promise 'the happiness of those with knowledge' (D 450). After
millennia of knowledge which simply led us into darkness, Nietzsche sees
physics as a '*relief* for the mind,' because '*here alone* we find consistency'
(N 1883/84, 24 [18]). Naturally, he defends himself against the 'Tartuffery of
scientificity [*Wissenschaftlichkeit*]' (N 1885, 35 [32]), and disapproves when,
out of vanity, scientificity is claimed in questions of representation and
method, or in the pretension to objectivity. But one should not overlook the
fact that Nietzsche's criticism of those who turn science into an attitude, who
'affect scientificity' (N 1885, 35 [31]), represents a defense of the true scientific
spirit. Correctly understood, science is a 'sign of strength and self-control'; it
shows that one can live without the 'healing and comforting worlds of illusion' (N 1887, 9 [60]). It follows that we must '*arrange* our life to *preserve* it.'
Why? In view of two later points I anticipate Nietzsche's answer here: we
must, because science leads to a 'kind of *practical reflection* about the
conditions of our own *existence* as knowers' (N 1884/85, 24 [18]).

Science is also indispensable from the perspective of the will to power.
Nietzsche defines it as 'the transformation of nature into concepts aimed

towards the control of nature.' As such, science is one of the essential 'means' by which the human being heightens or intensifies itself [*Selbststeigerung*] (N 1885, 26 [170]). Therefore, experimental philosophy also remains dependent on those means, and even adopts its essential procedures, i.e., hypothesis formation and experimental testing. Insofar as it wants to gain knowledge, insofar as it always wants to satisfy the curiosity of human beings, experimental philosophy belongs to *science* (cf. GS 51). In this case, no distinction between nature and culture is made. The experimental method is legitimate in *all* spheres of life, and it grasps, as any philosophy must, at *unities*, at concepts of life which are difficult to operationalize in an experimental way, according to exact measurements. This expansion corresponds to the fact that Nietzsche not only takes his bearings from the great physicists, but also especially idealizes the discoverers. Columbus appears to him as an early hero of the worldview of exploration. This, however, does not diminish his high regard for experimental research into particulars.

The *third* essential methodological strand of experimental philosophy, namely, that of *critique*, also has a close relation to modern science. *Skepticism* is the basic trait that Nietzsche demands of the philosopher, and *critique* is his most important instrument. By this he means the 'skepticism of audacious manliness,' which understands the art of 'destruction and dissolution,' and which has the 'courage and hardness of the analyzing hand' (BGE 209). Critical analysis alone is not sufficient: critique also involves the determination to draw consequences out of its results.

The 'philosophers of the future,' as one can read in *Beyond Good and Evil*, have to let themselves be called skeptics and critics, 'and certainly they will be men of experiments' (BGE 210). 'Critics in body and soul,' they will 'use the experiment in a new, perhaps broader, perhaps more dangerous sense.' The field of their experimentation is without limit. Everything that concerns human beings belongs to it. In this way, experimental philosophy is a critique of culture and its tradition, especially of the philosophical tradition, and particularly of science, morality, and knowledge.

But critique alone is not enough. Those who decree that 'Philosophy itself is critique and critical science – and nothing else!' do not reach far enough, according to Nietzsche: 'critics are instruments of the philosopher and for that reason, being instruments, a long way from being philosophers themselves' (BGE 210). The expectations placed upon experimental philosophy become immediately apparent when even Kant is counted as an instrument of the true philosopher: 'Even the great Chinese of Königsberg was merely a great critic' (ibid.).

To get beyond the role of the critic and to become a commander and legislator, the philosopher needs *teaching* [*Lehre*]. And with this I have arrived at the *fourth* basic feature of experimental philosophy: it has to integrate the results of science and the insights of critique into a *body of teaching* [*Lehrbestand*]. With this body, with this 'dogma' [*Dogmatic*], it steps beyond science and critique to create *new values*. After the teaching's *'positing* of values,' after its 'creation of values' – which become dominant 'for a time,' and can be called for this time 'truths' (BGE 211) – new orders are founded and new virtues set as an example.

This teaching is the visionary part of Nietzsche's experimental philosophical program. Through the mask of Zarathustra, some dogmas [*Lehrsätze*] are formulated, and in the remarks about the great liberation, the great health, and the extensive justice, outlines are hinted at. However, teaching involves not only the elements of a practical knowledge, not only the organizational principles of a newly shaped life, but also the insights that are the foundation of such a knowledge. Thus the 'teaching of the will to power' is already a genuine part of it, as is the consciousness of the constant flux of all events. Against the background of Becoming and the will to power, a fully unfolded teaching, with its temporary 'truths' and 'principles,' remains bound up with Nietzsche's conception of experimental philosophy. For even the distinctive monumentality [*Monumentalität*] of an epoch cannot withdraw from the processive and perspectival character of all events.[12]

If one thus adds Becoming and the will to power to the dogmatic stock of experimental philosophy, then it includes a considerable 'knowledge.' This knowledge is the expression of an experience that should henceforth determine how we philosophize and live. And this correspondence of teaching and philosophical attitude is fundamental for the self-understanding of experimental philosophy.[13]

The outrageous [*unerhörte*] kind of thinking that has left everything behind, and that should now become decisive, has already incorporated the teachings of Becoming and the will to power. Experimental philosophy has to abandon the securities of this world as well as those of the beyond. It can only rely on what it encounters as actually effective and what is founded in its own movement: that is, the in-itself compulsively tensed outburst of the will to power, agonistic, pluralistic, individual, mobile, and momentary, relative through and through, an outburst that admits of no world but at most only perspectives on the world, that admits of no beings but only instrumental relations, hierarchies [*Rangverhältnisse*] and mutual representations. Philosophizing is called for under such conditions, a philosophy which does not suppress the fact that there 'is' no world, a philosophy which not only recognizes the will to power, but which also acknowledges itself only as an expression of the will to power, a philosophy without secure presuppositions, without an absolute starting point, without any trust in a divine or historic goal, indeed, without the support of a general binding method, a philosophy which overcomes everything and especially itself, in short: a philosophy of risky self-testing, of the unconditionally attempted intensification of power [*Machtsteigerung*].

Where does the origin of this demand lie? How does the experimental philosopher know about the impulse which he seeks to obey?

To ask in this way is already to make the crucial step towards an answer. It leads at the same time to the next, the *fifth*, point, and therewith to the methodological starting point of experimental philosophy, a starting point which determines everything and which is in principle unavoidable: the fact that the origin of all sensation and empirical knowledge lies in *human experience*.

In Nietzsche we find a striking confirmation of Kant's dictum that all questions of philosophy finally lead back to one question: What is the human being? This is verified – in spite of Nietzsche's explicit insight that we 'always only recognize *ourselves*' – by his attempt to separate himself from the perspective of the human being and gain a distanced view on human matters from the outside. He insists on 'dehumanizing' the phenomena (N 1881, 11 [238]); he experiments with ideas to place himself 'outside mankind' (N 1881, 11 [35]), and speaks of the 'attempt to distance oneself from everything that is human and to understand it as a point in the process of becoming – not to construct everything around it' (N 1882–83, 6 [1]).

But despite all his attempts to 'gain' the epistemological 'advantages of a dead person' (N 1881, 11 [35]), he nevertheless again comes to the conclusion: 'the human being veils the things from us' (N 1880, 6 [432]). Despite attempts to be objective, we realize 'not the nature of things, but our nature' (N 1881, 6 [418]). All abstraction creates forms in the image of the human being, all science is an attempt 'to humanize things as faithfully as possible' (GS 112). Likewise whatever one investigates and deduces: in all 'thinking [the human being] refers back to itself,' everything is laid out ready for us 'as an event for the eye and the sense of touch'; not even the boldest abstraction leads beyond the inventory of 'human experience' (N 1883–84, 24 [17]); all understanding happens through translation into the language of the senses, and thus into the 'prejudices of the senses' (N 1888, 14 [79]). There is no escape from the human horizon; all testing, all intensifying, every development 'under "favorable circumstances"' takes place within this closed field of vision (N 1885, 34 [74]). The decisive attempt of Nietzsche's teaching to overcome the external world of physical powers is only accomplished by him after he determines: 'It's no use: one must understand all movements, all "appearances," all "laws," only as symptoms of an internal event, and use the analogy of the human being to its end' (N 1885, 36 [31]). That is how Nietzsche arrives at the concept of the will to power. In this way, not only the teaching of the will to power, but also experimental philosophy as a whole, is in its origin (and in its consequences) an *anthropology* – a conceptual self-interpretation of the human being, which always finds itself in everything.[14]

Experimental philosophy as *anthropo-logy*, i.e., as the human being's conceptual expression of itself, is conducted by Nietzsche, naturally, according the principle of experiment and temptation. Here also, the 'magic of the extreme' is at work (N 1887, 10 [94]). When the human being becomes the topic, seduction, which practices all extremes [*Äusserste*], becomes powerful, because 'we are *the most extreme*' (ibid.). There is thus no interest in determining the average human being. That which is human shows itself in the 'highest specimens.' Only the great goals open up the future, only the heroically self-overcoming individual permits a new taxonomy of the human being. Anthropology – and I don't say philosophical anthropology, because this is a pleonasm – is here conducted from the extreme position of the individual. And one cannot deny that finally everything human is decided by the individual.

But the individual does not function here merely as a kind of epistemological premiss; it also shows a fundamental interest in itself. It involves itself in events with all its pathos, and seeks in everything an *expression of its existence*. Therefore, in my *sixth* point, at the risk of misunderstanding, I describe experimental philosophy as a *philosophy of existence* [*Existenzphilosophie*]. It is a philosophy of existence in the best possible sense, because it limits itself to the present moments of existence and does not point to transcendence. To set high goals and perish because of them – this is a maxim dating from Nietzsche's early years (N 1873, 29 [54]; cf. UDH 9), which he later holds onto with an explicitly experimental intention: 'we instinctively seek a *potentialized* life, the life in danger . . .' (N 1888, 15 [94]). This refers especially to the 'new philosophers, philosophers of the dangerous maybe in every sense' (BGE 2). They have to use their 'dangerous hours' (D 460), they have to understand what 'wanting to be by oneself, being able to be different, standing alone, and having to live independently' means: 'He shall be greatest who can be loneliest, the most concealed, the most deviant . . .' (BGE 212). 'Bravery' [*Tapferkeit*] is demanded of the philosopher, and '*that he stand firm*' (N 1887, 10 [103]). Not only the 'method' is important, but also 'courage' [*Muth*] (BGE 210). Therefore philosophy is something that has to be understood and lived: 'experimental philosophy is how I live it . . .' (N 1888, 16 [32]). Under a new title, Nietzsche returns to an earlier thesis: the unity of philosophy and life. 'The product of the philosopher,' as it says in the notebooks of 1873, 'is his *life* . . .'; his life – 'this is his artwork' (N 1873, 29 [205]).

But this aestheticizing shouldn't be seen in opposition to an existential earnestness towards life. The aesthetic appeal only comes into play when we remain aware that we aim at the whole. Here, climaxes and finales are one. We speak of humans who are 'unconditioned' [*unbedingt*], and who 'know no mercy.' Those exceptional beings whom Nietzsche praises (with a pathos which also spurs himself on), those beings who should no longer be taught through circumstances are already dedicated to the principle of experiment and temptation: '*We do not want to build too early, we do not know whether we are even able to build, and whether it is perhaps best not to build.*' Therefore, those human beings who put the measure of their critique 'to everything,' and who like to 'sacrifice' themselves for the truth, above all only want to be called 'destroyers' (N 1875, 5 [30]).

In sacrificing itself for the truth, of course, the life of the human being doesn't remain isolated, but points beyond itself and becomes an example for others. With this I come to the *seventh* point of my reconstructive sketch: experimental philosophy does not mediate itself according to preformulated institutional norms, and it does not trust any regulated communication, but is based on the sympathetic announcement of exemplary achievements. It can therefore only become effective where it proves itself as *exemplary philosophizing* – and thus as *exemplary living*. This is the seventh point: experimental philosophy aims at what is unique; it aims at the unique example of the philosophical existence.

'I profit from a philosopher,' it says as early as the third *Untimely Meditation*, 'only insofar as he can be an example' (SE 3). Nietzsche holds onto this when he later emphasizes the fact that philosophy itself *cannot be taught* (BGE 213), when he emphasizes in addition to this the total independence of the free spirits, and when he proposes the extensive agenda of experimental philosophy only 'for his equals.' Who 'his equals' are cannot be established through external conditions; only those who, through their own greatness, are receptive to the extraordinary, even from a great distance, are able to take Nietzsche's model as an example.[15]

It becomes obvious that the communication of exemplary achievements is based on preliminary practical advances. In view of this, experimental philosophy stays related to the conduct [*Lebensvollzug*] of singular individuals. That leads me to the *eighth* point, which is probably self-evident, and which I therefore only want to mention briefly: in its explicit bond with life, in its orientation towards the unfolding of being, experimental philosophy cannot be anything other than a *practical* philosophy. It is a practical philosophy that does not accept a theoretical philosophy alongside it. '*Theory* and *praxis*: a disastrous distinction, as if there exists a *drive to knowledge* which, without consideration for questions of usefulness and harm, blindly goes for truth . . .' (N 1888, 14 [142], see also 14 [107]). That it nevertheless makes sense to call experimental philosophy – a philosophy which aims at usefulness and the enhancement of life, towards a new organization of being, towards legislation and judicial decision-making – a practical philosophy is suggested by Nietzsche's own words. The 'most insidious question of all' is for him this: 'whether science can *furnish* goals of action after it has proved that it can take such goals away and annihilate them – and then,' he continues, 'experimentation would be in order that would allow every kind of heroism to find satisfaction – centuries of experimentation . . .' (GS 7). And this experimentation would remain fundamentally tied to 'practical interests' in the broadest sense. The knowledge that belongs to this is called 'wisdom.' This too refers to the tradition of practical philosophizing.

However, no excellent practical power [*Vermögen*], neither practical reason nor pragmatic cleverness, can decide about this practical life-connection. With the renunciation of substantial being, as well as any absolute [*unbedingt*], commanding, intelligible authority, Nietzsche lacks a standard by which he can measure the practical efficacy of his experimental philosophy. This, of course, must not be spoken of as a fault: the renunciation of higher criteria is virtually constitutive for experimental philosophy, which believes that it wins room to move [*Spielraum*] only through the 'great liberation' from all conventional norms. Nevertheless, 'criteria,' i.e., discriminating, form-giving moments, are necessary if new values and different orders of rank are to be created successfully. Here aesthetic productivity comes into operation. It is art in the widest sense that will be expected to fill the empty place of the absolute. In view of its inner moment of organization, it is therefore justifiable to call experimental philosophy an *aesthetic philosophy*. This is the *ninth* characteristic that plays an incalculable role in Nietzsche self-portrayal and in the reception of his work. It cannot be estimated highly enough if we want to understand the peculiar consistency within this tragedy of philosophical self-contradiction.

However, the distinctive mark of aesthetic philosophy does not primarily have to do with the type of the so-called artist-philosopher. Here, in my opinion, Nietzsche is always over-rated. Seen as literature, *Zarathustra* is more of a curiosity than anything else, and Nietzsche's musical compositions show his effusive mediocrity. Only as a poet has he achieved something artistically outstanding, and he is, of course, a master of the aphorism, of short, polished aphoristic prose. But I wouldn't elevate this to the criterion of aesthetic philosophizing. Rather, I'm thinking about what Nietzsche himself sought to achieve as a standard of thinking and living: it is a standard that he tried to find in states of *consciously enhanced lust*, which he thought he recognized in *play* and *love*, further, in *the personality that productively solves inner contradictions*, and in general, in the figures that easily overcome the greatest oppositions, as well as themselves. Where out of illusions new illusions arise, where the tensions between fictions are dissolved in a richer and more rigorous fiction, that is where Nietzsche finds the real reality [*die eigentliche Wirklichkeit*]. 'Being' is not graspable [*greifbar*] anymore; reality can only be found in 'appearance.' We need only think Nietzsche's critical approach to knowledge through to its end to realize that, finally, everything has to lead to aesthetics, to a teaching of sensual appearance.[16]

Likewise, the human being opens up an access through itself. It is the human being which experiences itself as a 'shape and rhythm creating being,' which experiences in itself the difference between gravity [*Ernst*] and play, and which knows the happiness that can lie in the coherence of contradictory stimuli and in the intensification of its greatest strengths [*Krafte*]. So, for example, the human being 'knows' through its own productivity – independently of any absolute authority – what 'perfection' [*Vollkommenheit*] is. Perfection, as a highest measure, can be determined completely from the moment. In Nietzsche's words: 'Perfection: that is the extraordinary expansion of the feeling of power, the richness, the necessary overflowing of all brims . . .' (N 1887, 9 [102]). It lies also in the 'over-richness of the means of communication' [*Mittheilungsmitteln*] that allows it to enjoy the closed form [*die geschlossene Form*] and the conciseness of an expression, but also to enjoy the surplus as elegance, rigor [*Konsequenz*], style, or ornament.

Also in this regard, the experimental philosopher can use the 'analogy of human beings,' and is able to interpret all events as art. '*Art*,' as we read in a note from the seventies, '*doesn't belong to nature, but only to the human being.*' It 'is based entirely on humanized nature [. . . and] does not comprehend the nature of things, because it is entirely tied to the eye and ear' (N 1876–77, 23 [150]). In this sense, the body is declared an artist, life appears as a continuing aesthetic production, and the whole event becomes part of the closed cycle of the eternal return [*Wiederkunft*]. Even the thought of the eternal return is an expression of the essentially aesthetic character of experimental philosophy.[17]

My last and *tenth* point is, strictly speaking, only the recurrence [*Wiederkehr*] of the first: experimental philosophy is *philosophy*, clearly following the tradition of conceptual knowledge. In keeping with this tradition, it tries to measure the whole of Being, which we decipher through ourselves, and prove its *permanence* as *Becoming*, its *reality* as *appearance*, and its direction towards a *general goal* as *meaningless*. Experimental philosophy keeps referring to this whole when, under these new circumstances, it tries to create a meaning for existence which is obviously still required. This meaning is one that is only connected to the life of the human being, an existentially needed, exemplarily communicable meaning, a meaning which is only valid practically and justifiable aesthetically. But nevertheless, it is a *metaphysical* meaning. 'Why,' Nietzsche rightly asked, 'should one not be allowed to *play metaphysically*? And to use all of one's enormous creative strength doing it?' (N 1878, 29 [45]). In fact, he proceeded in exactly that way. Only later on, he no longer admitted these playful dealings to himself, and with his worn-out polemics, he fell back into his century's shallow critique of metaphysics.[18] It is regrettable, because even today many of his readers follow him in the false belief that with Nietzsche the age of metaphysics has come to an end. But he occasionally estimated the true effect of his thinking in a very apt way: 'I believe I have, through my critique of religion, art and metaphysics, enhanced their value: they are sources of power [*Kraftquellen*] more than ever' (N 1877, 22 [128]).

In his third *Untimely Meditation*, Nietzsche designated those activities as metaphysical which give meaning to existence. In this sense his experimental philosophy is a *metaphysics*, and in my eyes it is only because of this – and that should be my *tenth* point – that it becomes a philosophy that is relevant to us.

These ten points can be no more than clues for the reconstruction of experimental philosophy. There is not enough space here to elaborate on this any further. In conclusion, I simply want to draw attention to one more consequence which seems important, not only with regard to our position to Nietzsche, but to philosophy in general: supposing that my characterization is accurate, a well-known and thoroughly traditional motive appears behind the pretended modernity and exaggerated futurism of experimental philosophy. Nietzsche's entrance is not as ground-breaking as he himself wanted or feared, and as some of his followers would still like to have it today. Of course, he presents something new; after Kant and Hegel, after Romantic nihilism on the one hand and scientific socialism on the other, he opens up numerous interesting perspectives. But there is reason to doubt whether he is truly successful with his 'great liberation.' And even if we come to the conclusion that his judgment about himself is justified, we have to ask ourselves whether he does not remain, at least in that respect, tragically enslaved to the tradition, in that he expects a little too much from philosophy, despite his insight into the limitedness [*Bedingtheit*] of the mind.

We may doubt whether, in the daybreak of a new era, it will be experimental philosophy that will perform the prelude to the future. And we may doubt whether it will be the philosopher, who, appearing on the stage with his hammer, actually forges this future instead of just making plans for it. All the same, after Nietzsche's excessiveness, we have one more human reason to behave more modestly. That is especially true for a philosophy that does not want to give up the claim to think the whole.

Notes

1. I refer, for example, to the often-quoted books of Arthur C. Danto, *Nietzsche as Philosopher* (New York: Macmillan,1965), and Bernd Magnus, *Nietzsche's Existential Imperative* (Bloomington: Indiana University Press, 1978). In the later, clarified sense, one can mention the works of Josef Simon, 'Friedrich Nietzsche,' in Ottfried Höffe (ed.) *Klassiker der Philosophie*, Bd 2 (Munich, 1981), pp. 203–24, Joan Stambaugh, *Untersuchungen zum Problem der Zeit bei Nietzsche* (The Haag: Martinus Nifjhoff, 1959) [English version: *The Problem of Time in Nietzsche* (Philadelphia: Bucknell University Press, 1987)], Mary Warnock, 'Nietzsche's Conception of Truth,' in Malcolm Pasley (ed.) *Nietzsche: Imagery and Thought* (Berkeley: University of California Press, 1978), pp. 33–63, and Catherine Zuckert, 'Nature, History and the Self: Friedrich Nietzsche's Untimely Considerations,' in *Nietzsche-Studien* 5, 1976, pp. 55–82. Günter Abel understands his large-scale interpretation explicitly as reconstruction in *Nietzsche: Die Dynamik der Willen zur Macht und die ewige Wiederkehr* (Berlin/New York: Walter de Gruyter, 1984). Cf. Volker Gerhardt, 'Gipfel der Internität,' in *Nietzsche-Studien* 16, 1987, pp. 444–66.

2. Cf. Paul Natorp, *Psychologie nach kritischer Methode* (Freiburg i. Br., 1888), pp. 88ff., who considers 'objective science' as 'constructive,' and psychology that draws from 'subjective sources' as 'reconstructive.'

3. Cf. Bertrand Russell, *Principles of Social Reconstruction* (London: Allen and Unwin, 1916).

4. Rudolf Carnap, *Der logische Aufbau der Welt* (Vienna, 1928), p. 99.

5. John Dewey, *Reconstruction in Philosophy* (New York: Mentor Books, 1950), Introduction, p. 8.

6. See E. Baumgarten, *Der Pragmatismus* (Frankfurt-on-Main: V. Klostermann, 1938); Baumgarten, *Das Vorbild Emersons im Werk und Leben Nietzsches*

(Heidelberg, 1957). The influence of Pragmatism, especially the stronger effects of Dewey, becomes clearest through the references in Richard Rorty's book, *Philosophy and the Mirror of Nature* (Princeton: Princeton University Press, 1979).

7. Ralph Waldo Emerson, 'Circles' in *Emerson's Essays* (New York: Harper & Row, 1951), p. 225. In the translation of the *Essays* by G. Fabricius read by Nietzsche (Hanover, 1858, p. 234), it reads: 'so lasst mich den Leser erinnern, dass ich nur ein Experimentirender bin. Legt nicht den geringsten Werth auf das, was ich nicht thue, noch den geringsten Misskredit auf das, was ich nicht thue, als ob ich mir anmassen wollte, irgend etwas für Recht oder Unrecht zu erklären. Alles ist für mich unbeständig. Keine Facta scheinen mir geheiligt zu sein; keine profan; ich für mich thue weiter nichts, als dass ich experimentire, ein endloser Sucher, mit keiner Vergangenheit auf meinem Rücken.'

8. Voltaire (*Treatise on Metaphysics*, 1734) and Hume (*A Treatise of Human Nature*, 1734), explicitly demand an experimental method for philosophy as well. Kant not only speaks about the 'experiment of reason,' but also uses the term 'experimental philosophy' (*Critique of Pure Reason* A 425/B 542). The term is brought up again by Friedrich Schlegel in his letters on 'Transcendental Philosophy' (1800/01). And even later it still remained in the discussion, e.g., Hülsemann's accusations against Hegel (*Über die Hegelsche Lehre*, 1829, anon.). See Ernst Behler, 'Friedrich Schlegel und Hegel,' in *Hegel-Studien* 2, 1963, pp. 203–50, here p. 235.

9. Works of Nietzsche are cited in the text by abbreviation of English title, followed by aphorism number: SE = 'Schopenhauer as Educator' and UDH = 'On the Uses and Disadvantages of History for Life,' from *Untimely Meditations*, trans. R.J. Hollingdale (Cambridge: Cambridge University Press, 1983); HATH = *Human, All Too Human*, trans. R.J. Hollingdale (Cambridge: Cambridge University Press, 1986); AOM = *Assorted Opinions and Maxims*, ibid.; D = *Daybreak*, trans. R.J. Hollingdale (Cambridge: Cambridge University Press, 1982); GS = *The Gay Science*, trans. Walter Kaufmann (New York: Vintage Books, 1974); BGE = *Beyond Good and Evil*, trans. Walter Kaufmann (New York: Vintage Books, 1966); GM = *On the Genealogy of Morals*, trans. Walter Kaufmann (New York: Vintage Books, 1967); AC = *The Antichrist*, in *The Portable Nietzsche*, ed. and trans. Walter Kaufmann (New York: Viking Penguin, 1954). References to the *Nachlass* from the *Kritische Studienausgabe* [henceforth, KSA], ed. Giorgio Colli and Mazzino Montinari, 15 vols (Berlin: Walter de Gruyter, 1980) are cited as N. Translations of published works are R.J. Hollingdale's and Walter Kaufmann's with occasional minor alterations; translations of the *Nachlass* are ours. – Trans.

10. Cf. also N 1880–81, 10 [B 42]: 'humans also need *experiments*, as Darwinism does' (KSA 9, 42). Experiment and breeding are already connected in the seventies in Nietzsche. In 1881 it says with a certain solemnity: '*Whole parts* of the earth could *dedicate* themselves to the *conscious experiment*' (N 1881, 11 [276]; KSA 9, 548).

11. Cf. also esp. Friedrich Kaulbach, *Nietzsches Idee einer Experimentalphilosophie* (Cologne/Vienna: Bohlau, 1980), pp. 15ff., 131ff.

12. For an exploration of this teaching, see Volker Gerhardt, *Vom Willem zur Macht: Anthropologie und Metaphysik der Macht am exemplarischen Fall Friedrich Nietzsches* (Frankfurt–Main: Walter de Gruyter, 1996).

13. It should be remembered that *Zarathustra* was written and published when the project of 'experimental philosophy' had already taken form.

14. The briefly mentioned notion of a philosophy as conceptual self-interpretation of the human being does not presuppose a definite concept of the human being. 'Human being' here represents only the unity to which we have to refer in linguistic communication if some common agreement (practical, as well as theoretical) is to be accomplished. 'Human being' is the concept that is always agreed upon in the common self-reference of linguistic subjects. Naturally, the so-described being which we

know ourselves as could also be determined by methods of empirical anthropology. See also, e.g., B. Hassensten, 'Das spezifisch Menschliche nach den Resultaten der Verhaltensforschung,' in Hans-Georg Gadamer and Paul Vogler (eds) *Neue Anthropologie*, Bd 2 (Stuttgart: Deutscher Taschenbuch Verlag, 1972), pp. 60–97.

15. Cf. also Reinhard Löw, *Nietzsche: Sophist und Erzieher* (Weinheim: Acta Humaniora, 1984), pp. 160ff.

16. That 'art has to be understood as the organon of philosophy' and 'play' as integral to the 'whole of human activity' is shown by Mihailo Djurić in *Nietzsche und die Metaphysik* (Berlin/New York: Walter de Gruyter, 1985), pp. 116ff. and 148ff. How deeply Nietzsche was indebted to the (literary) art theories of his time is shown by Helmut Pfotenhauer in his philological study *Die Kunst als Physiologie* (Stuttgart: J. B. Metzler, 1985).

17. Only by considering its aesthetic content, I think, can one gain the moral/practical significance of the thought of the return, which is ascribed to it in Bernd Magnus' *Nietzsche's Existential Imperative* and Friedrich Kaulbach's *Nietzsches Idee einer Experimentalphilosophie*, pp. 116ff.; *Sprachen der ewigen Wiederkunft* (Würzburg: Königshausen and Neumann, 1985).

18. To mention only one example: 'Metaphysics is a natural ally of those imaginations that despise reality and seek satisfaction in other-worldly conceptions.' Eugen Dühring, *Der Werth des Lebens* (Breslau: E. Trewendt, 1865), p. 121. On the critique of metaphysics, see Volker Gerhardt, 'Metaphysik und ihre Kritik,' in *Zeitschrift für philosophische Forschung* 42, 1988, pp. 45–70.

46

Man as His Own Creator (Morality)*

Karl Jaspers

*Source: Karl Jaspers, *Nietzsche: An Introduction to the Understanding of his Philosophical Activity*. Translated by Charles F. Wallraff and Frederick J. Schmitz, University of Arizona Press, 1965, pp. 139–62.

Man's 'freedom' means that his alterability involves more than changes in accordance with those natural laws that apply to all existence: he is responsible for his own transformation.

During the entire course of history this transformation has been brought about by *morality*. We apply the term 'moral' to those laws to which human conduct and attitudes have been subjected in order that men may thereby for the first time become what they are. The contemporary world claims to acknowledge Christian morality. When one's faith wavers, he still regards 'morality' as self-evident. As modernism becomes godless, it regards morality as a solid ground upon which it still stands and by whose laws it lives.

Nietzsche attacks morality in every contemporary form in which he finds it, not in order to remove men's chains, but rather to force men, under a heavier burden, to attain to a higher rank. He becomes aware that the *value* of morality poses a significant problem. In all the stages of philosophy (even the skeptical), morality was considered to possess the highest value. All creeds were very much alike in this respect. 'He who is willing to dismiss God clings all the more firmly to the belief in morality.' Consequently once the problem of morality is posed, it becomes, in Nietzsche's opinion, so radical as to call in question what for thousands of years has been too obvious to be challenged.

By assailing and disavowing the moral law and freedom, both of which have been vital realities within human experience, he hopes to issue *a new challenge* which will arouse what is genuinely and distinctively human. What was called freedom becomes '*creation*' (*Schaffen*). He wishes to substitute '*nature*' for duty, the '*innocence of becoming*' (*Unschuld des Werdens*) for what the Christians call grace and redemption from sin, and *the historical reality of the individual* (*die geschichliche Individualität*) for what is accepted as universally valid by men in general.

Nietzsche's Attack on Morality

At any given time his attack depends upon what aspect of morality is under consideration. First of all he takes as his object the fact of the *plurality of moralities* and the possibility of investigating their *origins*, then he passes on to the *claim to absoluteness* which is advanced by moral demands.

The plurality of moralities and their origins: The fact of moral pluralism appears to rob every kind of morality of its supposed universal validity. The singularity and exclusiveness of each kind signifies that no group of moral judgments is to be explained in terms of the existence of the human species, but 'rather in terms of the existence of peoples, races, etc., and, in fact, of peoples that have had to assert themselves *in opposition* to other peoples and *classes* which wished to be set off sharply from those in the lower ranks.' Hence every distinct kind of morality is historically separate as one historically actualized possibility among others.

Still this argument need not lead Nietzsche to reject morality in its entirety, for a moral demand in its historical singularity might possess compelling and warranted obligatoriness for specific men at specific moments. And it is not necessary to renounce the universal validity of a law for man as man, but only the timeless universal validity of definite contents of that law. The demand for lawfulness in general, understood as agreement with the source of man as such, may remain indefeasible, even though its content is inexpressible and the possibilities that it opens to us are numerous.

One should distinguish between moral conduct and moral *judgment* concerning conduct. Nietzsche rejects the truth of moral judgments without qualification. His psychological observations concerning the origin and development of such judgments are inexhaustible. Among other things, he unmasks the pleasure taken in causing pain, the release of impotent instincts for revenge, the habit of furtive self-aggrandizement, the joy in feelings of power, and the mendacity of all moral indignation and the presumptuous judgment in all moral pathos. His magnificent 'ridicule of all the moralizing of the present day' is conclusive.

This psychology of the usual moral judgment, instructive as its truth may be to everyone, need not by any means be taken to impugn morality itself. Even though moral judgment – especially judgment passed upon others – may be impossible insofar as it lays claim to dogmatic finality, morality itself may still, in consequence, remain an even more decisive intelligible actuality.

According to Nietzsche it is the *Socratic* and *Judaeo-Christian* morality (which he regards as identical) that is accepted as valid in Europe. He attacks this morality by exposing its origin and development. He refers to it as the 'sum of the conditions of survival of an impoverished and partly or wholly ill-grown sort of man.' He calls it 'slave-morality.' The powerless, too, have their will to power: it is 'the instinct of the *herd* opposed to the strong and independent, the instinct of the *sorrowful* and poorly endowed opposed to the fortunate, the instinct of the *mediocre* opposed to the exceptional.' In spite of their impotence, all of them find in morality the means to mastery and to the creation of an internal (and eventually an external) power. For these moral values are fundamentally evaluations, by inferior people, of behavior patterns that afford them protection; and wherever these values prevail, the existence of their creators and bearers, namely the inferior people, attains increased value while that of the intrinsically powerful and radiant people is depreciated. 'The slave-insurrection of morality begins when *resentment* itself becomes creative and gives birth to values.' Insofar as the strong and successful ones, who are always in the minority, accept the evaluations of the crowd, the powerful are subjugated to the congenitally weak and infirm.

Still, insofar as such arguments from *origin and development* appear *in every sense* to annul the validity of morality, Nietzsche counters with the statement: 'He who has gained insight into the conditions under which a moral judgment has arisen has not thereby even touched upon its value.' This value 'remains unknown even when one is well aware of the conditions under which it arises.'

Such assertions by no means re-establish the view that, in spite of everything, there is an absolutely valid morality; they only show that *some other consideration* must prove decisive in connection with the question of the *value* of any given moral system. For if 'no morality is intrinsically valuable,' and the concept of morality 'is not even so much as relevant to man's worth,' still this adverse judgment passed upon morality would be impossible unless *some positive value were presupposed* to provide the standard of judgment. The question is: What is the intention and purpose of Nietzsche's dissolution of morals? He tells us that he wishes to attain 'the greatest power, depth, and splendor of which the human type is capable.' But when this demand is stated with such earnestness as that of Nietzsche, it is as decisive and absolute as any moral demand. Consequently his attack is not aimed at morality in general; it is directed at one specific morality from the standpoint of another.

So far as the derivation particularly of *Christian* morality from resentment is concerned, it should be made clear that, on the one hand, many specific occurrences within Christendom are indeed understandable in these terms, while, on the other hand, the moral evaluations that are perverted through resentment are subject to these perversions only because they derive from some other source. Nietzsche himself stopped short (an astonishing fact!) before the figure of Jesus. Here he finds the actualization of a way of life in which everything is genuine and without pretense or falsehood. 'Basically there was only one Christian, and he died on the cross.' It is an 'irony of world-history' that 'mankind prostrates itself before the very opposite of the source, significance, and justification of the gospels.'

In other words, Nietzsche's attack upon morality first presupposes an *indefeasible value* that is above every special morality (i.e., it presupposes the source of Nietzsche's own morality), and, second, it leaves open the possibility that a spurious morality may have originally come from a genuine *source*.

Moral claims as unconditional: Nietzsche is confronted with versions of morality – both religious and philosophical – whose demands are *unconditional* and whose contents are taken to be *universally binding*. *Christianity* bases its morality upon the law of God: 'Christianity assumes from the outset that man does not and cannot know what is good and what is bad for him. Man believes in God who alone knows these things. Christian morality is a command issuing from a transcendent source. It is beyond all criticism; it has truth only if God is the truth. It stands or falls with the belief in God.' *Philosophically* morality depends upon itself as a capacity of reason. It does not rest its case upon derivation from anything external, but upon a growing mental awareness of its source in the supersensuous nature of man. It heeds the law, not as a divine command, but as its own demand in which it is at one with itself and with every rational being. What is revealed in morality is not simply the existence of man as a being that is determined in its type by nature, but rather man's transcendent origin.

Nietzsche does not merely deny that moral acts are objectively discoverable (which Kant also denies, since he holds that the rightness of an act does not necessarily attest to its moral character but merely its legality); he also denies the sense and validity of the inner moral demand to act in conformity with the moral law. (Whether this ever really happens or not, i.e., whether morality is actual or simply springs from motives of utility, inclination, and concern with extraneous ends, can, according to Kant, never be objectively settled by empirical means.) Nietzsche goes on to deny not only the universal validity of specific contents of moral demands, but the law of the lawfulness of conduct as being identical with moral conduct itself. He impugns the *unconditionality* of morality – whether in self-sufficient original philosophic form or in the form of its religious derivative – on the following bases:

(1)   *Morality as alien to reality.* If morality is *unconditional*, then its demands possess *absolute* validity. Its content must be *discovered* or *heard*, not as an empirical but as an intelligible fact. In opposition to this, Nietzsche asserts: There are no moral facts. Morality is simply a *construction* placed upon certain phenomena; more precisely speaking, it is a misconstruction. In other words: 'There are no moral phenomena, but only moral interpretations of phenomena.' Moral matters have nothing to do with things 'in themselves'; they are simply matters of opinion. They are part of the world of appearance.

Now if morality is nothing but interpretation, there must be *something* to be interpreted. *What* could it be that is thus morally interpreted? One of Nietzsche's answers is: 'Morality is a sign-language of the feelings,' and these feelings in their turn are a sign-language of the functions of everything organic. Early in his career Nietzsche asks whether, like dreams and other psychological phenomena, 'our moral judgments and evaluations are only images and phantasies of a physiological process unknown to us.' At a later date he provides the answer by saying that he has accustomed himself 'to see in all moral judgments a bungling kind of sign-language by means of which certain physiological facts might be communicated.'

In this way, Nietzsche expresses in concise biological terms what he calls in the broadest sense *reality, actuality,* or *nature.* It is of these that morality provides a sort of *interpretation.* In his attack, he arrives at the conclusion that moral judgments make us falsify ourselves and become less real because they *pass reality by* and, consequently, lead us astray. Instead of letting us master nature in a natural fashion, morality ensnares us in vain imaginings and thereby makes us fall victim to an unseen and undesired actuality. As a result, so long as we act morally, we, in fact, miss the possibilities that are real to us and thus allow 'chance to become a law unto us.'

Since morality is alien to the actual and is bound to remain unreal because of the very principle on which it rests, Nietzsche views moral philosophy as nothing more than a creature of the imagination occupying itself with vain conceits: 'In the whole history of moral development, truth does not once make its appearance: all its conceptual components . . . are fictions, all its psychological interpretations . . . are falsifications, all the logical formulations which are dragged into this kingdom of lies are sophisms. The badge of the moral philosopher himself is a complete absence of any kind of cleanliness.'

In the first place, this attack presupposes that it is possible to know what reality is and also to know that this reality exists in such a way that I can deal with it as something simply given. But still, throughout the whole of Nietzsche's philosophy, *all reality is itself only interpretation*[1] – a kind of exegetical construction beyond whose limitless variations nothing else exists. I have only *one kind* of consciousness of reality; I do *not* know reality as an independent existent outside of myself.

In the second place, Nietzsche presupposes the *absolute value* of this reality which he calls nature. But he cannot maintain this either, insofar as to him every value can be only the value of *one* single reality as a way of interpreting this very reality.

Certain specific aspects of Nietzsche's attack, based upon the irrelevance of morals to reality, appear plausible: he hits upon the psychological truth about certain ways of behaving that pretend to be 'moral,' points out the ever present disparity in all human conduct between what is intended and willed and what actually occurs as a consequence of the deed, or strikes at the irresponsible practice of acting on principle and producing evil in a blind urge to sacrifice while finding comfort in leaving the successful outcome to God. But the root of the import of the absoluteness that moves men to act is not reached by Nietzsche. In Nietzsche's thought, then, one must always distinguish between the psychological truth that relates to the specific phenomena of human existence, and philosophic expressions of the truth that concern the source itself, for this latter alone is in question when we wish to come to grips with the roots of morality.

(2) *Morality as contrary to nature.* For morality to be 'unconditional' means that it ought to exist only for its own sake. It need not justify itself by reference to something external to which it is a means; rather it is itself the measure of all existing things – the measure by which they are to be accepted or rejected. But to rest the case for the ultimate value of morality upon the formula 'morality for morality's sake' is, according to Nietzsche, not only to accept its complete lack of realism, but also to pay the price of devaluating actuality itself. Nowhere does actuality pass the test of morality; adjudged by this test it is simply immoral and opposed to value and, consequently, something which ought not to exist. Like 'beauty for beauty's sake' and 'truth for truth's sake,' 'the good for its own sake' is a 'form of the evil eye for the actual,' 'for since life is essentially something immoral, it must constantly and unavoidably be in the wrong from the standpoint of morality (especially Christian, i.e., unconditional, morality).'

Nietzsche concedes that the value-distinctions and rank-orders which morality provides are defensible – but only as rank-orders of that which is actually living and, in this capacity, as indicators of the conditions underlying the existence and progression of some particular form of life. But as revelations of a higher world – which they have to be if they are to be unconditioned – they turn into the very opposite of life and acquire a life-destroying character. To insist that everything become moral 'would mean to rob existence of its *greatness*, and to castrate mankind and reduce it to a miserable mass of nondescript Chinamen.'

This attack, which claims that morality is 'contrary to nature,' is annulled, however, when Nietzsche, reversing himself, also speaks of *morality* as '*part and parcel of nature.*' Everything belongs to nature – even that which appears to be opposed to it. The modifications of nature's existence are very numerous. Of any moral system one can say: 'It is a fruit that betrays the soil from which it grew.' Morality is thus changed into a mere set of opinions held by one or the other type of man. It is not a source but a consequence – it is itself a product of nature. As such a consequence of the development of a particular type of man, morality in every one of its forms should be viewed as a natural phenomenon. These two ways of viewing morality – both as contrary to nature and as itself perfectly natural – thus appear to annul one another.

Nietzsche, in seeking to reject any '*unconditionality*' can do this only on the basis of a new unconditionality. He himself knows this to be unavoidable. Whenever we value something unconditionally our experience is moral, and, contrariwise, whenever our experience is moral in nature, we are dealing with something unconditional. It is 'simply not possible to relativize a moral experience; it is essentially unconditioned.' Hence, in unconditionally opposing the value accorded to 'nature' to the unconditionality of morality, Nietzsche himself does precisely what he condemns: he pronounces an absolute value-judgment. The basis for 'absolutistic morality' expressed in such words as 'my evaluation is final' is also the basis on which Nietzsche involuntarily – though knowingly – proceeds.

The Double Circle

The unambiguous arguments against morality can thus all be robbed of their decisive effect by an appeal to certain of Nietzsche's other tenets. He has a new way of raising critical questions – more ambiguous ones – by moving in inescapable circles. First he asserts that morality is itself a product of immorality, and then he urges that the criticism of morality itself derives from the highest kind of morality.

(1) *Morality as a product of immorality*. Nietzsche believes that, from the very beginning, the moral has come from something immoral, viz., the will to power. Morality 'is a special case of actual immorality.' For him this is psychologically discernible in individual cases: 'One does not become moral *because* he is moral! Subordination to morality can be slavish, or proud, or selfish, or thoughtless, but intrinsically there is nothing moral about it.' On the contrary 'our morality rests on the same foundation of lies and misrepresentation as our wickedness and selfishness.' Historically this can be seen on a grand scale: 'All the means by which mankind up to now was to be made moral were fundamentally immoral.' An indication of this is 'the *pia fraus*, that heirloom of all philosophers and priests who "improved" mankind. Neither Manu, nor Plato, nor Confucius, nor the Jewish and Christian teachers have ever doubted their *right* to lie.' Consequently 'to *create* morality one must have the unswerving will to the very opposite.' 'Morality has remained in good standing for so long only thanks to immorality.'

Even if the contentions here argued for were correct in their entirety and not merely to a large extent, they would still not be convincing, since it is true, here as elsewhere, that the manner in which something develops and reaches fruition is not decisive for the significance and value of the finished product. But insofar as it is asserted that all morality in its entirety is a product of development rather than a matter of individual developmental relations, the very meaning of morality as something specific, with a source of its own, is obliterated by a reduction of all being to *one* kind of being (nature, reality). It is not the moral that is unconditioned but rather actual nature.

(2) *The derivation of the critique of morality from the highest morality*. That Nietzsche's radical rejection of morality is itself a consequence of his moral involvement is consciously asserted in the following circle: Moral development is bound to have the result that the truthfulness demanded by *morality* finally calls in question the very morality in which it is rooted; morality becomes suspect for purely moral reasons. Judged by the truthfulness which morality itself demands, morality is reduced to mere semblance, and it therewith forfeits its right to condemn pretence. Thus this 'self-overcoming of

morality' occurs only in moral men: 'The critique of morality represents a high stage of morality.' 'In us morality achieves its own self-destruction.' Just because 'one of the highest and most potent efflorescences of the moral sense is the sense for truth itself,' morality, by insisting on truthfulness, has 'placed around its own neck the noose with which it can be strangled – its own last moral demand is the suicide of morality.'

But in these circles the self-assertion as well as the suicide of morality appears. For just as we are left, in the first case, with self-assertive immorality within the circle that reduced morality to a special case of immorality, so, in the second, *morality* becomes the basis for the circle that derives the destruction of morality from *morality itself*. In neither case does the negation strike the heart of the matter, though it presents origins and lines of descent concretely. Without such concrete presentation the circles are merely formal. Their consequence – not logical but rather derived from existential ground – can be self-sufficiency in self-assertion as well as self-negation through the suicide of morality.

Because Nietzsche's critique of morality transcends the specific and penetrates to the outermost limits, he is in fact compelled either to annul his statements in consciously constructed *circles* or to leave them standing in unrecognized *contradictory* opposition to each other.

At the start, Nietzsche had intended the two *circles* as attacks whose results would be final: the first by reducing morality itself to its opposite; the second by demanding the rejection of morality on the highest moral grounds. But when Nietzsche views reality (nature) as neither moral nor immoral, but rather as the encompassing being, he is, as a consequence, driven to reject in turn his own condemnation of morality: Moral condemnation is in itself simply a fact within nature; when I now condemn one single thing within nature, I condemn the whole of it, since everything is involved with everything else. It follows that when I condemn this condemnation, as I do, I am doing precisely the thing for which I just reproached those who play the moral judge: I am condemning the whole. I can and must say Yes to nature by affirming even the moral condemnation that I just now rejected. In this circle all positions annul one another, and there is no escape.

But if one retains these positions, they remain in inescapable *contradiction*, so that while one is being expressed the other has to be left out of consideration. We hear that 'it is not possible to live outside of morality,' as well as the contrary, that 'one can live only with an absolutely immoral way of thinking.' Or again, morality 'is the only interpretative scheme with which man can endure' and, on the other hand, 'the world, morally interpreted, is unbearable.'

Nietzsche's Demands

If we place before us the *fundamental meaning* of Nietzsche's total attack on morality (something that cannot be comprehended from any single argument), we find that it involves more than the attack on the Christian interpretation, which regards human conduct as sinful, and more than the attack on the codification of ethics accepted by philosophers or on the moral conventions within society. The attack proceeds victoriously against *all* fixated and derived phenomena of generally accepted morality and points beyond to the source of morality itself in a universally valid *ought*. Only thus can we understand how Nietzsche is aware of the awesome implication of his position (because of him 'the history of mankind is broken in two'): 'The lightning flash of truth has struck precisely that which stood highest up to the present. He who understands what was thus annihilated can see whether or not he has anything at all to cling to. . . . He who exposes morality thereby brings to light the worthlessness of all the values in which men believe or have believed.' Nietzsche's critical questioning is extraordinary, but it is not the culmination of his thinking and experiencing: the questioning cannot be understood unless we sense the *genuine positive demands* that struggle within it for recognition. Nietzsche's reflections upon morality are far from being exhaustively expressed in a series of aggressive statements which formally refute each other. On the contrary, his formalism contains hints of a depth of intention whose existential significance we must bring into focus.

Nietzsche's *demands* cannot be of the sort that set up definite prescriptions and proscriptions which could guide the purposeful will. He starts much deeper because he wishes to reach the possible *Existenz* of man through indirect illumination of those *modes of existential actualization* which he envisages. This appeal of Nietzsche, which seems to express the very substance of his being, will be elucidated in four directions:

(1) *He champions the individual in opposition to the universal.* The morality which he opposes is founded upon a substance common to all men, upon the Deity, or upon reason. Nietzsche counters by saying: 'My morality would consist of decreasing man's universality more and more and making him more specialized . . . and less understandable to others.' As it is so essential to Nietzsche 'that there is no single morality that alone can make us moral,' he wishes to place the individual ahead of all moral and rational universals. But he does not intend to give the isolated individual as such free scope for his self-centered caprice. Rather he reaches into the depths of existential historical reality (*existentielle Geschichtlichkeit*) to make us aware of the law in the form in which it becomes audible in the concrete situation of *Existenz*. Thus by the word 'individual' he means, not the isolated private person, but the single human being who always knows that 'we are more than individuals; we are also the entire chain and charged with the tasks of all the futures of the

chain.' It may be said of this potentially existing single being that 'each individual is an attempt to reach a species that is higher than man.'

Still Nietzsche's statements abound in individualistic phrases which, when taken by themselves, lose their existential sense.

(2)   *The innocence of becoming.* From his attacks on morality Nietzsche draws the following conclusion: If it is true that insofar as we believe in morality we condemn life, then we must 'annihilate morality in order to liberate life' and 'attempt to be as amoral as nature.' If man, when his powers are fullest and noblest, is part and parcel of nature, then the important thing is to *bring him back* to nature and the truths that she contains. Nietzsche speaks of this demand as his 'assault against two millennia of perversion of nature and of desecration of man.'

Still, if everything is nature and even morality is a product of a certain kind of nature, then all demands are nonsensical. When whatever exists and occurs must belong to nature, nothing may ever properly be commanded to rise above nature, and there is nothing that we can stigmatize as unnatural with a view to its rectification.

Nietzsche does in fact arrive at this last conclusion when he revokes every demand and *demands that all demanding cease.* Here he succeeds for the first time in regaining complete innocence and effecting a great liberation for all human behavior: 'The opposition has been taken out of things; the homogeneity of all events is preserved.' He no longer needs to exclude anything and is simply concerned to unite opposites. As a result of this liberation, he has no desire to annihilate even what he attacks. While the will to one single morality would amount to the tyranny of its adherents over all other types of men, Nietzsche concedes that he has 'not declared war against the anaemic ideal of Christians with a view to annihilating it. . . . The continuation of the Christian ideal is one of the most desirable things there is. . . . We immoralists thus need the power of morality: our instinct of self-preservation demands that our opponent remain strong.'

In this way Nietzsche gains insight into what he calls the 'innocence of becoming' (*Unschuld des Werdens*) – an insight that conquers all other moralities with their dichotomy of good and bad or good and evil.

Wherever indignation and the urge to discover the guilty party predominate – wherever attempts are made to fix responsibilities – there 'existence is robbed of its innocence.' We need not blame others – neither God nor society nor parents and ancestors; we need not succumb to our instinct for revenge, to our urge to shift the blame for all our discomforts to a scapegoat, or to any other stultifying impulses. Rather we have the right to an absolutely affirmative view that embraces everything – even what we momentarily reject – within the total chain of events.

Whenever we blame ourselves, we are succumbing to the bigotry of moral narrowness. Nietzsche wishes to achieve a consciousness of innocence. Why does he take such pains to prove in every possible way the complete innocence of becoming? 'Was it not simply in order to create for myself the feeling of complete irresponsibility – to place myself beyond every kind of praise and blame, to make myself independent of everything connected with yesterday and today – so that I could pursue my goal in my own way?' The seal of the attainment of freedom is 'being no longer ashamed of one's self.' When knowledge of the innocence of becoming is gained, then for the first time the highest possibilities present themselves: 'It is the innocence of becoming alone that gives us the greatest courage and the greatest freedom.'

Nevertheless, when Nietzsche attempts to reconcile all opposites, to see nature merely *as* nature and all things as natural, and to acquire the innocence of becoming, he cannot but discover that nothing follows from mere contemplation: no demand, to be sure, but also no impulse. Thus he returns to the thesis: 'No impulse can be derived from nature as known.' A 'beyond good and evil,' maintained merely as such, would in fact be just as empty a beyond as any known to metaphysics. Man must will something, move toward its realization, and receive guidance from its direction. This direction is not provided by becoming per se; it is always contained *within* becoming in the form of a real act through which one shows what he is and what he wills and through which he immediately becomes again subject to demands in the face of opposites and able either to hearken to the law or to turn a deaf ear to it.

Nietzsche's philosophizing is not intended to allow thinking man to sink peacefully into the undisturbed innocence of becoming. On the contrary, he should be able, by listening to the source of the possible, to learn what is historically called for by his own specific situation. Insofar as Nietzsche's thinking is intended to lead us through these self-destructive antitheses into the clarity of the audible, where the concrete and determinate law gives way before the encompassing law that becomes known only historically, this thinking must itself lose all definiteness. Hence Nietzsche is not content with such final statements as 'the innocence of becoming has been restored,' or 'all is necessity – all is innocence' rather he wishes to hit upon the productive factor in this extreme freedom. He calls it 'creation.'

(3) *Creation (Schaffen)*. Creation is the highest demand; it is authentic being, the ground of all essential activity:

Creation is *evaluation*: 'Without evaluation the nut of existence would be hollow!' 'Change of values – that is change of the creators.' 'As yet no one knows what is good and bad – except the creator! – He is the one who creates the goal for mankind and gives the earth its meaning and its future: the one whose *creativity* makes it possible for something to be good or bad.'

Creation is *faith* (*Glaube*). The sterile lack faith. 'But he who was driven to create always had his prophetic dreams and astrological portents – and had faith in faith!'

Creation is *love*: 'All great love ... still wishes to create – the object of its love!'

In creation is *annihilation*: 'It is only as creators that we can annihilate.' All creators are hard. 'To my love I sacrifice myself, and my fellow-men as well – this is the language of all creators.' The will to create is the will to become, to grow, and to shape, . . . but destruction too is involved in creation.' Together with the *creative* good, which is *the highest good of all*, 'goes the greatest evil.'

'All creation is *communication* (*Mitteilen*).' The moments of greatest creation are those of increased capacity for communication and understanding. 'Creation: that means to give of ourselves, leaving ourselves emptier, poorer, and more loving.'

Still, all aspects of creation together form a *unity*: 'The knower, the creator, and the lover are one.' The unity is 'the great synthesis of the knower, lover, and annihilator' or, again, it is called 'the unity, in power, of the creator, the lover, and the knower.'

The *condition* of creation is great pain and lack of knowledge. 'Creation – that is the great deliverance from suffering. . . . But if the creator is to exist, suffering itself is needed.' 'To see right through the perishable net and the last veil – that would be the greatest tedium and the end of all creators.'

In creation *authentic being is attained. 'Freedom* appears only in creation.' 'Our only happiness consists in creating.' 'As a creator you transcend yourself – you cease to be your own contemporary.'

The high value of the creator is *unconditional* for Nietzsche: 'Even the most trivial creative act is better than talking about what has been created.' 'Our salvation does not lie in knowing but in creating.' 'You should learn only for the sake of creating' : 'One even *ought* not to know more of a thing than what one can create. Furthermore the only way to *know* a thing truly is to attempt to make it.'

But it is as though the creator were *invisible*: 'The people have little conception of the great, that is, the creator. But they have an appreciation for all agitators and imitators of great things.'

Just what creation is remains *necessarily* indefinite. It is one of those *signa* of Nietzsche's philosophizing that, like 'life,' 'will to power,' and 'eternal recurrence,' is never conceptualized. Our thinking runs aground on them, either negatively, through becoming lost in a void or through misunderstanding due to simplification, or positively, by being translated into an actual impulse. In every kind of philosophizing we find these ultimate inconceivables that are aptly expressed but never conquered by words. Nietzsche always treats creation as though it were self-evident, but virtually never takes it directly as his theme. He does not develop and explain its nature. It is never a possible goal of the will. But his formulations have all the power of an as yet indefinite appeal to recall and to come to grips with authentic being.

Creation is absolutely primordial, but it is not a first beginning, as though nothing had ever been before. If, after the annihilation of morality, creation is the new morality, then it is precisely the creator who does *the preserving within the annihilation*. Consequently Nietzsche maintains throughout his thinking the position that he in no way intends to destroy morality by denying it.

Nietzsche is not simply hesitant: we must 'guard against rushing violently head over heels to exchange our customary morality for a new evaluation of things.' Rather he explicitly demands the preservation of traditional morality: 'We will be the inheritors of morality when we have destroyed the moral.' We possess 'the moral sense as a great legacy of previous generations.' 'We should not underestimate what a couple of millennia of morality have bred into our spirit!' Precisely in the case of the creative path-finder, 'a kind of wealth in moral inheritance must be presupposed.' 'We wish to be the heirs of all previous morality and *not* to begin anew. All our actions are simply morality reacting against its previous form.'

In the end Nietzsche bases the possibility of creativity of the heirs themselves on *the struggle against the pressure which Christianity has exerted* for thousands of years: through this struggle the thorough-going Christian morality has 'created in Europe a splendid spiritual tension . . . With so tense a bow one can now shoot to the most distant goals.' Twice the attempt has been made on a grand scale 'to relax the bow: once by the Jesuit Movement and again by the democratic enlightenment.' But Nietzsche, sure of still having the full tension of his own bow, wishes to preserve and increase the tension in the world as the source of a creation that will far outstrip all previous creation. What, in the critique of morality, is creatively destructive, must after all – since this is not the end of all things – assert itself in a new way as creative morality.

For *himself*, Nietzsche is aware that he lives on 'a rich moral heritage' and that he is in a position to treat morality as an illusion just because to him it 'has become instinctive and unavoidable' (to Fuchs, July 29, '88). To be sure, the morality that governs him and that enables him to reject morality does not derive from a timeless conscience but from a positive attitude that is at once original with him and historically inherited. As an immoralist he feels himself to be 'still related to the age-old German integrity and piety.' Being what he is, he would not be able to apply the conclusions that could conceivably be drawn from his own doctrine: 'It is all very well to talk about all kinds of immorality; but to live by them is another matter! For example, I could not bear to break my word or even to commit murder. It would be my lot to pine away for a shorter or longer time and then perish!'

(4) *Man as his own creator*. Nietzsche views man as more than a being that passively undergoes alterations: he never doubts that man is free and that he develops himself. His criticism of morality is intent upon making precisely this genuine freedom again possible. But man's freedom has its own specific meaning: the freedom of self-realization is simply creation. How man the creator is also the self-developer has been formulated by Nietzsche in three different ways:

(a) Since man is a creative being, in that he *appreciates, measures, and evaluates*, there are no absolute values that simply subsist as realities needing only to be discovered. Rather values are the form in which man, in a unique moment of historical actuality, lays hold not only upon the conditions of his existence but even those of his own self-being. Values are never final; at any given time they must be created. That is why Nietzsche, in the present moment of world history, assumes the task of a 'transvaluation of all values.'

(b)   Change, furthermore, comes about in connection with the fundamental relation that man assumes toward himself by seeing himself, evaluating himself, being deceived about himself, and giving form to himself. In this occurs, in addition to what is open to psychological investigation, something that is forever psychologically unobservable, although for self-being it constitutes the genuine assurance of its actuality: what I myself really am comes to me from without as though I were given as a present to myself. Hence Nietzsche tells us that behind every psychologically analyzable effect that man can have upon himself lies the incomprehensible riddle of a genuine depth which makes possible self-organization without repression and self-mastery without self-violation. As fundamental impulses emerge, I am carried, beyond all mere psychological actuality, to that from which the latter first acquires its meaning and its form. It is not a question here of grasping a psychologically discoverable measure and a mean between extremes, for what Nietzsche means by these words transcends the psychological. But self-being is far better attuned to it than to anything psychologically knowable: 'It is best never to speak *of two very great things: measure and mean*. Very few people know the powers and omens that come to them from *the mysterious paths and inner experiences* and conversions. They revere them as something divine and avoid noisy proclamations.'

(c)   Finally the change derived from the evaluative impulses within the medium of reflexive behavior can only be realized through a capacity for *motion within one's own nature* that does not exist as an entity, but has its being in the process of becoming through which it realizes itself. This is what Nietzsche regards as the phenomenon of the procreation of that which I already am in the sense of existential possibility, a phenomenon that transcends all psychologically visible conversions and all biologically knowable processes. Man as creator changes with the new evaluations that he assumes and at the same time becomes that which he really is. Thus Nietzsche makes Pindar's demand his own: *Become what you are!*

Nietzsche's stern earnestness paralyzes every sort of moral pathos. His kind of thinking cannot rest content with, or even find edification in, any proposition, demand, law, or specific content. It proceeds indirectly by demanding that one take seriously those profound inner depths that would simply be obstructed by appeal to any derived law and any fixed standard.

When one gives up the moral universal that makes its demands with logically inflexible unconditionality, no return is possible. One is threatened by the possibility of sinking into a limitless void. The loss of the resistance afforded by immutable moral laws may as easily be followed by abandonment to caprice and accident as by emergence from the source of an authentic and historically unique possibility.

In the end, the contradictory elements and circles in the movements of Nietzsche's thought are simply the means to touch indirectly upon what lies beyond form, law, and the expressible. Nothing can be at this boundary, and yet everything must be there. This thinking must always end with allusions to a ground from which my being will come toward me: allusions like 'the mysterious paths of inner conversions,' the 'belief in ourselves,' 'creation,' the actuality of life as the lightness of the 'dance.' But all formulae remain ambiguous and self-discrepant when they are involved with belief in a being whose becoming does not derive from what it is. In connection with what we ourselves basically are, this amounts to saying: 'Belief in ourselves is the strongest bond, the most compelling whiplash – and the strongest wing.'

Creation as Freedom without Transcendence

We must now examine in greater detail Nietzsche's idea that creation takes the place of freedom, or, in other words, *is* freedom. In the sense employed by the philosophy of *Existenz*,[2] freedom, whether Christian or Kantian, exists in relation to transcendence. Freedom is the potentiality of a finite being; it is limited by transcendence, and it depends on an incomprehensible source lying at this limit (whether this be called 'grace' or 'being-given-to-oneself'). The decision as to what has eternal significance is made through freedom. That is, freedom exists historically as the union of the temporal and the eternal and as the decision that is itself merely an appearance of eternal being.

Nietzsche rejects this freedom. He professes to follow Spinoza because the latter denies the freedom of the will, the moral order in the world, and genuine evil (to Overbeck, July 30, '80). The freedom that Nietzsche acknowledges and asserts amounts to being rooted in one's self and having the source of life within one's self without transcendence. Such freedom is both *negative* and *positive*. The way of freedom is *negative* insofar as it discards, breaks through, and denies what has been real and binding: 'To cut oneself off from his past (from fatherland, belief, parents, companions), to associate with *outcasts* (in history and in society); to topple what is most revered and affirm what is most strongly forbidden . . .' On the *positive* side, the fruits of freedom are of the nature of 'creation.' The positive cannot occur without the negative, because it can be attained only by traversing the negative way. The dialectic of the first discourse of Zarathustra shows that this way leads from service through the rejection of service to creation. But were the negative to detach itself from the positive and remain negative merely, it would amount to an empty and therefore spurious freedom. All negation is justified only by the creative positing to which it is preparatory and which it conditions or follows. By itself it is inferior to obedient service in accordance with tradition. That is why Zarathustra asks of all liberators who wish to remove man's chains for the sake of freedom as such: 'Free for what?' He is indifferent to 'freedom from' and expresses the opinion that 'there are many who discarded their last vestige of worth in throwing off their servitude.'

Since *negative* freedom is entirely inadequate, it is of paramount import-ance that negation should be carried out from the standpoint of *positive*, creative freedom. If positive creating were not the genuine ground of the annulment of existing obligations (and it is here the existential rather than the argumentative ground that is in question), then one could well exclaim in fear: 'Your wild dogs clamor to be set free.' By the same token, mere restraint of one's own unbridled impulses is not enough, when this springs from the inane denial of anything having instinctive existence and not from the sense of positive creative substance: 'You have conquered yourself. But why do you behave solely as the vanquished? I want to behold the victorious one . . .' This latter is the creator.

Thus Nietzsche's freedom without transcendence is by no means intent upon simply returning to mere life; it aspires to the life of authentic creation. Just as Nietzsche's denial of morals does not mean the annulment of all morality but a laying hold upon what is *more than merely moral*, so here his sole intention is to stimulate man to higher achievement. To be sure, without God, Nietzsche's purpose seems to lead to the radical loss of all bonds: what remains is just to live as before and to allow life to continue as always. But this is to turn Nietzsche's idea into its very opposite. Its challenge is tremendous, for the entire burden is laid upon the individual. He requires each of us to follow the insecure and thus dangerous new path of the individual who is not yet sustained within a stratified society and who must find the source of his ties within himself. Nietzsche is asking those who abandon morality to bind themselves by still higher and more inexorable bonds. After all, morality is no longer real; it is only an empty and deceptive show. Threateningly, he exclaims: 'If you are too weak to give laws to yourselves, then let a tyrant lay his yoke upon you and say: "Obey! Gnash and obey!" and all good and evil will be drowned in obedience to him.'

One can find decisive evidence for this interpretation of his doctrine. In a moment that led to his later, lonely, existence, he found it unbearable that his 'immoralism' could be confused with the 'less than moral' by a person whom he had believed to share his conception of a philosophy that lives through creation at a level above morality. 'You have within you,' he wrote, 'that impulse to a sacred selfishness which is the impulse to obey the highest com-mandment. You must at first have confused it, under the spell of some curse, with its opposite: the selfishness and delight in plunder of a cat that *desires nothing beyond being alive. . . .*' But the meaning of this mere life is simply 'feeling for life in a void; . . . something I find extremely repugnant in man' (correspondence with Lou, Nov. 1, '82). Nietzsche expresses the contrast even more tersely: 'She told me herself that she had no morals – and I supposed that hers, like mine, were stricter than anyone's' (correspondence with Rée, '82). This high claim that no one can fully live up to does not exist, to be sure, as a definable duty, and it cannot be fulfilled by acting in accordance with a specific law. Still the expression of this new morality clearly intends the very opposite of mere amoral living.

To be sure, Nietzsche characterizes the new, higher, and still wholly indeterminate morality as 'that of the creating ones,' but he does not express it in terms of any definite contents. The creative transvaluation of all values must bring forth his new 'morality': 'Who will create the *goal* that stands high over all humanity as well as over the individual?' The path can no longer be that of previous morality which intended merely to 'preserve.' Now that there is no goal for all, 'an *experimental* morality is called for: *setting* one's self a goal.' What is meant is 'a substitute for morality through the will to our goal and consequently to the means to this goal.' It is the substance of the future that is to become free: 'They will call you the destroyers of morality, but you are really only the finders of yourselves.' Everyone is made to rely on himself. A new self-sufficiency must develop: 'We must free ourselves of morality in order to be able to live morally,' or again: 'I had to invalidate morality in order to realize my moral will.'

When Nietzsche makes his magnificent claim on a deeper unattained source, he believes that *it can be reached only without God.* 'To rule and no longer be God's vassal – this is the means left to us for ennobling man.'

Because Nietzsche wishes to define, circumscribe, and interpret the creative source apart from transcendence, it constantly comes about that, in spite of his will to something more-than-life, he suddenly finds in his hands mere nature in the sense of what is biologically knowable, or he is left with only the corresponding mere psychological or sociological actualities. The new morality is to be a 'natural' morality, and this is affirmed in spite of all the thoughts that should render it untenable when he says: 'Every naturalism in morality, that is, every *sound* morality, is governed by an instinct for life.'

For example, the demand, '*Become what you are!*' illustrates the way in which Nietzsche's formulations lead him involuntarily from *the appeal to an existential source* to the mere assertion of *natural facts* (and hence of particular investigable existents within the world). In seeming correspondence with the above exhortation, Nietzsche, by ascertaining the nature of this developing being instead of demanding a certain nature of him, is able to say: 'One becomes a decent man just because he *is* a decent man, i.e., because he is born with a capital of good instincts and favorable conditions. . . . Today we know better than to regard moral degeneracy as something separate from the physiological.' Now it is certainly impossible at the level of existence to separate the physiological or causal (to say nothing of the psychological and sociological) from *Existenz*: whatever we come to know about ourselves through scientific investigation is so intimately bound up with us that we could not exist without it. But, inseparable from this observable existence that we know ourselves to be, there is also something else: the source of man himself, which transcends science. Only the clarity of conceptual distinction removes the ambiguity of a being that allows existential possibility and physiologically and psychologically investigable actuality to appear as identical rather than merely as involved with each other: (1) The being that I 'ought' to become may simply have the significance of *just-being-that-way* (with the consequence of withholding oneself on the basis of the principle that is really born of despair: I just happen to be that way); *ought* then no longer has any real meaning but is an inexorable *must*. Or (2) the being that I ought to become means as well the *encompassing force of possibility (das Umgreifende der Möglichkeit)* which I can never know as something fixed and determinate and which no one else can know. This possibility remains open and reveals again and again what I am (while self-withholding only leads to ever-recurring confirmation of the same inferiority or imagined excellence). On the plane of psychological facts, Nietzsche himself denies 'unchangeability of character' and condemns the 'average man's belief in himself as in a fully developed and completed state of affairs.' Psychologically, 'we are free' to choose among possibilities. But this source from which it is decided 'what we are free' to do – this being that cannot be identified by objective procedures of characterology but which we ourselves most truly are – is that to which the demand 'Become what you are!' is directed. This demand, which would be meaningless if it referred merely to an innate just-being-so as a psychological state of affairs, becomes 'dangerous' when taken seriously because it is directed at the still indeterminate source of my being and is exposed to all kinds of misunderstanding. For it is not a definite law and an objectively derivable obligation that decides, but rather reliance on the 'creative' source in me, and this may be lacking. Hence when Nietzsche says, 'Become what you are: that is a challenge which is permissible in the case of only a few men but is superfluous in the case of only the very fewest of those few,' even this challenge may become meaningless when one reverts to the view that man has an objectively identifiable nature. But the meaning of that true and willed existential danger that creativity may never come forth – a danger present to Nietzsche's consciousness with extraordinary urgency and persistence – is audibly conveyed.

Immanence Reverses Itself

Whenever anyone has been sure of possessing the kind of freedom that Nietzsche denies, he has viewed it as inseparable from himself, and, in being thus free, he has experienced both nullification and security in confronting transcendence. But creation, which Nietzsche substitutes for existential freedom as the sole immanent actualization of his kind of freedom, ends within itself or is lost, since it has only itself to depend on. The creating individual, whether he runs into obstacles or is able to continue on his way, has, according to Nietzsche's philosophy, an awareness of destiny rather than a relation to transcendence. In the place of transcendence Nietzsche puts 'necessity,'[3] metaphysically so conceived that every accident that happens to me and every impulse that stirs within me appears as meaningful in relation to the totality of my development as a *creator*. Necessity, thus conceived, is not wholly unlike the freedom which he denies, though it differs essentially from the causally interpreted necessity of a psychical and biological order of occurrences. In spite of everything, the one affords Nietzsche a transcending consciousness of being within the whole, while the other offers merely a relative knowledge of particular relations within the world.

Creation without transcendence, or self-being without God, must lead to two conclusions that Nietzsche actually draws. When human finiteness ceases to be evident *as* finiteness because it is no longer enclosed by any infinity, i.e., when creative freedom faces nothingness instead of transcendence (for that which has nothing outside of itself is everything, with the result that its finiteness cannot be taken seriously), then either (1) creation is *absolutized as a temporal actuality* to which no valid standard applies, or (2) it is *deified*. Naturalizations express the first conclusion, hybris the second. Neither of these relates to transcendence; each is, instead, a way in which confidence becomes evident at the boundary which is no longer a boundary but a fulfillment. Nietzsche has expressed both consequences in a singularly daring language in which all logical thinking reverses itself:

(1)   In assuming a position outside of morality, Nietzsche believed that he was *in agreement with Jesus*. 'Jesus took sides against those who judge: he wished to be the destroyer of morality.' 'Jesus said: . . . Of what concern is morality to us who are sons of God!' Nietzsche saw in Jesus the anticipated realization of his own idea (blurred in the process of deification) of what is more than morality and, hence, what he himself desired to be: 'God, conceived as the state of being liberated from morality, compressing within Himself all the fullness of life's contrasts, redeeming and justifying them in divine agony: God as beyond . . . good and evil.' It is in accord with the nature of this conclusion that Nietzsche in the early stages of insanity signed himself 'The Crucified' as well as Dionysus.

(2) Essentially the same self-confidence in transgressing all determinate morality appears as if reversed in its nature when aimed not at the source (there being nothing but nature and actuality) but *at triumphant effectiveness* within the world: 'We immoralists are today the strongest power: the other great powers need us. We construe the world in our own image.' Whatever has the appearance of validity seems to have gone by the board when there is nothing left but mere brutal actuality in its immediacy, in which such self-confidence seeks nothing but victory for itself. Then one begins to wonder whether we are left, not with the more-than-moral, but rather with the less-than-moral –

the mere existence of the forces of nature. This self-confidence does indeed become inseparable from demonic triumph in these awesome statements: 'We immoralists are today the only power that needs no allies in order to attain victory. . . . We do not even need the lie. . . . Even without the truth we would come to power. . . . The magic that fights for us is that of the extreme.'

Neither of the above expresses any longer the ethos of finite beings that go their way in tension with transcendence and bound by historical reality. Because these last demands of Nietzsche leave no room for the spirit who feels himself bound because of his knowledge of finiteness, both deification and sinking into the extremes (as an overpowering efficacy) are possible. Where finitude, confinement of the finite, and possible *Existenz* appear eliminated in this manner, finite creatures like ourselves are shut out. It is as though freedom in Nietzsche's thinking becomes transformed into creation, which, in its ambiguous indeterminacy, offers us no solid ground to stand on, while creation in turn is consumed in an explosion which leaves only a phantom deity or nothingness behind.

Finally it is always like a return from deification and devilization to find determinacy and concrete range of application in Nietzsche's thinking. Then, in opposition to deification and the immoderation of the extreme, he seems always prepared to come back to his acceptance of the statement: it is essential for manliness 'that we do not deceive ourselves about our *human* position: rather let us proceed strictly according to *our measure*'. But man must find his own limitation in the world by following *a way of life*. In seeking to find a way, Nietzsche accomplishes man's task of setting limits to himself.

To be sure there are times when he finds this way hopeless. His situation, which does not permit him either to live with morality or to live without it, he characterizes as follows: 'Perhaps a devil invented morality in order to torture men through pride, and a second devil at some time took it away from them to make them suffer from self-contempt.' The impossibility of escape from this makes it seem that 'perhaps man must simply perish as a result of his morality.'

But actually the way remains open to Nietzsche: 'We who again dare to live in an *amoralized* world – we pagans – . . . realize what heathen belief is: to have to conceive of beings higher than man.' Nietzsche believes that these beings that transcend humanity *can only be expected to emerge from the man* who transforms himself within the world. In place of the deity and of all morality, it is the *image of man* that becomes significant in propelling us upward.

Notes

1. Cf. pp. 184ff., 287ff.
2. Jaspers uses the term *Existenzphilosophie* to characterize his own view (*Philosophie*, III, p. 217; Von der Wahrheit, p. 165), while he prefers to use the word *Existentialismus* to signify a view which he rejects (*Philosophie*, I, xxiii) – Trs.
3. *Vide infra*, pp. 356ff.

47

Morality and Sublimation*

Walter Kaufmann

*Source: Walter Kaufmann, *Nietzsche: Philosopher, Psychologist, Antichrist*, Princeton University Press, 1988, pp. 182–97, 383–4.

The central conception of Nietzsche's later thought, the will to power, is introduced in Zarathustra's speech 'On the 1001 Goals': 'A table of virtues [*eine Tafel der Güter*] hangs over every people. See, it is the table of its over-comings; see, it is the voice of its will to power.' This passage has already been considered in passing in the preceding chapter [Kaufmann, *Nietzsche: Philosopher, Psychologist, Antichrist* (1988) Chapter 6], but only now are we ready to consider some of its systematic implications – especially Nietzsche's conceptions of morality and of sublimation. These in turn will make possible a proper estimation of the remainder of his philosophy of power.

The passage cited suggests nothing less than a generic definition of morality, i.e., an attempt to crystallize the common essence of *all* moral codes. Nietzsche himself, as we have seen, offers four illustrations – namely the codes of the Greeks, the Persians, the Jews, and the Germans. And instead of stating any preference, he stresses the common generic element, self-overcoming.

What is at stake is clearly something different from any attempt to develop a system of ethics. Even a very brief contrast of Kant and Mill shows this. Kant insisted that man is not morally good unless his conduct is marked by the total absence of any psychological inclination and motivated solely by respect for reason[1] – and Kant opposed all other views of morality as sheer perversions. John Stuart Mill, on the other hand, did not similarly repudiate Kant's ethics: rather he claimed that 'to all those *a priori* moralists who deem it necessary to argue at all, utilitarian arguments are indispensable' – and adduced Kant's moral philosophy as his prime example.[2] To this extent at least, Mill – instead of opposing his own utilitarianism to other conceptions of morality – seems to have advanced it as a formulation of the essence of *all* moral codes.

Nietzsche's generic conception of morality is best understood in terms of a brief contrast with the rival utilitarian definition. (In a later chapter, the pleasure principle and power standard will have to be contrasted in more detail in a different context.) Mill could include Kant's ethics within the fold of utilitarianism only on the basis of a crucial misunderstanding of Kant.[3] For expediency was not a matter of concern for Kant at all: moral worth was, to his mind, solely a function of the rationality, i.e. consistency, of the maxim according to which an action was resolved. Any inconsistency, he thought, might be made explicit by universalizing the maxim and determining whether its universal adoption would give rise to a situation in which the maxim could no longer be applied. To the extent to which he did consider consequences, he was thus concerned not with their utility but only with a formal property: was the maxim self-defeating? Whether Kant's ethics is preferable to Mill's is not the question here, but as a *generic* definition of morality, utilitarianism would fail to include Kant's morality. Nor is Kant's the only one. The force of his ethics is due in large measure to the fact that he crystallized elements which had long been implicit in the Western religious tradition which commanded man to do the good because God willed it, regardless of the consequences. And more recent studies in anthropology have brought to light a host of other moral codes which defy explanation in terms of expediency.

If actions inspired by love of God, fear of divine wrath, or a less clearly defined sense of awe should all be referred to expediency, then it might indeed be true that moral conduct is always 'expedient.' The word 'expediency,' however, is then given so wide a meaning that *all* conduct might well be called expedient and the distinguishing characteristic of moral conduct is lost. As a generic definition of moral goodness, the utilitarian definition must therefore be rejected.

Now one might well distinguish between the expediency of an act motivated by fear and the expediency of simply acting on impulse, but this distinction only confirms that expediency as such is not the essence of morality. There is another element which distinguishes the moral from the nonmoral – and this, says Nietzsche, is self-overcoming.

That Kant's ethic as well as, say, the Ten Commandments exhibits this characteristic seems clear; and the element of self-overcoming is no less essential to the utilitarian position. The force and plausibility of utilitarianism are inseparable from its insistence that the individual must overcome himself and subordinate his own interests to those of the greatest number. In so-called primitive moral codes, too, the element of self-control and the disciplining of the inclinations is invariably present. Self-overcoming may thus be considered the common essence of all moral codes, from 'totem and taboo' to the ethics of the Buddha.

So general a statement should not be founded on induction alone, as only a fraction of the evidence could be surveyed here. Nietzsche's position can be established more firmly by considering the form which a moral code would have to take to elude his generic definition. Such a code could not place any restraint on the individual and would have to permit him to act on impulse. While this position is conceivable, it would be in accordance with common usage to refuse to call it 'moral.' A man who adopted it might state his case thus: I repudiate morality and prefer to act on impulse.

This position should not be confused with classical Greek hedonism, which considered pleasure the aim of conduct, but did not identify pleasure with the gratification of every impulse which presents itself. Man was told to control his impulses for the sake of his ultimate happiness, which was conceived in refined and spiritual terms – usually as the pursuit of philosophy.

Wherever man is found he imposes restraints on himself; and it seems empirically sound to call man not only – as the Western tradition has usually done, following Aristotle – a 'rational animal' but also a 'moral animal.' The two epithets are inseparable. The general concepts which are the character-istic function of reason involve the transcendence of the merely given, includ-ing impulses which can thus be criticized reflectively. Such self-criticism – i.e. man's critical reflection on his own intentions and actions – is the core of morality.

Of course, an action which is not impulsive is not necessarily good. If a crime was committed 'in cold blood,' that is not an extenuating circumstance. In such a case, however, the criminal has acted as a moral agent, and his act was in that sense moral – though morally evil. A small baby who acts on impulse, on the other hand, is not immoral but simply not a moral agent yet; and a man urging us to yield to our every impulse would be telling us neither to act morally nor immorally, but – as babies do, i.e. amorally.

That a generic definition of morality does not reveal whether particular acts are good or evil is only to be expected: for specific moral codes are not in agreement on such matters, and a generic definition can only crystallize what is common to all the members of the genus. Morality always consists in not yielding to impulses: moral codes are systems of injunctions against submis-sion to various impulses, and positive moral commandments always enjoin a victory over animal instincts. Expediency, on the other hand, is no more than an important characteristic of some moral codes, conceivably of the best – but not, like self-overcoming, the very essence of morality itself.

Specific differences between particular moralities may be due to divergent conceptions not only of the aim and sanction, but also of the manner of self-overcoming. Thus the classical ideal was that reason should control the inclinations, while Kant insisted, as we have seen, that inclination must be overcome to the extent that it may not even be a co-motive of action. Had Nietzsche developed his own earlier dualistic tendencies, he might now have spoken of reason's control over the will to power, of Apollo's victory over Dionysus, or of Ormazd's triumph over Ahriman. His repudiation of any such dualism through the mouth of his Zarathustra, however, rules out any such approximation of the classical and Kantian views. In fact, Nietzsche's monism raises the question as to how there can be any control whatever. Asked what in the world could overcome the will to power, Nietzsche would have to reply that there is no other principle besides the will to power, and that the will to power must therefore overcome itself. Thus the conception of self-overcoming gains an entirely new significance. But one may question whether it is still meaningful.

The demand that reason should overcome inclination, or that consideration for one's own future happiness or for the welfare of others should restrain our impulses, is easily comprehensible. In each case, we can point out how a man might have acted in a certain specified way, how he 'overcame himself,' and how he then acted differently. That seems much more difficult in the case of the alleged self-overcoming of the will to power. After all, the simile of overcoming – and we must not forget that the word is metaphorical – implies the presence of two forces, one of which overcomes the other. 'Self-overcoming' is conceivable and meaningful when the self is analyzed into two forces, such as reason and the inclinations. Apart from such a duality, apart from the picture of one force as overcoming and controlling another, self-overcoming seems impossible.

One must therefore ask in all seriousness whether Nietzsche was possibly led astray by language and deceived by his own metaphorical expression. Perhaps the dualism which he had repudiated was still in the back of his mind and vitiated his argument. Perhaps Nietzsche presupposed a duality of the Dionysian and Apollinian or, as in the *Dawn*, of strength and reason. (M 548).

Those who have written about Nietzsche have rarely taken him seriously enough philosophically to ask such questions; and it is the great merit of Klages' book on Nietzsche that he has, to some extent, made Nietzsche's problems his own and attempted to think them through. His conclusion, however, is untenable, though other authors have failed to refute Klages' critique and ignored his plausible objection to Nietzsche's philosophy.

Klages' fundamental objection is the one just outlined: Nietzsche's monism is held to be inconsistent with the *Überwindungsmotiv*, the theme of self-overcoming, which permeates his philosophy. In this conception of self-overcoming, Klages recognizes a Christian motif, incompatible with Nietzsche's profession of monism. It so happens that Klages would repudiate 'the Christian in Nietzsche,'[4] that he attacks Nietzsche's 'Socratism,'[5] and that he opposes the will to power as spirit (*Geist*) in disguise.[6] It is striking that one of the leading irrationalistic thinkers of our time should have repudiated the will to power as a Christian conception in disguise, finding in it a principle essentially opposed to irrationalism; but our concern here is only with Klages' assertion that Nietzsche was inconsistent, not with Klages' preference for one of the two allegedly contradictory positions.

There are then two entirely distinct problems which require careful consideration. First, one should ask how Nietzsche himself would picture the 'overcoming' of the impulses: whether he meant that they should be extirpated, abnegated, controlled – or whether he had in mind yet another way of mastering them. Secondly, one should inquire how Nietzsche would deal with the special problem which is inherent in his monism, i.e. the problem of *self*-overcoming – and this question will be taken up in the next chapter. Neither of these two questions can be answered summarily. Each requires detailed consideration. Once both have been answered, however, the fundamentals of Nietzsche's philosophy will be clear.

II

Nietzsche proposed to explain all human behavior in terms of the will to power, and some of his earlier reductions have been presented in the last chapter. One may now quote him specifically: 'our drives [*Triebe*] are reducible to the will to power' (XIV, 287). This is the result of Nietzsche's 'small single questions and experiments' by which he penetrated human motivation far more deeply – so he thought – than any of the more systematic philosophers had done before him: they had all been impeded by the conventionally moralistic presuppositions of their systems:

> All of psychology to date remained stuck in moral prejudices and apprehensions: it did not dare go into any depths. To comprehend it [psychology] as the morphology and *theory of the evolution of the will to power*, as I comprehend it – that nobody has come close to doing yet even in thought: namely, insofar as it is permitted to recognize in what has so far been written a symptom of what has so far been kept secret.
>
> (J 23; cf. XVIII, 339)

In 1872 Nietzsche had penned the sentence: 'Those of his [man's] abilities which are awesome and considered inhuman are perhaps the fertile soil out of which alone all humanity . . . can grow' (II, 369). The essay, however, in which Nietzsche had sought to elaborate his meaning had remained a fragment; and it has been shown in previous chapters why he had not yet been ready to make good this ambitious claim. Now, however, after the discovery of the will to power, Nietzsche is ready to present the 'doctrine of the derivability of all good drives from the bad' (J 23).

It is important to note that this 'doctrine' does not entail the termination of Nietzsche's experimentalism:

> In the end, it is not only permitted to make this experiment: it is demanded by the *methodological* conscience. Not to assume several kinds of causality as long as the experiment to get along with a single one has not been pushed to its final limit (to the point of nonsense, if one has leave to say so): that is a moral of methodology and follows 'from its definition,' as a mathematician would say. The question is in the end whether we really

recognize the will as *efficacious* [*wirhend*], whether we believe in the causality of the will: if we do this – and at bottom our belief in *this* is precisely our belief in causality itself – then we *must* make the experiment of positing the causality of the will hypothetically as the only one. 'Will' can, of course, affect only 'will' – and not 'materials' (not 'nerves,' for example). Enough, one must risk the hypothesis whether will does not affect will wherever 'effects' are recognized – and whether all mechanical happening, insofar as a force becomes active in it, is not will-force, will-effect. Supposing, finally, that one succeeded in explaining our entire impulsive life as the unfolding [*Augestaltung*] and ramification of one basic form of the will – namely, of the will to power, as *my* thesis says; supposing that one could reduce all organic functions to this will to power and would find in it also the solution of the problem of generation and nourishment – it is one problem – then one would have thus created the right for oneself to define *all* efficacious force unequivocally as: *will to power*.

(J 36)

One may doubt the cogency of Nietzsche's argument in places – one will have to admit that in the book which followed *Zarathustra*, Nietzsche still thought experimentally and not as a prophet or a legislator.

Of the many questions involved in Nietzsche's thesis, only one shall be considered in the present chapter. The problem of the causality of the will will be taken up briefly later on; and the question, not touched upon in our long quotation, how one and the same force can be the cause of so many diverse manifestations – a problem which was not unknown to philosophers and theologians of the past[7] – will be considered in the next chapter. At the moment, only the specific psychological problem which we find here shall be examined. Not the *possibility* of *self*-overcoming, but the actual process of the overcoming of the impulses and the kind of control which Nietzsche had in mind are to be considered here.

This process and control Nietzsche defines in a single word as – *sublimation*. It is almost incredible that Klages, who has written the only book which purports to present and analyze in detail Nietzsche's *psychologische Errungenschaften*, has ignored Nietzsche's conception of sublimation completely. Jaspers and Morgan, in the two most thorough and scholarly philosophic accounts of Nietzsche's thought, mention this conception – but give no recognition to its central significance for Nietzsche's later philosophy, nor do they mention that Nietzsche's conception anticipated Freud's.[8] Oehler's two-volume index to the works omits *sublimieren*. Under the circumstances it is perhaps not surprising that Brill should have claimed, in his Introduction to *The Basic Writings of Sigmund Freud*, that 'sublimation' is 'another term coined by Freud.'[9] The founder of psychoanalysis himself, to be sure, had been more modest – not because he had read Nietzsche and found the term in his writings, but because the word is older than either Freud or Nietzsche. It was used even in medieval Germany as an adaptation of the Latin *sublimare*; and in modern times, Goethe, Novalis, and Schopenhauer employed it. Yet it was Nietzsche who first gave it that specific connotation which it has today. Goethe had said that 'human feelings and events' could not be brought upon the stage 'in original naturalness' – 'they must be wrought, prepared, sublimated.' Novalis had written: 'The coarse Philistine imagines the joys of heaven as a fair. ... The sublimated one turns heaven into a magnificent church.' 'As the world is quasi a deposit of human nature, thus the world of gods is its sublimation. Both happen *uno actu*.' And Schopenhauer had spoken of 'representations' as 'sublimated into abstract concepts.'[10] When Nietzsche first used the word in the first aphorism of *Human, All-too-Human* (1878), he still intended the same meaning. In the second volume of the same work, however, he spoke of 'sublimated sexuality' (95), thus giving the word the connotation which is generally associated with it today.

This is altogether characteristic of Nietzsche's 'coinages': the *Bildungsphil-ister*, the cultural philistine of the first meditation, also had been known before, though not prominently, and Nietzsche only gave the term a new and lasting meaning. The same is true, as we shall see, of the *Übermensch*. One may add that Nietzsche uses the word 'sublimation' off and on in his later writings (IX, 422, 437; M 202); that in a discussion of the Platonic Eros and the *Symposion* he refers to the 'sublimated sex impulse' (XI, 259) – and that almost the same use is made of the word in a discussion of Christian love (J 189; cf. GM II 7); while in *The Will to Power* Nietzsche speaks of the artist's sublimation of his impulses (677), thus making clear the connection between Goethe's usage and the modern one.

The important issue, to be sure, is not who used what word when and how, but what it is that Nietzsche had in mind. There is always the danger of believing that a new term may solve an ancient problem, when actually no word or phrase can accomplish that much. Nietzsche, however, did not depend on the mere word 'sublimation' but rather on the conception which he sometimes – though by no means always – designated in this way. One should therefore inquire what happens when impulses are sublimated.

Nietzsche believed that a sexual impulse, for example, could be channeled into a creative spiritual activity, instead of being fulfilled directly. Similarly, the barbarian's desire to torture his foe can be sublimated into the desire to defeat one's rival, say, in the Olympic contests; it can even be sublimated into the rivalry of the tragedians who vie with each other for the highest prize, or into the efforts of a Plato to write more beautifully than the poets – and the entire Socratic dialectic could be construed as a sublimation of the same ancient striving to overwhelm one's foe.[11]

Can one properly speak of the sublimation of one and the same impulse? Instead of doing one thing, a man does another – and the continuity of the original impulse seems problematic. Now Nietzsche was definitely not one to speak glibly of the coarseness of the sex impulse, while recommending 'simple' sublimation. There is a long aphorism in the *Dawn*, entitled *Selbst-Beherrschung und Mässigung ihr letztes Motiv*, 'self-mastery and moderation as its ultimate motive' – though *Mässigung* would be best translated by a Greek word: Plato's *sophrosune*. The aphorism begins: 'I find no more than six essentially different methods to fight the violence of a drive' – and in the end Nietzsche summarizes:

> Thus: dodging the opportunities [for its satisfaction], implanting regularity in the drive, generating oversaturation and disgust with it, and bringing about its association with an agonizing thought – like that of disgrace, evil consequences, or insulted pride – then the dislocation of forces, and finally general [self-] weakening and exhaustion – those are the six methods.
>
> (M 109)

Nietzsche does not confuse the last of these six methods with sublimation – one need only consider his account of it:

> Finally sixth: whoever can stand it, and finds it reasonable, to weaken and depress his *entire* physical and psychical organization, will of course attain thereby also the goal of weakening a single violent drive: as do, for example, those who starve out their sensuality and thereby indeed also starve out and ruin their fitness and, not seldom, their mind [*Verstand*], like ascetics.

In other words, Nietzsche does not mistake self-mortification, or self-exhaustion by athletics or sports for 'sublimation.'

It may seem that it is the fifth method which constitutes sublimation:

> One brings about a dislocation of one's quanta of strength [*Kraftmengen*] by imposing on oneself an especially difficult and exacting task or by subjecting oneself intentionally to a new stimulus or delight and thus diverting one's thoughts and the play of physical forces into other channels.

Closer examination, however, shows that this fifth method can be reinforced by the preceding four: and one may take it that sublimation, as conceived by Nietzsche, involves all of the first five methods. In a later passage, Nietzsche himself concludes:

> One can dispose of one's drives like a gardener and cultivate . . . the seedlings of wrath, pity, brooding, and vanity as fruitfully and usefully as beautiful fruit on espaliers; one can do it with the good or the bad taste of a gardener and quasi in French, or English, or Dutch, or Chinese manner;

one can also let nature rule and look only here and there for a little ornament and clean-up. . . .

(M 560)

Now one may still press the point that 'sublimation' covers up a logical
confusion and that, if a man does one thing instead of another, a substitution
takes place while the original impulse is canceled or subdued, but not sublimated. This criticism might be relevant, if Nietzsche maintained that only the
energy remains, while the objective of the impulse is changed: for the energy
is as nondescript as Aristotle's matter, while the objective appears to define
the very essence of an impulse. Nietzsche, however, insists – in conformity
with tradition – that what remains is the essence and what is changed is
accidental. He considers the will to power, which remains throughout, the
'essence,' while 'all "ends," "objectives," ' and the like, are merely accidental
and changing attributes 'of the one will,' 'of the will to power' (WM 675). In
other words, not only the energy remains but also the objective, power; and
those so-called objectives which are canceled are only accidental attributes of
this more basic striving: they are, to use one of Nietzsche's favorite terms,
mere 'foregrounds.' Thus Nietzsche's theory of sublimation avoids one of the
most serious difficulties of its psychoanalytic equivalent – and an explicit
contrast between the will to power and the sex drive may clarify this point.

When Nietzsche began to consider the will to power as possibly the basic
human drive, he also thought of the sex drive; and in his notes one finds on the
same two pages which contain the second and the third mention of the 'will
to power,' in the order of Nietzsche's writings, also the following sentences:

Sexual stimulation in the ascent involves a tension which releases itself in
the feeling of power: the will to rule – a mark of the most sensual men; the
waning propensity of the sex impulse shows itself in the relenting of the
thirst for power.

The reabsorption of semen by the blood . . . prompts perhaps the stimulus
of power, the unrest of all forces toward the overt coming of resistances.
. . . The feeling of power has so far mounted highest in abstinent priests
and hermits (for example, among the Brahmins).

(X, 414f.)

One may also recall a famous epigram from *Beyond Good and Evil*: 'The
degree and kind of the sexuality of a human being reaches up into the ultimate pinnacle of his spirit' (75). Yet Nietzsche did not decide to reduce the will
to power to a sexual *libido*; for sexuality is that very aspect of the basic drive
which is canceled in sublimation and cannot, for that reason, be considered the
essence of the drive. Sexuality is merely a foreground of something else which
is more basic and hence preserved in sublimation: the will to power. The
feeling of potency is essential, while its sexual manifestation is accidental;

and thus the feeling of sexual potency can be sublimated into that ultimate feeling of power which the Brahmin king Vicvamitra derived 'from thousands of years' of abstinence and self-control and which made him undertake 'to build a new heaven' (M 113). Sexuality is not basic, though it *may* be base.

That sexuality need not be base, Nietzsche emphasizes constantly. In fact, much of his polemics against Christianity is based on his opinion that Christianity has tended to consider sexuality as necessarily base – an opinion which may seem merely perverse today but can be explained in terms of Nietzsche's interest in Paul, Augustine, and early Church history: the period on which his friend Overbeck was an expert. Instead of seeing that the sex drive might be sublimated, Christianity – according to Nietzsche – repudiated it (G V 1–4). Looking for a symbolic representation of this attitude – as Nietzsche always likes to do – he finds Jesus' dictum (Mark 9.43ff.) that if a part of your body 'offend thee' you should 'cut it off.'

> The logic is: the desires often bring great harm, thus it follows that they are evil and to be rejected. . . . That is the same logic as: 'if a member offend thee, pluck it out.' . . . In the case of sexual irritability, unfortunately it does not follow that a member is missing, but the character of man is *emasculated*. And the same goes for the moralists' mania which demands not the control but the extirpation of the passions. Their conclusion is ever: only the emasculated man is the good man.
>
> (WM 383; cf. A 45)

This contrast of the abnegation, repudiation, and extirpation of the passions on the one side, and their control and sublimation on the other, is one of the most important points in Nietzsche's entire philosophy.

Nietzsche is ever insisting that for the Greeks 'the *sexual* symbol was the venerable symbol *par excellence*' and that 'only Christianity . . . has made something unclean out of sexuality: it threw *filth* upon the origin, upon the presupposition of our life' (G X 4).

> A dogma of the 'immaculate conception' . . .? *But with that conception is maculated.*
>
> (A 34; cf. A 56)

> How can one put a book into the hands of children and women which contains that vile word: 'to avoid fornication, let every man have his own wife, and let every woman have her own husband. . . . It is better to marry than to burn.'
>
> (A 56)[12]

> The sex impulse can be base, but it is 'capable of great refinement.'
>
> (XI, 258f.)

Ecstasies are different in a pious, sublime, noble man, such as Plato, and in camel drivers who smoke hashish.

(XVI, 320)

III

Some of Nietzsche's ideas which have generally been misconstrued are comprehensible if only this contrast of sublimation and emasculation is taken into account. It is, for example, a common misconception that Nietzsche admired Cesare Borgia and glorified him.[13] Nietzsche found it ridiculous to consider a Cesare Borgia unhealthy in contrast to an emasculated man who is alleged to be healthy (J 197). When Nietzsche was criticized on that account, he clarified his point in another book, three years later (G IX 37). He now explained that he did not favor 'the abolition of all decent feelings' but that he was not sure '*whether we have really become more moral.*' Perhaps we have just become emasculated, and our failure to do evil is to be ascribed merely to our inability to do evil. Perhaps we are just weak. To be moral is to overcome one's impulse; if one does not have any impulses, one is not therefore moral. In other words, Cesare Borgia is not a hero, but – Nietzsche insists – we are no heroes either if our own impulses are merely too weak to tempt us. A few months later, in his last work, Nietzsche insisted once more that his point was merely that there was more hope for the man of strong impulses than for the man with no impulses: one should look 'even for a Cesare Borgia rather than for a Parsifal' (EH III 1). Translators and interpreters have not always minded the *eher noch*: '*even* for a Borgia rather than a Parsifal.' This *eher noch* leaves no doubt that Nietzsche considered Cesare Borgia far from admirable but preferred even him to the Parsifal ideal (cf. A 46, 61; WM 871).

Nietzsche believed that a man without impulses could not do the good or create the beautiful any more than a castrated man could beget children. A man with strong impulses might be evil because he had not yet learned to sublimate his impulses, but if he should ever acquire self-control, he might achieve greatness. In that sense, there is more joy in heaven over one repentant sinner than over ninety-nine just men – if the latter are just only because they are too feeble ever to have sinned.

There is a section in *The Will to Power* where this point is discussed at great length (WM 382–88). There Nietzsche insists throughout that we must 'employ' (*in Dienst nehmen*) our impulses and not weaken or destroy them.

Instead of employing the great sources of strength, those impetuous torrents of the soul that are so often dangerous and overwhelming, and economizing them, this most shortsighted and pernicious mode of thought, the moral mode of thought, wants to make them dry up.

Overcoming of the affects? – No, if what is implied is their weakening and extirpation. But employing them: which may also mean subjecting them to a protracted tyranny (not only as an individual, but as a community, race, etc.). At last they are confidently granted freedom again: they love us as good servants and go voluntarily wherever our best interests lie.

Moral intolerance is an expression of weakness in a man: he is afraid of his own 'immorality,' he must deny his strongest drives because he does not yet know how to employ them. Thus the most fruitful regions of the earth remain uncultivated the longest: – the force is lacking that could here become master.

(383–85)

Nietzsche's few references to the 'blond beast' – *blonde Bestie* – are to be understood similarly. The Borgia and the beast are both ideograms for the conception of unsublimated animal passion. Nietzsche does not glorify either of them. He derides emasculation and scorns the Church for having 'hunted down' the Teutonic barbarians – 'blond beasts' – only to put them behind bars in monasteries (G VII 2). This alleged historical process, however, is viewed supra-historically as an allegory or symbol of the extirpation of the impulses. The 'blond beast' is not a racial concept and does not refer to the 'Nordic race' of which the Nazis later made so much. Nietzsche specifically refers to Arabs and Japanese, Romans and Greeks, no less than ancient Teutonic tribes when he first introduces this term (GM I 11) – and the 'blondness' obviously refers to the beast, the lion, rather than the kind of man. It may be well to add that, right after denouncing the Church for its alleged emasculation of these beasts, Nietzsche denounces the way in which the 'Law of Manu' dealt with the outcastes, saying that 'perhaps there is nothing that outrages our feelings more' (G VII 3), and concludes:

These regulations teach us enough: in them we find for once *Aryan* humanity, quite pure, quite primordial – we learn that the concept of 'pure blood' is the opposite of a harmless concept.

(G VIII 4)

The long exposition of the same ideas in the notes of *The Will to Power* culminates in the dictum: '*the Aryan influence* has corrupted all the world' (WM 142).

This conclusion may suggest that Nietzsche was something of a racist after all, though the very antipode of the later Nazi movement. As will be seen later on, however, this interpretation would be false; Nietzsche did not interpret history racially; and the violent dicta about 'Aryan humanity' and 'Aryan influence' must be understood as *ad hominem* arguments against contemporary racists. Nietzsche attacks them by saying that, if one were to accept such categories as Semitic and Aryan, the so-called Aryans would appear in the worst light. This notebook material is then introduced into a published work, the *Götzen-Dämmerung*, right after the criticism of the Christian Church – apparently because Nietzsche wanted to guard his critique of Christian practices against any misinterpretation by those who might claim that it was a 'Semitic' religion which had broken the fitness of the Teutonic tribes. '*Aryan* humanity,' says Nietzsche, is even worse – and one may note that what he objects to so much is precisely the 'Aryan' 'concept of "pure blood"'' which was invoked by Manu – and might be invoked again some day – to justify or rationalize the oppression of 'non-Aryans.' In the *Genealogy*, in the other paragraph in which the 'blond beast' is mentioned – Nietzsche is similarly careful to insist that 'between the old Germanic tribes and us Germans there exists scarcely a conceptual relation, not to speak of a blood relation' (G I 11).

Nietzsche's over-all contention is crystallized in the title of that chapter in the *Götzen-Dämmerung* where the treatment of the 'blond beasts' by the Church and of the outcastes by the Law of Manu is considered: 'The "Improvers" of Mankind.' Nietzsche claims that the self-styled improvers have always tried to make man sick and to emasculate him. His polemics as well as a vast number of his positive assertions can be understood only in terms of his own ideas about the way in which the impulses should be 'overcome': not by extirpation, but by sublimation.

Looking back on Nietzsche's early philosophy, one finds that an idea which was basic even then has now been strengthened and elaborated. The conception of 'culture as another and improved physis,' which was the culmination of the second meditation and the leitmotif of the third, is now reenforced by the more detailed account of sublimation. Nietzsche's difference with Rousseau – as the symbol of the 'return to nature' – could now be restated in terms of the important distinction between abandonment to the impulses and sublimation. It becomes clear what it may mean to 'organize the chaos' or to conceive of 'culture as a harmony of living, thinking, appearing, and willing' (U II 10), and what the 'transfigured *physis*' (U III 3) might be.

Our impulses are in a state of chaos. We would do this now, and another thing the next moment – and even a great number of things at the same time. We think one way, live in another way, and appear still different; we want one thing and do another. No man can live without bringing some order into this chaos. This may be done by thoroughly weakening the whole organism or by repudiating and repressing many of the impulses: but the result in that case is not a 'harmony,' and the *physis* is castrated, not 'improved.' Yet there is another way – namely, to 'organize the chaos': sublimation allows for the achievement of an organic harmony and leads to that culture which is truly a 'transfigured *physis*.'[14]

Notes

1. '. . . Without any inclination, solely from duty, only then does it have genuine moral value.' *Grundlegung*, section 1.

2. *Utilitarianism*, Chapter 1, paragraph 4.

3. The same may be said of R. B. Perry's subsumption of Kant's conception of moral value under his own generic definition of value as 'any object of any interest.' Kant's view of value is not an instance of 'Value as the Object of Qualified Interest,' if interest is defined as a feature of the 'motor-affective life' (*General Theory of Value*, 1926). For Kant the locus of moral and aesthetic value is in a setting which is defined by the total absence of any such interest.

4. *Nietzsches psychologische Errungenschaften* (1926), 196; chapters IX, XI, XIV, XV *passim*.

5. *Ibid.*, chapter XIII.

6. Cf. also Klages' *magnum opus*: *Der Geist als Widersacher der Seele*, 3 vols. (1929–33).

7. Cf. e.g. St. Thomas Aquinas, *Summa Theologica*, I. 47. 1; Maimonides, *Guide of the Perplexed*, II. 22; *Meister Eckehart*, ed. Karrer (1923), 218. The same problem appears in Plotinus, sixth *Ennead*, IV. 6, in Neoplatonism generally, and especially in Nicolas de Cusa, *Dialogus de Genesi* (1447), entire, where the problem is put thus: '*quomodo Idem ipse est omnium causa: quae adeo sunt diversa et adversa.*' Nietzsche's problem is not nearly so different from that of the Neoplatonic tradition as it may seem at first glance. This will become more apparent in the next chapter.

8. Jaspers, *op. cit.*, gives only half a page of his comprehensive study to an exposition of sublimation. Morgan gives a little more space to it (*op. cit.*, 99f., 128ff., 180f.). Somehow, not one of his quotations contains the word 'sublimation,' though some of the passages referred to in his footnotes do.

9. Modern Library Giant, 18.

10. Cf. Grimms' *Deutsches Wörterbuch*, art. *sublimieren,* where, however, Novalis and Freud are omitted, while Nietzsche is represented by a single reference, dated 1895, which gives no indication of the slight, but significant, shift in meaning which the word experienced in his writings. Cf. also Paul Fischer, *Goethe-Wortschatz* (1929). The Novalis quotations are from *Blütenstaub*, fragments 77 and 96. Cf. also *Hegels theologische Jugendschriften*, ed. Nohl, 308.

11. Cf. the fragment *Homers Wettkampf* (II, 367ff.); the lecture on Heraclitus, IV, 303; and V, 232; VII, 191; M 113, 544; XI, 299; XIV, 129, 261, 263; G II 8.

12. I Corinthians 7, 2, 9. The omission here is Nietzsche's.

13. E.g., von Martin, *Nietzsche und Burckhardt*, 3rd rev. ed. (1945), 93, 119, 137f. On p. 264 the author identifies Nietzsche's view of Cesare Borgia with 'the will "back to the animals"' and 'back to the natural uncontrolled character of the "animal-man."'

14. Only relatively few of the numerous passages in which Nietzsche develops the conception of sublimation have been referred to in the text. The following aphorisms may be consulted further as particularly relevant to this topic: S 37, 53; M 30, 110, 204, 502, 503; J 225, 229, 230, 260; GM III 8; G V 1–4; G IX 22; WM 255, 800, 801, 805, 806, 815, 820, 1025.

48

Infectious Reading: Health and Illness in Novalis and Nietzsche*

David Farrell Krell

*Source: David Farrell Krell, *Infectious Nietzsche*, Indiana University Press, 1996, pp. 197–212, 270–2.

> What if I should become the prophet of this art?
>
> (Novalis, in 1799–1800; *2*, 828)

> Whoever is not at one with me on this point I take to be *infected* [infiziert].
> . . . But all the world is not at one with me. . . . In all so-called 'beautiful souls' there nestles at bottom a state of physiological affliction [*Übelstand*]; – I won't tell everything, otherwise I'd become medi-cynical [*medi-zynisch*].
>
> (Nietzsche, *Ecce Homo*)

Infectious *laughter* is catching, highly contagious, and – Father Guillermo learned – almost impossible to bring under control. Likewise, I suspect, infectious reading. In what follows I pursue the metaphors of health and illness in Novalis's and Nietzsche's texts, with brief references to Schelling and Freud. My object in the present chapter is to pursue the problem of physiological decadence, whether such decadence plays a role in an inventory of genealogical-critical techniques or in a thinking of eternal recurrence of the same. Once again I shall call on Novalis for assistance, inasmuch as his meditations on health and illness anticipate to an uncanny extent many of Nietzsche's insights and obsessions. I shall focus on Novalis's philosophical-scientific notebooks of 1798–1799 and Nietzsche's *Ecce Homo*.[1]

In the *Poetics* Aristotle asks what sorts of people are good at writing tragedies and at creating poetry in general. His answer, at 1455a 21ff., appears well before the section on λέξιϛ, or 'diction,' in which he seems to reduce the art of metaphor to syllogism. Before the elevation of syllogism and reduction of metaphor, this is what he says about the talents of the poet and tragedian:

> In constructing his plots and using diction to bring them to completion, [the poet] should put [the events] before his eyes as much as he can. In this way, seeing them most vividly [ἐναργέοτατα], as if he were actually

present at the actions, he can discover what is suitable, and is least likely to miss contradictions. . . .

As far as possible, [the poet should] also bring [his plots] to completion with gestures. Given the same nature, those [poets] who *experience* the emotions [to be represented] are most believable; that is, he who is agitated or furious [can represent] agitation and anger most truthfully. For this reason, the art of poetry belongs to the genius [εὐφυοῦς] or the madman [μανικοῦ]. Of these, the first are adaptable [εὔπλαστοι], the second can step outside themselves [ἐκστατικοί].

There is a long tradition, however, that says that those who are most gifted or talented, the supple, subtle, pliant, and plastic geniuses, are precisely those who often 'step outside themselves' and succumb to infection, illness, and madness. As though the esemplastic power celebrated by Coleridge were a daimonic force that wrenches a poet out of herself or himself; as though the truly gifted were *vergiftet*; as though the makers of infectious reading materials were themselves infected writers – ecstatics, mantics, manics, and maniacs. Such as Nietzsche. Or those who suffer from deadly infections – for example, tuberculosis. Such as Friedrich von Hardenberg (Novalis).

A Poetics of the Baneful

Novalis's notes on illness and health appear principally in the context of his *Enzyklopädistik* (*I*, 477), an ambitious attempt to synthesize – or 'sym-philosophize' – the findings of all the sciences, whether natural or historical, with a transcendental philosophy and a universal poesy. His dream is to translate all lore, from the fairy tale to the findings of chemistry and physics, into a common code, which he calls the *lingua romana*. In the 'Preliminary Studies' (*Vorarbeiten*) of 1798 Novalis writes:

The world must be romanticized. In this way one will find its original meaning once again. Romanticizing is nothing other than a qualitative raising to the powers [*Potenzirung*]. The lower self is identified with a better self in this operation. Thus we ourselves are a kind of qualitative sequence of powers. This operation is still altogether unknown. Whenever I give the common a higher meaning, the usual a mysterious aspect, the familiar the dignity of the unknown, the finite an infinite appearance, in this way I romanticize it – Opposed to that is the operation for the higher, unknown mystical, infinite – by connecting these matters we find their logarithms – They receive a customary expression. Romantic philosophy. *Lingua romana*. Alternate elevation and degradation.

(*2*, 334)

Between 1798 and 1800 Novalis sketches out his project for 'the romanticizing of the world,' a project he shares with his friend Friedrich Schlegel.[2]
Here the lower and higher elements of the world are viewed as reciprocally
and even genetically related, forever in transition from low to high and high
to low. A privileged instance of the communication of high and low is, as
we learned in the preceding chapter, human sexuality. If philosophy, the
love of wisdom, begins with a kiss and is itself the first kiss, its search for
the human soul culminates in the sex act, itself conceived of as an ingest-
ing and engendering of soul and body. For Novalis and Schlegel, to be
sure, the Roman or Romantic tongue is less what Hegel calls 'the prose of
the world' than cosmic, universal poesy – albeit poesy of an 'algebraic' and
'logarythmic' sort. One of the consequences of the project – the only one
that I shall develop here, in preparation for a reading of *Ecce Homo* –
is the radical relativizing of the concepts of health and illness, illness
being 'indirect health,' and health 'indirect illness,' each in transition to the
other:

> Just as illness is a symptom of health, so must health manifest symptoms
> of illness.
>   1.   *Direct health* – 2.   indirect health. 3.   Direct illness – 4.   *indirect*
> *illness.*
>   No. 1 elides with 4, as no. 3 elides with 2.
>   Repeated *indirect illnesses* ultimately elide with direct illness, and vice
> versa – repeated indirect health elides with direct health. Indirect health
> follows direct illness as surely as indirect illness follows health.
>
> (*2*, 452)

A note from *Das allgemeine Brouillon* ('The Universal Sketchbook') of
1798–1799 reads: 'The utility of illness – *the poesy of illness*. An illness cannot
be a life, otherwise the *connection with illness* would have to *elevate* our existence. Continue this bizarre thought' (*2*, 475). The 'bizarre thought' occurs to
Novalis that the connection between life and illness might be elevating rather
than distressing and depressing. No doubt he is thinking of the imbricated
structures of sensitivity, excitability or irritability, and reproduction, as
developed in the physiological systems of the Scots physician John Brown
and his German disciples Karl Friedrich von Kielmeyer, A. A. Marcus, and
J. A. Röschlaub, all associated with Schelling during the period of his influential work, *Von der Weltseele* (1798), a work that both Novalis and Goethe
read with enthusiasm.

For the most part, Schelling's *Von der Weltseele* avoids discussion of illness
and death.[3] Yet it is clear that when the decline and demise of the individual
organism is introduced it will be in the context, and as a consequence, of
sexual reproduction. The formation of the reproductive organs and the mat-
uration of the sexual function occur only when the growth of organism is

completed, and in many animals – Schelling mentions insects, which are relatively close to plant life – reproduction leads to demise. If growth is continuous individualization, such individualization reaches its zenith in sexual maturity; yet once the zenith is surpassed, only the nadir is left, and sexual maturity ultimately occurs 'at the cost of individuality.' When living things go to seed, they go to seed. In his next work, *Erster Entwurf eines Systems der Naturphilosophie* (1799), which Novalis also may have read, Schelling elaborates at greater length the sexual function in living organisms. Sexual reproduction seems to him both the 'culminating moment' of natural development and the revelation of nature as a sequence of 'failed attempts.'[4] Whether the sexual function, the establishment of genus and species through two sexes, and the demise of the individual organisms reveal a monistic or dualistic structure in nature is Schelling's undecided and undecidable question. The obsessive and interminable footnotes to the text oscillate back and forth, sometimes toward a monism, but first and last veering away from all monism to a fundamental dualism. For dualism, duplicity, and polarity always gain the upper hand, as Schelling manages to preserve his identity against the one who will become Hegel. Whereas the Hegelian philosophy of nature will culminate in the identification of sexual reproduction as impregnation with the seed of death, and sexual division as original illness, wicked infinity, and the impotence of nature, so that a monistic philosophy of spirit can arise only from the ashes of nature,[5] Schelling refuses to abandon duplicity. Yet relinquish a common, universal cause, relinquish monism once and for all he cannot:

> **Thus a common cause of universal and organic duplicity is postulated.** The most universal problem, the one that encompasses all of nature, and therefore the *supreme* problem, without whose solution all we have said explains nothing, is this:
>   **What is the universal source of activity in nature? What cause has brought about the first dynamic exteriority [*Außereinander*],** with respect to which mechanical exteriority is a mere consequence? **Or what cause first tossed the seed of motion into the universal repose of nature, duplicity into universal identity, the first sparks of heterogeneity into the universal homogeneity of nature?**
>
> (*1/3*, 220)

It is at this point in the *Erster Entwurf* that a long discussion of illness supervenes. While the Brownian trinity of sensitivity, irritability, and reproduction provides the terms for the discussion of illness, a certain ambivalence concerning life in nature shows itself: while life relies on the duplicity of irritability, on the relation of the excitant to the excited, so that health may be defined as the continuous restitution of duality and death as 'absolute homogeneity,' it also makes sense to say that 'life is a continuous illness, and death mere convalescence from it' (*1/3*, 212 n. 2). Schelling thus anticipates the problem of the 'exquisite dualism' in Freud's *Beyond the Pleasure Principle*, which struggles to maintain the impossible distinction between the life and the death drives, impossible inasmuch as drives as such can only be thought of as erotothanatotic, that is, as matters of lifedeath, *la vie la mort*.[6] Schelling defines illness in terms of the graduated relationship between 'exciting powers' and the organism's excitability or irritability. While he specifies the inverse ratio of sensitivity and irritability, he neglects to draw the third aspect of the triad – reproduction – into his account, perhaps because in sexual maturity culmination and demise lie too close for comfort. Hegel will not fail to draw the consequences that Schelling allows to hang in suspense, and if Schelling does manage to preserve his identity over against Hegel, it is as the one who never managed to draw the full consequences of that education he got in public. But to return briefly now to Novalis and his 'bizarre thought' that illness might elevate rather than depress life – and that malady may lie at the conjunction of high and low, and thus at the heart of the Romantic philosophy.

The equally bizarre thought occurs to Novalis that, no matter how elevating illness in general might be, the soul itself, the very principle of life, may serve to aggravate the worst illnesses of the body. Indeed, Novalis, who knows the secret ambivalence of all φάρμακα, now speculates that the soul itself might be the most poisonous of entities:

> Among all *poisons* the *soul* is the strongest. It is the most penetrating, the most diffuse stimulus. All the effects of the soul are therefore supremely harmful when it is a question of local illness and infection.
>
> A local illness often cannot be cured except by means of a general illness, and vice versa.
>
> Curing *one illness* by means of *another*.
>
> (*2*, 706)

Finally, the utterly bizarre thought occurs to Novalis that sheer *love* of illness can transform malady into 'supreme, positive pleasure,' that illness may be a means toward higher synthesis, a means of returning to intimacy with nature. To such intimacy the poet gives the name of his dead fiancée, *Sophie*. Such uncanny thinking would involve, to repeat, *eine Poetik des Übels*, a poetics of the baneful and malignant. 'Does not the best everywhere begin with *illness*?' Novalis asks, setting for his poetics the theme 'On the attractive force of the dire' (*2*, 628). In one of the final notes, he elaborates as follows:

> Illnesses are surely a *supremely important object for humanity*, for they are numberless, and each human being has to struggle with them so often. It is only that we know so little about the art of using them. They are probably

the most interesting stimulus to our meditation and our activity. . . . What if I should become the prophet of this art? [*Wie wenn ich Profet dieser Kunst werden sollte?*]

(2, 828)

The Biopositive Effects of Infection

The immediate context for my remarks on Nietzsche's *Ecce Homo* is the second chapter of Pierre Klossowski's *Nietzsche et le cercle vicieux*, on the 'valetudinarian states.'[7] However, whereas Klossowski raises the question of Nietzsche's thought as a periodic battle with migraine, I wish to relate his thought to the matter of infection. What *is* infection? Even for allopathic medicine, which takes it to be an attack *from without*, an invasion by a bacillus or virus, the threat to the organism is always elaborated *from within*. Infection represents a kind of fifth column, the betrayal or treason of the body, or parts of the body, against the body as a whole. Such betrayal threatens to terminate the body's irreversible life history. Here the Freudian detour becomes the royal road to irremediable demise; here the body goes to meet the primeval Chaos out of which, according to the myth in Plato's *Statesman*, it is said to have arisen and to which it returns. Infection would therefore comprise at least a part of Nietzsche's 'secret phantasm,' as Klossowski describes it: Nietzsche dreams of investigating a culture that functions according to nonlinguistic forces (*des forces de la non-parole*). Pursuing such investigations and writing up their results would require a *language* that tries to make itself heard and understood at the expense of reason – something like a *lingua romana*, if indeed romance invariably falls in love with demise and death.

Inevitably, Freud's speculations on the economy of lifedeath in the 1895 'Project' and the 1920 *Beyond the Pleasure Principle* form a more distant yet haunting context for any infectious reading. So too do the speculations of biologists such as Eugen Korschelt on the role of disease and decline in the life span of individual plant and animal species. Heidegger cites these speculations at a crucial moment in his *existential* analysis of death, even though fundamental ontology prides itself on the distance it believes it can take from mere biology.[8] Finally, the speculations of the psychiatrists who have involved themselves in 'the Nietzsche case' constitute an irritating, insistent context. The principal sources here are Poul Bjerre, the Swedish psychiatrist writing in 1905, and Karl Jaspers and Wilhelm Lange-Eichbaum, writing in the 1930s. Curt Paul Janz summarizes their findings – and speculations – at the outset of volume two of his three-volume biography. The psychiatrists suggest that there is evidence of 'biopositive effects,' at least for a poet and thinker such as Nietzsche, of infection with *Lues* or syphilis.[9] Adopting their voice, Janz writes:

Precisely in the case of luetic infection, as with other infections such as tuberculosis, research teaches us that certain life functions are at least for a time stimulated and enhanced; that an effect similar to that of certain narcotics – alcohol, for example – is produced, such that specific energies and possibilities of fantasy are released, energies and possibilities otherwise suppressed or repressed in the 'normal' organism.[10]

Janz's question is: What if the suppression or repression of the energies that are necessary for the 'free play of the spirit' were the condition of good health, so that well-being necessitates a dulling of the creative edge, a certain benevolent torpor; what if, from the point of view of the harmonious interplay of the creative faculties at the highest level, after the manner of Kant, robust good health were in fact the genuine psychopathogenic disturbance? Janz embraces the thought that so affrights Jaspers: not that Nietzsche's thought is sick, but that 'sick' is impossible to define in sheer opposition to biopositive effects. Whereas Jaspers feels constrained to admit that the factor of illness 'not only disturbed but also perhaps even made possible what otherwise would never have come to be' – meaning the writings of the 1880s, from *Daybreak* to the *Dionysos-Dithyrambs*, Bjerre, Lange-Eichbaum, and Janz affirm the biopositive effects of illness with some enthusiasm, albeit with trepidation.

Poul Bjerre had speculated early in the century on 'the chronic, mild, intoxicating effect [*Rauschwirkung*]' of luetic infection, as though Dionysian rapture were dependent on noxious chemical secretions of a particular bacillus or spirochaeta, *Treponema pallidum*. From some unknown original moment of infection – whether in the mid-1860s while a student at Bonn or Leipzig, or in 1870 during the Franco-Prussian War, or in 1876–1877 while on ill-health leave in Sorrento, and so on, seemingly endlessly, as the speculations run – up to the collapse on January 3, 1889, the infection would have exerted a biopositive influence, as though both instigating and helping to combat the migraines, the vomiting, and the approaching blindness.

Lange-Eichbaum himself waxes lyrical, even as he diagnoses.[11] He detects 'the euphoric mood,' the 'uninhibitedness,' and the 'manic traits of Nietzsche's writings, especially *Ecce Homo*. He appeals to both classical pathology and the tradition of *Existenzphilosophie*, which has taught him that 'to the existence of human beings the morbid too belongs, something that acts as a ferment, a stimulus, keeping the living flame in motion, just as sourdough is indispensable for bread, and shadow and the dark for light.' It is after all 'the inner disquiet in the blood' that spurs thinking and poetry. And, in the midst of the doctor's own sober analysis, armed to the teeth with the technical jargon of the pathologist's *lingua franca*, if not *romana*, the parade of metaphors marches by, and all of them mixed, all of them wildly catachretic: flames that walk, sourdough with chiaroscuro, and disquiet in the blood. Infectious reading is here a delectation for the Thomas Mann of

Doktor Faustus and *Der Zauberberg*, something for the European twilight and dusk of the 1920s and 1930s.

When the doctors set their metaphors in motion alongside their Latin and Greek germs, we nowadays may be inclined to laugh or to shout, paraphrasing Emerson, 'Doctor, infect thyself!' It does seem a mystification, for the usual purposes of manipulation and control, and our 'social-critical' and 'humanistic' impulses alike rebel.[12] Yet we are unnerved by the doctors even as we shout. For we recall Nietzsche's letter to his doctor, Otto Eiser, in early January 1880 (KSAB, *6*, 3–4). After a veritable litany of complaints, the distraught patient adds this postscript: 'As a whole, I am happier than ever before in my life.' To be sure, no chemical secretion on its own produces either *The Gay Science* or *Zarathustra*. And, at all events, neither the *lingua romana* nor the *lingua franca* of modern medicine is advanced enough to specify the chemical name of the specific intoxicant – assuming there is only one. Lange-Eichbaum does not give us the equivalent of Freud and Ferenczi's trimethylamine, the elixir of 'Irma's injection' and of *Thalassa*. Yet it does seem, as both Jaspers and Janz suspect, that especially after 1880 something dismantles 'the threshold of inhibition' in Nietzsche; it does seem that something enhances the euphoria and gradually illumines the transfiguration to the burning point. Perhaps some molecular; miasmic Mistral blows in the halcyon skies of Nietzsche's most exhilarating writing?

Admittedly, we have no way to *think* this biopositive impact: either we reduce Nietzsche's creativity to the crudest sorts of objectivist, positivistic determinations, or we idealize his productivity and snatch it away from his body. Worse, after the research and speculations of Weismann, Bernstein, Korschelt, Simmel, and Freud, we hardly know what to make of pathogenesis in general: if death is immanent in and intrinsic to life, if life is the economy of lifedeath, then what *are* infection, disease, dissolution, and demise? If Spinoza's mosquito (carrying malaria, no doubt) imagines itself the center of the universe, what sorts of airs will the bacillus and virus put on – the virus in its free and infectious state being a non-self-replicable yet eminently successful scion of life? Whether we emphasize the allopathic germ theory of disease, with its sepsis, antigens, and antibodies, or the homeopathic account, which lays more stress on the receptivity of the soil than the virulence of the seed, we are unaccustomed to taking seriously the reaction of thought *to* and *in* the diseased body, the body forever ill-at-ease, the body whose mind hovers on the very verge of delirium. Yet if Klossowski is right, this relation is what Nietzsche most wanted to think. If Novalis is the prophet of this new art, Nietzsche is its Messiah, or at least its Anti-Donkey, par excellence.

Fiancées, Physiology, and Infections Rhetoric

Allow me to revert to Novalis, and to the infectious rhetoric of biography. After Sophie's death – two days after her fifteenth birthday, of tuberculosis of the liver and lungs – Novalis is plagued, we are told, by sexual torments. One well-known editor and biographer of Novalis, Gerhard Schulz, cites an apparently laconic yet well-nigh frenzied observation from the notebooks – an observation that is quite representative of Novalis's jottings during the months following Sophie's death: 'The voluptuous phantasy of this morning occasioned this afternoon an explosion.'[13]

The same biographer now goes on to mix in a curious way sexuality, tubercular infection (of which Novalis himself was to die less than four years later), and the defense mechanisms of a beleaguered spirit (*Geist*):

We can descry not only in such notes [on the 'explosion'] but also in his works the fact that Friedrich von Hardenberg was tortured [*heimgesucht*] in more than usual measure by sexual representations and dreams. That is not unusual or surprising in the case of human beings who, like Novalis, are carriers of the germ of tuberculosis [*den Keim zur Tuberkulose in sich tragen*] and who without surcease have to struggle against a weak constitution. Yet commentators have gladly overlooked the fact that his thought and the world of his poetic representations received strong impulses from the sexual sphere. Above all, one must not forget that his intensified exposure to the pulsional [*das verstärkte Ausgesetztsein an das Triebhafte*] also mobilized the defenses of his mind [*die Abwehrkräfte des Geistes*] against such domination. In many respects, such exposure alone led Novalis to the achievement of his œuvre.

Note the biographer's use of the full family name, Friedrich von Hardenberg, when it is a question of autoerotic torture, and only later the literary pseudonym, Novalis, as though thereby negotiating the mysterious straits between 'the man' and 'his work'; note also the problematic phrases 'tortured in more than usual measure,' 'carriers of the germ,' 'weak constitution,' 'intensified exposure to the pulsional,' 'the defenses of the mind,' and 'such exposure alone. . . .' What begins as the tubercular infection of a labile constitution becomes a well-nigh parasympathetic infection through contact with the young woman who can have infected him in no other way, the fiancee whom he once admits loving 'precisely on account of her illness,' and ends as the achievement of a robust – though besieged and defensive – spiritual production. But let us turn now to Nietzsche.

Two further contexts might be mentioned with regard to Nietzsche's views on health and illness, the first arising from his 1886 prefaces to the second editions of several of his works (the prefaces that we examined in the opening chapters of the present book), the second from letters written during the autumn of 1888. Of course, one could also simply lose oneself in the noted books from the years 1887–1888, where the themes of health and decadence, the physiology of art, and 'the great health' prevail. However, let us examine the well-known prefaces to the 1886 editions of *The Birth of Tragedy*, *Human, All-Too-Human* (Parts I and II), *Daybreak*, and *The Gay Science*, where questions of health and illness are omnipresent. For such questions involve what Nietzsche calls *die nächsten Dinge*, the closest things, in parody of the eschatological 'four last things,' *die letzten Dinge*. Nietzsche first mentions 'the closest things,' I believe, in 'The Wanderer and his Shadow,' written, as *Ecce Homo* reminds us, at the nadir of Nietzsche's own health – when he truly believed that he was ready to follow in his father's footsteps toward the apocalyptic four last things. Yet diet, climate, locale, and solitude or (more rarely) companionship replace death, judgment, heaven, and hell as the philosopher's ultimate things. For these are crucial not only to the philosopher's health and well-being but also to his or her *thinking* and *writing*.

However, it is high time I introduced the central paradox or double-bind of infectious reading. If Nietzsche's struggle for health enables him to pursue his study of physiological decadence, that struggle dare not abate. If attention to the 'closest things' replaces terror in the face of the eschatological 'last things,' such vigilance dare not replace apocalypse with complacency. The search for health is and remains dalliance with disease and madness. It is not, as both Nietzsche and Klossowski would have it, a *periodicity* of illness and respite, with clearly marked peaks and valleys, but an awful coextensivity, a dreadful contamination. It is what both Schelling and Novalis know as *contagium*.

Indeed, it is high time I reached a bit farther with the thought that was elaborated in chapter 3, 'The Decadence of Redemption.' If the thought of eternal return smacks of consolation, of piety and piety's ressentiments, it nevertheless has to do with connections that are not so easily broken. Deleuze stresses that we do not know what a human being stripped of ressentiment would look like: *rancune* is not something we can drop from our lives with the application of personal discipline and mental hygiene, a change in diet and a crash course in transcendental meditation. For *res-sentiment* is that which is *felt again*, precisely that which *re-turns*. In other words, we may have underestimated the *structural* relation of ressentiment and return. It may not be a mere contingency that Freud invokes eternal return of the same in the context of re-experiencing trauma. If war neurosis consists in the effort to discharge the excessive energy of the traumatic event through repetition of the original event in active remembrance, if in repetition compulsion the traumatic event is *felt again*, is *re-sented*, it may well be that recurrence is essentially bound up with ressentiment. Not the supreme euphoria of Dionysiac possession can shatter the imbrication – the disastrous dovetailing – of ressentiment and return. Not the grandest of great healths can escape the contagion of chronic indirect illness. Perhaps this is the insight toward which Nietzsche's prefaces to his works of convalescence are headed, however much they may boast of exuberant health.

In his 'Attempt at a Self-Criticism' (*I*, 16) Nietzsche wonders whether madness might be a sign of something other than degeneration or senescence. 'A question for the psychiatrists: Are there perhaps neuroses of health [*Neurosen der Gesundheit*]'? Was Plato's *Phaedrus* right when it attributed mortals' best blessings to μανία, divine madness? The preface to the second edition of *Human, All-Too-Human*, Part I, describes Nietzsche's literary corpus to date in terms of convalescence (*die Genesung*). Convalescence consists of recuperation *of* the self *from* the self ('*zur Erholung* von mir,' in which the emphatic *von* expresses both the subjective and the objective genitives); convalescence relies on the cunning of self-preservation (*die List der Selbst-Erhaltung*) in the face of the inimical self (2, 14). Nietzsche's very life is an attempt at temptation, tempting health itself in the direction of what he calls 'the great [or grand] health' (*die große Gesundheit*) (2, 18). Section 5 of the preface begins: 'One step further in convalescence: and the free spirit sidles up to life once again – slowly to be sure, almost in revulsion [*widerspänstig*], almost distrusting.' The section ends as follows: 'And, to speak seriously: it is a thoroughgoing *cure* of all pessimism (of the cancerous lesions of the old idealists and flagrant liars) to be ill after the fashion of these free spirits, to remain ill a good long while, and then, over a still longer stretch of time, to become healthy – I mean "healthier."' As Novalis had prophesied, it is always a matter of one illness battling another, of what one might call *chronic* indirect health. Nietzsche concludes this passage, which mixes the metaphors of health and illness by pitting one form of illness against another; the illness of suspicion – as though suspicion were a free-range scavenger – against the cancer of idealism, with the following remarkable piece of wisdom: 'There is a wisdom – a life-wisdom – that consists in prescribing health itself for a long period of time in tiny doses only [*die Gesundheit selbst lange Zeit nur in kleinen Dosen zu verordnen*]' (2, 19).

The preface to *The Gay Science* speaks of the convalescent's gratitude and of the '*drunkenness* of convalescence [*von der* Trunkenheit *der Genesung*]' (3, 345). No wonder so many highly irrational and foolish things come to light in and through a gay science, including the extravagant tenderness the scientist comes to feel for even the spiniest moral-psychological problems. Among the principal problems, Nietzsche avers, is the fact that in the history of philosophy the sick thinkers have prevailed (*3*, 347). As if anyone could now straightforwardly declare what is healthy, what noxious! *The Gay Science* of 1881, which concludes with Part IV (Part V having been added in 1886 for the second edition), ends with the *Incipit tragoedia* of *Zarathustra*. Five years later, in 1886, with the second edition, Nietzsche warns us that tragic thinking is in his view and for his practice always a parodic thinking also: '*Incipit parodia*, no doubt.' He then writes one of the strangest self-referential remarks in all his œuvre: *Aber lassen wir Herrn Nietzsche*: pay him no mind:

what does it matter to us that Herr Nietzsche grew healthy again?' (*3*, 347). Yet if by 1886 all the oppositional logic has been purged from the metaphorics of health and illness, is not every assertion touching them – especially the claim of a successful convalescence – essentially parodic and paradoxical, merely tightening the knot of the double-bind? What can it mean that Herr Nietzsche got well? Did he surrender the essential – and essentially noxious – weapons of genealogical critique? Did he get well the way Socrates did, by sacrificing his rooster to Asclepius? Cock-A-Doodle-Doo?

An aphorism on the 'health of the soul,' in Book III of the first edition of *The Gay Science*, merits our attention in this regard. (No doubt it was an important aphorism for Foucault, who insisted on the auto-da-fé of all knowers.) Here Nietzsche doubts whether virtue constitutes the health of the soul, or whether the health of the soul can be defined at all. 'For there is no health-in-itself, and all attempts to define something of that sort are wretchedly misconceived' (FW, 120; *3*, 477). There are countless varieties of health in soul and in body. Indeed, the very multiplicity of the states and conditions of health and illness ruins any possible blueprint for health, subverts any regimented regimen, especially for the one who practices genealogical critique:

> Ultimately, we have to leave an important question open, namely, the question as to whether we can *renounce* illness, even for the development of our virtues, and in particular whether our thirst for knowledge and self-knowledge does not need the sick soul as much as the healthy one: in short, whether the will to health, taken by itself, is not a prejudice, a piece of pusillanimity, and perhaps a matter of refined barbarity and atavism [*ein Stück feinster Barbarei und Rückständigkeit*].
>
> (Ibid.)

The long penultimate aphorism of the second (1886) edition of *The Gay Science* is entitled '*Die große Gesundheit*' (FW, 382; *3*, 635–37). Nietzsche thought so highly of this aphorism that he reproduced it in his account (in *Ecce Homo*) of the gestation of *Thus Spoke Zarathustra* (*6*, 337–39). It too is a reflection on health and illness in terms of two types of ode – *Tragödie* and *Parodie*. Nietzsche proclaims himself the prematurely born infant of an as yet undemonstrated future, so premature that he will later have to concede the 'posthumous' nature of his birth. Yet this posthumous 'preemie' has as his most urgent need a new health, a health that is 'stronger cleverer tougher more reckless and more hilarious' than any prior sort of health – in a word, 'the *great health*.' It is a health that always needs to be attained, because it is always and again surrendered during the sea voyages of genealogical critique and transvaluation. As 'human-superhuman well-being and benevolence,' such health 'often enough appears *inhumane*,' especially when it poses as 'the incarnate, involuntary parody' of everything that heretofore has been held to be sacred. An *involuntary* parody, precisely in its '*great earnestness*,' marks the inception (and not the end and cap) of the tragedy. Nietzsche, the genealogist, has a highly developed sense of the extent to which he and all the sons and daughters of Christendom are still pious – which is to say, still infected with ressentiment by and from the origin. He has a highly refined sense of the mutual contamination of biopositive and bionegative effects in genealogical science. His parodic question to his own practice, which is ostensibly always in service to *life*, is whether that practice makes the practitioner worthier . . . to *live*. One is often tempted to think that the multiple voices, the minidramas, and the tropes of even the most prosaic texts of Nietzsche's œuvre are attempts to withstand or to dodge the incessant recoil of such contagious parody, which is always prelude to such relentless tragedy.

Including the Ecce

Ecce Homo is not the most prosaic of texts. How shall we initiate a discussion of it, or rather, an infectious reading of its discourse on health and illness? Initially, perhaps, by hearing several brief extracts of letters from the period in which it was written, letters that parody, letters that warn.

On 6 November 1888, to C. G. Naumann, Nietzsche's publisher: 'Between October 15 and November 4 I carried out an extremely difficult task: I recounted my self, my books, my views, all in fragmentary form, presenting only what was called for. I believe that *this* will be heard, perhaps heard too much [das *wird gehört werden vielleicht zu sehr*]. . . . And then all would be in order. . . . The new text is called

Ecce Homo
How One Becomes What One Is' (KSAB *8*, 464).

On 13 November 1888, to Franz Overbeck: '. . . the manuscript of *Ecce Homo: How One Becomes What One Is* is already at the printer's. This work, of absolute importance, provides some psychological and even biographical materials about me and my literature: they [the readers] will *behold* me all at one go [*man wird mich mit Einem Male* zu sehen bekommen]. The tone of the text is cheerful and fateful [*heiter und verhängnißvoll*], as with everything I write' (KSAB *8*, 470).

On 14 November 1888, to Meta von Salis: 'For I myself am this homo, including the ecce; the attempt to spread a bit of light *and fright* about me seems to me to have succeeded almost too well [. . . *Dieser homo bin ich nämlich selbst, eingerechnet das ecce; der Versuch über mich ein wenig Licht* und Schrecken *zu verbreiten, scheint mir fast zu gut gelungen*]' (KSAB *8*, 471).

Let me now refer to five passages in *Ecce Homo*, proceeding regressively from back to front. First, a passage from 'Why I Write Such Good Books' tells us how, during the period in which *Human All-too-Human* was written, *circa* 1877–1880, Nietzsche's ill health actually rescued him from his earlier lifestyle and thus contributed to the composition of the œuvre (*6*, 326). Nietzsche writes:

> At that time my instinct decided relentlessly against any further concessions, collaborations, or confusions-of-myself-for-someone-else. Every form of life, the most unfavorable conditions, illness, poverty – all seemed preferable to me to that undignified 'selflessness' into which I had been plunged unwittingly from my *youth* onward, and in which I was later stuck by sheer inertia and the so-called 'feeling of duty.' – What came to help me, in a way that amazes me more than I can say, and in the nick of time, was that *dire* legacy from my father's side – at bottom, the predetermination to an early death. Illness *slowly undid the fetters*: it spared me every breach, every violent and offensive step. I sacrificed no one's good will toward me, and in fact I gained even more good will. Similarly, illness gave me the right to a complete reversal in all my habits; it allowed me, *commanded* me, to forget; it bestowed on me the *compulsion* of lying still, remaining at leisure, waiting, being patient. . . . But that, of course, is what we call thinking! . . . My eyes alone put an end to all bookwormery – in German, *Philologie*. I was liberated from the 'book,' and for years 1 read nothing more – the *greatest* benefit I ever granted myself! My nethermost self, buried alive, as it were, and silenced by the constant need to listen to other selves (– and that, of course, is what we call reading!), roused slowly, shyly, full of doubt – but in the end *it spoke again*. Never have I been so happy with myself as during the periods of greatest pain and illness in my life: one only has to examine *Daybreak* or 'The Wanderer and His Shadow' in order to grasp what this 'return to *myself*' implied: a supreme sort of *convalescence* as such! The other convalescence merely followed in its train. –

If illness undid the fetters, it nevertheless remains true that Nietzsche sought recuperation and liberation from his drastic liberator. And if at the end of the passage he appears to collapse back into a traditional spiritualism – with corporeal convalescence 'merely following in the train' of the intellectual or scriptural convalescence – it also remains true that illness and the predetermination to an early death mark the very life of this perturbèd spirit.

A second and a third passage (*6*, 289–90, and 282–84) in 'Why I Am So Clever' recount Nietzsche's response to Wagner and his path to 'reason' in terms of health and illness. He praises Wagner's *Tristan und Isolde* as the great poison and antidote (*Gegengift*) of his life. 'The world is poor for one who has never been sick enough for this "voluptuosity of hell,"' he exclaims. Further, he condemns Wagner's own convalescence from *Tristan*, with *Die Meistersinger* and *Der Ring*, as sheer regression: those who are as thoroughly decadent as Wagner was should not even try to recuperate. As for Nietzsche's own 'cleverness,' it arises from his illness, which alone shocked him out of all the bad habits of diet and lifestyle he had accumulated. Illness alone is responsible for Nietzsche's health: 'Die Krankheit *brachte mich erst zur Vernunft.*'

Perhaps the most famous of Nietzsche's reflections on the question 'Why I Am So Wise' is the passage in which he declares that he is both decadent and antidecadent at once. It is the passage that serves as the conclusion to the first draft of *Ecce Homo*, the final words of the so-called *Ur-Ecce Homo* (*6*, 266–67; cf. *13*, 631–32).:

For, apart from the fact that I am a decadent, I am also its contrary [*dessen Gegensatz*]. My proof for this, among other things, is that I always instinctively chose the *correct* medicament against dire conditions, whereas the decadent as such always chooses the medicament that will hurt him. As *summa summarum* I was healthy; as niche, as specialty, I was decadent. That energy for absolute isolation and for the dissolution of customary relationships, that compulsion against myself, not allowing myself to be dithered over, doted on, *doctored* any longer – it betrays an unconditioned certitude of instinct concerning *what it was* at the time that was necessary for me above all else. I took myself in hand, made myself healthy again: the condition for that – as every physiologist will concede – is *that one at bottom be healthy*. A creature that is morbid by type cannot become healthy, still less make itself healthy; as opposed to that, for one who is healthy by type, illness can be an energetic *stimulans* to life, to more life. Indeed, that is how the long period of my illness *now* appears to me: I discovered life anew, as it were, including myself; I tasted all good things, even the most minute, as others could not readily taste them – out of my will to health, to *life*, I made my philosophy. . . . For pay heed to this: the years of my lowest vitality were the years when I *ceased* being a pessimist: the instinct for self-restitution *forbade* me to embrace a philosophy of poverty and discouragement. . . . And, at bottom, how does one recognize whether a human being has *turned out well* [*die* Wohlgerathenheit]! By the fact that one who has turned out well pleases our senses: that he is carved from wood that is hard, tender, and fragrant. Only what is conducive to him [*ihm zuträglich*] pleases him; his delight, his pleasure, ceases whenever the measure of what is conducive is exceeded. He unearths pharmaceuticals against injuries, uses baneful accidents to his advantage; whatever does not kill him makes him stronger. He instinctively gathers from everything he sees, hears, and experiences, *his* quantum: he is a selective principle, he lets many things fail the test. He is always in his *own* company, whether he tarries with books, human beings, or landscapes: he honors things by *choosing, admitting, trusting*. He reacts slowly to every sort of stimulation, with a slowness that is bred by long-practiced caution and a willed pride – he probes the stimulus that is approaching, far be it from him to approach it. He believes in neither 'misfortune' nor 'guilt': he knows how to put things behind him, whether they involve himself or others; he knows how to *forget* – he is sufficiently strong to *make* everything serve him for the best. – Well, then, I am the *counterpart* [*das* Gegenstück] of a decadent: for the one I was only now describing is precisely *me*.

If Nietzsche is the contrary (*Gegensatz*) of a decadent, he is also the decadent's counterpart (*Gegenstück*), the σύμβολον of the decadent. The very fortune (*Glück*) of his existence is to be both commencement and decadent; if no 'local degeneration' can be found in him, his life is nevertheless convalescence and regression, 'the periodicity of a kind of decadence' (*6*, 265). If Nietzsche is *experienced* in questions of decadence, if he has spelled the word forwards and backwards, if he has developed a finger for nuances and a gaze that sees around corners and down into the secret recesses of the decadence instinct, if, in short, Nietzsche has mastered the optics of the ill (*Kranken-Optik*), then no typology of the 'essentially healthy' type, no conceptual procedure, no therapeutic pose, no clever maneuver, no taking-oneself-in-hand will surgically sever the pathogenic from the biopositive effect, no eye will descry and distinguish the peaks from the valleys of periodicity, no nose will know the perfume of hard oak from the sweet corruption of watery cottonwood.

To repeat, *Ecce Homo* is not the most prosaic of texts. How shall we broach a discussion of it? In the first place, no lines of the text lend themselves to a straightforward analysis of health and disease. While one easily spots the inflated, megalomanic, sardonic, or euphoric passages, even the halcyon passages, the passages that are beautifully *composed*, in both senses of the word, must now give us pause. Thus, for example, even the untitled exergue of the book, *An diesem vollkommnen Tage*, which at first perusal seems undeniably in the full flush of exuberant health, slips into an odd state of suspension. In such suspension, questions of *infection* give way to vagaries of *inflection*, and to doubts about whether and how one can *read* the words:

> On this perfect day, when everything is ripening, and not only the grapes are turning russet, a ray of sunlight fell across my life: I looked back, I looked ahead, and never did I see so many things and such good things at once. Not in vain did I bury today my forty-fourth year: I was *allowed* to bury it – whatever was of life in it has been rescued, is immortal. The first book of the *Transvaluation of All Values*, the *Dionysos-Dithyrambs*, and, for recuperation, the *Twilight of the Idols*, are all gifts of this year, even of its last quarter. *How should I not be grateful to my entire life?* – And so I shall narrate my life to myself.

Is Nietzsche's *vollkommner Tag* a day on the autumnal earth, an earth to which one remains doggedly faithful, or is it a day of *infinite* consummation?

A day of mortal harvest or of divine – that is to say, *decadent* – redemption? Are the grapes russet or bronzed? Is it happy birthday or happy burial day? As for Nietzsche's locution, *ist gerettet, ist unsterblich*, one can hardly suppress an 'Alleluia, Alleluia.' Does something decadent, something reactively nihilistic, something *resentful* and redolent of *rancune* conceal itself in the negative form of the affirmation, *Wie sollte ich nicht . . .*? Finally, how does one *read* the quasi-reflexive self-recounting of one's own life to oneself? Is the emphasis to fall on the *recounting* or on the *to myself*? Is the question to be inflected liltingly, whimsically? Or defiantly, as though rushing to the barricades? Or piously, that is, paralytically? Or, to end the list, *infectiously*?

Conclusion and Postscript

My meager conclusions are these:

1   Novalis's poetics of the baneful moots something like a periodicity of *indirect* health and illness, in which the soul is the most virulent poison, but poison 'the most interesting stimulus to our meditation.'
2   The biopositive effects of infection may be an invention of hokey medicine, but that invention will haunt those of us who know that in order to do good work you just about have to kill yourself.
3   Infectious rhetorics – for example, in the biographies of literary figures – are nests of prejudices concerning the body, sexuality, and spiritual hygiene. They have to be dirtied.
4   'The great health' is both parodic and tragic. It expresses a double-bind in our reading and writing, including the *ecce*: infectious rhetoric is as unreadable as illness and health 'in themselves' are undecidable – at least until death do us part.

Postscript

No doubt there is something vaguely (if not flagrantly) sentimental about this entire venture. Perhaps it only helps us to measure our own distance from the *lingua romana* of Novalis, the Schlegels, and Schelling. By now, long after the 1960s, madness has lost most of its charisma. In *Human, All-Too-Human* (2, 122), Nietzsche himself writes: 'Because people observed that an excitation often made the head more lucid and induced lucky inspirations, they came to believe that extreme excitations would enable one to share in the luckiest inspirations and windfalls of the mind: and so they honored the insane as the wise and oracular. At bottom, this was a false deduction.'

In the Age of AIDS, tertiary syphilis seems a dose of the old down-home: we can view it with a certain fondness, familiarity, and nostalgia. In the Age of AIDS, tuberculosis means a mutant, more highly resistant and resilient bacillus, one that defeats the lingering romanticism of 'biopositive effects.'

We never dreamt that when Nietzsche's Zarathustra said, 'The human being is something that must be overcome,' a highly mobile virus was preparing to undertake the task quite literally, as though it missed the metaphor. Will anything appear in any future of ours that will allow some living creature ages hence to speculate on the 'biopositive effects' of AIDS? Or has *our* romance language become a truly *dead* language? And is it the mortification of our romance tongue that best explains why the slightest allusion to sexual desire in our time is grounds for lawsuits, denunciations, and recriminations?

The death of God never troubled us, because we believed that God died so that Eros might live. Now that Eros is in its final throes, not merely poisoned by the culture of Christendom but in our own secular and infectious age administered the lethal dose, one wonders what could possibly keep Thanatos at bay a while longer; what could possibly prolong the detour that is leading us to endless stasis by one more turn, one more round.[14]

Notes

1. I shall continue to refer to Novalis, *Werke Tagebücher und Briefe Friedrich von Hardenbergs*, 3 vols., especially vol. 2, *Das philosophisch-theoretische Werk*, ed. Hans-Joachim Mähl (cited in note 3 of chap. 8). On the question of health and illness in Novalis's theoretical work, see the important study by John Neubauer; *Bifocal Vision: Novalis's Philosophy of Nature and Disease* (Chapel Hill: University of North Carolina Press, 1971), passim. As for Nietzsche, a word about editions of *Ecce Homo*, the composition of the work, and related materials in the notebooks. No other work of Nietzsche's is as complex in its printing history as *Ecce Homo* is. No single edition, not even the historical-critical edition by Giorgio Colli and Mazzino Montinari, suffices. The most useful edition is a facsimile of Nietzsche's holograph, with a transcription and commentary: F. Nietzsche, *Ecce homo, Faksimileausgabe der Handschrift, mit Transkription und Kommentar*, ed. Anneliese Clauss, Karl-Heinz Hahn, and Mazzino Montinari, Edition Leipzig, 1985. For details on the printing history of the text, see the extensive and authoritative account in the *Kritische Studienausgabe, 14*, 454–512. Nietzsche composed and corrected the text in six main phases, beginning on October 15 and finishing by the end of December, even though the bulk of the writing was completed by November 4. The most important alteration was the substitution of an entirely new section 3 for Part One, 'Why I Am So Wise,' mailed to C. G. Naumann on December 29, 1888. There are surprisingly few related materials in the notebooks, apart from the so-called *Ur-Ecce Homo*. The final page of notebook 23 (Mette-Nr.) contains the untitled exergue of the work, *An diesem vollkommenen Tage*. Fragment I of notebook 24, some eighteen pages, presents the *Ur-Ecce Homo*. The material there corresponds for the most part to *Ecce Homo* Part Two, 'Why I Am So Clever,' although sections 1, 2, and 4 of Part One are also sketched out here. Let this one passage offer something of the flavor of these notes. It is 24 [6] (*13*, 633):

The perspicacity of my instinct consists in my sensing the truly calamitous conditions and dangers for *me* as such.

likewise, in my surmising the means by which one avoids them *or* arranges them to one's own advantage and reorganizes them, as it were, about a *higher* intention.

Finally, fragment 6 of notebook 25 offers a first draft of Part Four; 'Why I Am a Destiny,' which begins '*Ich kenne mein Loos . . .*' In sum, to repeat, the relevant notebooks are 23–25, in KSA, *13*, 613–35.

2. See esp. no. 116 of Friedrich Schlegel's 1798 *Fragmente*, which begins: 'Romantic poesy is a progressive universal poesy,' and which ends: '. . . for in a certain sense all poesy is or should be romantic.' Friedrich Schlegel, *Werke in zwei Bänden* (Berlin and Weimar: Aufbau Verlag, 1980), *2*, 204–5.

3. F. W. J. Schelling, *Von der Weltseele. eine Hypothese der höheren Physik zur Erklärung des allgemeinen Organismus* (1798), in *Sämmtliche Werke* (Stuttgart and Augsburg: J. G. Cotta, 1856), Abteilung 1/2, p. 534.

4. See *Sämmtliche Werke*, Abteilung 1/3, pp. 44–65 and 220–40.

5. See G. W. F. Hegel, *Enzyklopädie der philosophischen Wissenschaften (1830)*, ed. Friedhelm Nicolin and Otto Pöggeler (Hamburg: F. Meiner, 1969), §§367–76.

6. I have cited the sources and discussed them in some detail in chap. 7 of my *Daimon Life: Heidegger and Life-Philosophy*. (Bloomington: Indiana University Press, 1992).

7. Pierre Klossowski, *Nietzsche et le cercle vicieux*. (Paris: Mercure de France, 1969), p. 40. The quotations appear on pp. 40 and 51.

8. Once again, see chap. 7 of *Daimon Life*.

9. The term *lues* arises from an early designation of the particular germ that was thought to cause syphilis: *Cytorryctes luis*. The more commonly accepted term for the bacillus is *Treponema pallidum*. See on all these questions Claude Quétel, *History of Syphilis*, trans. Judith Braddock and Brian Pike (Cambridge, England: Polity Press, 1990), passim.

10. Curt Paul Janz, *Friedrich Nietzsche Biographie*, 3 vols. (Munich: Deutscher Taschenbuch Verlag, 1981), *2*, 10.

11. Wilhelm Lange-Eichbaum and Wolfram Kurth, *Genie, Irrsinn und Ruhm: Genie-Mythus und Pathographie des Genies*, 6th ed. (Munich: Ernst Reinhardt, 1967 [first ed., 1927], pp. 244–46.

12. Yet no matter how 'social-critical' we are, we no doubt prefer the humanistic explanations of creativity, which keep illness, whether physical or psychological, at arm's length. See, for example, Albert Rothenberg, M.D., *The Emerging Goddess: The Creative Process in Art, Science, and Other Fields* (Chicago: University of Chicago Press, 1979), passim; see esp. pp. 135–36 and 351–57 (on the distinction between creative processes and psychopathological symptoms), and pp. 142–44 on the creativity and 'great healthiness' of Nietzsche. However, whether or not the proximity of genius and illness occurs only in extreme or 'dramatic' cases, as Rothenberg avers, the question of the biopositive effect of *infection* remains altogether undiscussed by him – although the material on 'anxiety and arousal' (pp. 351–57) might well lend itself to an infectious reading. (I am grateful to Professor Carl Hausman for recommending Rothenberg's text to me.)

13. Gerhard Schulz, *Novalis* (Reinbek bei Hamburg: Rowohltt Monographien No. 154, 1969), pp. 66–67.

14. A thoughtful critic at the University of Toronto, where I presented a version of this chapter as a paper in May 1994, rightly noted that AIDS should not be used as material for a peroration – that it must stand at the *front* of a paper and be confronted more directly and courageously. I accept that criticism. All it will take on my part to do that is more insight into what has changed for us in this terrible time, and more courage in order to face it. At all events, my gratitude to that unknown critic, who will rightly find it even worse that I have reduced this matter to an endnote – meant, however, as a promissory note, a hostage to our common endangered future.

49

The Spirit of Revenge and the Eternal Recurrence: On Heidegger's Later Interpretation of Nietzsche*

Wolfgang Müller-Lauter

Translated by R. J. Hollingdale

*Source: *Journal of Nietzsche Studies*, issue 4/5, 1992–3, pp. 127–53.

No philosopher has had so profound an influence on the course of Heidegger's thinking as Nietzsche.[1] It is true that it was only after the publication of *Sein und Zeit* that Nietzsche became for Heidegger a 'decision': but it was precisely out of the existential analytic of Dasein presented in that book that there grew the demand that, returning from its resolute moving forward to what existed formerly, it 'chose for itself its heroes' (385). That which preserves itself in the structures of the historicity of Dasein in general formally receives its determining content round 1929–30 through Heidegger's 'repetition' of the understanding of actual history which he found in Nietzsche. What became decisive for him in this was Nietzsche's saying 'God is dead.'[2]

Characteristic of Heidegger's *earliest reception of Nietzsche* is undoubtedly the affirmation of 'will' and 'power' – as the handing-over of the future to men – resulting from the acceptance of this saying which he saw come into effect in 1933–34 with the emergence of National Socialism.[3] The *second phase* of Heidegger's interpretation of Nietzsche began with his lectures of 1936; after an initial basic orientation (and one wholly intent on carefulness in interpretation), these lectures were much informed by an increasingly *critical* posture towards Nietzsche, though at the same time they emphasised his greatness as the consummator of metaphysics – a metaphysics to be overcome, to be sure – and did so most impressively, perhaps, in the lecture *Der europäische Nihilismus* of 1940. Heidegger afterwards interpreted his Nietzsche lectures as a confrontation with National Socialism.[4]

In his writings and lectures of 1942–1944 Heidegger's polemic against Nietzsche is intensified to such a degree that it allows us to speak of a *third phase* of his consideration of him. The idea of the *consummation of metaphysics* associated with his thought appears in this phase almost unreservedly as a *decline*.

That the *fourth phase* of Heidegger's involvement with Nietzsche at the beginning of the 1950s has received relatively little attention is undoubtedly due to the worldwide effect produced by the publication in 1961 of his Nietzsche lectures, supplemented by later texts on the history of metaphysics: it was thought that Heidegger's definitive interpretation of Nietzsche was already to be found in these lectures, i.e. in the 'second phase', its being in particular overlooked that in this matter they differed significantly from talks and lectures of Heidegger's published earlier but delivered later (*Was heisst Denken?*, winter semester 1951–52, and *Wer ist Nietzsches Zarathustra?*, 1953, both published 1954). The material difference between these texts and those of the second and third phases is, however, obvious.[5]

II

In the last named texts Heidegger attains to a new relationship with Nietzsche's thought (in particular with *Thus Spoke Zarathustra*[6]). The renewed positive assessment of Nietzsche which grew out of this is to be detected in his observations regarding an individual aspect: Heidegger's interpretations of Nietzsche in the 1950s emphasised Nietzsche's clear-sightedness and foresight with regard to the future to an extent that seems to transcend his consignment to the expiry of metaphysics. Since, however, the placement of Nietzsche in Heidegger's conception of modern metaphysics as history of the truth of Being suffers no fundamental change, there arises a tension between that Nietzsche who was incapable of surveying and seeing beyond the world of technology which, though he could not comprehend it, he had nonetheless advanced, and the other Nietzsche who was supposed to have reflected on the devastation of the earth.

Before I investigate Heidegger's attempt to resolve that tension I ought to exhibit it with all possible clarity and rigour. To that end I shall first quote some of Heidegger's observations from the 1940s and then contrast them with his interpretations of 1951 and 1953. In the Heraclitus lectures of 1943 and 1944 Nietzsche is to Heidegger, more markedly than in the earlier Nietzsche lectures, the philosopher through whom reality was exposed as will to power, which in the late phase of modern times meant in the mode of technologically determined objectivisation. In Nietzsche's metaphysical 'connection with reality' 'the machine gun, the camera, the "word", the poster' possess 'the same basic position of the securing of objects'. Of importance for the understanding of *language* which broke through with Nietzsche is that 'the technological precision of the word' is 'the counterpart to the decay of language into a device of communications technology' (*Her* 71: see 105ff.). That a philosophy which ties together power and technology can understand Being, which Heidegger's reflections are concerned with, merely as the last vapour of an evaporating reality, as Nietzsche had written in *Twilight of the Idols* (*Her* 83; cf. *KGW* VI 3, 70), once more confirmed the decline of metaphysics grounded in the history of Being.

> It lies in the inexorable logicality of Nietzsche's metaphysics, which accepts 'truth' only as a 'value', as one cipher among others, that all philosophical thought should be misinterpreted as a writing of codes,

Heidegger says in allusion to Jasper's reading of Nietzsche (*Her* 180). Even though in the will to will which, according to the conclusion of Heidegger's 1944 lecture, was to find its most extreme metaphysical form in Nietzsche's doctrine of will to power, there was still to be 'detected a trace of the initial nature of Being'. Heidegger is nonetheless concerned to show that the distance in the history of Being between Heraclitus and Nietzsche cannot be exaggerated. It comes to light, for example, in the fact that Nietzsche left behind and gave currency to the most dreadful mis-interpretation of what Heraclitus thinks' (*Her* 5). In any event, in these observations Nietzsche is regarded solely as the thinker who, *blind* to the *essence of technology*, advances and legitimates the technological to its last extreme.

From 1951 onwards much has changed. To Heidegger Nietzsche is now the one who became aware of the death of the metaphysical world. 'More clearly than anyone before him' Nietzsche had perceived the danger that man was making himself (technologically) at home on his superficies, and he had been 'the first' to be aware both of the 'danger' and the 'necessity of a transition' (WD 24, cf. 62f.). It was even possible that he had known 'that precisely his thought would first have to produce a devastation, in the midst of which . . . one day and from elsewhere springs would here and there emerge' (*WD* 21). According to Heidegger's interpretation, in Nietzsche's saying 'the desert is growing' there is announced a total desolation of the earth. He finds some-thing more basic expressed in this saying than is expressed in the twentieth-century social critique employing Nietzsche's insights of the kind produced by, for example, O. Spengler and K. Sedlmayr (*WD* 11, 14; cr. 61): Nietzsche had conceived this saying 'seeing far beyond all of this from the most elevated position . . . as early as the eighties of the last century' (*WD* 11). His saying is 'a true saying' (*WD* 14).

Heidegger's late concession to Nietzsche's thought does not alter the fact that, seeing him as the thinker of *transition*, he sets him 'as a whole to one side', namely to that of metaphysics. Nietzsche may possibly have known that he himself was a *precursory* transition who everywhere pointed ahead and cautioned back and thus would be bound to remain 'ambiguous'. To Heidegger he is, to be sure, the only one to have 'thought through' the danger – but, unavoidably, he still did this 'metaphysically' (*WD* 21–25). The tension referred to thus experiences a relaxation to the extent that even Nietzsche's far-sightedness is held to remain confined within the bounds of metaphysics and to be aware of the need for a transition only at the extremist limit of its vision.

III

The later Heidegger wants to show that in Zarathustra's observations on the doctrine of eternal recurrence Nietzsche has reached the extreme limit of his thought. What is held to lead to the 'fundamental idea' contained in it, and thus 'into the core of his metaphysics', is 'Nietzsche's question about revenge' (*WD* 37f.). Heidegger's interpretation is in its essence orientated towards two guiding principles in *Zarathustra* II: 'this, yes, this alone is *revenge* itself: the will's antipathy towards time and time's "It was" ('Of Redemption': *KGW* VI 1, 176); and 'For *that man may be freed from the bonds of revenge*: that is the bridge to my highest hope and a rainbow after protracted storms' ('Of the Tarantulas': *KGW* VI 1, 124). On the basis of these, and occasionally drawing on other Nietzsche texts, Heidegger explains that the will becomes 'free from the antipathetic "It was" if it desires the continual return of all "It was" ' (*WD* 43). In Zarathustra's sense this is quite correct: problems emerge only when Heidegger proceeds to a detailed interpretation. Before going into them I would record my view that, because Heidegger considered the doctrine of recurrence – together with the doctrine of the overman which belongs with it – 'from their unified questionable ground' (*WD* 45), his interpretation seeks on the one hand to serve Nietzsche's philosophy, whose inner unity and strength he would like to demonstrate, while on the other hand he is concerned to show its inadequacy as regards the history of Being. Nietzsche is the *consummator* of metaphysics. Its end is 'as consummation [of] the bringing together into the extremist possibilities' of thought in the 'present style' (*SD* 63; cf. *WD* 21). It is with regard to this that Nietzsche's greatness is held to be demonstrated. But as the consummator of *metaphysics* he is to Heidegger at the same time one who presses against the frontier of metaphysics without being able to cross it.

Heidegger's late Nietzsche interpretations are marked by this double-sidedness in such a way that his reconstructed *going along with* Nietzsche and his critical *distancing from* him often pass barely perceptibly over into one another. Perhaps one is entitled to say that Heidegger goes along with Nietzsche (though it is a Nietzsche interpreted in his own way) up to that last extreme at which on the one hand he leaves him behind and on the other retains him for something still open. With regard to the theme I am addressing now it may be asserted as a fact that Heidegger sees as a failure Nietzsche's effort to derive metaphysics from the spirit of revenge, while conceding that the idea of recurrence may possibly have a future.

This parting company from Nietzsche on the one hand and being caught up with him on the other, which in the succeeding logical steps came to mark

Heidegger's *final* 'examination of and dispute with the case of Nietzsche' (*N*1 10), will here be presented only in their essentials. *First step*. Heidegger explains that Nietzsche understands revenge *metaphysically* (*WD* 45, *VA* 11 1f.). In support of this proposition he invokes both definitions which accord with Nietzsche's concept of metaphysics and, undermining these, definitions which grow out of his own understanding of metaphysics. At first he even concedes to Nietzsche the right to describe present thinking as being *dualistically* determined by the spirit of revenge. That Plato already called the transitory *mê on* shows that from time immemorial the independence of eternity from time was regarded as characteristic of metaphysics. That is why Nietzsche found 'the profoundest revenge . . . in that thought which posits what is the ideal in a supratemporal sense as absolute ideals measured against which what is temporal must relegate itself to that which really has no Being' (*VA* 116f.). *More basic* metaphysically than such a dualism, however, is, Heidegger gives us to understand, that which is willed in revenge as counter-will (aversion) (*WD* 45), and *even more basic* metaphysically 'every relationship of man to Being as such' (*VA* 112). – In a *second step* Heidegger includes Nietzsche's thought in precisely that metaphysics which the latter opposed. Heidegger's thesis is that Nietzsche himself falls victim to the spirit of revenge: he therewith enters into the field of an immanent critique of Nietzsche. He rejects 'superficial appearance', it is true; he assesses Nietzsche as the 'most essential part' of that which the latter wants to 'overcome'. Heidegger desires to preserve himself from any such 'agitation of the desire to refute', for 'the path of a thinker' never leads to it. What is essential to the matter, however, is his interim conclusion that Nietzsche's thought itself moves 'within the spirit of present thinking'. This statement, understood out of its context, contains within itself a twofold meaning: in the sense both of Nietzsche's own understanding of metaphysics and that of Heidegger, Nietzsche remains imprisoned within metaphysics (see *VA* 121f.). – Nietzsche's alleged self-entanglement permits Heidegger to take a *third step* with and against Nietzsche. If Nietzsche's understanding of metaphysics is itself still metaphysical it may be asked whether the 'decisive sense of the spirit of present thinking is hit on at all when it is interpreted as spirit of revenge'. Even in 1953 Heidegger still leaves this question 'open' (*VA* 122). Such a leaving open is, to be sure, rather a concession to *that* Nietzsche whom Heidegger still desires to go along with on the path of thought. Fundamentally his question already constitutes a denial. – Consequently Heidegger is able, in a *fourth step*, to sever the spirit of revenge from the doctrine of recurrence. The former sinks as a special peculiarity of Nietzsche's interpretation in the modern history of metaphysics as Heidegger understands it. The doctrine of recurrence, however, is that towards which this history has always been orientated. According to Heidegger it constitutes that 'of which Schelling says all philosophy strives after, namely to find the highest expression for primeval Being as will' (*WD* 47; cf. 35, 77; *VA* 113f.)[7]. If the history of metaphysics was to attain to its extreme limit by developing and exposing itself expressly as *will to will*, by which Heidegger understands the *essence* of will to power,[8] then this extreme limit would have finally to come to light in that doctrine of Nietzsche's. But, as Heidegger frequently explains, in will to will the *essence* of technology reveals and conceals itself, and for this reason must be considered in the light of the idea of recurrence. In the *fifth step* Heidegger draws this conclusion: 'the constantly rotating recurrence of the same brings to light the essence of technology' (*WD* 47). For 'what else is the essence of the modern engine but one form of the eternal recurrence of the same?' (*VA* 126). Now, this doctrine has, to be sure, been taken up in the nineteenth and twentieth centuries with respect to the technological–economic view of the world both together with, and after, Nietzsche. To extend Nietzsche's ideas in this direction may have its own justification. We also find similar reflections on the history of ideas in other authors.[9] Here, however, our concern is to pursue Heidegger's examination of and dispute with Nietzsche. What emerges is that he leaves behind him not only *what Nietzsche says about revenge* but in the end *what Nietzsche understands by the doctrine of recurrence* as well. 'That Nietzsche interpreted and experienced his most abysmal thought from the Dionysian point of view suggests only that he still had to think it metaphysically and only metaphysically', he says finally (*VA* 126). – Heidegger's *sixth step* points to the future: the doctrine of recurrence is 'shrouded in a darkness before which even Nietzsche had to draw back' (*WD* 46). To us today, too, what is essential in this doctrine is still *hidden*, and it is so precisely because the *essence* of the present and the coming age finds expression in it. As yet 'no thinker' has appeared who is equal to the fundamental thought of *Thus Spoke Zarathustra*. Nietzsche's 'most abysmal thought' conceals, according to Heidegger, 'something unthought . . . which at the same time closes itself to metaphysical thinking' (*WD 21; VA* 101, 125).

IV

The still unthought in what Nietzsche thought is preserved by Heidegger as that which is to be thought about in the future. So far as that which Nietzsche said fails to fit in with what Heidegger demands he ignores it, after first having reduced it to contemporary influences (see also *VA* 81f.). Yet the question arises whether Heidegger has adequately appreciated that Nietzsche whom he leaves behind. This question should be discussed in response to those arguments which Heidegger adduces to demonstrate his thesis that Nietzsche was himself captivated by the spirit of revenge he had only apparently overcome. This thesis constitutes the prerequisite for Nietzsche's being integrated into Heidegger's own understanding of metaphysics. In support of his thesis Heidegger adduces several pieces of evidence: here we can deal with only his two most important objections.

In 1952 Heidegger refers to a much quoted sentence in the *Nachlass* fragment *WM* 617 (*KGW* VIII 1, 320f.[10]):

> That *everything recurs* is the closest *approximation of a world of becoming to a world of Being*: high point of the meditation.

It is understandable that Heidegger should say of this 'high point' that it rises up 'not in clear and firm outline in the brightness of transparent aether but remains 'enveloped in heavy clouds' (*WD* 46). Heidegger's impression of unclarity is no doubt also clarified here by the fact that in the *Zarathustra* texts quoted he had been looking at Being in the form of 'It was', as Being that returns again and again, to be sure, but – more essentially – Being that is again and again (and with endless finality) overcome in the *abolition of its immovability.* Precisely the 'rigidity' of Being counted as that which provoked the spirit of revenge (cf. *WD* 43). Now, however, the doctrine of recurrence is presented under the opposite aspect of Nietzsche: approximation to the *constancy* of Being here appears as virtually the ultimate and actual meaning of the idea of recurrence. For Heidegger's endeavour to demonstrate Nietzsche's own spirit of revenge the passage quoted is, however, inadequate. Reference to a constancy which requires for its recurrence a constant self-dissolution, and to a becoming and passing away which in its revolving within itself eternally consolidates itself, may perhaps allow one to demonstrate that Nietzsche's doctrine is ambiguous, if not actually self-conflicting;[11] that the spirit of revenge triumphs in that passage, however, even Heidegger cannot say. It is no doubt for this reason that a year later Heidegger cites in support of his thesis another passage from *WM* 617: ' To *impose* upon becoming the character of Being – that is the *supreme will to power*' (*VA* 120).[12] Heidegger finds expressed in the character of the *imposition* that therewith 'all becoming' is taken 'into the care of the eternal recurrence of the same events'. He asks:

> Is there not nonetheless still concealed in this imposition a will *repugnant* to the mere fact of passing away and therewith a highly spiritualised spirit of revenge?
>
> (*VA* 121)

The question first of all demands that we establish that in *WM* 617 revenge is not at issue at all. What is involved in both the passages now cited by Heidegger is the relationship between *becoming* and *Being*. Naturally that does not prevent its being brought into connection with the guiding proposition from *Zarathustra* from which his late interpretation of Nietzsche takes its start.

An adequate answer to Heidegger's question demands, of course, the more detailed examination deferred up to now of Zarathustra's remarks on revenge and of Heidegger's interpretation of them.

1. In 'Of Redemption' Zarathustra speaks of the intolerability of the *actual* 'It was' that cannot be altered. Powerlessness 'against that which has been done' constitutes his 'most solitary affliction'. Powerlessness towards that which has happened becomes 'wrath', 'ill-temper', revenge on all that can suffer. Such revenge is, however, profoundly different and far removed from that antipathy towards *passing away as such*, towards *transitoriness*. This antipathy appears, according to Zarathustra, only when the 'foolishness' of ill-temper 'acquired spirit', which 'up to now has been mankind's chief concern'. Interpreting Nietzsche, we can say that from Anaximander to Schopenhauer 'cloud upon cloud' has 'rolled over the spirit'. Nietzsche's interpretation of the spirit up to now addresses itself to the fact of passing away, and decisive for this interpretation is the idea: 'Where there was suffering there was always supposed to be punishment.'

2. It is only the development of the idea of revenge into that of punishment (as it were revenge to the second power) which, according to Zarathustra, leads to the *theme of transitoriness as such*. It is 'madness' that preaches 'Everything passes away, therefore everything deserves to pass away!' The desire for 'redemption from the stream of things and from the punishment "Being"', which would like to abolish willing altogether, is nothing but a 'fable-song of madness'. Of this Zarathustra speaks in the passage cited by Heidegger only insofar as he is concerned to unharness the will 'from its own folly', to unlearn 'the spirit of revenge and all teeth-gnashing'.

3. Zarathustra's concern is to take the past up into the *creating will*. Here he is so little concerned with passing away as such that he realises he has unreservedly to affirm the *actual* 'It was' as 'fragment', 'riddle', dreadful 'chance'. That such an affirmation beyond all 'reconciliation with time' includes within itself: Thus I willed it, thus do I will it, thus shall I will it – in face of this idea of the recurrence *of the same events* Zarathustra is here still 'seized with the extremist terror'.

The transitoriness of passing away and the insistence of what is past belong together and yet have to be separated from one another and their relationship carefully considered. With the elaboration of the existential of *Gewesenheit* in *Sein und Zeit*, Heidegger brought out the ontological priority of that which persists over the 'flux of time'. Not that these two characters of time were not distinguished from one another in his Zarathustra analyses. Thus Heidegger finds Nietzsche's redemption from revenge to reside in the fact that 'the past does not rigidify in the mere "It was" and as such stare at willing with unmoving rigidity' (*WD* 43). The counter-will (aversion) is 'against passing away insofar as it causes the past to be only past and to freeze in the rigidity of finality' (*WD* 42). Aversion disappears if the past does not 'sink' into *nothing but* 'It was' but goes *and* returns (*WD* 43). On this point only a shift of emphasis between interpreter and him he interprets is needed to establish that according to Heidegger's interpretation of 'redemption' the 'rigidity' is dissolved, the past abolished as 'finality', insofar as it is taken up into the *mobility* of passing away and returning. Zarathustra's terror, however, derives from the fact that the 'Thus I willed it' is demanded of him as 'Thus shall I eternally will it (again)'; he sees himself at the mercy of what is past in such a way that it will occur again and again in that agonising 'rigidity' which has been and is Zarathustra's 'most intolerable' burden – but which is foreign to Heidegger.

In Heidegger's analysis of Nietzsche's understanding of time, passing away gains priority (as against that which is past).[13] This can now be made clear here only by referring to his interpretation of the 'and' in Zarathustra's discourse on antipathy 'towards time and time's "It was."' To Heidegger the 'and' possesses only a clarificatory significance: it signifies no more than 'and that means' (*VA* 116). It refers to the 'It was' *of* time (*WD* 39). Heidegger therewith gets it right, but at the same time he leads into error. It is right that the 'It was' belongs to time. But it is an error that 'with the "It was"' Nietzsche was not asserting 'an isolated determination of time' but was accepting the latter 'in its whole temporal essence . . . passing away' (*WD* 39). Against this is to be said: the 'and' separates *within* time as nonetheless belonging together with it. The will's aversion is directed against time as passing away ('flowing off') *and* – above all – against that which has run away in such a flowing off, which as '*Thus* it was' *remains and returns*.

At the same time we must observe that to Nietzsche *becoming* (and passing away) *and Being* are antitheses only in an 'absolute' sense. In his view becoming takes place solely on the presupposition of *suppositions* (of Being). These alone push becoming forward. 'Every event, or movement, or becoming [is] to be regarded as a firm establishing and fixing of relationships of rank and force, as a *struggle*' (*Nachlass*, *KGW* VIII 2, 49). Nietzsche emphasised again and again in his works the unavoidability of the determining [*feststellenden*] constant (regardless of its *deceptive* character in regard to 'reality'). According to him *becoming* is so little a 'streaming away' and a 'new emerging' that it is brought about rather by the 'alteration' of the said determinations.[14] That which firmly establishes is each time will to power. Is it not logical, then, to assume that the supreme will to power would have to consist in imposing upon becoming and passing away the character of Being, as happens in the doctrine of recurrence? Revenge *on life* cannot be what is meant by such an imposition even if only because life itself (and therefore becoming) is real only *as imposition* (in context with counter-impositions).

V

We must leave aside the question whether Heidegger became aware of the inadequacies of his *immanent* critique of Nietzsche's understanding of revenge. In any event he saw himself obliged, in his examination and dispute with Nietzsche, to go beyond the concept of revenge as *revenge on life*. With the aid of etymology he produces a concept of revenge *in general* whose provisional definition is: 'Revenge is a subverting and belittling hunting-after' (*VA* 113, cf. *WD* 33ff.). The universality of this definition leaves undecided *against what* the subverting (the counter-will) is directed and *what* is belittled. Its formal character allows us to include in it equally counter-will against life *and* counter-will against enmity towards life.

Heidegger's *expansion* of the concept of revenge, undertaken in opposition to Nietzsche's understanding of the concept, nonetheless lays claim to being in accord with Nietzsche's thought – interpreted as being metaphysical – insofar as with this thought the full *metaphysical essence of revenge* is held to have first come to light.[15] Nietzsche himself had 'brought the intrinsic metaphysicality of his thought to the extremist form of counter-will – and did so, indeed, in the last lines of his last book, *Ecce Homo* . . . "Have I been understood? – *Dionysus against the Crucified* . . ." ' (*VA* 123; *KGW* VI 3, 372). – In the end Heidegger extracts from this 'formula' of Nietzsche's only an answer to the question posed in his lecture of 1953: *who is Zarathustra?* He regards him as 'the advocate of Dionysus', as 'the teacher who in his teaching of the overman and for this teaching teaches the eternal recurrence of the same events', in which the latter is supposed to denominate 'the Being of beings' and the former the name for the 'human being who corresponds to this Being' (*VA* 123ff.). – That Nietzsche's thought had been vanquished with the 'formula' of metaphysically understood revenge was to Heidegger beyond all doubt. The problems his thesis raises will not be considered, though we shall of course be able to highlight only a few fundamental aspects of Nietzsche's late philosophy.

1. As original counter-willing, as power-wills against one another, the definition of *against* is a fundamental constitutive element in Nietzsche's understanding of becoming, as has already been explained (see above). Even Heidegger's interpretation, which, to be sure, hardly considers this aspect, does not aim to show that in Nietzsche the against-one-another in general is to be equated with the counter-will as revenge. The character of the latter is supposed to be found in the 'formula' to the extent that 'the extremest form of counter-will' finds expression in it. The counter-will attains this through its *against-what*.

2. This against-what is designated the *Crucified*. Under this name Nietzsche comprehends quite generally *Christian morality*, of which he says, e.g. two pages before the 'formula' in *Ecce Homo*, that it is 'the idiosyncrasy of *décadents* with the hidden intention of *revenging themselves on life* – and successfully', as history showed (*KGW* VI 371).[16] Under the name of justice 'with revenge the *reactive* affects in general and one and all are subsequently brought into honour' (*On the Genealogy of Morals KGW* VI 2, 325f.; *cf. op. cit.* 296f.). In *The Anti-Christ* Nietzsche says that the disciples of Jesus, far from '*forgiving* his death', were driven by '*ressentiment*': 'the most unevangelic of

feelings, *revengefulness*, again came uppermost' (*KGW* VI 3, 211f.). That *ressentiment* is held to pertain not only to Christianity but to characterise many *décadence* movements as well can be no more than mentioned here. – With this we already find ourselves confronted by the problem raised by Heidegger's expansion. If revenge is no longer only (as it is for Nietzsche) revenge on life in his sense, but belittling and subverting hunting-after in general (cf. *WD* 32ff.), then what evidently appears here is *revenge against revenge*.

3. To bring out fully his objection to Nietzsche let us stay with Heidegger's definition of revenge. A reading of the final section of *Ecce Homo* alone makes it apparent that Nietzsche far outdoes Voltaire's *Ecrasez l'infâme*, to which he refers at the conclusion: what he is concerned with is the *annihilation* of Christianity. Nor do we have to go into the question whether in the last resort Nietzsche really wanted to publish his 'Law against Christianity'[17] to discover in that '*Curse on Christianity*' represented by *The Anti-Christ* – which is, after all, the only book of the 'Revaluation of All Values' – belittling and subverting in plenty.

4. How seriously, especially in his last active year, Nietzsche took his 'war to the death' (*KGW* VI 3, 251) with Christianity, which for its part represented in his view 'mortal hostility towards life' (*Ecce Homo, KGW* VI 3, 372), also emerges with all possible clarity from his letters and drafts of letters of this time. His later self-descriptions[18] evidenced an over-estimation of the influence he was able to exert – an over-estimation which became pathological – but it brings no alteration to his assessment of the necessity for the 'revaluation'. From this point of view Nietzsche regards himself not as one Anti-Christ among others but as *the* Anti-Christ, which title is, as Salaquarda has convincingly shown, equated with the positive sense of a morality which has not grown out of *décadence*.[19]

5. Proceeding from this 'positive' a more penetrating understanding of the 'formula' is possible. In Nietzsche's later work the 'two types: *Dionysus* and *the Crucified*' are repeatedly related to one another. Seen as a whole they designate the antithesis between the fundamental Yes and the fundamental No to life. According to the nature of the matter under discussion Nietzsche understands this antithesis in a very wide or a narrower sense (which, however, does not exclude the wider sense). – A note of spring 1888 asserts the 'type of a well-constituted and ecstatically overflowing spirit', 'a type which takes into itself and *redeems* the contradictions of existence', to be that of the man of pagan religion who accounts '*Being as holy enough*' to 'justify even a monstrous amount of suffering'. Nietzsche finds such justification, which affirms 'even the harshest suffering', represented in '*Dionysus* of the Greeks'. – As opposed to him, the 'Crucified as the innocent one' counts for Nietzsche 'as an objection to this life, as a formula for its condemnation', i.e. revenge. What constitutes the difference between the two types is not the *martyrdom* they undergo but the *affirmation* or *denial of this world* which is held to be the *meaning* of it (*WM* 1052; KGW VIII 3, 57–59).

6. It is true that Nietzsche says there has been 'no *affirmative* philosophy, no *affirmative* religion'; nonetheless he finds 'historical signs of such movements', of which 'the pagan religion' is one. He also names 'Dionysus against the "Crucified" ', and finally 'the Renaissance. Art . . .' (*WM* 401; *KGW* VIII 3, 113). – The 'ideal' of the antithesis to denial of life is described by Nietzsche in, e.g., *Nietzsche contra Wagner*:

> He who is richest in abundance of life, the Dionysian god and man, is able to allow himself, not only the sight of the frightful and questionable, but even the frightful deed and every luxury of destruction, subversion, denial – in his case the evil, senseless, ugly seems as it were permitted.
>
> (*KGW* VI 3, 423)

Cruelty, which 'constitutes the great festive pleasure of earlier mankind', appears 'naïvely' and is as innocent as it is natural (*On the Genealogy of Morals, KGW* VI 2, 317ff.) – as opposed to that *ressentiment* cruelty which Nietzsche finds in Tertullian and in Thomas Aquinas (*loc. cit.*, 297ff.).

7. According to Nietzsche that naturalness of 'war' and cruelty is alien to the character of revenge rooted in *ressentiment*. Nor does the secondarily motivated hunting-after which Heidegger describes as revenge in the metaphysical sense correspond to Nietzsche's understanding of the Dionysian. What is involved in the latter is a *primary* power-willing (out of its own nature) whose intention is the enhancement of life and its long endurance. That the active and formative forces of which Nietzsche frequently speaks in this connection are able (indeed ought) to employ the devices of prudence and cunning cultivated during the course of history occasionally (at first sight) leads to their being confused with the postures of *ressentiment*.

8. The unbridgeable chasm which, according to Nietzsche, exists between reaction to the original natural action *and* action in the sense of primary power-willing as against secondary reaction is revealed with all possible clarity when, in *Twilight of the Idols* (also written in 1888), we find commended the 'spiritualisation of enmity', to which prudence, thoughtfulness, even forbearance towards the enemy are said to pertain. Such a posture presupposes that one 'profoundly grasps the value of having enemies'. One should act and think 'in the reverse of the way' in which one formerly did: if, e.g., the church again and again desired 'the destruction of its enemies', the 'immoralists and anti-Christians' for whom Nietzsche here speaks see that it is 'to their advantage that the church *exist*'. For, to Nietzsche's profounder understanding, the enemy is that upon which the power-willing is dependent – as upon the antithesis which must necessarily itself be strong if the power-will is to be strengthened (*KGW* VI 3, 78). Thus, according to a note of 1887, to the declaration of war on the 'chlorotic Christian ideal' there pertains the imperative desire for its 'continuance': 'to become *strong*' one's own ideals

must 'have *strong* opponents' (*Nachlass, KGW* I VIII 2, 189). This conception receives a final intensification in Nietzsche's 'evocation of the enemies' who are needed for the sake of one's own ideal. One elevates and transforms oneself when one transforms 'the enemies that are one's equals into gods' (*GA* XIV 274; *Nachlass, KGW* VII 1, 540).

9. Inasmuch as in the name of Dionysus Nietzsche simultaneously pursues the destruction of his enemies and their deification, the question arises whether or not his philosophy possesses an inner unity. His idea of the eternal recurrence of the same brings about the reconcilability of the extremes: the Dionysian affirmation of life, which, since the frightful, destructive and deny-ing pertain to life, must include these in its affirmation, cannot in the last resort deny even the denial directed against life – for this is (according to Nietzsche's presuppositions) itself an expression of life. Nietzsche notes: 'by approving of everything one also approves of all present and past *approvals* and rejections!' (*GA* XIII 74; *Nachlass, KGW* VII 2, 103). He even goes beyond approval of that which should be denied in that he imposes upon the hoped-for overman the demand that its unending repetition should be his *highest desideratum* – in doing which he asks of him the extreme of extensivity and intensity in the accommodation of the idea of recurrence.[20]

VI

The formula 'Dionysus against the Crucified', from which we started in order to test the legitimacy of Heidegger's objection that Nietzsche himself falls captive to the spirit of revenge which he claims to overcome, has proved to be ambiguous. Heidegger's interpretation has turned out to be an inadequate simplification of a very complex ideational structure. Its ambiguity comes to light in the differing ways of defining the 'against . . .' through which the characteristic quality of 'Dionysus' is concretised on any given occasion. Nietzsche's Dionysus has many faces. To the one 'the Crucified' appears as him whom Dionysus is to fight and destroy without reservation: to the other this opposition takes the form of a forbearance towards the enemy which even has as its goal the enemy's strengthening, in which it is revealed that for its own sake Dionysian strength requires a strong opponent and which can he taken to the point of the deification of this opponent. And in the final analysis the 'against' is for Dionysus no longer an opponent at all but that which is *taken into* the Dionysian nature. Even *décadence*, and even in its form of unreserved *denial* of life, is drawn into his natural life-affirmation by Dionysus. In this process the '*against*' of denial becomes an *element* of the Dionysian.

If one wants to do something more than simply indict Nietzsche for inconsistency one has to draw distinctions. The idea set forth here can be interpreted as a *succession* of philosophical positions. Dionysus, who in the final formula of *Ecce Homo* enters the lists against the 'Crucified', appears first of all as him who is concerned to *destroy* his opponent. In this sense Dionysus is Anti-Christ without his nature being limited to this 'Anti-'.[21] Deeper penetration into the nature of the Dionysian reveals that what is beneficial to one's own force and strength is not the destruction but the preservation, indeed the enhancement of the strength of one's opponent. And finally Dionysian life-affirmation finds its supreme expression in the inclusion of even the powers that will denial of life. The 'highest desideratum' is that everything that has been and is should return as it has been and is. In accordance with the Dionysian 'faith' 'only what is separate and individual may be rejected' here, while 'in the totality everything is redeemed and affirmed'. When Nietzsche finally says of this 'highest of all possible faiths' '*it no longer denies*' (*Twilight of the Idols*, *KGW* VI 3, 146), the formula 'Dionysus against the Crucified' appears to have been cancelled by Nietzsche himself. But we have to read meticulously. Nietzsche does not say that faith denies *nothing* any longer (thus does not deny 'what is separate and individual'): for, as an aimless 'play of forces and waves of forces' the unceasing struggle constitutes the 'world of the eternally self-creating, the eternally self-destroying' (*WM* 1067; *KGW* VII 3, 338f.).

In such a progression by stages Nietzsche's philosophy proves to be more coherent than they are willing to admit who, by referring to superficial contradictions or to his criticism of systems on principle, want to brand Nietzsche a romantic aphorist or an 'artist-philosopher'. Nonetheless, with regard to the inner compatibility of the ideas of the later Nietzsche many questions do remain open. But it is beyond question that Nietzsche did not in the end fall captive to the spirit of revenge which he had opposed in *Zarathustra* as Heidegger thinks he did. Moreover, Nietzsche resisted on principle any attempt definitively to tie him down to anything he had said: for in his view every philosophy is a 'foreground philosophy' which *conceals* an (other) philosophy. 'Every opinion is also a hiding-place, every word also a mask.' According to Nietzsche one ought to 'doubt whether a philosopher *could* have "final and real" opinions at all, whether behind each of his caves there does not and must not lie another, deeper cave – a stranger, more comprehensive world beyond the surface, an abyss behind every ground, beneath every "foundation"' (*Beyond Good and Evil*, *KGW* VI 2, 44).

Notes

1. Abbreviations employed in the text for editions of Nietzsche: *KGW* (*Nietzsche: Werke. Kritische Gesamtausgabe*, ed. G. Colli and M. Montinari, 1967ff.); *GA* ('*Grossoktav-Ausgabe*': *Fr. Nietzsche: Werke*, 1894ff.); *WM* (the *Nachlass* compilation *Der Wille zur Macht* in the arrangement in *GA* XV and XVI; the numeral in the text is in each case the number of the aphorism). – *GA* and *WM* are referred to because they

formed the basis of Heidegger's reading of Nietzsche. Abbreviations employed in the text for Heidegger's writings: *Hu* (*Über den Humanismus*, n.d. [1947]); *WD* (*Was heist Denken?*, 1954); *VA* (*Vorträge und Aufsätze*, 1954); *N1* (*Nietzsche*, Vol. 1, 1961); *SD* (*Zur Sache des Denkens*, 1969); *Her* (*Heraklit. Vorlesungen* 1943, 1944, *Gesamtausgabe*, Vol. 55, 1979).

2. On the foregoing see O. Pöggeler: *Der Denkweg Martin Heideggers* (1963), 104; *ibid*: *Philosophie und Politik bei Heidegger* (1972), 26, 106.

3. See, e.g., his rectorial address *Die Selbstbehauptung der deutschen Universität* (1934). On the transformation of the existential of *resolution* after *Sein und Zeit* (1927) via its definition as *will to self-responsibility* (in the address mentioned and again in Heidegger's lectures of 1935) to *abolition of the willed* in the later Heidegger's concept of resolution, see A. Schwan: *Politische Philosophie im Denken Heideggers* (1965); and the author's 'Das Willenswesen und der Übermensch. Ein Beitrag zu Heideggers Nietzsche-interpretation', in *Nietzsche-Studien* 10 (1981).

4. '*Spiegel-Gespräch*' with Martin Heidegger: *Der Spiegel* 30 (1976), Vol. 23, 204

5. See the author's 'Das Willenswesen und der Übermensch', *op. cit.*, 165ff.

6. We can only indicate here the transformation Heidegger's understanding of *Thus Spoke Zarathustra* underwent between the 1930s and the 1950s. According to his interpretation of 1937, Nietzsche's poem about the figure of Zarathustra is much influenced by the 'making tangible of the idea of recurrence', it is intended to represent (abstract) truth in sensory form and 'consequently as a symbol': hence 'the figure of the teacher' can in the end 'be comprehended only from the teaching', even though this has, conversely, required 'the fashioning of the teacher'. But this fashioning nonetheless remained for the earlier Heidegger only the *preliminary stage* of the essential steps which Nietzsche took *after Thus Spoke Zarathustra* (*N1*, 286–288) – in 1953 the question 'Who is Nietzsche's Zarathustra?' becomes the fundamental metaphysical question (*VA* 101ff), especially since 'nowhere else in the history of Western metaphysics' was the 'essential form of its current thinker . . . specifically . . . thought out' – except perhaps for Parmenides (*VA* 123). The chapter central to Heidegger's interpretation of 1951–53, 'Of Redemption', receives only a casual mention in the lecture of 1937 (*N1*, 289); since the theme of revenge was not raised at that time, the sentence from 'Of the Tarantulas' (see above) was also ignored.

7. Heidegger refers to Schelling's book of 1809 on the essence of human freedom, in which be says that will is 'primeval Being' to which alone 'all predicates of the same' are appropriate: groundlessness, eternity, independence of time, self-affirmation' (*Schellings Werke*, ed. M. Schröter, IV 242).

8. On this see the author's 'Das Willenswesen und der Übermensch', *op. cit.*, 146ff.

9. I refer to W. Benjamin's remarks in the *Zentralpark* fragments, where he says, e.g., that the idea of recurrence owes its 'sudden topicality' to a trail 'of economic circumstances'; also to his proposition: 'The doctrine of eternal recurrence is a dream of the tremendous inventions imminent in the domain of reproduction technology!' (in Walter Benjamin's *Charles Baudelaire*, ed. R. Tiedeman [1974], 159, 176). – Benjamin refers to Blanqui and to Baudelaire, for whom the idea of recurrence possessed, he says, considerable importance (e.g. *op. cit.* 169). – It can only be mentioned here that this idea has during the nineteenth and twentieth centuries been taken up from widely differing approaches.

10. I can refer only in passing to the fact that Heidegger cites a draft of Nietzsche's (for the preface to *The Gay Science*) as evidence that the latter conclusively succumbed to the spirit of revenge. As Heidegger quotes him, Nietzsche finds in himself 'a kind of sublime malice and ultimate wantonness of revenge – for there is *revenge* in it, revenge on life itself, when one who suffers deeply *takes life under his protection*' (*GA* XIV 404f.; *Nachlass*, *KGW* VIII 1, 144). Nietzsche's thought that among the forms

assumed by revenge on life is that of being relatively *favourably inclined* towards it certainly deserves serious consideration. As a psychologist Nietzsche expended a great deal of care on exhibiting the varying forms in which preservation of life is in truth intent on its *gradual* destruction. According to the *Genealogy of Morals* the 'ascetic priest', for example, 'revenges' himself on life in this fashion. If we regard Nietzsche's portrayal of types of *décadent* (among whom as at once *décadent* and 'healthy man' he classes himself), we can only be surprised to see that Heidegger draws from the sentence he quotes the conclusion: 'Zarathustra's teaching does not bring redemption from revenge' (*VA* 122). What is also astonishing about this conclusion of Heidegger's is that he makes no distinction between Nietzsche's description of the state of his existence at this time or that (the significance of which for his work is uncontested) and the 'ideal' demands of Nietzsche's 'fictional' character Zarathustra (cf. *VA* 123). How necessary this is is shown by, e.g., a note of Nietzsche's of the end of 1882: 'I do not want life *again*. How have I endured it? Creating. What makes me bear the sight of it? The sight of the overman, who *affirms* life. I have tried to affirm it *myself*. – Ah! (*Nachlass*, *KGW* VII I, 139; *GA* XII 359). – In any event, it is all the less permissible to deny the validity of Zarathustra's teaching of redemption from revenge by appealing to Nietzsche's self-analysis if (as the later Heidegger does) one sees in the former the fabricated image of self-consummating Western thought.

11. From the point of view of Nietzsche's doctrine of the overman I have, in *Nietzsche. Seine Philosophie der Gegensätze und die Gegensätze seiner Philosophie* (1971), especially 186ff., demonstrated the ambiguity of the doctrine of recurrence.

12. Heidegger, who quotes Nietzsche from *GA*, remarks, *op. cit.*, that *WM* 617 belongs 'to the time immediately after the completion of *Thus Spoke Zarathustra*, 'to the year 1885'. *KGW* assigns the note to the period 'end of 1886–Spring 1887'. – Heidegger further remarks: 'the note carries the underlined heading *"recapitulation"*. Nietzsche is here with an uncommon clear-sightedness assembling the principal elements of his thought into a few propositions.' Yet this heading does not derive from Nietzsche; it was added by P. Gast (see *GA* XVI, 508). – Whether or not the said heading is appropriate to the notes Nietzsche has put together here remains to be seen: in any event what is involved is a *Nachlass* fragment of outstanding importance. We would, to be sure, need to view the various tendencies which Nietzsche ventilates in what is only apparently a disconnected way in their mutual reference and relevance, which would naturally demand an interpretation in detail. Here I can only adduce the themes which in their turn and in their own ways could forward the ascent to the 'high point of the meditation': falsification in all cognition; the fallacy of knowledge of oneself; the necessity of determining that which is thought of as 'life' under the name 'will to power'; the opposition of all becoming things to one another as their numbers vary; the unusability of present world-interpretations; Zarathustra's parodistic posture towards present evaluations. – The 'heavy clouds' in which Heidegger saw this high point enshrouded would presumably have cleared a little if he had not supported his interpretation solely with the two most prominent sentences of the fragment (and this, moreover, in the light of his own particular pre-judgement in the realm of the history of metaphysics).

13. Heidegger's analyses of Nietzsche's concept of revenge are in 1951–52 and 1953 nourished by his reference to the 'long familiar idea of time as a passing away', 'as a flowing off of one-after-the-other, as a rolling up and rolling away of every "now"' (*WD* 40). They give him a further opportunity of deriving Nietzsche's thought, in this case his understanding of time, from the history of Western metaphysics. Let us leave aside whether or not the basic experiences of temporality are not more natural and original than those of any interpretation of history, whether or not Aristotle and Augustine, Kant and Hegel, 'asserted and advanced various lines of interpretation of

its factual content' because this factual content is given with the Being of man and cannot be gone beyond, and not because the boundaries of interpretation were fixed by the history of metaphysics, as Heidegger seeks to demonstrate (*WD* 38ff.). The later Heidegger here stands opposed to the Heidegger of *Sein und Zeit*. – In any event, 'the concepts of ordinary language concerning time' seem even in regard to the natural sciences and even as regards the theory of relativity to be 'More stable and solid' than 'the precise concepts of the language of science', which are always in danger of being applicable 'only to a very restricted portion of reality' (W. Heisenberg: *Physik und Philosophie* [Frankfurt-am-Main, 1959, 168ff.).

14. On the problems arising from this see my book *Nietzsche, op. cit.*, 10–32.

15. Heidegger prepares this expansion through a reflection of fundamental importance on the true nature of *metaphysical reversal*. His *reversal* must be distinguished from Nietzsche's *revaluation*. *Revaluation* still stays more enclosed within the metaphysical domain than does the *reversal* imagined by Heidegger. Thus, e.g., according to Heidegger the antithesis of the supra-sensory and the sensory still persists even when the 'Platonic order of rank' between them is 'reversed' (*VA* 122). *Revaluation* in Nietzche's sense remains for him only foreground, if not appearance. As is well known, Heidegger frequently employed the interpretational metaphor of reversal: by regarding processes of change in the history of philosophy as events occurring within metaphysics he is able to ignore what is distinctive and new in whatever comes to light in the course of this change. Thus, e.g., Marx (together with Nietzsche) is dismissed to the extent that his thought remains, as metaphysical reversal, within metaphysics and does not lead beyond it (*Hu* 23f.), just as Sartre's reversal of a metaphysical proposition (that in the case of man existence precedes essence) remains a metaphysical proposition and does not touch on what is solely essential in the history of Being (*Hu* 17). Thus, according to Heidegger, Nietzsche's reversal of the antithesis of a supra-sensory and sensory also undergoes no essential modification from the fact that in Nietzsche the sensory 'is experienced more essentially and broadly in a sense designated by the name *Dionysus*': as 'the superabundance after which Zarathustra's "great longing" is directed', the inexhaustible continuance of becoming as which the will to power wills itself in the eternal recurrence of the same events' (*VA* 123f.). If, however (thus Heidegger), considered metaphysically nothing happens in the reversal of order of rank other than that supra-sensory and sensory change places, one cannot see why the counter-will can be directed (by the representatives of the supra-sensory) only against life (the sensory) and could not, in accordance with the relationship of reversal, also display itself as revenge, e.g., on Platonism and Christianity.

16. By the symbol 'the Crucified', just as by the symbols 'God on the Cross' or 'Christ on the Cross', Nietzsche does not mean the *historical Jesus*, he means decadent morality as 'the basic trend of later Christianity ... as whose actual founder Nietzsche designates Paul', as J. Salaquarda correctly says ('Dionysos gegen den Gekreuzigten, in Nietzsche', ed. J. Salaquarda [1980], 296ff.). Salaquarda points to the 'untenable consequences' to which it must lead if one understands the great opponent of Nietzsche's Dionysus to be *Jesus*, as K. Jaspers and *mutatis mutandis*, P. Wolff do (*op. cit.*, 317). – For Nietzsche's understanding of Paul, H. Lüdemann's 'Anthropologie des Apostels Paulus' has been considerably influential, as Salaquarda and – independently of him – M. Jacob, employing Nietzsche's excerpts, have shown (*op. cit.*, 29ff., 314f., 321f.). We can also agree with Salaquarda that, beside his reading of Dostoevsky, Wellhausen and Renan, Tolstoy's *Ma Religion* provided 'the final impetus for distinguishing in principle between Jesus and Paul' such as Nietzsche emphasized in the 'psychology of the redeemer' in *The Anti-Christ* (*op. cit.*, 292).

17. See M. Montinari's note in *KGW* VI 3, 161.

18. Cf. M. Montinari: *Chronik zu Nietzsches Leben. Kritische Studienausgabe* (1980), Vol. 15, 181ff.

19. In 'Der Antichrist'. *Nietzsche-Studien* 2 (1973), 105ff.

20. See the author's *Nietzsche, op. cit.*, 139ff.

21. See J. Salaquarda: 'Der Antichrist', *op.* cit., 105ff. – As soon as the first review of *Zarathustra* I appeared it was clear to Nietzsche that he could at first be understood only in his exoteric popular anti-Christian aspect. Salaquarda has demonstrated this through two letters of Nietzsche's to P. Gast and F. Overbeck at the end of August 1883 (*op. cit.*, 103): the deeper meaning of Nietzsche's anti-Christianity would have to be reserved for the 'philosophers of the future' (*cf. op. cit.*, 106).

50

Opening and Closing the Possibility of a Feminine Other*

Kelly Oliver

*Source: Kelly Oliver, *Womanizing Nietzsche*, Routledge, 1995, pp. 10–32, 202–4.

Freud's Femininity: Fear of Birth

> Throughout history people have knocked their heads against the riddle of the nature of femininity – Heads in hieroglyphic bonnets, Heads in turbans and black birettas, Heads in wigs and thousand other Wretched, sweating heads of humans. Nor will you have escaped worrying over this problem – those of you who are men; to those of you who are women this will not apply – you are yourselves the problem.
>
> (Sigmund Freud, 'Femininity')

Many feminists have wondered whose sweating heads have knocked against the riddle of femininity. To whom is Freud speaking? To whom is femininity a mystery? And who can we trust to solve this riddle? This riddle cannot be solved by contemporary science or psychoanalysis (Freud, F 114). Freud tells 'us' all he can about femininity, but admits that it is 'incomplete and fragmentary.' Freud says that we will have to wait for the scientists or turn to the poets to solve the riddle of femininity (F 135). In other words, even if he cannot solve it, there are other men who might be able to. It seems clear that Freud addresses himself to other men about women. Women and femininity are his object but not participants in the discussion.

Sarah Kofman argues in *The Enigma of Woman*, however, that Freud did not want to 'speak among men' and exclude women from his discussion of femininity. First, she posits that Freud explicitly addresses himself to a 'mixed public': 'Ladies and Gentlemen . . . ' Second, she asserts that Freud is trying to 'establish complicity with the women analysts so as to clear himself of the suspicion of "antifeminism"' (104). Third, she maintains that Freud cannot be excluding women because that assumes that women are the opposite of men, which is what Freud is arguing against with his bisexuality thesis – Freud claims that all humans, especially women, are innately bisexual, both masculine and feminine.

I disagree. In spite of Freud's ironic 'ladies and gentlemen' and his flirtation with the women analysts – I will come back to the bisexuality thesis – it seems undeniable that he makes women the objects of his investigation while men are the subjects: 'Nor will *you* have escaped worrying over this problem – those of you who are men; to those of you who are women this will not apply – you are yourselves the problem' (Freud, F 113). Kofman admits that Freud makes women his accomplices in their own objectification, oppression, and silencing (see *EW* 47, 222). And even though she defends Freud as addressing women as subjects, Kofman argues that Freud creates women as the type of object for psychoanalysis that he takes them to be; he/ psychoanalysis makes women into hysterics. I maintain that Freud not only makes women into a particular kind of object of psychoanalysis, the hysteric, but also excludes the possibility of women subjects in his discussion of femininity.

One of Kofman's most powerful examples of how Freud turns women into hysterics is her interpretation of Freud's dream of Irma's injection. Freud interprets the dream to be a manifestation of his wish not be responsible for Irma's continued pains. At one point in the dream, as Freud recounts it, Irma refuses to open her mouth and Freud attributes her reluctance to 'female recalcitrance.' Kofman argues that what Freud's dream tells him is that he has injected his female patients with a dirty solution, psychoanalysis, that makes their sexuality dirty and shameful:

> If Freud has such an urgent need to excuse himself, it is because he knows perfectly well that he himself is the criminal. Not only because he has not yet cured Irma, but, as another part of the dream indicates, because he himself (a transgression attributed in both the dream and the interpretation to his friend Otto) has infected her with his symbolic-spermatic 'solution' – trimethylamin – injected with a dirty syringe. The term 'trimethylamin' brings to mind the learned solutions he has thrown in his patients' faces: if Irma and all indomitable women refuse to open their mouths and their genitals, it is because Freud has already transformed each of these organs into a 'cavity filled with pus,' has closed women's mouths himself, has made them frigid, by injecting them with a learned, malignant, male solution.
>
> (*EW* 47)

Kofman suggests that the dream of Irma's injection is another manifestation of Freud's fear of femininity and his fear of listening to women; he is afraid of the terrifying sight of open female genitals or their open mouths.

Many of his feminist critics argue that Freud fears feminine sexuality (for example, Cixous, Irigaray, Gallop).[1] His bisexuality thesis might be further evidence of this fear. In 'Female Sexuality' he argues that women are more bisexual than men because the have two erotic zones, one masculine and one feminine; they are hermaphrodites of a sort (FS 228). Freud claims that the women in his audience who are intelligent enough to understand him are more masculine than feminine (F 116–17). But the bisexuality of men goes unanalyzed. What of the feminine in men? Freud protects himself against this radically other sexuality, feminine sexuality, this 'Minoan-Mycenean civiliz-ation,' as he calls it, by always comparing the situation of women to the situation of men, by turning women into men.

There are many ways in which Freud turns women into men, femininity into masculinity. He maintains that for both boys and girls the first love object (with which they identify) is the phallic mother; this makes the mother masculine and it makes infants of both sexes masculine-identified. In add-ition, Freud claims that there is only one libido, masculine libido. Also, he defines all sexuality, both masculine and feminine, in terms of castration, having or not having the penis.[2] He reduces the clitoris to an inferior penis – never mind that this contradicts his claim that women are already castrated. In 'Female Sexuality' he explicitly claims that 'it will help our exposition if, as we go along, we compare the state of things in women with that in men' (FS 227).

It will be profitable at this point, in order to analyze Freud's troubled relation to the feminine, to enter a debate between Irigaray and Kofman over Freud's equation of phallus and logos. Luce Irigaray argues that by turning women into men and femininity into masculinity, Freud excludes women and the feminine from culture, from logos (*SOW* 14). In *The Enigma of Woman* Sarah Kofman, in the name of 'intellectual honesty,' defends Freud against Irigaray's powerful criticism of 'Femininity.' She maintains that 'nothing in the text ['Femininity'] justifies Luce Irigaray's reading (according to which Freud, like Aristotle, deprives women of the right to the logos and phallus alike). We have seen that things are not that simple. And even supposing that Freud wished to speak among men of the enigma of femininity (which is not the case), that would not suffice to condemn him as a metaphysician' (104). While Kofman is right that Freud's text is fraught with ambiguities, there is plenty in his 'Femininity' to justify Irigaray's claim that his theory deprives women of the right to the logos and phallus. And Irigaray does not 'condemn Freud as a metaphysician' because he speaks among men about women. Rather, Irigaray condemns Freud as a metaphysician because of the central-ity of presence in his account of the evolution of subjectivity and sexual difference: for Freud everything hinges on the sight/presence of the male organ; both masculine and feminine sexuality are defined in terms of its presence.

Irigaray's 'condemnation' of Freud as metaphysician, however, is not unambiguous. She maintains that Freud makes a double move in relation to metaphysics:

Thus Freud would strike at least two blows at the scene of representation. One, as it were, directly, when he destroys a certain conception of the present or presence, when he stresses secondary revision, over-determination, repetition compulsion, the death drive, etc., or when he indicates, in his practice, the impact of so-called unconscious mechanisms on the discourse of the 'subject.' The other blow, blinder and less direct, occurs when – himself a prisoner of a certain economy of the logos, of a certain logic, notably of 'desire,' whose link to classical philosophy he fails to see – he defines sexual difference as a function of the a priori of the same, having recourse, to support this demonstration, to the age-old pro-cesses: analogy, comparison, symmetry, dichotomic oppositions, and so on. When, as a card-carrying member of an 'ideology' that he never ques-tions, he insists that the sexual pleasure known as masculine is the para-digm for all sexual pleasure, to which all representations of pleasure can but defer in reference, support, and submission.

(SOW 28)

So while in one move Freud exposes a crisis in the metaphysics of presence, with a second move he closes off the possibility of acknowledging the impact of that crisis. The primary processes call into question the metaphysics of a fully present subject, but the identification of those primary processes with the masculine libido closes off all possible discussion of difference. Irigaray argues that Freud leaves us with an economy of representation of the same, a hom(m)o-sexual economy. Kofman, on the other hand, takes issue with Irigaray's claim that Freud invokes science in the name of this masculine economy of the same. She argues that Freud does not invoke science to reassert sameness, as Irigaray claims, but rather to undermine popular opin-ions and stereotypes with regard to the sexes, especially the notion that the feminine is passive while the masculine is active (*EW*, 112, 115).

Yet, if we look at the passage in which Freud most insistently invokes science and denies the connection between femininity and passivity and mas-culinity and activity, it becomes clear that even while Freud sets out to break down popular prejudice, he reinforces it through his rhetoric. He points out that 'the male sex-cell is actively mobile and searches out the female one, and the latter, the ovum, is immobile and waits passively. This behavior of the elementary sexual organisms is indeed a model for the conduct of sexual individuals during intercourse. The male pursues the female for the purpose of sexual union, seizes hold of her and penetrates into her' (F 114). Then he warns that this reduces masculinity to aggressiveness and that in some species the females are stronger than the males; so it is 'inadequate ... to make masculine behavior coincide with activity and feminine with passivity' (F 115). Immediately after claiming that we should not associate masculinity with activity and femininity with passivity, Freud does so anyway. He argues that though mothers exhibit activity, their activity is a sort of active passivity necessary to carry on the species. Next he makes a distinction between passivity and having passive aims. He suggests that even though the female has passive aims, this does not make her passive. He qualifies the later claim by pointing out that we should not underestimate social customs that condition women to have passive aims. But no sooner has he issued this warning than he says, 'There is one particularly constant relation between femininity and instinctual life which we do not want to overlook'; this constant is masochism (F 116). So every time that Freud warns us against the prejudices of science in the very next breath he reiterates them.

Although Kofman is right that Freud allows for women to enter society and have the right to the logos and the phallus, women do so only through the masculine. It is only Freud's bisexuality thesis that allows him to admit women into the order of the logos, because for Freud the feminine is antithetical to the logos and the phallus. To feminist ears Freud sounds outrageous when he says: 'For the ladies, whenever some comparison seemed to turn out unfavorable to their sex, were able to utter a suspicion that we, the male analysts, had been unable to overcome certain deeply-rooted prejudices against what was feminine, and that this was being paid for in the partiality of our researches. We, on the other hand, standing on the ground of bisexuality, had no difficulty in avoiding impoliteness. We had only to say: "This doesn't apply to *you*. You're the exception; on this point you're more masculine than feminine"' (F 116–117). Ultimately Kofman explains the ambiguities in Freud's writings on femininity as manifestations of his fear of death. In the following paragraphs, I will explain them as manifestations of Freud's fear of birth.

The riddle of femininity is really the riddle of masculinity. The question that is really at stake for Freud is how is masculinity possible – how can the male, who was once part of the female/mother, be masculine? It is necessary that Freud explain femininity in order to safeguard masculinity. If he can't guarantee that the masculine is not identified with the feminine, one possible safeguard is to make the feminine masculine after all. In this way even if the masculine is identified with the feminine (or the mother), it is not threatened.

I maintain that Freud's solution to this problem is the fetishist's solution. He argues that little girls are in the beginning little men. That is, their sexuality is phallic and they are more masculine than feminine. In fact *this* is the mystery of femininity: how do masculine little girls, little men, become women? For Freud a little girl's erotic zone is masculine and her clitoris is a small penis: 'Anatomy has recognized the clitoris within the female pudenda as being an organ that is homologous to the penis; and the physiology of the sexual processes has been able to add that this small penis which does not grow any bigger behaves in fact during childhood like a real and genuine penis' (OSTC 217). The clitoris operates as a penis equivalent. Hers, however, as Freud tells us, is obviously inferior. Why is it inferior if it functions in the same way and brings the same phallic pleasure, and if, as Freud says, 'frequent erections of that organ make it possible for girls to form a correct judgment, even without any instruction, of the sexual manifestations of the other sex' (TE 219–20)? As Kofman points out it can only be the size of the girl's 'penis' that makes her inferior. Sexual difference, then, is not a matter of kind or quality, but a matter of degree or quantity – unless at a small enough size the penis becomes feminine. Perhaps this is Freud's fear. He is afraid that the masculine is really feminine.

This is always the fear of players in what Irigaray calls the 'game of castration' (*ML* 80). Within the economy of castration there is no qualitative difference; everything is measured in terms of quantity. Irigaray criticizes the economy of castration because within it there can be no depth: 'To simulate depth in the guise of the bigger or the smaller. To bring erection and limpness into the game of castration. And the other into the same: a comparison between the bigger and the smaller, the harder and the softer, etc., until it becomes impossible to evaluate anything except in terms of *less* and *more*' (ML 80–81). Playing the game of castration Freud reduces all sexual difference to a question of less and more.

Like the fetishist who cannot bear the mother's castration and substitutes another object for the mother's missing penis in order to protect the mother from castration (and ultimately reassure himself that he is not castrated), Freud substitutes the clitoris for the missing penis. Oddly enough, it is the impossible combination of women's castration and inferior penis that erects masculine sexuality. As Kofman says, 'only the Freudian solution, that of granting woman an incomplete sexuality envious of man's penis, makes it possible at once to recognize woman's castration and to overcome one's own castration anxiety' (*EW* 89). 'Woman's genital organs arouse an inseparable blend of horror and pleasure; they at once awaken and appease castration anxiety' (*EW* 85).

Like the fetishist, Freud has it both ways. The mother is both castrated and phallic. This ambiguity is necessary for Freud to imagine that masculinity is possible at all. The real problem for Freud is, how is it that the male, once part of the woman's body, becomes masculine? His concern for how the female performs the difficult task of changing both erogenous zones and love objects covers up the prior concern for the male's transition from literal identity with a female maternal body and a psychic identification with the mother to not only a separate body but also a separate sexual identity. One way that Freud explains this transition is to invent the masculine mother, the mother who is either phallic or castrated, but never feminine. So Freud's conflicted theory of femininity and the phallic/castrated mother can be read as symptoms of the fetishist's logic. And these symptoms can be read as manifestations of a fear of birth; man fears his birth out of the body of a woman. For Freud there is nothing more frightening than the thought of being buried alive, which is the fear of internment in the maternal womb.

Freud turns all sexuality and all desire into masculine sexuality and desire.

While he opens up the discussion of sexual difference, at the same time he closes off the possibility of sexual difference. In this way, as Irigaray suggests, Freud makes a double move to both challenge and protect a metaphysics of presence that favors the presence of the phallus. He resorts to the fetishist's logic in order to ensure that the phallus is present in both sexes. So while he opens up the discussion of an other to representation – the unconscious, repressed and over-determined – at the same time he closes off the possibility of a specifically feminine other. Freud's psychoanalytic theories invite attempts to represent the other but, like more traditional theories of representation, continue to exclude the feminine from representation.

Nietzsche's Wisdom: A Dagger through the Heart[3]

> Would a woman be able to captivate us (or, as people say, to 'fetter' us) whom we did not credit with knowing how to employ the dagger (any kind of dagger) skillfully against us under certain circumstances? Or against herself; which in a certain case might be the severest revenge (the Chinese revenge).
>
> (Friedrich Nietzsche, *Gay Science*)

Like Freud, Nietzsche in his way opens up the discussion of representing the other and yet closes off the possibility of representing the feminine other. He opens up the possibility of interpreting otherwise, but he excludes woman from the process of interpretation. As an example, I will read *On the Genealogy of Morals* as a call for a type of reading and writing that engage in active interpretation which is not the product of traditional philosophical rationality. There Nietzsche describes a process of reading and writing otherwise that is sensuous and bodily. Yet for Nietzsche, as for Freud, the body out of which reading and writing surge is always a male body. Like Freud's, Nietzsche's writing denies any place for woman or the feminine except as objects. As we will see, this is evidenced by all (necessarily awkward) attempts to answer the question 'As a woman, how can I read Nietzsche's text?'

Nietzsche begins the third essay of *On the Genealogy of Morals* with an aphorism from *Thus Spake Zarathustra*: 'Unconcerned, mocking, violent – thus wisdom wants *us*: she is a woman and always loves only a warrior' (*OGM* 97 III 1).[4] What is the relationship between Nietzsche's warrior and the woman, wisdom? Provocatively, Nietzsche suggests that this aphorism is part of a lesson in reading. We cannot learn, however, Nietzsche's lesson in reading unless we explore the relationship between the warrior and the woman, wisdom.

In the preface to *On the Genealogy of Morals*, Nietzsche claims that the third essay is an exegesis of Zarathustra's aphorism. The connection between the third essay and the aphorism, however, is far from obvious. In the preface

Nietzsche suggests that he is giving us a lesson in 'reading as an art.' As always, Nietzsche leaves his reader to learn the lesson the hard way, to take up the place of the warrior and do violence to the text, in order to create some connection between this aphorism and the apparent topic of the third essay, the meaning of the ascetic ideal.

The title of the third essay is 'What Is the Meaning of Ascetic Ideals?' – a question that Nietzsche asks over and over throughout the essay. He does not repeat the question in order to emphasize some particular characteristic of the ascetic ideal. Rather, he repeats the question in order to emphasize a particular style of reading, genealogy, which diagnoses *the meaning* of various cultural symptoms. The third essay is as much about meaning as it is about ascetic ideals; the meaning of ascetic ideals is a pretext for a performance of reading as interpretation, reading as an art. Not only is Nietzsche artfully reading the meaning of ascetic ideals, he is also reading the meaning of Zarathustra's aphorism – his analysis of the meaning of ascetic ideals poses as an exegesis of Zarathustra's aphorism. More than this, he is reading the meaning of meaning itself: what does it mean to ask about the meaning of the ascetic ideal? What does it mean to do genealogy?

Nietzsche's redoubling of meaning is a *performance* of the dynamics of reading. 'What does that *mean*?' asks Nietzsche, 'for this fact has to be interpreted: *in itself* it just stands there, stupid to all eternity, like every "thing-in-itself"' (*OGM* 107 III 7). To answer the question 'What does it mean?' we have to interpret. Yet the question 'What does it mean?' is the screw upon which the ascetic ideal itself turns; the ascetic ideal requires that life and suffering have a meaning. 'What is the meaning?' is the ascetic question par excellence. Nietzsche turns the ascetic ideal back on itself in order to ask 'What is the meaning of ascetic ideals?' or 'What is the meaning of demanding some meaning?'

In *Nietzsche and the Question of Interpretation*, Alan Schrift suggests that Nietzsche uses meaning 'not in the epistemological sense of uncovering the true referent or the accurate representation of a state of affairs, but rather in the psycho-genealogical sense of *deciphering* the significance which these ideals hold as a symptom of the health or disease of the will to power that has posited them as ideal' (173, my emphasis).[5] Because we have to interpret even Nietzsche's theory of meaning, however, Nietzsche's use of 'meaning' can be read *both* in the epistemological sense of uncovering the true referent – the rhetorical maneuver that Schrift himself makes when he claims to uncover the true referent of Nietzsche's use of 'meaning' – and in the psychogenealogical sense of deciphering the significance of ideals. It depends on how we read. I will link these two types of reading with the two types of morality that Nietzsche describes in *On the Genealogy of Morals*. I will associate uncovering meaning in the epistemological sense with the slave morality and uncovering meaning in the psychogenealogical sense with the master morality.

We could say that just as Nietzsche proposes an active and a reactive morality in *Genealogy*, he proposes an active and a reactive reading. He describes the logic of slave morality as reactive – imaginarily reactive at that – and the logic of the master morality as active (*OGM* 36–37 I 10).[6] Unlike the slave, the master affirms him directly without a hostile external world. He is unconcerned about differences and this is his potency. He is strong enough not to feel threatened by what is outside himself, what is not he: – 'While every noble morality develops from a triumphant affirmation of itself, slave morality from the outset says No to what is outside, what is different, what is not itself; ... [the noble valuation] acts and grows spontaneously, it seeks its opposite only so as to affirm itself more gratefully and triumphantly – its negative concept low, common, bad is only subsequently-invented pale, contrasting image in relation to its positive basic concept – filled with life and passion through and through' (*OGM* 36–37 I 10).

Like the noble morality, the artful reader does not say no to difference in order to affirm only the self same.[7] Like active morality, active reading affirms itself directly and is therefore open to differences. Whereas active reading opens and multiplies the text, reactive reading closes and narrows the text. Just as the slave can only affirm himself in opposition, as a reaction, to a hostile external world, the reactive reader requires an interpretation that puts itself forth against all other interpretations as the only possible truth of the text. This reading is a reaction to what the reader takes to be the transcendent meaning of the text, its true referent. By claiming to have discovered the transcendent meaning of the text, the reactive reader can claim authority for his interpretation alone. Ascetic interpretation is reactive reading at its limit: 'The ascetic ideal has a goal – this goal is so universal that all the other interests of human existence seem, when compared with it, petty and narrow; it interprets epochs, nations, and men inexorably with a view to this one goal; it permits no other interpretation, no other goal; it rejects, denies, affirms, and sanctions solely from the point of view of its interpretation ... it submits to no power, it believes in its own predominance over every other power – it believes that no power exists on earth that does not first have to receive a meaning, a right to exist' (*OGM* 146 III 23).

If we apply Nietzsche's analysis of ascetic interpretation to reading texts as well as reading epochs, nations, and men, then we get a description of something like a naive view of reading as an exercise in looking through words to their meanings, what for now I will call 'simply reading' as opposed to interpretation. This is uncovering meaning in the epistemological sense of looking for the true referent. But the aphorism is not 'understood' when it is simply read in this way; this is reactive or passive reading.

Genealogy is one alternative to reactive reading in that it combines interpretation with diagnosis; this is uncovering meaning in the psycho-genealogical sense described by Schrift. Genealogy not only interprets the meaning of the 'text' (ascetic ideals in this case) but also diagnoses what Jane Gallop calls in another context 'the symptomatic effects produced by the presumption that the text is in the very place "where meaning and knowledge of meaning reside."[8] In this sense active reading is distinguished from reactive reading in that it involves a recognition of the investment the reader makes in the text's meaning and diagnoses the symptoms of that investment. Reactive reading, on the other hand, assumes that words are transparent windows onto the text's or the author's meaning. In the preface to *Daybreak* Nietzsche describes the art of reading well as an art that 'does not so easily get anything done, it teaches to read *well*, that is to say, to read slowly, deeply, looking cautiously before and aft, with reservations, with doors left open, with delicate eyes and fingers . . .' (D 5).[9] Genealogy is a way of reading that opens on to the other of a text. Yet within Nietzsche's genealogy, that other is not permitted to be feminine.

In Nietzsche's setup in *On the Genealogy of Morals*, however, it is impossible to ask the question of reading without asking the question (Freud's question) '*Was will das Weib?*' 'What does woman want?' Nietzsche's lesson in artful reading is an exegesis of the answer to the question 'What does woman want?'[10] Nietzsche sets it out, in order to learn his lesson in reading, we first have to interpret Zarathustra's aphorism, which asks the question 'What does woman want?' And answers it, 'She wants a warrior.' The relationship between the question of reading and the question of woman, however, points to the impossibility of both for Nietzsche. We cannot answer the question of reading – How do we read? – without answering the question 'What does woman want?' Yet we cannot answer this question without first reading Nietzsche's aphorism, if not woman's desire itself. Reading, pure and simple, in order to *see through* words to their meaning is not possible. Reading is always necessarily interpretation. We are caught in the hermeneutic circle.

We encounter the impossibility of reading on another level. If wisdom is a woman and therefore wants us to be courageous, unconcerned, mocking, violent, then we *cannot ask* the question 'What does woman want?' To ask this question is to be *concerned* with her desire, something a warrior would not do. For once we inquire and show our concern, we are no longer unconcerned and therefore we are no longer desirable readers. As Arthur Danto points out, wisdom does not love those who love her (14). Wisdom does not want a reader, her reader is impossible; she wants (her desire) to be known by heart. This *Weib* wants a carnal knowledge and not a conceptual knowledge. Her love is a sensuous passion far from platonic love. This *Weib* is of doubtful morality. She wants to be had by force. She wants violence [*gewalttätig*]; she wants to be violated [*vergewaltigen*]. She wants a violent, indifferent warrior who cannot reciprocate her love. Wisdom wants a dagger through the heart.

If wisdom is this loose woman, then whom does she love? *How* is it that she wants *us*? Who are *we*? How are we to read the relationship between wisdom and the warrior? Although I will analyze Nietzsche's warrior later, I passionately disagree with Alexander Nehamas, who says that 'the conception of the writer as warrior, and not the identification of wisdom with woman, is the crucial feature of this aphorism.' Nehamas reads essay III as an application of the aphorism which precedes it. He argues that essay III is a 'declaration of war' on the ascetic ideal in which Nietzsche tries to put his own values in the place of ascetic values (115). In his reading, Nietzsche is the warrior waging war against the ascetic ideal (114). Nietzsche is wisdom's beloved. The joint on which this reading turns, however, is the thesis that essay III is waging all-out war against the ascetic ideal. A close reading of essay III reveals that Nietzsche is extremely ambivalent toward the ascetic ideal. Nietzsche is diagnosing the *meaning* of the ascetic ideal in its various modalities rather than condemning it outright.

Most Nietzsche critics and scholars choose to ignore Nietzsche's woman. Like Nehamas, they don't take her seriously. Yet, as I will argue, if we attend to Nietzsche's woman, then our reading of Nietzsche must change drastically. Unlike Nehamas, who engages the warrior but not the woman, I want to investigate the relationship between the two. After all, in Zarathustra's aphorism it seems that the lesson which we are to learn comes from the relationship between the warrior and the woman or the writer/reader and wisdom.

The relationship between the warrior and wisdom can be read, as Michael Newman suggests, as an inversion of the philosopher's love of the Forms in Plato's *Phaedrus*. For Nietzsche, like Plato, love is the means to the noble or aristocratic soul; but Nietzsche inverts the Platonic notions of noble and base.[11] For Nietzsche an elevation to nobility is not an elevation to transcendent Forms which brings with it self-knowledge and a turn away from sensuousness. Rather, for him an elevation to nobility is an elevation to sexual sublimation which brings with it self-mockery and a turn away from ascetic ideals.

Plato's characterization of the ascent to nobility is as bloody and violent as Nietzsche's. In the *Phaedrus* Plato paints a gory picture of the self-violence necessary to overcome baseness in the self and reach the level of nobility in the soul. The black, wanton steed, which represents sensuality in Plato's metaphor, must be violently beaten as if to death so that the soul might overcome its base passions. It is interesting that in Plato's metaphor methods that we might associate with bodily passions and physical violence are associated with the intellect and reason. The Charioteer, reason, uses bodily violence against the black steed, bodily passion. Whereas in Plato's metaphor the methods of physical violence associated with bodily lust are turned against bodily passion, in Nietzsche's genealogy the methods of argument and derision associated with the intellect and reason are turned against reason. In *Genealogy* the white steed receives the whipping.

In addition to the parallel between *Genealogy* and Plato's *Phaedrus*, Nietzschean Eros can be read against Socratic Eros as the latter is articulated in the *Symposium*. In the *Symposium* Socrates claims to have learned from a woman, Diotima, that Eros is the intermediary between ignorance and wisdom and between mortal and immortal or human and divine. In Nietzsche's aphorism, love is the intermediary between wisdom and the warrior, wisdom's love brings them together. Nietzsche not only inverts the sensuous and transcendent in their relationship through Eros, he also inverts the positions of lover and beloved. In both the *Phaedrus* and Socrates' speech in the *Symposium*, the lover uses his wisdom to conquer both his own lust and his reluctant beloved. Nietzsche, on the other hand, puts the warrior in the passive position; wisdom or woman is the lover and the warrior is the conquered beloved. This inversion, however, is unusual in Nietzsche's texts – which is why it seems more promising for a feminine subject. Recall the preface to *Beyond Good and Evil* where Nietzsche asks us to suppose that truth is a woman who is sought after by dogmatic philosophers. Here truth/woman is the beloved hopelessly lost to the impotent lover – what a joke.

The fact that in Zarathustra's aphorism the woman, wisdom, is the active lover and the warrior is the beloved is overlooked by most of the scholars who comment on this passage. As I indicated above, Alexander Nehamas claims that the woman is unimportant in this passage (114). And even Michael Newman, who seems at least interested in the relationship between the warrior and the woman, chooses a course which is 'expedient rather than satisfactory' in order to steer clear of the 'vexed question of "Nietzsche and woman"' (279 n. 7). While acknowledging that the warrior is the passive beloved of wisdom, Newman restores a more properly Platonic relationship between lover and beloved, warrior and woman, by asking 'who, or what, then, does the warrior or noble love?' (264). He restores the warrior to the position of lover. He then positions Zarathustra as the noble warrior/lover; and he answers the question 'Who does the warrior love?' by indicating that Zarathustra speaks the warrior's desire when he says that 'of all that is written I love only what a man has written with his blood' (264). Newman's warrior is both the writer, Zarathustra (Nietzsche), and the reader who loves only what he himself writes with (his own?) blood. In Newman's reading the warrior loves a reader who does not seek to understand but rather learns by heart – recall that Zarathustra proclaims that 'whoever writes in blood and aphorisms does not want to be read but to be learned by heart.' Love, after all, is a matter of heart. The beloved reader is necessarily a passive reader who submits to a 'branding' with burning aphorisms (cf. Newman 265).

Through the process of reading by heart, the reader is transformed into the noble warrior. By submitting to the text, the reader becomes active. This self-transformation does not take place through Socratic self-knowledge but through 'rumination,' as Nietzsche says in the preface to *Genealogy*. Newman maintains that *Genealogy*'s 'quasi-scientific accounts can also be read as myths for the purpose of the self-education of the reader: indeed for the transformation of the "knower" into a "reader" who "ruminates"' (Newman 267). In this way Nietzsche creates his own reader, who, as we have seen, is necessarily as masochistic and sadistic as his lover, who writes not only with his own blood but also the blood of his readers.

Like Newman, Arthur Danto emphasizes the violence that Nietzsche's texts do to their readers. The aphorism is the best weapon of the philosopher since, like a dagger traveling fast, it lodges itself in its reader. As Danto says, the aphorism is 'implanted' in the reader and 'metabolized' (15–16). Because Nietzsche's aphorisms are painful, we remember them; like the tortures he describes in book II, they are mnemonic shocks that jolt the memory. On Danto's reading violence is not instrumental but essential to Nietzsche's warrior; this warrior is fighting for the sake of fighting, unconcerned for any cause (Danto 14). In the end, Danto seems to turn Nietzsche into Kant when he claims that to be unconcerned is associated with will and that Nietzsche's goal is to redirect the will – which, of course, prevents Nietzsche from being an unconcerned warrior: 'But that is what he would like to have achieved: . . . to replace a morality of means with a morality of principle: to act in such a way as to be consistent with acting that way eternally: to stultify the instinct for significance' (27–28). On Danto's reading, then, the reader and the writer as unconcerned warrior must act in such a way as to 'stultify the instinct for significance'; he must engage in the impossible battle, which must be fought for its own sake.

Nietzsche wants a sensuous, violent reading and writing that come from the body.[12] But it seems that this body, for Nietzsche and his commentators, is always only the male body. What happens, however, when unlike Danto, Newman and Nehamas we shift our attention from the warrior to the woman? Remember that Nietzsche's aphorism reads, 'Unconcerned, mocking, violent – thus wisdom wants *us*: she is a woman and always loves only a warrior.' What happens when woman/wisdom becomes the lover? She becomes the active agent and the warrior becomes the passive beloved, the object of her love. What kind of love belongs to her? Is hers necessarily the violent love? And what does her love teach us about reading and writing? When we read woman/wisdom as the active lover, then what can we learn from Nietzsche's lesson on reading and writing? Furthermore, what happens when Nietzsche's reader is a woman? What happens when a woman takes the place of the warrior seeking favor with wisdom?

It doesn't seem that Nietzsche imagines that wisdom's beloved – this warrior who writes and reads with blood – could be Athena. Certainly Nietzsche's woman reader must laugh or she will feel wounded by his texts. Perhaps, like Irigaray, she can't help but mock Nietzsche for his own fear of the body, of his own body as well as hers. And certainly images of a woman reading and writing with her blood will bring with them very different interpretations of the process of reading and writing.

What would it mean for a woman to write and read with her blood? In *Marine Lover of Friedrich Nietzsche*, Luce Irigaray laments that Nietzsche overlooks woman's blood: 'Something red was lacking, a hint of blood and guts to revive the will, and restore its strength' (79).[13] Irigaray suggests that Nietzsche forgets the blood of life, maternal blood, which still makes 'a stain, a spot. No one is supposed to notice the opening onto the stage of sameness

. . . which is no longer possible without suppressing the whole body' (*ML* 81). Although Nietzsche advocates writing and reading as bloodletting in the manly warrior, he forgets about women's blood that flows into new life without the knife, without self-mutilation or the mutilation of others. Perhaps interpretation can be of the body and fecund without also being violent. The image of a woman reading and writing with her blood promises a creativity that is neither sadistic nor masochistic, that does not require violence toward the reader or self-violence.

As I elaborate later, Irigaray indicates that Nietzsche's texts always promote sameness even when they sing the praises of difference, because Nietzschean difference is always merely difference as defined by the same, or is what she calls 'the other of the same' rather than 'the other of the other.' Another way to say this might be that Nietzsche's notions of active morality and active reading are always merely reactions to the reactive morality and reactive reading. Irigaray claims that Nietzsche denies the fundamental difference of sexual difference. He overlooks woman's difference. In particular, Nietzsche's texts deny the maternal body out of which all human beings are born; and in order to cover over this murder of the maternal body, to wipe away the blood and wash away the stain, he must deny the body altogether. The body always reminds us of that first body, the maternal body, which sustained us; it reminds us of the maternal blood out of which we were born (cf. *ML* 96). For Irigaray to imagine woman's blood is to imagine difference; but Nietzsche cannot imagine woman's blood or what it would mean for a woman to read and write with her blood because the bloodstains on his texts are the result of a murder, matricide – the blood of death and not the blood of life. Woman is not the warrior whom wisdom loves.

So although Nietzsche proposes a way of reading and writing that opens onto its other, a reading and writing from the body, this body is always a masculine body. It becomes clear from attempting to put woman into the subject position as the reader or writer within Nietzsche's discourse that in that place she is out of place. Like Freud, Nietzsche makes woman and the feminine into an object for a masculine subject. Like Freud, while Nietzsche opens philosophy onto the other, the body, he closes off the possibility of a specifically feminine other and there by eliminates the possibility of sexual difference.

Derrida's Feminine Operation: Philosophers in Drag

'Would you like me to dress up as a woman?' I murmured.
(Jacques Derrida, *Glas* 223, 243)

I am a woman and beautiful.
(Jacques Derrida, 'The Law of Genre')

In most of his texts Derrida plays with/as woman.[14] In addition, in many of his texts he criticizes his predecessors (Kant, Hegel, Heidegger) for excluding woman. Yet how is a woman to read these texts? Where is she in these texts? Where is her desire? Derrida's texts suffer from the same symptoms as Nietzsche's texts and in some respect Freud's texts as well. It is clear that in his lectures on femininity Freud is speaking to men about women. Women are his objects and the texts give voice to a masculine desire for this feminine object. Although Nietzsche's case is less clear, the awkwardness, if not impossibility, of reading or writing as a woman becomes clear when we examine the metaphors with which Nietzsche describes the processes of reading and writing. In Nietzsche's text the operations of reading and writing can even be interpreted as man doing violence to woman, the violent warrior taking the loose woman. And although Derrida begins his *Spurs* by proclaiming that 'it is woman who will be my subject,' in that text she is never afforded any subject position; rather she is used to deconstruct a unified subject position (*S* 37). Like Freud and Nietzsche before him, and so many others, Derrida seems to be speaking to men about women; his case, however, is fraught with ambiguities.

Like both Freud and Nietzsche before him, Derrida is concerned with opening a space for the other. For Freud the other was the unconscious. For Nietzsche the other was the body. For Derrida the other is difference itself. Following Levinas, in order to open philosophy onto difference Derrida shifts from a conception of language as a means of coming to know ourselves, and thereby possessing ourselves, to a conception of language as a means of exposing the other whom we cannot possess. This Levinasian shift is a move from a philosophy of the subject to a philosophy of the other. Derrida is not concerned with the correspondence between philosophical thinking and things in themselves; rather he is concerned with what has been excluded from philosophical thinking.

In an interview Derrida says that his 'central question is: from what site or non-site can philosophy as such appear to itself as other than itself, so that it can interrogate and reflect upon itself in an original manner? Such a non-site or alterity would be radically irreducible to philosophy. But the problem is that such a non-site cannot be defined or situated by means of philosophical language' (RK 108). Much of Derrida's writing addresses ways in which traditional philosophical language attempts to conceptualize difference, exteriority and otherness. Operating according to a type of Hegelian logic (without the crucial negation of the negation of difference or particularity) in which the self consolidates itself at the expense of the other, traditional philosophical discourse tries to eliminate all difference, exteriority and otherness. As Derrida claims in 'Tympan,' philosophy insists 'upon thinking its other: its proper other, the proper of its other, an other proper? In thinking it as such, in recognizing it, one misses it. One reappropriates it for oneself, one disposes of it, one misses it, or rather one misses (the) missing (of) it, which, as concerns the other, always amounts to the same. Between the proper of the other and the other of the proper' (T xi–xii). Ultimately, in much of his writing, Derrida suggests that philosophy closes off the possibility of listening to any other because it always operates within an economy or logic of the proper, making all difference into its own property (T xvi). But how is it possible to relate to any other without making it your own; isn't any object of consciousness an object *for us*? How does Derrida confront this problem? Following the later Heidegger, he makes the problem one of address rather than consciousness.

In 'Psyche: Inventions of the Other' Derrida suggests that deconstruction opens a place for the other. As I indicated earlier, he argues that we cannot invent the other or the place of the other because insofar as it is radically other we have no access to it; we do not speak the same language. Yet this other invents us through its call: 'For the other is always another origin of the world and we are (always) (still) to be invented' (Psy 61). This is what Derrida calls the paradox of invention. Invention is only possible through the invention of the other, or something other; and yet inventing something other out of the same is impossible. So he formulates the process as originating with the other's call or invitation to 'come.' This call is a Heideggerian call to thinking. When thinking opens onto the other, then the impossible is possible; invention takes place. Beyond this, however, is the ethical concern that Derrida finds lacking in Heidegger and finds in Levinas. Deconstruction does not open up just the possibility of invention but also the possibility of justice. Derrida says that 'to address oneself to the other in the language of the other is, it seems, the condition of all possible justice' (FL 17). Yet, speaking/ writing to the other in its own language is as impossible as inventing the other. How can we speak/write in a language that by definition we do not know?

The first step is to expose what makes it possible to speak/write in our language. Speaking, writing, reading are dialogic; they need an other, in the form of another person, meaning, or a text. Only the other makes language possible. Signification brings with it responsibilities, ethical responsibilities: 'We are invested with an undeniable responsibility at the moment we begin to signify something (but where does that begin?). This responsibility assigns us our freedom without leaving it with us, if one could put it that way. And we see it coming from the Other. It is assigned to us by the Other, from the Other, before any hope of reappropriation permits us to assume this responsibility in the space of what could be called *autonomy*' (PF 634).

Signification brings with it a responsibility to and from the Other. There is no signification in isolation, no private language. We are born into a system of signification where, although it is not determined and unchanging, meaning is beyond us. Julia Kristeva identifies meaning as the Other within signification. In the shadow of both Heidegger and Levinas, Derrida describes a type of invitation from the Other that both opens up the possibility of communication and obligates us. Following Heidegger, Derrida sees what he calls the 'come,' the call, from the Other as the very possibility of signification or meaning. We are indebted to this other beyond us because it opens up the possibility of any language, thought or meaning. Language itself and our relationship to it opens up the possibility of our asking both ontic and onto-logical questions. Following Levinas, Derrida sees the 'come' from the Other as an obligation, ultimately an ethical call.

So, following Levinas, Derrida insists on the responsibility to try to speak (to) the other. In the case of inventing the feminine other, however, Derrida is caught in an impossible place, both dressing up as a woman and parodying all attempts to do so. As self-conscious as Derrida's masquerade appears to be, it is still important to diagnose the ways in which his discourse effectively closes off the very space that it attempts to open up. Like Freud and Nietzsche before him, Derrida closes off the possibility of listening to a feminine other even while he is attempting to hear, to speak of/as that other.

When Derrida says that woman will be his subject, he is playing with woman. While she is the subject of his discourse, he also suggests that her position is *his* subject position. Yet Derrida does not identify with the woman in his text. In effect endorsing some of Nietzsche's proclamations about woman, Derrida not only quotes Nietzsche but also reaffirms that woman is 'so artistic'; her effect is at a distance; she will not be pinned down and yet one cannot help looking for her (*S* 47, 55, 71). When a woman reads these pas-sages, where is her position? Is she, like Nietzsche and Derrida, caught look-ing for the irresistible but elusive woman? Herself? Is her effect a distance from herself? Whose desire is given voice in this text? This is not a woman's desire. When women desire women qua women, they cannot have the kind of distance from themselves that Derrida describes without experiencing a kind of self-alienation to the point of psychosis. Perhaps, then, *Spurs* is merely 'the advice of one man to another: a sort of scheme for how to seduce without being seduced' (*S* 49).

Like Nietzsche's view of reading and writing as the violent warrior's rela-tion to woman, Derrida's view of reading and writing also suggests a violence toward woman. In *Spurs* he proposes that if style is a man, then writing is a woman (*S* 57). Derrida's spurring operation, which he has identified with the feminine operation, is a violent operation on woman's body itself. Style is the spur that violently penetrates into the material of writing in order to have its way. And woman's body is sacrificed to style. The grand style is a type of violent (self-)mocking warrior. 'At this point, where it pierces the veil of truth and the simulacrum of castration in order to impale the woman's body, the question of style must be measured against the larger question of the interpretation of Nietzsche's text, of the interpretation of interpretation – in short against the question of interpretation itself' (Derrida, *S* 171–73, my emphasis).

For Derrida it is the point at which style impales the woman's body that the question of interpretation comes to the fore. In this passage Derrida raises the question of whether this violence *belongs* to the interpretation of Nietzsche's texts and the larger question of whether violence necessarily belongs to interpretation.[15] Does interpretation necessarily impale woman's body? Where does woman belong in interpretation, in reading and writing?

Below I will read Derrida's insistence on self-parody, self-violence, as a violence against the masculine 'for the sake of' the feminine. Deconstruction's autocastration emasculates style in order to pose as woman. And as Derrida underlines in both *Spurs* and *Glas*, the operation of posing itself is feminine; posing is the feminine operation (see *Glas* 246, *S* 69). One possible answer, then, to the question of where woman or the feminine belongs is that each belongs to man; he is feminine so there is no need for woman.

In addition, within Derrida's discourse, affirmation, particularly double affirmation, is another operation of woman. Discussing Blanchot in 'The Law of Genre,' Derrida maintains that saying 'yes, yes,' a double affirmation, is 'usually' performed by 'women,' 'beautiful women' (not 'woman,' but women). So perhaps deconstruction's self-referential, self-parodying self-denials are self-affirmations of the double gesture of deconstruction; deconstruction says yes to self-parody by saying yes to parody. It says yes to itself through its parody of itself. Like Nietzsche's ascetic priest whose no to life becomes a series of 'tender yeses,' deconstruction's self-violence becomes a twisted self-affirmation. Within the logic of his 'Law of Genre,' deconstruction's self-referentiality – which is always a self-affirmation no matter what else it might be – is itself a feminine operation because it is a double affirmation. But Derrida provides the ground for yet another possible reading of his feminine operation in *Glas* when he asks: What would it mean for a man to want to become a woman? In a detour through Kant in his analysis of Hegel, Derrida answers his question (for Kant?): 'What would it mean, for a man, to want to be a woman, seeing that the woman wants to be a man in proportion to her cultivating herself? That would mean then, apart from the semblance of a detour, to want to be a man, to want to be – that is to say, to remain – a man . . . either the man who wants to be only a man wants to be a woman inasmuch as woman wants to be a man; so he wants to be a woman in order to remain what he is. Or else the man who wants to be a woman only wants to be a woman since the woman wants to be man only in order to reach her womanly designs. To wit, the man' (*Glas* 130). All this is to say that 'woman wants to be a man, the man never wants to be a woman' (*Glas* 130); and the man who wants to be a woman is suspect. On Derrida's reading of Kant, the man who wants to be a woman is suspected of really only wanting to be, to remain, a man. And sometimes the best way to do that might be through the detour of woman. Taking the place of the other may in fact guarantee that one has a place. Gayatri Spivak calls this double movement – assigning the other the displaced position on the margin and then appropriating that place – which shows up in *Spurs* and *Dissemination*, 'double displacement.'[16] She argues that the deconstructive philosopher (Derrida) usurps the 'place of displacement' and thereby doubly displaces woman. That is, he takes even her already displaced place.

More recently, however, Spivak has suggested a way to reappropriate Derrida's use of 'woman,' a way to deconstruct Derrida's deconstruction of 'woman.' She describes a way that we can use deconstruction politically in the project of overcoming oppression. Spivak points out that deconstruction is both a naming and an unnaming. It is misnaming since within its discourse names have no 'adequate literal referent.'[17] And this is part of Derrida's project to show that there are so many names for her that there is no woman; there is no literal referent to the 'woman' of philosophical discourse. While maintaining her suspicions of Derrida's 'woman,' Spivak suggests that those of us concerned with emancipation from oppressive categories can use this deconstructive naming device politically in order to motivate a continual process of naming the unnamed and thereby unnaming the named (FD 220). Naming, she reminds us, is the effect of particular historical circumstances. If we name 'woman' the disenfranchised woman whom we cannot imagine as a literal referent, then in a sense, we have named the unnamable. But, at the same time, as soon as the name conjures some sort of image, the literal referent, always inadequate, begins to fade. The hope of this politicized deconstruction, claims Spivak, is 'that the possibility for the name will be finally erased' and its material conditions destroyed (FD 220). In other words, through the use of a deconstruction of names or categories, we can not only give a voice to experiences previously denied a name, but also unname experiences that have been defined only in patriarchal terms. In this way the term 'woman' can be used provisionally, subject to continual deconstruction, so that eventually it will no longer refer to the second sex or an oppressed group. What Spivak's analysis suggests is that the continued exclusion of the feminine other and woman is not inherent to the deconstructive methodology.

As Spivak points out, for Derrida 'woman' is the name for the double-bind which is at the heart of naming itself. The double bind is the non-truth of truth, the fact that all naming is misnaming. If Derrida calls this double bind 'woman,' then woman must be used against itself. In other words, if the very foundation of deconstruction is this double bind called 'woman,' then in order to deconstruct 'woman' we must use 'woman' against 'woman.' As Sally Robinson argues in another context, 'man' is not subject to change.[18] Rather, in a metaphorical sense, 'woman' is pitted against 'woman' in order to maintain the economy of masculine desire.

For Derrida 'woman' becomes the most convenient target in the deconstruction of the subject. Here 'woman' is seen as an arbitrary sign which results from relations within a sign system whose phallocentric economy has led to essentialism. 'Woman,' then, through its ambiguous referent, tentative subject position, and marginal status, becomes a prime exemplar of the status of signs and subjects in general. The predicament of 'woman' is the predicament of the subject. In this context, Derrida claims that there is no such thing as a 'woman' ('*Il n'y a pas une femme*'), because there is no truth or essence of 'woman' (*S* 100). And, on the other hand, anyone who occupies a tentative position in relation to the phallocratic sign-system, occupies the place of 'woman.'

Against Derrida I will argue that even if the attempt to do away with 'the unified subject' is a desirable goal, it should not begin with the deconstruction of 'woman.' After all, in some situations it is still necessary for feminists to rally around the identity of 'woman.' Some of his followers may defend Derrida by arguing that his goal is not just to deconstruct 'woman,' but also 'man' and the woman/man dualism. In fact, Derrida intends (if that word is appropriate for him) to show that hierarchy is inherent in dualism and that we need, therefore, to deconstruct dualism. Yet the target in the deconstruction of the woman/man dualism is woman and not man. The privilege of man's position in this hierarchy is not in itself deconstructed. To aim the deconstructive mechanism at 'woman' is a different operation than aiming it at 'man.' It is much different to disempower the *powerful* than it is to disempower the *powerless*.[19]

The question once again is where is the position of woman in Derrida's text? How does a woman read these texts? How does a woman write? If it is the operation of simulation that makes an operation feminine, then are women to simulate men or women? On my reading it seems that within the economy of deconstruction only men can be women. And women can neither play with the position of woman in the same way as men can nor play within the position of man. In Derrida's reading of Kant, all women want to be men. But if the feminine position, woman's position, is always the position of an object and never the position of a subject, is it necessary for woman to take up the position of man in order to be a subject? Is it true, as Luce Irigaray argues, that any theory of the subject is always appropriated by the masculine?

Derrida reads an answer to this question in Kant: 'In fact, even if she truly wanted to, which is not the case, woman could never be a man. The masculine attributes with which she adorns herself are never anything but fake, signifiers without signification, fetishes' (*Glas* 130). While the man's transvestism is not only passable but highly amusing, the woman's transvestism is not passable. She is easily called out. She is called a feminist: 'And in truth, they too are men, those women feminists so derided by Nietzsche. Feminism is nothing but the operation of a woman who aspires to be like a man' (Derrida, *S* 65). Men can perform the feminine operation, an operation that no 'real' woman can perform, yet women cannot take up the subject position, traditionally masculine, without being derided as 'feminists' just trying to emulate men.

This still leaves us with the question 'What belongs to woman in Derrida's text and where does woman belong?' I will come back to this question again.

Notes

1. See Hélène Cixous's 'The Laugh of the Medusa,' *Signs* 1, 875–99; reprinted in *New French Feminisms*, E. Marks and I. Courtivron (eds.) (New York: Schocken Books, 1980), 245–64; Irigaray's *Speculum of the Other Woman*; Jane Gallop's *The Daughter's Seduction* (Ithaca: Cornell University Press, 1982).

2. Both Elizabeth Grosz and Sarah Kofman argue in different ways that Freud's theory presupposes castration in order to set up castration in the girl. See *Jacques Lacan: a Feminist Introduction* (New York: Routledge, 1990).

3. I would like to thank Daniel Conway and Alan Schrift for generous comments on an early version of this section. I would also like to thank Kathleen Higgins, Elissa Marder, and Johanna Seibt for their invaluable help and suggestions. A version of 'A Dagger through the Heart' was previously published in *International Studies in Philosophy*, Summer 1993.

4. Friedrich Nietzsche, *On the Genealogy of Morals*, trans. Walter Kaufmann and R. J. Hollingdale (New York: Random House, 1967); referred to as *OGM* in the text from now on followed by the page number and then the section number.

5. Alan Schrift, *Nietzsche and the Question of Interpretation* (New York: Routledge, 1991).

6. For an impressive account of the difference between active and reactive forces and their relation to the master and slave moralities, see Gilles Deleuze, *Nietzsche and Philosophy*, trans. Hugh Tomlinson (New York: Columbia University Press, 1983).

7. Nietzsche is a bad reader insofar as he denies sexual difference.

8. Gallop is quoting Shoshana Felman's 'To Open the Question,' *Yale French Studies* 55–56 (1977): 5–10. Gallop is applying Shoshana Felman's distinction between two aspects of psychoanalysis – interpretation and transference reading. Gallop suggests that an analysis of the text that recognizes the operations of transference in reading – investing the text with the authority of meaning – can open up the process of reading beyond mere interpretation. In this context, Gallop means something more specific by interpretation than my use of 'interpretation' in this essay. She uses 'interpretation' in a way akin to my use of reactive or simple reading which I oppose to interpretation. I use interpretation to designate something like what she calls a reading that includes the recognition of transference; that is, a reading that diagnoses the symptoms of investing the text with the authority to mean. See Jane Gallop, *Reading Lacan* (Ithaca: Cornell University Press, 1985).

9. John Walchak suggests that my distinction between active and reactive reading is similar to Roland Barthes's distinction between writerly reading, through which the reader creates a new text, and readerly reading, through which the reader closes off possibilities for further investigation in the text. See Roland Barthes, *Writing Degree Zero*; Noëlle McAfee suggests that my description of active reading is similar to Simon Critchley's description of deconstructive reading. See Simon Critchley, *The Ethics of Deconstruction* (Blackwell, 1992). I will make the connection between Nietzsche's style and Derrida's style in chapter 2.

10. This question is echoed in Freud's lecture on femininity. There Freud asks '*Was will das Weib?*' in order to read sexual difference, and ultimately the very possibility of difference itself. Nietzsche's lesson in reading is a lesson in reading difference. It is the ascetic ideal that insists on one reading and excludes the very possibility of difference.

11. Michael Newman makes this argument in his thought-provoking, if problematic, essay 'Reading the Future of Genealogy: Kant, Nietzsche, Plato,' in Keith Ansell-Pearson (ed.), *Nietzsche and Modern German Thought*, 264.

12. For an insightful discussion of Nietzsche's writing styles, see Gary Shapiro, *Nietzschean Narratives* (Bloomington: Indiana University Press, 1989). For a discussion of Nietzsche's bodily metaphors see Eric Blondel, *Nietzsche: The Body and Culture*, trans. Seán Hand (Stanford: Stanford University Press, 1991).

13. Luce Irigaray, *Marine Lover of Friedrich Nietzsche*, trans. Gillian Gill (New York: Columbia University Press, 1991).

14. In *Gynesis*, Alice Jardine presents a very nice summary of Derrida's positions on woman and the feminine in some of his essays. Although she raises many questions for feminists, she neither answers these questions nor criticizes nor deconstructs Derrida's texts from a feminist perspective.

15. I will analyze the centrality of the question of belonging in *Spurs* in chapter 3 below.

16. Gayatri Chakravorty Spivak, 'Displacement and the Discourse of Woman,' in Mark Krupnick (ed.), *Displacement: Derrida and After* (Bloomington: Indiana University Press), 171.

17. Gayatri Chakravorty Spivak, 'Feminism and Deconstruction, Again: Negotiating with Unacknowledged Masculinism,' in Teresa Brennan (ed.), *Between Feminism and Psychoanalysis* (London: Routledge, 1989), 215.

18. Sally Robinson, 'Misappropriations of the "Feminine,"' in *SubStance 59* (1989).

19. Sally Robinson argues that Derrida's appropriations of the feminine and 'woman' operate within a masculine desire to avoid castration and protect the phallus. See 'Misappropriations of the "Feminine."' Given Freud's analysis of fetishism, we must remember that it is not just any woman but the mother who is fetishized. I suggest that this is because the male child was once part of his mother's body (a castrated body) and therefore he must deny her castration in order to deny his own.

51

Modernity, Ethics and Counter-Ideals: *Amor Fati,* Eternal Recurrence and the Overman*

David Owen

*Source: David Owen, *Nietzsche, Politics and Eternity*, Sage Publications, 1995, pp. 105–31.

> The problem I raise here is not what ought to succeed mankind in the sequence of species (– the human being is an *end* –); but what type of human being one ought to *breed*, ought to *will*, as more valuable, more worthy of life, more certain of the future.
>
> (AC §3)

At the same time as Nietzsche addresses modernity as nihilism and decadence, he also addresses modernity as the condition of possibility for a particular range of human types. Nietzsche presents his understanding of the possibilities for being human immanent within modern culture through the dramatic contrast of two ideal-typical figures which mark the limits of the range of possible types: the dystopian figure of the *Last Man* and the utopian figure of the *Overman*. As Laurence Lampert astutely comments: 'Last man and superman [i.e., Overman] represent the two extremes made possible by the malleability of man, "the as yet undetermined animal"' (1986: 24). This chapter will follow on from Nietzsche's account of modernity as *nihilism* and as *decadence* in which human beings are characterised by the affective dispositions of *nausea* and *pity* in order to show how Nietzsche seeks to articulate the overcoming of modernity by providing the conceptual resources (the doctrine of *eternal recurrence*) and communicating the affective dispositions (*heroism* and *irony*) necessary to such a task. In particular I will argue that through the contrasting figures of the *Last Man* (as the completion of modernity) and the *Overman* (as the overcoming of modernity) Nietzsche attempts to seduce his readers into adopting his perspective by providing a counter-ideal to the ascetic ideal in which the will to nothingness is displaced by the will to *amor fati.*

Amor Fati and the Overman

A consequence of Nietzsche's understanding of human beings as members of a linguistic community, a form of life, is that the construction of an ideal is necessarily disclosed in terms of the cultural resources of that community. In the context of his genealogical reflections on modern culture, Nietzsche argues that two distinct ideals – the Overman and the Last Man – can be formulated in modern culture which are consonant with both the collapse of the appearance/reality distinction and the capacities of modern individuals. In this section, I will focus on Nietzsche's recommendation of *amor fati* and the Overman as a counter-ideal and, in the next section, I will address the idea of eternal recurrence as the ethical rule appropriate to this *telos*. In the following two sections, I will seek to specify the characteristics which Nietzsche assigns to the Last Man, before going on to raise the question of the capacities of modern man to pursue these ideals.

Let us start, perhaps slightly obliquely, with a section from *The Gay Science* entitled 'Elevated Moods':

> It seems to me that most people simply do not believe in elevated moods, unless these last for moments only or at most a quarter of an hour – except for those few who know at first hand the longer duration of elevated feelings. But to be a human being with one elevated feeling – to be a single great mood incarnate – that has hitherto been a mere dream and a delightful possibility; as yet history does not offer us any certain examples. Nevertheless history might one day give birth to such people, too – once a great many favorable preconditions have been created and determined that even the dice throws of the luckiest chance could not bring together today. What has so far entered our souls only now and then as an exception that makes us shudder, might perhaps be the usual state for these future souls.
>
> (GS §288)

Despite the apparent pessimism expressed in this passage, my suggestion is that Nietzsche is concerned to facilitate the cultural conditions of possibility of such a future people and that he focuses on the affective disposition or mood which he calls *amor fati* and which is given incarnate form in the figure of the Overman.

We can begin by recalling that Nietzsche's account of the ascetic ideal – and his central objection to it – focuses on its devaluation of this-worldly existence; by contrast to the noble who affirms the sensuous relationship between self and world, the slave rejects this world in the name of a metaphysical world. Consequently, Nietzsche's product of reconstituting noble culture in the context of the deconstruction of metaphysics begins with the recognition that the ideal which he formulates must involve an affirmation of our sensuous this-worldly existence. It is at this juncture that Nietzsche's reflections on *amor fati* (love of fate) become significant:

> My formula for greatness in a human being is *amor fati*: that one wants nothing to be different, not forward, not backward, not in all eternity. Not merely bear what is necessary, still less conceal it – all idealism is mendaciousness in the face of what is necessary – but *love* it.
>
> (EH 'Why I Am So Clever' §10)

And, on a more personal note:

> I want to learn more and more to see as beautiful what is necessary in things; then I shall be one of those who make things beautiful. *Amor fati*: let that be my love henceforth! . . . And all in all and on the whole: some day I wish to be only a Yes-sayer.
>
> (GS §276)

But what is the experiential character of *amor fati* as an affective disposition? And what is the logical character of the concept of *amor fati*? What is the relationship between *amor fati*, eternal recurrence and the Overman? To explicate Nietzsche's notion of *amor fati*, we need to address these questions, and this will be my task in the remainder of this section and the following section.

In specifying the experiential character of *amor fati*, Nietzsche seems to have in my mind that form of experience which we might term 'ecstatic epiphanies', moments of utter wonder and overflowing joy, moments of sublime rapture such as the moment when Nietzsche was struck by the revelation of the thought of eternal recurrence – 'six thousand feet beyond man and time' (EH 'Thus Spoke Zarathustra' §1): 'Immortal is the moment when I produced the recurrence. . . . For the sake of this moment I *endure* the recurrence' (cited in Thiele, 1990: 204). I think that it is relatively straightforward to depict the type of experience to which Nietzsche is referring by giving a few examples.

1   Lying in the grass on a summer's day, I am suddenly overwhelmed by a feeling of oneness with nature in which I 'see' myself as part of a shimmering, vibrant whole which makes my soul resonate, laugh and sing. In this moment, melancholy is stripped from my being and redeemed in wonder and joy.
2   Writing this book, I am suddenly grasped by a sense of utter clarity in which thought, being and word processor become continuous. I am simultaneously at one with this process and separate from it, watching myself as part of it. In this moment, all the blocks, frustrations and despair fall away like dead leaves and life breathes through me.

3 Playing tennis, I am caught in a sense of complete certainty that I can do no wrong and play without the need for conscious reflection on what I'm doing. The court, racket, balls and I are all one, flowing into and through each other, and I can somehow 'see' myself in this condition – knowing what to do without needing to reflect on it. All the days when the racket felt like an alien piece of wood are forgotten and redeemed in a moment of utter lightness of being.

While these elevated moods may be fairly commonplace in the sense that I suspect that everyone experiences such states at one time or another (often perhaps mistaking them for the presence of divinity), they are unfortunately also fleeting (at least in my experience – and I will return to this feature shortly), but I think that we can draw out certain features from these examples which help to illuminate what Nietzsche is gesturing towards.

Firstly, each of these examples points to the 'paradoxical' quality of this experiential state in which co-exist simultaneously a sense of the dissolution of subjectivity in an experience of 'oneness' and a sense of the presence of subjectivity in recognising and watching its own dissolution. We might express this paradox by saying that I experience the dissolution of subjectivity as an *actor* but that I experience the presence of subjectivity as a *spectator*. (As an aside, it is worth noting in this context that this distinction between unity and separation, dissolution and individuation, parallels Nietzsche's distinction between the *Dionysian* and the *Apollonian* in his first published book *The Birth of Tragedy*, in which he attributes 'Greek cheerfulness' to this type of experience as it is generated by Attic tragedy.) The second point we can develop from these examples can be specified by my reference to them as 'moments of wonder and joy', insofar as I would suggest that 'wonder' refers to our experience as *spectator* and 'joy' to our experience as *actor*. My suggestion is that our feeling of wonder is tied to a sense of *distance*, while our feeling of joy is tied to a sense of *passion* or erotic engagement. A third feature which can be drawn from these examples concerns the *redemptive* power of such moments of love of life, insofar as it seems to be a feature of these moments that we experience them as both a *liberation* from emotional states such as nausea and pity (to pick two random examples!) *and* as a *justification* of our past experience of these states. Thus, in a sense, we can suggest that the experience of *amor fati* implicitly involves the claim that one would suffer all the frustration, despair, etc., again as a condition of possibility of this rapturous moment.

These three features might seem pretty much to exhaust the elements of these examples cited, but I'd like to introduce a fourth feature which refers specifically to our second and third examples. The crucial difference between the first example and the other two is that while they all refer to human activities, the second and third examples refer to activities which are cultural practices involving specific skills.[1] To set out my claim, let us consider a comment by Nietzsche on *mastery*: 'One has attained mastery when one neither goes wrong *nor hesitates* in the performance' (D §537). If we recall the 'tennis' example cited above, it is notable that the features of the state described are captured by the sense that 'one can do no wrong' and has no need of 'conscious reflection' – 'knowing what to do without needing to think about it'. Indeed, it is a characteristic of such moods that as soon as something does go wrong or one is caught in hesitation, the mood is broken. This point suggests that the frequency and sustainability of such moments of *amor fati* is dependent on one's mastery of the activity in which one is engaged: to experience one's engagement in an activity as 'pure poetry' requires some degree of mastery of the activity (where our criteria of mastery are publicly constituted). Thus, for example, I suspect that – given his sublime genius – John McEnroe's experience of such moments is incomparably more regular and sustained than my rather infrequent and extremely fleeting experience of such moments *qua* the activity of tennis. We can confirm this relationship from the other direction by adducing a further example: having absolutely no mastery of dance entails that when I am engaged in this activity, I have to think about what I'm doing and, consequently, I am consumed with hesitation and a sense that what I'm doing is probably all wrong; whereas my partner surrenders herself to the music, I am utterly at sea and never experience (or expect to experience) moments of the type under discussion. The significance of this relationship between mastery and *amor fati* emerges if we consider that the tennis example, for instance, refers us to an affirmation of the relationship of self and world *qua* self as tennis player. The question which arises from this consideration is this: what would be required to affirm the relationship of self and world *qua* self as self, that is, to affirm one's self not simply with respect to one activity but with respect to the totality of one's activities? The obvious answer to this question, which is also the one that Nietzsche gives, is 'self-mastery', and we will illustrate this answer shortly.

At this stage, having sketched an understanding of *amor fati* as a mode of experience, we can turn to reflect on the conceptual character of *amor fati* within the context of Nietzsche's work. Let us begin by noting that *amor fati* represents love of life because Nietzsche posits the fateful character of existence. This identification is not the product of the philosophical claim that there is no freedom, only determination (not least because the freedom/determination antinomy is tied to the metaphysical realist position which Nietzsche rejects); rather it is an expression of the idea of becoming what one is (applied to both the individual and the cultural community). This point becomes clear if we note the relationship between the concepts 'fate' and 'character'.

Nietzsche's argument is that my actions express (and further constitute) my character (i.e., the narrative that is my self); thus, if I choose an action after long deliberation, both the chosen action and the process of deliberation are expressions of my character at this time, which is itself constituted by the previous actions and reflections which make up the narrative history of my self. (But perhaps this way of putting this point makes it sound as though 'becoming what one is' is a solitary activity; if given, this impression would be misleading because Nietzsche is in no way denying that my actions and reflections take place in the context of my relations with both my self and others, that is, within a dialogic context of intersubjective relations.) However, it might be objected to this expression of the notion of character that, in any given context, a number of different actions could express my character. This is a reasonable claim, but it does not undermine Nietzsche's argument since he can simply respond that the fact that I do act in one way and not another, that I act on the basis of one evaluation and not another, illuminates the ranking of the different (perhaps contradictory) features of my character: 'A human being's evaluations betray something of the *structure* of his soul' (BGE §268).

Consider for a moment our response to someone we know who acts in an unexpected way, who acts 'out of character'; typically, in such cases, we seek reasons – 'She's not herself at the moment because . . .' – and if we can't find reasons (and/or the reasons offered by the person concerned don't seem adequate), we are likely to think that our assessment of their character is mistaken – 'She has more of a temper than I thought' (consider further the identical form of one's response to unexpected actions by oneself). These considerations seem to support Nietzsche's claims about character and, thus, his argument that one is fated to act as one does because how one acts is what one is. Human beings are pieces of fate. Thus, to love one's own fate is to love one's life, to affirm the relationship of self and world.

However, in the same way that we talk about the character of a person, we also talk about the character of a culture, of humanity and of the world. Indeed, the piece of fate that I am is a part of the piece of fate that my culture is, which is part of the piece of fate that is humanity, which is, in turn, part of the fate of the world.[2] In other words, my narrative is part of the narrative of my culture, which is part of the narrative of humanity, which is part of the narrative of the world. Consequently, when Nietzsche talks about love of fate, we may suggest that he is not simply recommending love of one's own fate but love of the fate of one's culture, of humanity and of the world. A more precise way of putting this point would be to say that Nietzsche is arguing that the *total* love of one's fate requires the love of the *totality* of fate. This is not to say that one cannot love one's fate to different degrees, but simply to argue that the *highest* affirmation of the relationship of self and world involves the love of the fate of the world. Another way of putting this point is simply to say that *amor fati* represents our *maximal* possible feeling of power. To reflect on this claim, recall Nietzsche's characterisation of happiness as the feeling of the increase in power which attends the overcoming of resistances. In the context of this notion of happiness, love of the totality of fate reveals itself as the overcoming of all resistances to affirmation and, thus, as the maximal feeling of power.

Thus far, then, we have examined the experiential and conceptual aspects of Nietzsche's recommendation of *amor fati*, but what is the relationship between *amor fati* and the Overman? This relationship has already been gestured to by the passage on 'Elevated Moods' and is neatly expressed by Leslie Paul Thiele: '*Amor fati* is the disposition of the Overman' (1990: 200). Nietzsche gives lyrical expression to his vision of the Overman in the following passage, which is worth quoting at length:

> Anyone who manages to experience the history of humanity as a whole as *his own history* will feel in an enormously generalized way all the grief of an invalid who thinks of health, of an old man who thinks of the dreams of his youth, of a lover deprived of his beloved, of the martyr whose ideal is perishing, of the hero on the evening after a battle that has decided nothing but brought him wounds and the loss of his friend. But if one endured, if one *could* endure the immense sum of this grief of all kinds while yet being the hero who, as the second day of battle breaks, welcomes the dawn and his fortune, being a person whose horizon encompasses thousands of years past and future, being the heir of all the nobility of all past spirit – an heir with a sense of obligation, the most aristocratic of old nobles and at the same time the first of a new nobility – the like of which no age has yet seen or dreamed of; if one could burden one's soul with all of this – the oldest, the newest, losses, hopes, conquests, and the victories of humanity; if one could finally contain all this in one soul and crowd it into a single feeling – this would have to result in a happiness that humanity has not known so far: the laughter of a god full of power and love, full of tears and laughter, a happiness that, like the sun in the evening, continually bestows its inexhaustible riches, pouring them into the sea, feeling richest, as the sun does, only when even the poorest fisherman is still rowing with golden oars! This godlike feeling would then be called – humaneness.
>
> (GS §337)

In other words, the Overman is the being who can truthfully affirm the fate of the world and experiences in that affirmation of the maximal feeling of overflowing power. It is this affirmation that is the abysmal thought with which Zarathustra struggles for so long and finally comes to terms with at the end of part three of *Thus Spoke Zarathustra* in the section entitled 'The Seven Seals (or: the Song of Yes and Amen)' wherein Zarathustra's song, which marks his affirmation, echoes the disposition of the passage just cited in its refrain '*For I love you, O eternity!*'

However, given the relationship which I have claimed exists between *amor fati* and self-mastery, we can say more about the character of the Overman by suggesting that this figure represents a *perfectionist* ideal of self-mastery. This claim can be at least partially supported by Nietzsche's recommendation of self-mastery in the following passage, in which it is presented in terms of making oneself a work of art:

> *One thing is needful*: To 'give style' to one's character – a great and rare art! It is practiced by those who survey all the strengths and weaknesses of their nature and then fit them into an artistic plan until every one of them appears as art and reason and even weaknesses delight the eye. . . . In the end, when the work is finished, it becomes evident how the constraint of a single taste governed and formed everything large and small. Whether this taste was good or bad is less important than one might suppose, if only it was a single taste!
>
> (GS §290)

This passage suggests that becoming what one is can be likened to the process of creating a work of art in which the achievement of self-mastery is revealed as the constraint of style given content through a single taste. Our discussion of eternal recurrence will support and develop this relation to self-mastery, but before we move to this crucial discussion, we should note a possible line of objection to Nietzsche's recommendation of *amor fati*. Such an objection might proceed thus:

> In the context of twentieth-century history (let alone world history), isn't this idea of loving fate *obscene*? How can Nietzsche seriously recommend an ideal which seems to require the affirmation of, for example, the Holocaust? Moreover, in the context of the re-emergence of fascism and neo-Nazism in Europe (America, of course, has its own home-grown Christian varieties), isn't it utterly irresponsible (not to say abhorrent) to propagate the ideas of such a thinker?

These are serious questions and, while I think they are based on a misunderstanding of what Nietzsche means by 'affirmation' and 'love of fate', we should recognise the necessity of addressing these concerns. In order to take up this task, and to support earlier claims in this section, let us turn to Nietzsche's notion of eternal recurrence.

The Thought of Eternal Recurrence

There seems little doubt that Nietzsche regarded the thought of eternal recurrence as the linchpin of his mature thinking; however, there is considerable disagreement among Nietzsche scholars as to the form and function of this thought.[3] Typically such disagreements focus on the relationship between the ideas of will to power, eternal recurrence and the Overman which are often held to be incompatible in some way or other.[4] In this context, the need to situate the concept of eternal recurrence with respect to the concepts of will to power and the Overman becomes an important concern for any attempt to do justice to Nietzsche's thought; indeed, it was for this reason that I felt constrained to take up the question of the necessity of a counter-ideal by addressing the question of how Nietzsche thinks about the form of ethical reflection. It will be recalled that one of our conclusions was that, for Nietzsche, ethical reflection entails the provision of an ontological account of human beings, a set of ethical precepts and ascetic practices, and a *telos*. In this context, let me propose the following schema:

1   Ontological account: the thesis of will to power.
2   Ethical precept: the 'rule' of eternal recurrence.
3   Ascetic practices: self-overcoming – any form of artistic work on the style of one's character, the narrative unity of the self, consonant with the 'rule' of eternal recurrence; the practical cultivation of ethical virtues.
4   *Telos*: the Overman and *amor fati*.

In a sense, we have already explored arguments for the first and fourth dimensions of the schema but, in order to tie them into the second and third dimensions, I will spend this section arguing for the cogency of this way of thinking about the central concepts in Nietzsche's philosophy by focusing on the idea of eternal recurrence.

Let us begin by specifying the tasks involved in this project. Firstly, it is necessary to set out the formal character of eternal recurrence and its relationship to *amor fati*. Secondly, we need to develop the claim that eternal recurrence and *amor fati* are tied to self-mastery. This will involve clarifying the claim that *amor fati* represents our maximal experience of will to power. Thirdly, we must fulfil our commitment to explaining the sense of 'affirmation' revealed in this idea. We will leave the question of whether or not modern individuals have the capacity to pursue the ideal of the Overman through the thought of eternal recurrence until after our discussion of the Last Man.

What kind of thought is the thought of eternal recurrence? How does it relate to *amor fati*? Consider the following passage:

> *The greatest weight* – What if, some day or night, a demon were to steal after you into your loneliest loneliness and say to you: 'This life as you now live it and have lived it, you will have to live once more and innumerable times more; and there will be nothing new in it, but every pain and every joy and every thought and sigh and everything unutterably small or great in your life will have to return to you, all in the same succession and sequence – even this spider and this moonlight between the trees, and even this moment and I myself. The eternal hourglass of existence is turned upside down again and again, and you with it, speck of dust!'
> Would you not throw yourself down and gnash your teeth and curse the

demon who spoke thus? Or have you once experienced a tremendous moment when you would have answered him: 'You are a god and never have I heard anything more divine.' If this thought gained possession of you, it would change you as you are or perhaps crush you. The question in each and everything, 'Do you desire this once more and innumerable times more?' would lie upon your actions as the greatest weight. Or how well disposed would you have to become to yourself and to life *to crave nothing more fervently* than this ultimate confirmation and seal?

(GS §341)

This passage is characterised by a lyrical simplicity of expression which conceals the complexity of its character. Let us begin by noting that this passage does not disclose a *cosmological* thesis but poses a *hypothetical* question: can you affirm (i.e., will) the eternal recurrence of your life? Nietzsche's reference to 'a tremendous moment' when one could make such an affirmation directs us to the moments of *amor fati* already discussed because we experience such moments as a *justification* or *redemption* of our being what we are (with all that this entails). In this context, we can grasp the relation of eternal recurrence to *amor fati* in this passage in a twofold sense. Firstly, the thought of eternal recurrence embodies the conceptual structure of *amor fati* in drawing our attention to the fact that to affirm the fleeting moments of the experience of *amor fati* entails not only affirming all the moments of one's life prior to this experience and as such constitutive of its possibility but also affirming the *necessity* (eternal recurrence) of one's being what one is. Secondly, the thought of eternal recurrence acts as a test of our *present* capacity to love fate, to embrace the necessity of our being what we are, by posing the question 'Do you desire this once more and innumerable times more?' If we reflect on these two aspects of the thought of eternal recurrence, we can note that insofar as it reproduces the conceptual structure of the experience of *amor fati*, so too the experiential structure of the affirmation of eternal recurrence reveals itself as the experience of *amor fati*; it is this which makes the thought of eternal recurrence a test of one's capacity to love fate. In other words, our capacity to experience *amor fati* is tied to our capacity to affirm the thought of eternal recurrence; to affirm this thought truthfully is to experience *amor fati*.

Of course, to experience a moment in which one can affirm the thought of eternal recurrence is not to say that one can go on affirming this thought; such moments are all too fleeting. But insofar as we can both identify the affirmation of the thought of eternal recurrence with the experience of *amor fati* and recognise the *telos* of human existence in the ideal of a human being who is *amor fati* incarnate (the Overman), then the thought of eternal recurrence acts as an ethical imperative: 'act always according to that maxim which you can at the same time will as eternally recurring'. We can give this alternate expression by referring to the thought of eternal recurrence as the rule of an *eroticised asceticism*: 'erotic' because it does not abstract from the embodied and embedded character of human agency, and 'ascetic' because it places a purely formal constraint on the expression of our erotic nature, it channels the activity of willing towards the formal architectonic goal of the Overman. In this sense, the thought of eternal recurrence acts both as a test of our *present* capacity to love fate and as an ethical rule for our *future* actions – but what of our past actions? Does the thought of eternal recurrence have any significance here?

Consider the following passage from *Thus Spoke Zarathustra*, in which Zarathustra comments on the relationship between willing and the past:

> Will – that is what the liberator and bringer of joy is called: thus I have taught you, my friends! But now learn this as well: The will itself is still a prisoner.
>
> Willing liberates: but what it is that fastens in fetters even the liberator?
>
> 'It was': that is what the will's teeth-gnashing and most lonely affliction is called. Powerless against that which has been done, the will is the angry spectator of things past.
>
> The will cannot will backwards; that it cannot break time and time's desire – that is the will's most lonely affliction.
>
> (Z 'Of Redemption')

It is worth noting that the image of the will's 'teeth-gnashing' in Zarathustra's remarks recalls Nietzsche's phrase 'Would you not throw yourself down and *gnash your teeth* and curse the demon who spoke thus? (GS §341, my italics) from the presentation of eternal recurrence discussed above. Whatever we make of this similarity of expression, it seems clear that Zarathustra is drawing our attention to the fact that past actions and events have the character of *necessity*; however much we feel ashamed of our past actions and, thus, regret them, we cannot change either these actions or the fact that they are partially constitutive of what we are. Thus we may imagine that, confronted by the thought of eternal recurrence, one might be overwhelmed with nausea and pity – nausea because we regret these actions and pity because we recognise that we cannot change them. In such an all too imaginable situation, it seems likely one would feel crushed by the thought of eternal recurrence. But does the feeling of shame which attends our recognition of the ignoble character of certain of our actions have a *necessary* connection with the feeling of regret? In a remark from his 'positivist' period, Nietzsche comments:

> *Remorse* – Never give way to remorse, but immediately say to yourself: that would merely mean adding a second stupidity to the first. – If you have done harm, see how you can do good.
>
> (WS §323)

It is in this respect that I think that the thought of eternal recurrence is significant for past actions which one cannot in good conscience affirm, because in forcing us to confront the fact that our shameful past actions are constitutive of what we are, it reveals a way to redeem these actions by transforming them into motivational resources for overcoming our shame by *becoming* what we are through the pursuit of *amor fati*, that is, submission to the rule of eternal recurrence in its prospective role as ethical imperative. In other words, if the thought of eternal recurrence gains possession of us, we may experience this possession as feeling crushed (because we are ashamed of many of our past actions), yet precisely because this 'feeling crushed' is a feeling of a *decrease of power*, we are motivated to overcome this feeling and we recognise that we can overcome it by using it as an affective resource for performing noble actions in the future.

What is going on in this breaking of the connection between shame and regret? If we return to the example of my diet, which was deployed in our discussion of the necessity of a counter-ideal, we can see that the thought of eternal recurrence heightens my feeling of shame at failing to achieve my goal (my lack of self-mastery) by asking me to contemplate the eternal recurrence of this failure and the attendant feeling of shame. In the face of this abysmal prospect, I am motivated to overcome (and thus redeem) my failure by using my shame as a resource to embark on a new diet and to succeed in achieving my goal of weight-loss in the full recognition that my desire for sausage, bacon, egg and chips may overwhelm me once again. In this way, my feelings of *nausea* ('I regret failing. God, I'm feeble') and *pity* ('I wish I could change my past failure – what I am – but I know that I can't') are transformed into the dispositions of *heroism* which attends my embarkation on a new diet ('I am determined to succeed this time and redeem my past failure!') and *ironic cheerfulness* (or self-parody) which attends my recognition that, being what I am, I may fail again ('Once more unto the diet, dear friends . . .').

Having sketched the character of the thought of eternal recurrence and its relationship to *amor fati* by specifying it as the ethical rule of an eroticised asceticism, we can turn to the topics of self-mastery and will to power. Recalling Nietzsche's characterisation of self-mastery in terms of giving style to one's character, we can now see that the thought of eternal recurrence operates for Nietzsche as the law of stylistic constraint which constitutes self-mastery. Notably, it is in respect of this self-mastery that Nietzsche expresses his admiration for Goethe in a revealing passage:

[Goethe] did not sever himself from life, he placed himself within it; nothing could discourage him and he took as much as possible upon himself, above himself, within himself. What he aspired to was *totality*; he strove against the separation of reason, sensuality, feeling, will . . .; he disciplined himself to a whole, he *created* himself. . . . A spirit thus *emancipated* stands in the midst of the universe with a joyful and trusting fatalism, in the *faith* that only what is separate and individual may be rejected, that in the total-ity everything is redeemed and affirmed – *he no longer denies.*

(TI 'Expeditions of an Untimely Man' §49)

On the evidence of this passage, Nietzsche regards Goethe as the best exem-plar of the Overman that Europe has produced. Here self-mastery reveals itself as the maximal feeling of power since it denotes the overcoming of all resistances in the affirmation of the totality of what is: 'Yes and Amen!'[5]

Yet we should also note another feature of the activity of giving style to one's character (achieving self-mastery), namely, that Nietzsche is not con-cerned with specifying what the content of one's character *ought* to be, that is, the *taste* which guides one's stylistic activity. In other words, the thought of eternal recurrence is not concerned with *what* is affirmed, only with submis-sion to this law of affirmation. This point has been drawn out by Keith Ansell-Pearson through a comparison of Nietzsche's thought of eternal recurrence with Kant's categorical imperative:

Like the categorical imperative, the thought of eternal recurrence has a universal character or form, but unlike the categorical imperative, it does not posit a universal content. However, it might be argued in response that the categorical imperative too is a purely formal doctrine, for it has no determinate content. But the key point is that, although the categorical imperative is indeed formalistic, its willing does *presuppose* that the actions the autonomous will is to will are universal in content: always will in such a way that the maxims of your actions are capable of being universalized into universal natural laws. The eternal return, however, provides the form of universality in the act of returning, whereas what returns (the actual content) and is willed to be returned cannot be universal, since each life (each becoming) is unique.

(Ansell-Pearson, 1991: 198)

The importance of this point is that it raises the question of whether or not it is appropriate to describe the thought of eternal recurrence as an *ethical* imperative since it is unclear if it has any ethical content. Another way of putting this point would be to ask if self-mastery can properly be regarded as an ethical (hyper)good. Couldn't I quite consistently act in ways which most people would find morally abhorrent while willing the eternal recurrence of these acts? Appealing to will to power will not help us here since this onto-logical thesis is quite consistent with obtaining a feeling of power by tortur-ing others (recall the ancient noble); while appealing to *amor fati* or the figure of the Overman just restates the problem since I have argued that these notions are formulations of self-mastery and don't entail anything about the content of the self which is mastered. So in what sense, if any, does Nietzsche's notion of eternal recurrence involve an ethics?

Perhaps we can get some hints on this topic by noting the characteristics of the Kantian – God's-eye view – position which Nietzsche attacks, namely, impartiality and universalisability. With respect to impartiality, recall Nietzsche's comments on its epistemic correlate, namely, objectivity, which he argues should be 'understood not as "contemplation without interest" (which is a nonsensical absurdity), but as the ability *to control* one's Pro and Con' (GM III §12). On this analogy, impartiality is tied to self-mastery and means being able to consider 'a *variety* of perspectives and affective interpretations' in coming to an ethical judgement consonant with our being able to will its eternal recurrence. Thus, for example, if my mother and a great scientist are trapped in a burning lift and I can only get one of them out before they both die,[6] I can consider and weigh up a variety of perspectives against each other such as that of family loyalty and love versus utility to humanity. All that the law of eternal recurrence states is a rule which enables one to reflect on which evaluation one could will as eternally recurring, which evaluation one experiences under the aegis of this rule as *necessity*. Asked why I saved my mother or the great scientist, I respond 'Because I had to', and asked to expand on this statement, I respond 'Because that is what I am. I could not have lived with myself if I had not acted in this way.' We can note that this example reveals the reason for Nietzsche's attack on universality, namely, I cannot reasonably demand (as Kant's categorical imperative would have us do) that all persons should act in the way that I acted because other people may be committed to different evaluations (i.e., have different characters) which they experience as necessity under the aegis of eternal recurrence. This is Nietzsche's point when he comments:

> A word against Kant as a *moralist*. A virtue has to be *our* invention, *our* most personal defence and necessity: in any other sense it is merely a danger.
>
> (AC §II)

Reflecting on this critique of Kant's notions of impartiality (as impersonal neutrality) and universality (as applying to the content of moral action), we can suggest that Nietzsche's thought of eternal recurrence does seem to involve at least one virtue which is tied to self-mastery, namely, *integrity*. Indeed, this point seems intuitively obvious if we recall that we use 'personal integrity' to refer to someone's life possessing a coherence and 'ethical integrity' to refer to someone's life exhibiting a coherence in terms of his or her substantive ethical commitments.[7]

To elucidate this point, let us turn once more to my recurring diet. What is the nature of the commitment I make when I decide to go on a diet? It seems reasonable to characterise this commitment as a *promise* which I make to myself, and if I say to other people 'I promise to stay on my diet', keeping this promise to others is predicated on keeping my promise to myself. Insofar as I stay on my diet, I keep my promise to myself, and we refer to this keeping of promises to oneself as 'personal integrity'; however, we also refer to my staying on my diet, my overcoming of my desire for fattening, as 'self-mastery'. We should note that this example helps draw out the point that a feature of integrity is that it involves self-mastery in the sense of overcoming resistances; this can be clarified by noting that if I did not have a desire for fattening food, we would not appropriately refer to my avoidance of such food as an example of integrity. In other words, to make a promise to oneself entails having a reason for making a promise, that is, placing a constraint on oneself, and if I have no desire for fattening food, I have no reason for placing myself under this constraint. This point makes clear the relationship between integrity and self-mastery, which we can state thus: integrity is the exhibition of self-mastery since one's capacity to keep one's promises to oneself is dependent on one's mastery of one's self at this time and is also the ethical work one does on oneself to develop one's capacity for self-mastery. With respect to 'ethical integrity', we can simply note that my substantive ethical commitments (whatever they may be) are, like my commitment to dieting, promises I make to myself, and as such the same conclusions follow. We should make clear that this position does entail an ethical rule immanent to the concept of integrity, namely, 'if you make promises, keep them', since to break a promise to another person is to break one's promise to oneself to keep promises (of course, this does not entail that one must make promises to others, but what would a life which included no commitments to others consist in?).

We should stress that this discussion does not entail that one's ethical (or other) commitments may not change in the course of one's life either in terms of how they are ranked or in terms of what they consist in; it does, however, entail that we can give reasons for these changes in terms of our reordered or new ethical commitments which sustain our commitment to integrity as the *ruling* virtue (or, to put it another way, maintain the narrative unity of one's life). Recalling our discussion of will to power and the displacement of one conceptual scheme by another, we can suggest that it is a *necessary* feature of our new substantive ethical scheme (the ordered totality of our substantive ethical commitments) that it not only provides an overcoming of the reasons which led us to abandon our previous scheme, but also offers an adequate account of the reasons for the failure of our previous substantive scheme. To avoid confusion, we should probably re-emphasise the point which began our discussion, namely, that a plurality of substantive schemes are compatible with the formal scheme which Nietzsche offers in terms of will to power, eternal recurrence and the Overman.

Three brief final – and possibly obvious – points on this question of the ethical character of eternal recurrence. Firstly, we can note that this formal ethical rule – or *law of integrity* as we may now call it – constructs an ethical framework structured around the concepts of *shame* (lack of integrity) and *honour* (integrity). Secondly, we can see that keeping a promise (i.e., submitting to the law of eternal recurrence) is both an instance of honour and, concomitantly, part of the constitution of an honourable life. It is in this context that Nietzsche refers to the affective disposition of *reverence* – the valuing of, and respect for, honour – as an integral feature of noble morality (see, for example, BGE §§260, 265, 287), which also draws into the affective dimension of this ethical framework the opposite of reverence, namely, *disdain*. Thirdly, it is apparent that one exhibits one's nobility (self-mastery) *publicly* by acting in accordance with the commitments one espouses. In summary then, we can state that the law of eternal recurrence is an ethical rule and that the Overman is an ethical ideal but that this rule and ideal are formal in character. We can note in passing that this discussion indirectly clarifies why Nietzsche characterises self-mastery in terms of making the self into a work of art, because it is the defining feature of a work of art that it possesses internal coherence which we typically refer to as the integrity of the work.

At this juncture, let us turn to the objection posed to the idea of *amor fati* at the end of the preceding section, namely, that it is an abhorrent thought because it involves *affirming* events such as the Holocaust. Turning to this objection also draws our attention to the point that the thought of eternal recurrence does not entail simply becoming able to affirm one's own life but also becoming able to affirm the totality of fate (a feature somewhat elided in the discussion thus far). The point missed by this objection is that the act of affirmation does not occur outside of time but, on the contrary, is temporally situated and as such recognises the *necessary* character of past events, that is, our inability to will backwards – only the future is open to us. Consequently, Nietzsche's point is that rather than being consumed and, perhaps, paralysed by the remorse (nausea and pity) which attends our shame at humanity for committing such genocidal atrocities, we must *struggle* to redeem humanity by reflecting on such events in order to motivate us both to act with nobility ourselves and, concomitantly, to pursue the goal of a humanity characterised by nobility (in which such expressions of *ressentiment* are impossible). In other words, I think Nietzsche's commitment to the idea that *amor fati* requires the love of the totality of fate is tied to the argument that while as an individual I am accountable for my actions because these actions are constitutive of what I am, as a member of humanity I am accountable for the actions of humanity because these actions are also constitutive of what I am: the Holocaust is part of the conditions of possibility of my being what I am. This is a crushing thought and one might wonder what one can do to struggle to redeem humanity from its past and present barbarism or if one can do anything that makes a difference. Nietzsche's point is this: just as the performance of a noble action is partially constitutive of a noble life, so too the living of a noble life is partially constitutive of a noble humanity: in seeking to live noble lives ourselves (self-overcoming), we help to bring about the goal of a noble humanity, that is, we contribute to the self-overcoming of humanity. Thus, far from being ethically abhorrent, Nietzsche's teaching of eternal recurrence calls on us to take responsibility for ourselves and for humanity in developing an ethical culture characterised by honour and reverence.

The aim of this section has been to make plausible the ethical schema presented at its outset by reflecting on the thought of eternal recurrence and illustrating its connections to will to power, self-overcoming and the Overman as incarnate *amor fati*. The argument developed has suggested that we can grasp the rule of eternal recurrence as a law of integrity which tests our self-mastery (capacity to love fate) and enjoins us to cultivate an honourable life by seeking to overcome those aspects of ourselves which are ignoble, that is, involve dishonesty or self-deception (recall Nietzsche's noting of the fact that the ancient Greeks referred to themselves as 'the truthful'). This argument led to the conclusion that the law of eternal recurrence cultivates an ethical scheme characterised by the ethical virtues of honour and shame and, relatedly, as the valuing of honour and the devaluing of shame, the dispositions of reverence and disdain. We have also noted that the submission to the law of eternal recurrence is not a private, solipsistic activity but is a public activity in the sense of being subject to public criteria and exhibited through the consonance of actions and commitments, and as such is subject to public testing (I will return to the publicity of integrity in the next chapter). However, it must be stressed that we have said nothing about the capacity of modern individuals to submit to the law of eternal recurrence, to pursue the goal of the Overman; this topic is central to our concerns, but before we address it, let us turn to the other 'ideal' which Nietzsche specifies as immanent in modern culture: the Last Man.

'Happiness' and the Last Man

By contrast with the topics of *amor fati*, eternal recurrence and the Overman, Nietzsche says very little about the figure of the Last Man. However, since this figure emerges as a contrast to the figure of the Overman, we need to try to elucidate at least some of the characteristics of the Last Man. In opening this discussion, I want to make two claims which I think are necessary consequences of Nietzsche's deployment of the Last Man as a contrast to the Overman. Firstly, the Last Man must also be consonant with the collapse of the ascetic ideal and, concomitantly, beyond the legislative authority of the ascetic priest. Thus, for example, on this argument we cannot claim that Kantians are exemplars of the Last Man; while Nietzsche deeply objects to the Kantian position, he places it under the aegis of the ascetic ideal as an exemplification of an ascetic legislation. Secondly, insofar as Nietzsche is seeking to cultivate a feeling of reverence towards the figure of the Overman, he is also seeking to nourish a feeling of contempt towards the figure of the Last Man. Noting these claims, let us turn to the task of elucidating the characteristics of this figure.

The Last Man appears in *Thus Spoke Zarathustra* during 'Zarathustra's Prologue' and is explicitly presented by Zarathustra in terms of a contrast with the Overman. Zarathustra speaks thus:

> Behold! I shall show you the *Last Man*.
>
> 'What is love? What is creation? What is longing? What is a star?' thus asks the Last Man and blinks.
>
> The earth has become small, and upon it hops the Last Man, who makes everything small. His race is as inexterminable as the flea; the Last Man lives longest.
>
> 'We have discovered happiness,' say the Last Men and blink.
>
> They have left the places where living was hard: for one needs warmth. One still love's one's neighbour and rubs against him for one needs warmth.
>
> Sickness and mistrust count as sins with them: one should go about warily. He is a fool who still stumbles over stones or over men!
>
> A little poison now and then: that produces pleasant dreams. And a lot of poison at last, for a pleasant death.
>
> They still work, for work is entertainment. But they take care the entertainment does not exhaust them.
>
> Nobody grows rich or poor anymore: both are too much of a burden. Who still wants to rule? Who obey? Both are too much of a burden.
>
> No herdsman and one herd. Everyone wants the same thing, everyone is the same: whoever thinks otherwise goes voluntarily into the madhouse.
>
> 'Formerly all the world was mad,' say the most acute of them and blink.
>
> They are clever and know everything that has ever happened: so there is no end to their mockery. They still quarrel, but soon they make up – otherwise indigestion would result.
>
> They have their little pleasure for the day and their little pleasure for the night: but they respect health.
>
> 'We have discovered happiness,' say the Last Men and blink.
>
> (Z. 'Zarathustra's Prologue' §5)

In this speech Zarathustra presents the Last Man as a being whose intellectual horizons are defined by the displacement of a concern for truth and a feeling of wonder at existence in favour of a concern for happiness characterised in terms of material comfort and spiritual complacency; the Last Man is troubled by suffering (unhappiness) and seeks to banish it through morality – by affirming the equal worth of all persons – and through technology – by overcoming scarcity – but only as long as this doesn't require too much effort (Lampert, 1986: 24–5). Characterised by a sense that the quest to achieve any ideal other than the preserving of a comfortable security in which to pursue one's preferences is mad, the Last Man engages in arguments as intellectual entertainment but doesn't take such arguments as being practically significant. He is too ironic and such constraints on superficiality might upset his indigestion. (Notably Zarathustra's attempt to deploy this contrast between the Overman and the Last Man at this stage is an utter failure; his audience embrace the 'ideal' of the Last Man.)

But why does Nietzsche despise the Last Man? In what sense is the Last Man an ideal-typical character embodying the features for which Nietzsche feels greatest contempt? Two answers present themselves. Firstly, Zarathustra's speech outlines figures for whom integrity (which Nietzsche also refer to as 'intellectual conscience')[8] is sacrificed to comfort; the Last Men feel neither honour nor shame, their souls are too shallow for these ethical emotions:

> . . . at one in their faith in the morality of *mutual* pity, as if it were morality in itself and the pinnacle, the *attained* pinnacle of man, the sole hope of the future, the consolation of the present and the great redemption from all the guilt of the past – at one, one and all, in their faith in the community as the *saviour*, that is to say in the herd, in 'themselves'.
>
> (BGE §202)

Secondly, and relatedly, Nietzsche argues that the Last Man's desire to be free of suffering erodes the possibility of nobility:

> You want if possible – and there is no madder 'if possible' – *to abolish suffering*. . . . Wellbeing as you understand it – that is no goal, that seems to us an *end*! A state which renders man ludicrous and contemptible – which makes it *desirable* that he should perish! The discipline of suffering, of *great* suffering – do you not know that it is *this* discipline alone which has created every elevation of mankind hitherto?
>
> (BGE §225)

This second objection to the Last Man is related to the first objection since integrity requires suffering in the sense that it requires overcoming desires which one would like to indulge (think back to my diet and resistance to the temptation of fattening food). Together these reasons reveal the worry which Nietzsche confronts with respect to the Last Man, namely, that the erosion of intellectual conscience and the capacity to place oneself under constraint in the name of freedom and freedom from suffering undermines not merely the present nobility of humanity and thus the redemption of the past but also the possibility of the future nobility of humanity; the culture of the Last Man abrogates its responsibility both to redeeming humanity's past and to enabling the elevation of humanity's future.

We should note, however, that the Last Man does solve the problem of nihilism – the will to nothingness – posed by the collapse of the ascetic ideal, although it achieves this resolution in a curious way. Consider, to begin, that the Last Man as a post-ascetic ideal involves accepting the view of the self as a web of desires situated both culturally and historically, which also informs the idea of the Overman. But whereas the figure of the Overman is entwined with the rule of eternal recurrence as a law of integrity, the figure of the Last Man is interwoven with another rule: don't be cruel to yourself or others, don't inflict suffering on yourself or others, *or* – to put it another way – don't subject yourself or others to constraints, be 'free' and let others be 'free'. *This is an ethical position*: 'Be nice!'

It is important to note this point, namely, that the Last Man is a counter-ideal to the ascetic ideal, not least because, if it is expressed in this way, this ideal has a certain attraction which consists in its commitment to maximising pleasure and minimising pain within a framework of equal rights: 'Do what you want to do, express your emotions, your subjective preferences – just don't harm others!' The central claim of this position is that the collapse of the foundationalist project entails that all conceptions of the good are simply subjective preferences, and that since we lack grounds on which to decide between them, the only objective good we can specify in terms of the ethical interests of our public political culture is that anyone be able to pursue their preferences to the extent that this is compatible with everyone else being able to pursue their preferences. Or, to give this alternate expression, since persons are simply the conception(s) of the good which they pursue (their value-commitments) and we have no grounds on which to rank conceptions of the good, it follows that all persons are of equal worth and we recognise this fact in granting everyone equal rights.

As these comments may suggest, for Nietzsche, a culture characterised by Last Men is the fulfilment of the vision of 'the *autonomous* herd' (BGE §202), which he associates with liberalism, and I will be concerned to draw out the political aspects of the cultivation of the Last Man in the next chapter by arguing that the figure of the Last Man is given precise expression in contemporary political theory as the *postmodern bourgeois liberal* advocated by Richard Rorty. For the moment, however, having sketched the dystopian ideal which Nietzsche identifies as immanent in modern culture, we can turn to his arguments concerning the possibility of the Overman and the Last Man, that is, the capacity of modern individuals to pursue these ideals.

Culture, Capacities and Counter-Ideals

We have seen that the two ideals which Nietzsche presents involve very different features; whereas the Overman represents a utopian ideal of integrity, the Last Man is a manifestation of the dystopian (anti-)ideal of comfortable freedom – freedom to pursue desires and freedom from suffering. To explore the question of the capacities of modern individuals to attain these ideals, we can begin by noting that the context in which the quotations from *Beyond*

Good and Evil cited in the last section are drawn is a critique of modern liberal democracy. This context suggests that Nietzsche regards the Last Man as the product of a liberal culture shorn of its theological and philosophical foundations. I will explore this aspect of Nietzsche's thought in the next chapter, but I mention it at this stage because it points us to the claim that Nietzsche regards the Last Man as simply involving the capacity of the Christian and the metaphysical liberal for engaging in rational calculation about one's desires (but without the spiritual discipline) which is developed under the aegis of anti-erotic asceticism,[9] and, since the Last Man does not seem to entail much more than this calculative capacity, I will focus my attention on the question of whether or not modern individuals possess the requisite capacities to submit to the rule of eternal recurrence and pursue the perfectionist ideal of integrity towards which it is directed.

Are modern individuals capable of integrity? We can address the question by dividing it into two distinct queries: firstly, what capacities are required for the pursuit of integrity and, secondly, do we find these capacities in modern individuals on the genealogical account of the constitution of modernity offered by Nietzsche? To take up the first of these questions, we can note that integrity seems to presuppose two capacities: *truthfulness*, which is required if we are to stand in a meaningful relation to the question of eternal recurrence (to make asking this question meaningful entails that we are capable of giving an honest response to it), and *the will to truth*, which is required if we are to have an interest in posing the question of eternal recurrence (if we do not value truth and specifically the truth about ourselves, we have no reason to ask this question of ourselves). These answers are revealing with respect to our second query, namely, whether or not modern man possesses these capacities, because a moment of reflection on the analysis of nihilism which began this chapter indicates that while Nietzsche certainly believes that modern individuals have the capacity for truthfulness which was bred under the aegis of Christian asceticism and was responsible finally for its self-destruction, he regards the will to truth as having been undermined by our truthfulness – this is the *telos* of the logic of nihilism. To offer further support for the idea that the capacity for truthfulness is immanent within modern culture, we can simply note a remark from the section 'Our Virtues' in *Beyond Good and Evil*:

> Honesty – granted that this is our virtue, from which we cannot get free, we free spirits – well, let us labor at it with all love and malice and not weary of 'perfecting' ourselves in *our* virtue, the only one we have: may its brightness one day overspread this ageing culture and its dull, gloomy seriousness like a gilded azure mocking evening glow!
>
> (BGE §227)

However, the fact that we are capable of truthfulness does not entail that we value truth; rather we require a reason to value truth in order to deploy and develop our capacity for truthfulness. This reason is given in Nietzsche's tying of integrity (i.e., self-mastery) in the form of the ideal of the Overman to *amor fati* as the maximum possible experience of the feeling of power (recall my three examples of fleeting moments of *amor fati*). This is revealed clearly in a comment already cited when Nietzsche remarks: 'Immortal is the moment when I produced the recurrence. . . . For the sake of this moment I *endure* the recurrence' (cited in Thiele, 1990: 204). The rapturous experience of such moments of wonder and joy is the fish-hook on which Nietzsche hopes to catch modern individuals by presenting the ideal of the Overman as incarnate *amor fati* and, thus, presenting integrity as the condition of experiencing such moments with respect to oneself. Within this framework, the will to truth is the will to *amor fati*.

But why do we value the experience – however fleeting – of *amor fati*? It may seem intuitively obvious that we do value such moments, but it is not so immediately apparent that we will necessarily continue to do so. Thus, for example, it is apparent that Nietzsche's portrayal of the Last Man presents a figure for whom the experience of such moments is not worth the cost in terms of self-discipline. My suggestion is that Nietzsche is seeking to mobilise the fact that we do value such moments to tackle the problem posed by the question of the *pathos of distance*. In order to state this problem, let us begin by reflecting on Nietzsche's concern with the pathos of distance. It will be recalled that it has been argued that a condition of experiencing oneself as autonomous (the feeling of power) is to experience oneself as a unified subject (and not just as an unorganised collection of social roles), and this is clearly central to Nietzsche's concern with integrity, but it was also argued that a condition of possibility of unified subjectivity is the pathos of distance, since it is this pathos which is internalised as 'inner distance' (the feeling of power over oneself). This is Nietzsche's point when he comments:

> Without the *pathos of distance* . . . that other, more mysterious pathos could not have developed either, that longing for an ever-increasing widening of distance within the soul itself, the formation of ever higher, rarer, more remote, tenser, more comprehensive states, in short, precisely the elevation of the type 'man', the continual 'self-overcoming of man', to take a moral formula in a super-moral sense.
>
> (BGE §257)

What, then, is the problem which Nietzsche confronts? We can note two types of pathos of distance recounted in Nietzsche's genealogy of modernity. On the one hand, the 'inner distance' of the ancient nobles is predicated on the pathos of *social* distance: 'a concept denoting political superiority always resolves itself into a concept denoting superiority of soul' (GM I §6). On the other hand, the 'inner distance' of the slave is predicated on a pathos of *metaphysical* distance, which appears, firstly, as a simple inversion of the social order of rank and, secondly, in the context of the ascetic priest, as the distinction between soul/mind/reason (grace) and flesh/body/affects (corruption). The problem raised by reflecting on these two types of pathos of distance is that *neither* is available to modern man! On the one hand, modern culture is characterised by a commitment to formal equality entrenched within the political institutions of democracy; besides which Nietzsche's comment that while he recognises the superiority of the ancient Greek to modern man, he wants nobility without the causes and conditions of Greek nobility (WP §882), although an unpublished note does suggest that he is not interested in advocating some anachronistic return to antiquity. On the other hand, given the collapse of the ascetic ideal wrought by our truthfulness, we cannot appeal to the imaginary constructions of metaphysics. To clarify how Nietzsche avoids being trapped by this problem, we can note the twist introduced by the ascetic priest, in which metaphysical distance is divorced from any relation to social distance; this strategy suggests that, under the aegis of asceticism, the pathos of distance is constructed *reflexively* in terms of distinct aspects of the self (in this case, soul versus body) which serve to mark the extremes of 'height' (soul) and 'depth' (body) requisite for the constitution of 'inner distance'. My suggestion is that Nietzsche's distinction between the utopian ideal of the Overman and the dystopian ideal of the Last Man is a post-metaphysical version of the same twist, in which the capacity for the reflexive constitution of 'inner distance' draws on the fact that, on Nietzsche's account, the Overman and the Last Man are the limit-ideals immanent within modern culture and the products of this culture, namely, modern individuals. *But* this strategy can only work if we value the experience of *amor fati*; if this ceases to be the case, the distance between the elevated heights of the Overman and the subterranean depths of the Last Man collapses.

On the account offered in this section, Nietzsche's claim that both the Overman and the Last Man are immanent possibilities within modern culture is consonant with his genealogy of modernity; indeed, one of the advantages of this account is that it explains why Nietzsche felt it to be necessary to sketch a dystopian ideal as well as a utopian ideal. But this account does raise a further question which can be addressed by way of a comment from Max Weber in one of his more Nietzschean moments:

> Without exception every order of social relations (however constituted) is, if one wishes to evaluate it, ultimately to be examined in terms of the human type (*menschlichen Typus*) to which it, by way of external or internal (motivational) selection, provides the optimal chances of becoming the dominant type.
>
> (cited in Hennis, 1983: 169)

The topic raised by this Nietzschean remark[10] is expressed by Nietzsche in terms of the relation between politics (external selection) and culture (internal selection). Of course, external and internal processes of selection are not independent of each other but reciprocally bound, and this is precisely Nietzsche's concern, namely, that the political institutions and processes of modern culture frame and constrain our forms of agency in ways which mitigate against the production and reproduction of the Overman as a cultural ideal and in favour of the cultivation of the Last Man. Elucidating how Nietzsche seeks to come to terms with this *political* question will be one of the tasks of the next chapter and, more specifically, of the critique of postmodern bourgeois liberalism. At this juncture, however, we need to take up a question which has been suspended throughout this chapter, namely, how is Nietzsche's claim to authority grounded? In other words, we need to ask on what ground Nietzsche claims the authority to recommend a cultural ideal at all.

Exemplarity and the Claim to Authority

Is Nietzsche an ascetic priest? While he offers an erotic asceticism, isn't Nietzsche simply taking up the role of the ascetic priest in specifying a cultural or, indeed, universal goal for humanity? As early as *Daybreak* Nietzsche is concerned to articulate the difference between himself and the type of ascetic priest characteristic of Christianity:

> Only if mankind possessed a universally recognised *goal* would it be possible to propose 'thus and thus is the *right* course of action': for the present there exists no such goal. It is thus irrational and trivial to impose the demands of morality upon mankind – to *recommend* a goal to mankind is something quite different: the goal is then thought of as something which *lies in our own discretion*; supposing the recommendation appealed to mankind, it could in pursuit of it also *impose* upon itself a moral law, likewise at its own discretion. But up to now the moral law has been supposed to stand *above* our likes and dislikes; one did not want actually to *impose* this law upon oneself, one wanted to *take* it from somewhere or *discover* it somewhere or *have it commanded to one* from somewhere.
>
> (D §108)

This passage draws our attention to two points. Firstly, Nietzsche is concerned that we take responsibility for imposing our own law on ourselves, a point repeated in Zarathustra's injunction that the individual 'must become judge and avenger and victim of his own law' (Z 'Of Self-Overcoming'). Secondly, and more significantly for our current concerns, Nietzsche distinguishes between *recommending* a cultural ideal to us, that is, making a *claim* on us (in the way, for example, a work of art does), and *commanding* a universal ideal. This point suggests that Nietzsche's objection to the ascetic priest, quite apart from *what* he recommends (although related to it), is his activity as a *legislator.*

Of course, Nietzsche would object to this legislative activity on the part of the ascetic priest because the legislation of a goal for humanity presupposes a transcendental ground of authority – a God's-eye view – which is only possible on the presupposition of a metaphysical conception of truth (and is, thus, related to the devaluation of *eros*). In this respect, Nietzsche's cheerful acknowledgement that he can only recommend a cultural or universal ideal is a consequence of his post-metaphysical erotic theory of truth. But does this position entail that any recommendation of a cultural ideal has a claim to authority? What is at stake in this discussion may become clearer if we admit that any recommendation of a cultural ideal may claim authority (i.e., none can be ruled out *a priori*) but our concern is with the conditions under which such a claim to authority is recognised by the public community. There are, I think, two relevant considerations. Firstly, any recommendation of a cultural ideal must involve an acknowledgement of our ethical interests (in the same way that any theory claiming truth must acknowledge our cognitive interests). Although we may (and do) disagree about what these interests are and how to rank them, such disagreements are bounded by our form of life. Of course, this is a fairly weak constraint since it simply says that if a recommendation of an ethical ideal is to claim authority, it must be intelligible to us as an ethical ideal (i.e., address some ethical interest or set of interests). The second constraint provides a stronger criterion and we can draw this rule out by reference to a distinction which Max Weber makes between legislative prophets, who ground their claim to authority in a transcendental argument which legitimates their right to command a goal, and exemplary prophets, who ground their claim to authority in the exemplification of their ideal which legitimates their right to recommend a goal. If we transpose this distinction onto philosophical arguments, we get a distinction between legislative and exemplary forms of argument: in examining whether or not to grant the claim to authority of an argument, our question is whether or not this argument establishes *either* transcendental criteria of rational argumentation which guarantee its right to command *or* exemplifies in the structure of its reflection the cultural ideal which it seeks to recommend. Since we have already ruled out the possibility of specifying transcendental criteria of rationality (although this project has been interestingly – if, I think, still mistakenly – renewed in the recent work of Jürgen Habermas), we are left with the criteria of exemplification. 'But', it might be objected, 'why do we need any such criterion?' A straightforward response to this objection becomes clear once we recognise the logically isomorphic character of the claim to authority of the prophet and the claim to authority of argument: if I recommend a cultural ideal to you, and I, as a member of the same culture, do not exhibit my commitment to this ideal in my life, then I am engaged in a performative contradiction which utterly undermines not the ideal I recommend but the process of recommendation. In other words, you can only take me (assuming we are members of the same culture) to be recommending a cultural ideal if I show my commitment to this ideal, otherwise you have no reason to think that what I am doing is 'recommending' an ideal. The implication of this argument is that if Nietzsche's argument is to legitimate its right to recommend an ideal (if we are to recognise its claim to authority as a valid claim and this says *nothing* about the degree of authority it will be granted, only that it has established the right to be considered), it must exhibit in the performance of its argument the ideal which it seeks to recommend. But does it?

To address this question in detail would require a book in itself and consequently I shall confine myself to the attempt to make plausible the claim that Nietzsche's argument is an exemplification of its commitment to the ideal of the Overman and *amor fati*. To perform this task, I will focus very briefly on three topics: firstly, the exemplification of the cognitive commitment to truthfulness (and, thereby, the value of truth) in Nietzsche's strategies of argument; secondly, the exemplification of the affective commitment to heroism and irony in Nietzsche's stylistic strategies; and finally Nietzsche's reflection on this topic in *Thus Spoke Zarathustra*.

To establish the plausibility of Nietzsche's performance of a commitment to truthfulness, two points will suffice. Firstly, the relentless attack on idols which characterises his work is undertaken in terms of a valuing of truthfulness. To take but one example, consider the following passage:

> Even with the most modest claim to integrity, one *must* know today that a theologian, a priest, a pope does not merely err in every sentence he speaks, he *lies* – that he is no longer free to lie 'innocently', out of 'ignorance'. The priest knows as well as anyone else that there is no longer any 'God', any 'sinner', any 'redeemer' – that 'free will', 'moral world-order' are lies – intellectual seriousness, the profound self-overcoming of the intellect, no longer *permits* anyone *not* to know about these things.
>
> (AC §38)

The tone of moral indignation which characterises this passage may be less ironic than is typical of Nietzsche's voice, but it does seem typical of the commitment to intellectual probity which characterises his writing. The second point, which buttresses this claim, concerns Nietzsche's relationship to his own work, and here I simply want to refer back to our discussion of the section 'How the "Real World" At Last Became a Myth', in which it was noted that Nietzsche's critique of metaphysical accounts of truth develops through three stages which are characterised by an ongoing ethos of autocritique. This self-critical relation to his work is given clearest expression in the 'Attempt at a Self-Criticism' attached to his first book, *The Birth of Tragedy*, in 1886.

If we turn to the question of whether Nietzsche's stylistic performance exhibits the dispositions of heroism and irony, the plausibility of our case may be less immediately obvious. However, we can note in this context that Alexander Nehamas has pointed out that the most pervasive figure deployed in Nietzsche's writing is that most unscholarly of tropes, '*hyperbole*', going so far as to claim that 'Nietzsche's writing is irreducibly hyperbolic' (1985: 22).[11] Why is this significant? I think that two considerations are relevant. Firstly, on his own account, Nietzsche is writing for an audience characterised by decadence, by the experience of affective exhaustion. As such, a stylistic strategy predicated on provocation, on a trope of exaggeration, might seem a prerequisite for generating affective engagement with his readers. In this sense, we can read Nietzsche's hyperbolic expressions of disdain for modern individuals and, in particular, Germans as attempts to engender an erotic agonism in the souls of his readers which parallels the cognitive agonism constructed by the contrast of the Overman and the Last Man. Recalling our discussion of the pathos of style, we can note that this topic is particularly significant in terms of the reading practices of his audience. By insulting, cajoling and provoking his readers to pay attention to his stylistic performance – the texture, tempo and tone of his language – Nietzsche can be seen to be attempting to constitute the conditions of affective communication whereby an affective investment in overcoming decadence is 'transferred' to his audience. The second consideration which we can bring to bear on this topic concerns the *ambivalence* of hyperbole as a rhetorical figure which oscillates between the heroic and the ironic (or self-parodic). Commenting on this trope both generally and in relation to Nietzsche's texts, Magnus, Stewart and Mileur note:

> Hyperbole is . . . inflated language, and since what goes up must come down, it follows from this deflated language as well. But hyperbole is not just the language of heights aspired to and depths fallen to, it is also the language of detours, of errancy, extravagance, and even errantry. . . . Exaggeration, extravagance, errantry, quest – synonymous with want of due proportion as error – hyperbole is also the excess that leads to quality, sublimity, greatness.
>
> (1993: 139)

Attending to the ambivalence of hyperbole as simultaneously inflated and deflated language (a kind of figural equivalent of the aspect change exhibited by pictures like Wittgenstein's duck/rabbit drawing), we can draw attention to Nietzsche's hyperbolic 'autobiography' *Ecce Homo*, which has been read by Nehamas (1985), amongst others, as an exemplification of the heroic self-overcoming of nihilism and decadence in which the dramatic structure of the text reveals Nietzsche's achievement of the task of giving style to his character. However, as Daniel Conway (1993) has argued, alongside the heroic Nietzsche, *Ecce Homo* also reveals an ironic or self-parodic Nietzsche who recognises that he may be engaged in self-deception and is concerned to deconstruct the monumental idol which the heroic register constructs. The double character of this hyperbolic text is revealed, for example, in the opening three titles – 'Why I Am So Wise', 'Why I Am So Clever', and 'Why I Write Such Good Books' – which can be read as both an inflationary monumental construction of heroic authority and a deflationary critical and ironic undermining of such authority. Throughout *Ecce Homo*, I suggest, the figure of Nietzsche as heroic prophet is doubled by that of Nietzsche as ironic critic of idolatry through a deployment of the ambivalence of hyperbole which sets up a complementary relation between the heroic and the ironic as mutually limiting (Conway, 1993). Thus, against the dispositions of nausea and pity which characterise decadence, Nietzsche's play on the ambivalence of hyperbole may be read as attempting to communicate the dispositions of heroism and irony appropriate to the overcoming of decadence and, consequently, provoking an affective contest within the soul of the reader.

The final observations which will be brought to bear on this question of exemplarity concern Nietzsche's own reflections on the topic of teaching the Overman and the doctrine of eternal recurrence as these reflections are exhibited in *Thus Spoke Zarathustra*. Here I simply want to draw attention to some features of Zarathustra's journey and to make a claim on the basis of these observations. In the opening two parts of the book, Zarathustra comes down from his mountain to announce the death of God and to preach the vision of the Overman initially to the public and latterly to a small group of disciples. His attempt to present his clearly Nietzschean teaching to the public is a pathetic failure and he is mocked as a fool, while his teaching to his disciples is hardly less of a failure because they fail to understand him. This latter failure is contemporaneous with Zarathustra's recognition that he has not himself realised the implications of his teaching and he leaves his disciples in the realisation that he needs to be able to affirm this teaching himself before being able to teach it. In part three, Zarathustra struggles with the abysmal thought of eternal recurrence before finally overcoming his nausea at humanity and affirming this thought. Part four brings a series of bizarre visitors to Zarathustra, with whom he contests (in overcoming his pity for mankind), before ending on a note of climactic affirmation and preparedness to return to the world to resume his teaching.

Reflecting on this woefully schematic summary, we can note that in both parts one and two Zarathustra acts as an ascetic priest in attempting to legislate an ideal (the Overman). However, in announcing the death of God, Zarathustra undermines his claim to public authority, and this point is marked by the public's laughter at his preaching. His attempt to legislate for his disciples is similarly undercut by his failure to manifest the ideal which he preaches, and this point is marked by the failure of understanding which greets his pronouncements. In this context, parts three and four may be read as Zarathustra's coming to exemplify the ideal which characterises his teaching by overcoming both his nausea and his pity towards humanity (and himself). Thus, when Zarathustra commences once more to return amongst humanity and resume his teaching at the end of the book, he has found a way to recommend his ideal by exemplifying it. The suggestion which I want to attach to this claim is that Zarathustra can teach the Overman by doing precisely what Nietzsche has done in writing *Thus Spoke Zarathustra*, that is, offering an exemplary account of becoming what one is which manifests the ideal it recommends. In other words, I want to assert that, in his writings, Nietzsche is committed to the project of exemplarity which I have ascribed to him.

In summary, the purpose of this section has been to suggest that Nietzsche does not engage in ascetic acts of legislation, since he recognises both that he has no grounds on which to do so and that such an act undermines the ethics which he recommends. I have argued (or, perhaps, asserted) that a concern with exemplification can be found in Nietzsche's reflections on teaching his ethics as these are performed in *Thus Spoke Zarathustra*, and that by attending to his commitment to truthfulness and to communicating the dispositions of heroism and irony through his stylistic strategies, we can conclude that it is plausible to claim that Nietzsche's writing does exemplify the ideal it recommends.

Conclusion

The concern of this chapter has been to set out the counter-ideal to the ascetic ideal which Nietzsche elaborates and to try to draw out the ethical implications of this ideal. It has been argued that Nietzsche's ethical position can be best expressed in terms of the schema: will to power as ontological thesis, eternal recurrence as ethical rule, self-overcoming as ethical ascetics, and *amor fati* and the Overman as *telos*. I have claimed that the contrast between the Overman and the Last Man is an attempt to construct the pathos of distance requisite to this ethics and that the capacities required to pursue this ethics are immanent in modern culture. Finally I have argued that Nietzsche's claim to the authority to recommend the ideal of the Overman is grounded in the exemplification of the ethical commitments of this figure in his writing. At this stage, then, let us turn to the question of how this ethical counter-ideal is connected to Nietzsche's agonistic politics.

Notes

1. Of course we might make this claim of lying in the grass as well, but only, I think, as part of some practice such as relaxing or meditation which involves particular skills.

2. I am not going to develop this point here, but Nietzsche's argument expands to include the love of the fate of the world and, ultimately, the universe. This might have some interesting implications for human/non-human relations but this would require an argument which I do not have the space to develop.

3. Does the idea of eternal recurrence represent a cosmological thesis or a hypothetical thesis? Is it a statement of fact or an ethical imperative? Is it selective or non-selective?

4. For example, Erich Heller (1988: 12) argues that the Overman and eternal recurrence are contradictory, while Lawrence Lampert (1986) argues that Nietzsche drops the idea of the Overman in favour of the idea of eternal recurrence. While with respect to will to power and eternal recurrence Tracy Strong comments: 'The will to power and eternal return represent the greatest stumbling blocks in any interpretation of Nietzsche. Separately, they are obscure enough; but their relationship to each other leaves most commentators in the embarrassed position of having to make a choice' (1988: 218).

5. For a brilliant discussion of this 'Yes and Amen!', see Howard Caygill's essay 'Affirmation and Eternal Return in the Free-Spirit Trilogy' (1991).

6. I borrow this example from Anne MacLean's excellent attack on utilitarianism, *The Elimination of Morality* (1993).

7. For a fascinating discussion of integrity which clarified a number of issues for me, see Lynne McFall's article 'Integrity' (1987).

8. Nietzsche's advocation of integrity as tied to his concern with intellectual conscience is most clearly exhibited in GS §335.

9. In this context, the Last Man is rather like Hobbes' conception of human beings.

10. Weber's relation to Nietzsche has recently received much attention. I make my own view clear in 'Autonomy and "InnerDistance": A Trace of Nietzsche in Weber' (Owen, 1991).

11 Nehamas goes on from this claim to develop an extremely insightful discussion contrasting Nietzsche's use of hyperbole with Socrates' use of irony (1985: 22–41). For an insightful alternative reading of Nietzsche's style in terms of concinnity, which I do not think is incompatible with that stressed here, see Chapter 1 of Babette Babich's *Nietzsche's Philosophy of Science* (1994).

52

Behold Nietzsche*

Michael Platt

*Source: *Nietzsche-Studien*, vol. 23, 1993, pp. 42–79.

In what follows I shall offer an interpretation of one of the strangest philosophical books ever written. If I am right, Nietzsche's *Ecce Homo* is unlike any of the books it is designed to resemble, celebrates one new virtue, advances a new order of the virtues, is an indispensable preface to all of Nietzsche's work, the most authoritative account of his life there will ever be, the culmination of his life, and perhaps the culmination of his work.

I Nietzsche on Nietzsche

There is no Homer on Homer, no Moses on Moses, no Sophocles on Sophocles, no Aristotle on Aristotle, no Tacitus on Tacitus, no Aquinas on Aquinas, no Ibn Khaldûn on Ibn Khaldûn, no Chaucer on Chaucer, no Machiavelli on Machiavelli, no Giorgione on Giorgione, no Bach on Bach, no Kleist on Kleist, and no Thucydides on Thucydides. There is, however, Nietzsche on Nietzsche.[1]

Nietzsche is one of a small number of great souls who have presented an account of their own life. His *Ecce Homo* is his *Apology*, his *Commentary on the Civil Wars*, his Crucifixion and Last Words, his *Confessions*, his *Essais*, his *Discourse of the Method*, his *Autobiography*, his *Confessions* and his *Reveries of a Solitary Walker*, his *Prelude*, his *Poetry and Truth* and his *Conversations with Eckermann*, his *Point of View of My Work as an Author*, and his *Letter on Humanism*. *Ecce Homo* is also like Rembrandt's 'Self-Portrait of 1660', or Van Gogh's 'Self-Portrait of January–February 1888' in which the art portrayed is the same as the art employed to portray the artist. Nevertheless, the mode of composition is more musical than painterly. *Ecce Homo* is a joyful *da capo* hymn to himself such as no composer has attempted.

Ecco Homo is Nietzsche on Nietzsche, and Nietzsche on Nietzsche is unlike any other great soul on itself.

Throughout his life Nietzsche compared himself to Sokrates and near the end, in *Götzen-Dämmerung* (*Twilight of the Idols*), he came close to according the Greek pied piper an enigmatic depth equal to his own. Here his description of himself as a decadent who has overcome his malaise puts him with the Sokrates who, as Nietzsche noted, confessed he was a monster who conquered himself. 'Know thyself' was, however, not his maxim; to become himself, Nietzsche had to submit to an idea which has gathered up all his mistakes, illnesses, and fragments and now makes him a destiny. Nietzsche's δαιμόνιον does not restrain the philosopher, as Sokrates' did, but eggs him on.

Thus, the charges Sokrates answers in his *Apology* are ones Nietzsche is proud to plead guilty to. Not only does he question the god of Europe, he attacks him. 'Introduce' is too pale a word for the exuberant way Nietzsche hails the new 'divinity' or being, Zarathustra. Does Nietzsche corrupt youth? He would if he could, but when he wrote *Ecce Homo* he was an ignored man. In the agora of Europe, no one recognized his near-sighted and far-eared visage and no Aristophanes had satirized him. 'Put me on trial' his *Apology*, *Ecce Homo*, demands. 'Put me on trial so that I can corrupt the youth.' In the *Crito* Sokrates supports the laws of civil society, even those of the city that condemned him. In *Ecce Homo* and elsewhere, Nietzsche condemns the laws of European civil society, one of whose universities supported him with a professorship and later with a pension. Nietzsche was neither citizen nor citizen philosopher like Sokrates. To Aristotle's remark at the beginning of the *Politics*: 'That man who lives outside the city must be either a beast or a god', Nietzsche riposted: 'leaving out the third case: one must be both – a *philosopher*' (*Twilight of the Idols*, 'Maxims and Arrows' 3). Or, we must add: a hermit of Sils Maria, a walker in arcaded Turin, and a wanderer between Alp and Mediterranean Sea, for after resigning his Basel professorship in 1879 Nietzsche had no home, only various haunts, watering holes, and Alpine pastures, which he visited like brief habits. That he regretted his only deed as a citizen, volunteering as a nurse in Bismarck's swift war against France in 1870, is clear from the way he attacks Germany and lauds France in *Ecce Homo* and elsewhere. However, according to Nietzsche himself, *Ecce Homo* is a civil deed. By declaring that he is ready to rule the world, he refutes Sokrates – far from shunning rule, the best want to rule (Za, 'On Old and New Tablets' 21). If we are to believe Nietzsche's *Apology*, his attack on Europe is for the sake of a super-Europe, of which he is the first citizen.

The sentiment of *amor fati* in *Ecce Homo* makes it a kind of 'Confessions'. At the end of his *Confessions*, Augustine blesses every chance, every confusion, every evil, in his life and in life as a whole. So does Nietzsche. At the end of his *Confessions*, Augustine nonetheless strives to save the souls of others. So, in his way, does Nietzsche. Yet his 'Confessions' are addressed to no Creator-God. Their author is more solitary than Augustine and, thus, more fearfully dependent on himself. Augustine's *Confessions* are a love song to

God, Nietzsche's a solitary love song to himself. Augustine's *Confessions* tell us how he sought what he later knows as his Creator, how he came to see himself as a sinning creature, and thus readied himself for the graceful gift of salvation. It is a story of how an original sinner became the saint he truly was. It is the subtitle of Nietzsche's 'Confessions': 'How One Becomes What One Is' that hints at the story in *Ecce Homo*. It points to the section, the only one that arranges its material chronologically, about Nietzsche's 'so gute Bücher'. Clearly *Zarathustra* is the book in and by and through which Nietzsche became what he was. Yet precisely here Nietzsche's solitude seems to vanish; here his 'Confessions' become a love song not to himself, but to Zarathustra. Is *Zarathustra* something Nietzsche wrote and created? Or, is it something or someone that was revealed to him? In *Ecce Homo* Nietzsche says both. Nietzsche could almost say of Zarathustra what Augustine says of God, you were there hidden in my beginning guiding me. Almost, not quite. Zarathustra is not the God who watches every hair on an Augustine's head. What Augustine recounts would exist for him even if he never wrote – *Zarathustra* unwritten does not exist. Only as a writer then can Nietzsche bless his life. And also present it. Having lost the Watchful, Loving Creator-God, Nietzsche is more solitary than Augustine, but also more dependent on other men. To become what he was Nietzsche had to present himself in *Ecce Homo*. Nietzsche could have been wise and sagacious without writing, but he could not have been a destiny without writing the good books he did write. Just as the gift-giving Zarathustra of *Zarathustra I* needs men to give to, so Nietzsche needs readers; just as the pregnant Zarathustra of *Zarathustra IV* awaits his children, so the Nietzsche of *Ecce Homo* awaits public fame. Looking forward, Nietzsche in *Ecce Homo* tries to become a destiny looking backward, he loves fate.

Nietzsche wanted to love himself well and also entirely. Augustine wanted to love himself entirely and could not do so until he saw that God did (indeed always had). Sokrates was content to know himself, or try to, and love or despise himself accordingly.

The question of friendship links *Ecce Homo* with the *Essais* of Montaigne. In their meandering course, Montaigne reveals much about his intelligent, diverse and *ondoyant* self. His turning away from public life was no violent conversion. From his tower he did not expect to sight heaven; on its rafters are human maxims: '*Que sçay je?*' (What do I know?) and '*homo sum: humani nil a me alienum puto*' (I am a man and count nothing human alien to me). His *Essais* are a preparation for death addressed not to God, but to himself, and to friends, both dead and yet to live. Only once does the urbane, intelligent Lord of Montaigne grow entirely earnest, nearly ardent, almost reverent. What most deeply stirs him is the recollection of his dead friend Etienne de La Boétie. Nietzsche lived entirely in a tower and his 'Essais', his 'Of Friendship', *Ecce Homo*, is addressed to old friends still living. In it he tells them more about who he is than he had ever told them in letters. To them

Ecce Homo seems to say, 'Know me? – You never knew me. Know me now. Hail and farewell.' What Nietzsche would have been if he had had a friend, such as Montaigne had in Etienne, is hard to say.

Wagner is the only living candidate, but like Etienne he fell away. That he fell away by choice, by choosing to make peace with the decadent, with pity, with the German *Reich*, and with a coarse, enthusiastic public, is more trying to Nietzsche than his early death in his arms would have been. Disappointment with Wagner, regret at having served him, and a sense of betrayal by him, all touch Nietzsche, but he overcomes them in his celebration of their first meetings and in his ranking of them as the finest meetings in his life. Meetings, or near meetings? Nietzsche tells us that what they shared was suffering from life and from each other. At age seven, Nietzsche knew he was alone. Now he tells us solitude is a virtue.

If great gifts and virtues are required for friendship, no man was more apt than Nietzsche, but if such gifts are rare, no man was more likely to be solitary. In a letter, Nietzsche once wrote:

> Es lebt übrigens jetzt Niemand, an dem mir viel gelegen wäre; die Menschen, die ich gerne habe, sind lange, lange todt, z. B. der Abbé Galiani oder Henry Beyle oder Montaigne.

> [Actually, there's no one living whom I could care *much* about; those I really like are long, long dead, e.g., Abbé Galiani or Henry Beyle or Montaigne] (to Franziska and Elisabeth Nietzsche, 14 March 1885).[2]

That he delivered this judgment to a living person (rather than keeping it in his diary)[3] shows both his detachment from humanity and his suffering from it. The 'friend' most present in *Ecce Homo* is not Wagner, or Cosima, or Lou von Salomé, or Overbeck, or Peter Gast, or Burckhardt, but Zarathustra, someone who could not be described as 'long, long dead' because he was never really alive, certainly not as alive as Nietzsche. Nietzsche's understanding of friendship excludes intimacy, deliberately and reluctantly. You should not look upon your friend sleeping or try to guess her dreams. Towards dead friends like Montaigne or yet to live ones, say Heidegger, Nietzsche maintains a star friendship. In *Ecce Homo* Nietzsche is a burning light; occasionally a twinkle from such another star may reach him, but such lights never embrace; if they meet, it is only in collision. Yet this self-sufficient, solitary star needs a European public to become the destiny he is. He needs pupils, disciples, and followers more than he needs friends. Finally, one might ask whether the author of *Ecce Homo* is a friend to himself. Does he treat himself as a friend, even a star friend?

II Behold me, not them

Nietzsche's *Ecce Homo* is also related to three modern thinkers who have felt called to present themselves to the public: Descartes, Rousseau, and Kierkegaard.

Nothing is more prominent in Descartes' fabulously autobiographical *Discourse of the Method of Rightly Conducting the Reason* than the word 'I'. Descartes' proof of his own existence not only comes before his proof of God's, but grounds it. The God of Descartes springs from the ratiocinative head of Descartes and also never leaves it. God is the creature, indeed a servile one, and Descartes the creator. (If it were otherwise, He would be an evil genius.) It cannot be accidental that Descartes' *cogito ergo sum* is creative in the image of the creative God. The six parts of the *Discourse* remind us of the six days of Genesis; for God-Descartes they point to humanity's day of rest in which men will walk directly in the morning, plan cities at noon and geometrize in the evening forever and ever. Although the pre-methodical Descartes sets out as a resolute walker in a forest, he soon comforts himself by certifying his existence, by adopting the method, and by resolving to master nature. At the end of the sixth Discourse 'day', Descartes claims to be a soldier, indeed a general who has won the decisive battle, in a war to make courage superfluous. Descartes was something worse than a Last Man: a great man who wanted, after his great labors, to become a Last Man. The Nietzsche we meet in *Ecce Homo* walks vigorously in the morning and in the afternoon; in the night he sings; and all day and all night he loves himself too much to become God. *Ecce Homo* is not a conquest of death because it is a preparation for it. Descartes said, 'Seeing that I am imperfect and wish to be perfect, there must be a God', whereas Nietzsche seems to say, 'If there were God, how could I not be him.'

In *Ecce Homo* there is none of Rousseau's concern with displaying himself, and his sexuality, which makes the *Confessions* a vain exhibition of the author and a coy seduction of the reader. In the way modern Americans on a bus or a train talk loudly about their 'sex lives' to strangers, Nietzsche would have seen indelicacy, a lack of thresholds and a want of cleanliness. In *Ecce Homo* Nietzsche says nothing of such things, nothing about the disappointment in love he may have borne. Fräulein Lou von Salomé is mentioned only as the author of a fine poem; Frau Cosima Wagner is mentioned in an entirely veiled manner. That Freud complained of *Ecce Homo* that it did not say enough about the author's 'sex life' only reveals his dogmatic indelicacy and hostile incomprehension of all things noble.[4] Rousseau said man was born free and good, but in his own *Confessions* shows he was born slave and bad, and yet he shows this without shame. True, Nietzsche admits in *Ecce Homo* to being a decadent, but without the shameful details, because he thought the overcoming of the base to be the important thing.

Moreover, for Nietzsche shame is something noble; the highest men often hide the best things about themselves. Nietzsche's *Ecce Homo* bears more resemblance to Rousseau's *Reveries of a Solitary Walker* than his *Confessions*. In them Rousseau to some degree overcomes the *amour propre* he complains so much of and the compassion he suffered so much from. From an accidental meeting with a hurtling dog, Rousseau attained a blissful sentiment of his own existence. Jean Jacques forgot he was Rousseau. When he remembered who he was, he interpreted his collision as fated and loved the Creator who destined it – a moment that resembles Nietzsche's blessing all his accidents without, in his case, thanking a Creator and without desiring to forget who he was. Rousseau opposed happiness to history; Nietzsche sought to identify them. Rousseau's life was a distraction that seldom allowed him to dwell happily in that from which he was distracted; Nietzsche's was an experiment for the sake of thinking. The human task as Nietzsche saw it was to love history.

Like Rousseau and like Kierkegaard, Nietzsche feared misinterpreters. *Ecce Homo* is his 'Dialogues' and his *Point of View of My Work as an Author*, for in it he aims to set right all his readers, extant and yet to be. *Ecce Homo* is the first secondary work on Nietzsche and all later ones are by nature attempts to replace or confirm it. Most ignore it. You can lead a horse to water, you can, with brawn, force his head into it, but you cannot make him drink a drop from it. Then again, when a subtle, artful man suddenly says, 'Let me be frank with you; all along I have meant one thing', watch out; he is probably only half frank, and that half to cover the other. Both Kierkegaard and Nietzsche love the ironic Sokrates, both are artful, and both claim to be frank, but they may not be.

On the vacillating state of the West, Nietzsche and Kiekegaard agree; the West is not Christian and it is not something else. Nietzsche's remark that modernity is 'Eine *Zeitung* an Stelle der tägüche *Gebete*' ('a daily newspaper in place of daily prayers') would have pleased the suffering Dane.[5] His general description of contemporary Europe as 'Christian morals without the Christian God'[6] accords with Kierkegaard's general claim that it is more difficult to be a Christian in Christendom than in times of persecution. While Kierkegaard contrasts reasonable morality with Christian faith – Abraham being either a child-killer or a knight of faith – Nietzsche contrasts the natural love of life with the holy hatred of it; Nietzsche as pro-life.[7] As their perspectives differ, so do their solutions. Whereas Kierkegaard would restore the Christian God, Nietzsche would get rid of Christian morals. In Paul, Christ became the spirit of revenge incarnate. However, there is a twist at the end of Nietzsche's rope. Christian, that is Pauline, morals traduced the Christian God. There was only one Christian and he died on the Cross. Christian morals have always been without the Christian God. Not strangely, Kierkegaard would agree.

III Sokrates with the soul of Christ

It should not surprise us then that the words of Nietzsche's title, 'Ecce Homo', are the very words of Pilate beholding Jesus (John 19:5).[8] KGW, 7:2. Since Nietzsche is both the beholder and the beheld in *Ecce Homo*, this means he must be a kind of Pilate beholding Pilate, or a Christ beholding Christ, or perhaps Roman Pilate beholding the soul of Christ. Nietzsche's title then recalls the remark in his *Nachlass* (leftovers) about the *Übermensch* being 'Roman Caesar with the soul of Christ' (KGW VII 27[60]).[9] Thus, if Nietzsche's 'Ecce Homo' makes him a kind of Caesar/Christ beholding himself, Nietzsche must have overcome the incompatibility of Caesar, who ruled the world but did not suffer and bless it, and Christ, who suffered and blessed the world but would not rule it. In *Ecce Homo* Nietzsche does suffer and bless the world and he does declare his readiness to rule it. Yet in *Ecce Homo* there is something divine as well. In it Nietzsche enjoys the seventh day rest of a God strolling in the cool of autumn among his creatures. Because of his *Zarathustra* – the work of forty days and forty nights – he finds the whole of his creation very good or, what is the same for Nietzsche, 'very evil'. Heady with the cider of good and evil, this deluge-commanding Noah is ready for a free death.

The subtitle of *Ecce Homo*, 'How one becomes what one is', seems to yoke God and nature with violence. We create ourselves, yet we have a nature. This contradiction is resolved as follows: self-creating is not exnihilic. Man starts with the block he is and knocks off parts of it to get to nature. It is hardly easy. Like a sculptor cutting away stone to make his self portrait, a man must be hard on himself; to make 'what he really is' stand out, he must cut himself as he now is. All the foresight, cunning and energy once attributed to the out-of-nothing Creative God are needed by man to become what he is, but because man starts with something, not nothing, he must destroy to create. A clean, gentle, innocent beginning is not possible for man. Like God starting over with a flood, man must destroy much that was once dear to him to make anything good of himself. The union of Caesar and Christ that Nietzsche's title points to is both a work of art and a growth of nature.

That Nietzsche's *Ecce Homo* is divided into four parts, on his wisdom, on his sagacity, on his good books and on his destiny, allows us to distinguish Nietzsche on Nietzsche from all his predecessors, especially Sokrates, Plato and Christ.[10] For unlike the ignorant Sokrates, Nietzsche claims to be wise (EH, 'Why I am So Wise'), and unlike Sokrates before the Athenian court, Nietzsche claims to be sagacious (EH, 'Why I am So Clever'); also unlike Sokrates, Nietzsche claims to be made of good wood. Then in the third part of *Ecce Homo*, Nietzsche tells us that Plato used Sokrates to discover himself, just as Nietzsche used Schopenhauer; the third part itself shows that Nietzsche writes better books than Plato, for Zarathustra is better than Sokrates.[11] In the fourth part Nietzsche claims to be a destiny, who brings tidings of a great crisis, who like Christ 'breaks history in two' and who like Christ (Matthew 24:4) and John of Revelations foresees 'wars the like of which have never yet been seen on earth'. He too has his disciple Peter (Heinrich Köselitz) whom he too has renamed (Gast, Peter 'the Guest'). Like the Gospels then, *Ecce Homo* offers four overlapping accounts of a new divinity. Like Luke, Nietzsche is a physician and healer; as Matthew once did, he will soon collect taxes. Like John beloved by Christ, Nietzsche is beloved by his Zarathustra, and like John he is a theologian. The resemblance is deliberate on Nietzsche's part; of all previous figures to which Nietzsche invites comparison, one finally stands out: Christ. Like Christ, Nietzsche has an invisible genealogy; although you might think Christ had a Jewish father, really his father was heavenly. So likewise although you might think Nietzsche had German parents, really he is Polish. The fact that Nietzsche, like his Zarathustra, lasted beyond the 33 Christ died at, is not insignificant, for Zarathustra speaks of Christ as the one who died too young. Perhaps it is even significant that Nietzsche disappeared at 44, or 4 times 11 rather than 3 times 11.[12] More importantly of course, like Christ, Nietzsche is a healer, a teacher, a prophet, and a destiny.

Yet the greatest resemblance seems only to bring out the greatest difference; for Nietzsche concludes *Ecce Homo*: 'Have I been understood? – *Dionysus versus the Crucified*' (EH, 'Why I am a Destiny' 9). This is usually understood to mean Nietzsche is the Dionysus, but it may not be so. Dionysus and Christ, both gods, both suffer for man, but only Christ is a teacher and lover, as Nietzsche is; likewise his Zarathustra, whose greatest temptation is pity, whose greatest perturbation is nausea at man, whose greatest struggle is with regret, anger, vengeance and ressentiment, and whose greatest victory is the *amor fati* implicit in his loving celebration of eternity at the end of Part Three. All this is like Christ, not Dionysus. Moreover, since it is the task of Nietzsche, he would say his destiny, to unite all that is richest and yet most contradictory in the past of man so far, he would surely have to unite Dionysus and Christ. His *Zarathustra* shows such an attempt on Zarathustra's part and is such an attempt on Nietzsche's part. Although he suffers, as a teacher and a lover, Zarathustra does not perish, as Dionysus and Christ do. Perhaps he may be better described as a Sokrates with the soul of Christ, for the view of human things Zarathustra achieves in Part IV is comic, like Sokrates', and yet the virtue he achieves is, like Christ's, one of love. So, too, Nietzsche, in imitation of his hero, and his heroes, in *Ecce Homo*, tries to unite Dionysus, Sokrates and Christ. How this might be is hard to see.

Because no one else was like Nietzsche, Nietzsche cannot be finally and fully understood through others. To turn then to Nietzsche, let us return to *Ecce Homo* and read it.

IV *Ecce Homo* as a Preface

In being Nietzsche on Nietzsche, *Ecce Homo* is a guide for the living, a lesson for beginning readers, a preface to his works, and a warning to misreaders. In being a birthday present to himself, *Ecce Homo* is also an epilogue to his work, a fulfillment of work and of life, and a demonic weight on the reader. It will be convenient to treat *Ecce Homo* in this order.

Of course, it will be impossible to turn to this book and read it seriously, if we know it is not serious, if we know it is not a book, or if we think the risk of reading it too great.

As to the risk, it is hard to judge for others. Great books may be dangerous. The Platonic dialogues are dangerous; in them some grown-up, solid citizen is always being shown up as ignorant, some good young man is always watching, or getting the stuffing of good opinions knocked out of him by direct Sokratic interrogation. Aristotle wrote differently because he thought these dialogues dangerous. The Gospels may be dangerous too. Perhaps some later Christians wrote differently because they thought so. Dangerous too may be Nietzsche. Certainly his reputation suggests it. Some of his many students, such as Strauss, may have written differently as a consequence. Moreover, a few months after Nietzsche wrote *Ecce Homo*, he went mad, and for the next eleven years until he died sunk more and more in inarticulate suffering. Some think Nietzsche was already mad, or nearly so, when he wrote *Ecce Homo*, that the madness was already erupting in the book, or even driving Nietzsche to write such a thing; but others think that the thoughts in it and the writing of them led to the madness. Was madness the cause of the book, or did the book cause the madness? However, still others deny that there is any relation between *Ecce Homo* and the madness that overtook its author.[13] In any case, the only way to decide if there is madness in *Ecce Homo* is to read the book.

As to whether *Ecce Homo* is a book, the only way to find out is, likewise, to read it, and read it assuming that it is a book, that it is coherent, ordered, designed, neat, beautiful. Start with the opposite assumption and you will never find out if it is a book. As to whether it is serious, again the only way to find out is to read it, as if it *is* serious. Only this assumption encourages the reader to do the work a serious reader always has to do in order to be rewarded. The opposite assumption leads effortlessly to its own 'confirmation'. Effortlessly.

Let us begin with the title. It points two ways. The words 'Ecce Homo' announce that the subject is a man, one who both points to himself and steps forward to address us. Will this be like Tocqueville's *Souvenirs*, written primarily for the author's self-knowledge, or like Richard III's opening soliloquy on himself, uttered primarily to seduce us? Most people who want to tell us about themselves are bores, they do not know themselves, and thus cannot know anything else. However, right off Nietzsche comes to us because he serves some higher purpose. What will be his difficult demand? If we are not offended by Nietzsche's contempt for his contemporaries, we may side with him. Certainly he is witty. Perhaps we are fascinated. Or is he mad? What does it mean to die as your father and live on as your mother?[14] What does he mean, that Caesar or Alexander or Dionysus might be his father? Horatio thought Hamlet 'too curious' when he traced his dusty lineage to the same Plutarchian heroes. Is a hero ever a hero to his friend? Especially if he be witty?

Moreover, the interleaf that follows the Preface is a genuine soliloquy, something the man says to himself, something we only overhear. He tells his life to himself, on his birthday, because his whole life has been good. He is happy, so perhaps he means us well. Of Natasha at her first ball, Tolstoy says she was so happy she could not sin. Nietzsche certainly seems happy, so perhaps he can mean no evil. Also, it seems he tells us only what he tells himself. So, perhaps he is trustworthy.

Although the title of *Ecce Homo* points to someone other than the reader, the subtitle, 'How One Becomes What One Is', invites the reader, at least the reader who wants to become what he is, to seek instruction. It seems that by beholding this someone, by looking away from ourselves and beholding him, we will learn how to become what we are. Or perhaps we will learn what we are; after all, the title also says 'Behold Man', so maybe by looking at man, or this man, we will learn how to become a man. Nietzsche is who he is, no one else could possibly be him, but he is also *what* he is and that might permit imitation.[15]

Read before anything else of Nietzsche's, *Ecce Homo* has much to give us in the way of guidance. For one thing it tells us that the usual separation of life and work does not obtain. There is not the life on the one hand and the works on the other. Although distinct, they are not separate. Nietzsche's life was lived as an experiment and his books were written both as an expression of such living and as a part of it. The four parts of *Ecce Homo* make one instructive whole. The wisdom and sagacity (*Klugheit*) of the man are present in the good books he writes and all three, wisdom, sagacity, and books, make him a destiny.[16] Hence, such matters as whether one should drink coffee, or whether Nietzsche should, are connected to the history of the West or rather to the history of the whole earth. Hence also the linking of the proper names of Nietzsche's haunts and the dates he frequented them to such a momentous thing as the coming of the idea of the eternal return of the same. Life and work are so related that everything about Nietzsche is momentous. Nietzsche's illnesses, insomnia, and headaches are painful, but never trivial.

Here we are dealing with a man who claims to have achieved perfection in the life and in the work. Such a claimed unity would seem to justify the attention an interpreter might give to Nietzsche's letters and *Nachlass* (leftovers). (Of which more later.) However, Nietzsche says that he is one thing and his works another. The kind of perfection in each is not the same. Art is very important in life, and as we shall see, very important in Nietzsche's life, but he understood the difference.[17] Nietzsche's life was marred by inheritances, accidents, mistakes, burdens, disappointments, regrets, sufferings; he met them; he suffered them; he overcame them; his books show it; once he was fingered by fate, his books had nothing to do with accident. Yet they would not be perfect if his life were not good, so Nietzsche begins with his life. That is where the reader should begin, Nietzsche thinks. Is it right to ask of a demanding author, what does he demand of himself? What was his life like?

Since he has achieved a certain perfection in his life, Nietzsche claims to be our teacher. What does he tell us on first reading? First of all he tells us, in the proud, prankish titles of his four parts, that proper self-love is the fundamental theme and the fundamental virtue. Although he often praises courage, especially intellectual courage, and although he exhibits enormous intellect, and even sometimes praises it, still Nietzsche regards self-love as, the fundamental virtue. This virtue is at once something that depends on yourself and on reality. To be able to love yourself you have to be lovable. And then you must not leave your virtues and deeds in the lurch, by falling out of love with them.

In some degree this virtue is possible for all souls. However, there is an order of rank of souls, and the higher up the ladder of rank you climb, the more you may become something rare and even very rare – unique. Thus at the end of the four parts, Nietzsche himself is most Nietzsche and most a destiny, something whose commanding nature is evident to all men. He is most *who* he is and most *what* he is, both. Thus the virtues of the first two sections, wisdom and sagacity, are far more open to most men. No one will be the Nietzsche who is a destiny, few will write such good books as Nietzsche has, but quite a few may be as sagacious (*klug*) as he, and many may be as wise as he. You will notice that this reverses every other tablet of virtues we have heard of, for wisdom is not the end and crown but the beginning and base of the virtues. It also quite specifically reverses the Platonic quartet of virtues, in ways we shall examine specifically later. (We set aside for the moment whether the lower virtues are transformed by the higher ones.)

So, what is wisdom? What does the first part of the book, 'Why I am So Wise', tell us about wisdom? Upon first reading, it tells us that wisdom is right disposition toward the given, towards one's nature, towards one's parents, one's genealogy, and toward suffering. There is enough good in what you begin with so that you should feel gratitude, and enough evil so that virtue is an achievement – and for that too you should feel gratitude. Thus, Nietzsche is thankful for his body, for his fundamental health, for his parents, including his ghostly father, and for being born in Germany, in the modern era. Never do we feel that he would prefer any of this different.

Not that all of life is lovable. All life is suffering. Nietzsche's life has been one long, and increasing agony; pain and debility have haunted him, impeded him, and regret has accused him. Although he emphasizes the sufferings of the body, as is proper for an honest celebrant of the body, and an honest warrior against anti-nature, there are other sufferings he mentions, above all the disappointments of having made so many mistakes in life, of having to deal as a boy with those visited upon him, and later those he visited upon himself.[18] Other sufferings he only alludes to. The greatest is unrequited love. This man who possessed such great gifts was rejected by those he loved best. By Wagner, by Cosima, by Burckhardt, and by Lou von Salomé. This great teacher bearing such great gifts was rejected by nearly everyone. Or so it seemed to him. Certainly during his life there was an incommensurability between his gifts and his friends.

What is wisdom? In the beginning, in the boy and youth, it is a low sense; it is the sense of smell, the ability to sense what stinks, the strength to avoid it; in the young man, in the young teacher and writer, it is nausea, the rejection of what is base and yet not always the avoidance of it, but often the suffering of it. Not the opposing of it, except to suffer it, to take no counter-measures, but to endure it. Anger is a perturbation of the soul. No philosopher suffered more from anger than Nietzsche, or talked less of it. He preferred to talk of the virtue that casts it out, *amor fati*. This is not the virtue that casts it out.

You will note that with this virtue, as with sagacity to follow, the first signs of it are negative, or more exactly defensive. In life for a long time we know better what we do not like than that alone for which we were made. As it grows the virtue of wisdom must be heroic. It is heroic when it makes solitary war, the rules of which Nietzsche provides, and heroicly magnanimous when it conquers. Only then, in victory over oneself and in peace, can it become sweet, taking pleasure in things that would have been hindrances during war, with a moderation in regard to oneself that is nearly abstemious, and yet a display of these pleasures for others that is lavish. The exception should not insist on becoming the rule. And the extraordinary should not mind serving the ordinary sometimes.

Nietzsche tells us that wisdom is the love of this suffering. *Amor fati* is the love of everything you suffer for the sake of, everything that suffering drives you to achieve, to write, to be. Already we sense then, that Nietzsche could only write this part because the other parts, especially the third and fourth, follow. Still, for others, wisdom is possible with less than unique and less than great achievements. Self-love that includes love of your suffering is possible for all.

The link between Part One, on wisdom, and Part Two, on sagacity, is solitude. Suffering isolates. Pain isolates. You feel it and no one else. Pain is always your pain. Others can only increase it. The pity of others only increases your pain. Debility isolates even more. If you are Nietzsche, you have to stay indoors for days; you can't plan anything; all meetings are tentative, under the sign 'If I am well' and even under the sign 'If I am still alive'. And unrequited love isolates even more. But since the virtue of wisdom is self-love, attaining it means realizing that the solitude suffering exposes one to is good, is lovable. Finally, it means being impervious to whether your love is requited, so great is your self-love.

It is only in this solitude that knowledge of nature and of one's own nature is likely. It took suffering and solitude to teach Nietzsche what climate was good for him, what cuisine, what orders of the day, what daily exercises, and thus what way of daily life was best for him. This is sagacity, to know what habits, brief and long, are conducive to becoming what you are. Sagacity is Nietzsche's name for self-knowledge. First self-love, then through it self-knowledge, and then teaching and ruling, is the order of how the virtues become what they are in a man.

Only when you have become what you are could you possibly know yourself. *Nosce te ipsum* is not a command good for youth. It will only lead to something premature, some liaison, union, or job, some niche that will forever forestall becoming who you are. Endurance, discipline, patience are needed to keep going, to live through all the many sideroads, mistakes, fragments that will fall into their proper subordinate places when the 'organizing idea that is meant to rule' you finally takes command. Here Nietzsche accords with the experience of all inquiry. If you knew, knew fully, what you were seeking, you would have it now and not be seeking it. And if you knew nothing about what you were seeking, you wouldn't be seeking, and certainly wouldn't find it. In especial, this is true of the man, such as Nietzsche, who is to be someone the like of whom there has never been before. Toward such a destiny, no one, living or dead, can point the way.

If wisdom as Nietzsche understands it, including self-love and self-discipline, is a fundamental expression of nature in oneself, certainly in himself, someone made of good wood, then sagacity is a choice of virtue. Wisdom makes you endure well, with good spirits and good benefit, what you begin with, sagacity allows you to choose what is best for you. Thus in the one part Nietzsche expresses gratitude for home, homeland, and parents, in the other part, he chooses other cuisine, other climes, other places, and by implication other parents. Thus, he now prefers the cuisine of Piedmont to that of Thuringia; likewise, he now finds that dry, sunlit climes are best for a man with a spiritual task. Finally, we must count the four major authors he mentions under 'recreation' (Pascal, Stendhal, Heine, and Shakespeare) as his choices; these others replace parents for the mature man, and were perhaps important for the youth. What might be vital for a youth, say as misperceived but so important Schopenhauer was for Nietzsche, becomes recreation for the man who knows his task. Thus Nietzsche's sagacity will restrict the claims that even good things make on his time.

Sagacity is also, certainly for Nietzsche, the virtue that protects solitude. As knowledge of the right climate, cuisine, and habits, it substitutes for moderation in the Platonic quartet, and as protection of solitude, it substitutes for justice in the Platonic quartet, since like justice it is right relation to other people. Nietzsche's elevation of solitude as a virtue finds some agreement in Plato. In Book VI of the *Republic* (496 a) Sokrates mentions five ways a man growing up in a bad city – all extant cities are bad – might become a philosopher. The five are: 1) if a noble and well-reared nature is held in check by exile; 2) if a big soul grows up in a small village; 3) for the very few, if a man has an art and despises it from good nature; 4) or if he is sick, like Theages; 5) or if he has a daimonion, the case of Sokrates. Now Nietzsche had an art, philology, and out of good nature despised it; he grew up a big-hearted soul in small towns and smaller homes; he was also noble and yet in a sense exiled, first from Germany, then from Academe; and it may be that Zarathustra was his daimonion. However, it is the fourth way that is most pertinent, the way of Theages, the way of sickness. In Nietzsche, the decadent, it includes the rest. He could not heal others if he had not healed himself first, and he could not have done that if he had not first been sick, and yet also, as he claims, fundamentally greatly healthy.

V Truth Discovers Nature

In order to discover the fundamental basis of the new tablet of virtues Nietzsche teaches in *Ecce Homo*, we must turn to Part Four. In Part One, Nietzsche began by saying he was fated to be both decadent and healthy; in Part Two, on sagacity, he spoke of an organizing idea, which keeps one from knowing oneself until one knows it, even as it orders everything to itself, and at the end he declared his formula for greatness is to love one's fate. Now Part Four, 'Why I Am a Destiny', Nietzsche begins with the important declaration, which we have been waiting for: 'I know my fate.' The 'organizing idea' that drove young Nietzsche on his way was truth, his torment was the question, 'What is the relation of truth and life?', and eventually his task was to be the Revaluation of All Values. This was his fate; it was what he should love; and it is his destiny.

Naturally we wonder about the basis of this task. We wonder whether truth and life can be reconciled. In Part Four, especially in section 7, the theme of the whole work, and of Nietzsche's work, is given its polemical summation. Nietzsche makes spiritual war against all anti-nature teachings, especially those of the priest and the Christianity that had ruled the world since antiquity. Even on a first reading, such a polemical summation may also reveal the non-polemical theme of the work. That theme is nature; fundamentally it is nature that calls one to be what one is and that in such a man as Nietzsche actually achieves what it wants to. Nature is the will-to-power willing the wave, and Nietzsche is the wave and the lover of will and wave.[19] Φύσις loves *Geist*, and *Geist* loves φύσις.[20] In nature truth and life find their source. Nietzsche says that all he says here has been said in *Zarathustra*. That is true, but the proportion between theme and polemical summation is the opposite in that pacific work, which ends with a festival, not a war. Moreover, while *Ecce Homo* points above itself, to *Zarathustra*, *Zarathustra* does not point above itself, except to the Eternity that Zarathustra weds at the end of Part Three.[21]

VI How One Reads Good Books

However, all that Nietzsche has to tell us about how to lead our lives, what the virtues are, who he is, and why we should obey him as a Destiny, depends decisively on his authority. Why should we trust him? Certainly there is no reason to trust him without coming to know him, and since he is dead, we can only come to know him through his books. Nietzsche knew this and that is one reason why he has so much to say about reading. He also knew, from experience, that reading was a dying art, and he feared, from foresight, that it would soon die. Judging from the reading *Ecce Homo* has received, especially recently, one cannot say his fears were excessive.

Knowing the decline of reading, Nietzsche gives us guidance by teaching us how to read. Like other great writers, he gives us instruction in good reading by writing well. In addition, in this book, he notices the good writing in his books, criticizes some of their stylistic weaknesses, and through both explicitly teaches us what to look for in reading, above all what to enjoy.[22] This is not all.

Few thinkers of the first order have much at all to say about reading or writing. Reading Hume and reading Rousseau were important to Kant, but he gives us no readings of them and no reflections on reading. Aquinas and Heidegger give us abundant examples and bright models, but say little. Nietzsche does both. So do Maimonides and Schopenhauer, but they say less. Only Plato says as much as Nietzsche. The virtues required of those who read the only books worth reading – books that demand to be read slowly and invite us to learn them by heart – have never been better described than by Nietzsche in *Ecce Homo*:

> Wenn ich mir das Bild eines vollkommnen Lesers ausdenke, so wird immer ein Unthier von Muth und Neugierde daraus, außerdem noch etwas Biegsames, Listiges, Vorsichtiges, ein geborner Abenteurer und Entdecker. Zuletzt: ich wüßte es nicht besser zu sagen, zu wem ich im Grunde allein rede, als es Zarathustra gesagt hat: wem allein will er ein Räthsel erzählen?
>
> Euch, den kühnen Suchern, Versuchern, und wer je sich mit listigen Segeln auf furchtbare Meere einschiffte, –
> euch, den Räthsel-Trunkenen, den Zwielicht-Frohen, deren Seele mit Flöten zu jedem Irrschlunde gelockt wird:
> – denn nicht wollt ihr mit feiger Hand einem Faden nachtasten; und wo ihr errathen könnt, da hasst ihr es, zu erschließen . . .
>
> (EH, 'Warum ich so gute Bücher schreibe' 3)

[When I imagine a perfect reader, he always turns into a monster of courage and curiosity; moreover, supple, cunning, cautious; a born adventurer and discoverer. In the end, I could not say better to whom alone I am speaking at bottom than Zarathustra said it: to *whom* alone will he relate his riddle?

To you, the bold searchers, researchers, and whoever embarks with cunning sails on terrible seas –
to you, drunk with riddles, glad of the twilight, whose soul flutes lure astray to every whirlpool,
because you do not want to grope along a thread with cowardly hand; and where you can *guess*, you hate to deduce.]

It is as such a monster of curiosity and guessing, of pride and solitude, that Nietzsche himself reads his own books in 'Why I Write Such Good Books'. It is also as a sufferer that Nietzsche reads. Over his own books, as over Shakespeare, he sobs. And not because he has guessed wrong, no, because he guesses right. Reading was no diversion, no game for Nietzsche. Being the first reader to meet his own demands is not the least way he teaches us what it means to read him.

Ecce Homo guides the reader as yet unacquainted with Nietzsche's works in another way: by already before the fact attacking various misinterpretations Nietzsche expected to be foisted upon him. To those who would wish to call him 'holy', who would, for example, acknowledge the death of God and still call themselves Christian theologians, he declares himself to be an Antichrist. For those who would claim him as a fellow Jew-hater, he plainly expresses his contempt. To those who would enlist him in a war of the then-current German *Reich* to dominate Europe, he makes plain his championship of the French. (Anyone who tries to enlist him in favor of a bellicose Germany, headed by a Jew-hater like Hitler, is, therefore, a double-misreader of *Ecce Homo*.) The debasing misinterpretations of such movements as Marxism or Freudianism Nietzsche treats with high-peak silence. From Nietzsche's point of view the two are much the same – their ideal for man is to live warm in body and adjusted in soul, without suffering, courage, wisdom, or joy. Lest these mendacious misinterpreters have an excuse for claiming Nietzsche as their co-belligerent, Nietzsche declares war in *Ecce Homo*. Not against the Jews or against the French or against the unholy but against the spirit of revenge in its most virulent form. Nietzsche may be known by his friends; he is certainly known by his enemies.

Ecce Homo also offers positive guidance. In it Nietzsche treats his works roughly in the order of their publication; indeed, 'Why I Write Such Good Books' is the only part of *Ecce Homo* to be arranged chronologically. This procedure not only justifies reading them in such an order, as stages on a journey, episodes in an adventure, and steps toward a goal, but indicates that they tell the story of Nietzsche's life. If *Ecce Homo* tells how, in the words of its subtitle, Nietzsche became or becomes what he is, then Nietzsche became what he was in the course of writing the sequence of books that he comments on in 'Why I Write Such Good Books'. Here again *Zarathustra* is decisive; its writing or its inspiration made Nietzsche what he only dimly was in the works that precede it and deliberately refrained from seeming to be in those that followed.[23]

Ecce Homo offers its reader positive guidance by indicating the canon of Nietzsche's works. Clearly the peak is *Thus Spake Zarathustra* and the peak of the peak is its disclosure of the challenging and blessing thought of the eternal return of the same or, as he also calls it, *amor fati*. All the other works lie like foothills below *Zarathustra*. We are to read and interpret them in the light of *Zarathustra* or on the way to reaching it, which does not mean treating these easier prose works as a key to *Zarathustra*. Just the opposite. What appears easier, simpler, more palatable in them is ultimately to be put aside in favor of the inhospitable altitude of *Zarathustra*, however cold and thin, or hot and untouchable, it might prove for human, all too human, lungs and hands. According to the prose of *Ecce Homo*, the poetry of *Zarathustra* is higher than any prose Nietzsche wrote.

Nor does *Ecce Homo* leave us without guidance in reading *Zarathustra*. Of the eight sections Nietzsche devotes to *Zarathustra*, the first four tell the history of its writing; the fifth tells the consequences and the last three speak of the work itself. From this history we learn that *Zarathustra* was a work of inspiration and revelation. Though there is no God, there is revelation. Throughout his excited and happy retelling of how Zarathustra came, as happy and breathless as Pheidipides from Marathon, Nietzsche stresses the extraordinary character of the experience of inspiration, something unheard of in the nineteenth century, and fundamentally unknown in any. Throughout, Zarathustra is represented as a real being who visited Nietzsche and *Zarathustra* as something given and imposed upon Nietzsche, something he may have desired and courted but did not make or create. The unmade otherness of *Zarathustra* and the given rather than invented character of Zarathustra permit Nietzsche to praise *Zarathustra* and Zarathustra without offense; yet what are we to make of the fact that throughout Nietzsche also speaks of *Zarathustra* as his possession, one that he not only found but invented? What would otherwise be confusion or nonsense or fatal contradiction seems to be offered us as a mark of the exaltation of *Zarathustra* and of Zarathustra, whose coming cannot, it seems, be described without falling into contradiction. *Zarathustra* is Nietzsche's best book, he wrote it, but it was also the gift of Zarathustra, whose inspiration Nietzsche could not refuse. Sometimes then Nietzsche treats *Zarathustra* as if he is its father, sometimes he treats *Zarathustra* as if he is its mother, as for example in the prankish assertion that the eighteen months between August 1881 and February 1883, between the conception of the 'eternal return' and the birth of *Zarathustra I*, make

Nietzsche a female elephant.[24] Other times, Nietzsche seems to be the son of Zarathustra.

Is Nietzsche the creative contemplator he describes in *Frolicsome Science* No. 301, who does not know he creates, or is there genuine revelation and *Zarathustra* the highest example of it? Here in *Ecce Homo* he claims the latter. It seems that his sense of owning *Zarathustra* is not a claim to have created *Zarathustra*. Nietzsche's pride is then like the pride of a youngster who has received a wonderful gift. He feels delighted by it, singled out by it, as if it were made for him only, made to help him become what he always wanted to be, and thus he cannot feel he made it. Nietzsche's gratitude pre-supposes he did not make the gift of *Zarathustra*. Nietzsche's claim to have invented and written it merely does justice to the exertion and labor it takes to receive such a revelation. Unless, of course, Nietzsche's understanding of creation embraces these opposites by regarding spontaneous otherness as the mark of a created thing. It is when your creature overtakes you with a sudden gift of its own that you know yourself to be a creator. It is when a child gives his parents a gift they would not have given themselves, or perhaps thought to, although it fits their desire or aspiration exactly, that the parents most nearly understand procreation.

Be that as it may, there is a third thing we need to know about *Zarathustra* before we read it. In *Ecce Homo* Nietzsche never mentions Part Four.[25] *Zarathustra III* brings *Zarathustra* to a close. *Zarathustra I, II*, and *III* are a whole. Is Part Four, which was only sent to seven friends (or should we call them 'higher men'?), not, according to Nietzsche, a part of *Also Sprach Zarathustra*? Is it not even among the books that make Nietzsche such a 'good writer'? Is this a blushing denial of his work, or merely a reticence? Is even this most intimate and publicizing of Nietzsche's works, nonetheless, reticent? To know, one would have to read *Zarathustra*.

Even as a preface to Nietzsche's works, *Ecce Homo* poses a moral challenge to the reader. By exhibiting his joyful love of his fate so wittily, so lightly, so abundantly, Nietzsche challenges those approaching or passing forty-four to examine their own lives or what is left of them – can you love your life as I do? Can you affirm everything small, wasted, lost, pained, and foolish in it? Is there enough good in your life so that you can bless the whole of it? And to those far from forty-four his self-beholding and self-loving portrait warns – have you acted so that at forty-four you can love and bless as I do? Yet these questions are not sufficiently precise. Each reader must think of himself, review his own life, in minute detail, and judge it. Despite or rather because of its witty exuberance *Ecce Homo* can make a reader pensive and solitary; it is punctuated with 'one minute silences' for the reader. Suddenly you face a thought, yourself, your life. *Ecce Homo* is like a demon perching on our bed at night asking 'Could you bear to repeat this, this day, this week, this life?'[26] If we find our life wanting, we will find *Ecce Homo* unbearable and its author insufferably happy or, rather, 'proud, selfish, and wicked', as we like to say of those who offend our self-esteem. By exhibiting his life, Nietzsche's *Ecce Homo* is a fitting introduction to *Zarathustra*; in Nietzsche's affirmation of his own life, we already begin to meet with Zarathustra's most abysmal and most joyous thought, of the eternal return of the same.

By offering in *Ecce Homo* such positive yet challenging guidance to his would-be readers, Nietzsche also warns against a most powerful misinterpretation of his work, even though he could not have entirely foreseen it. Almost from the beginning of his reception, what Nietzsche did not publish has made his reputation as much as what he did. At first and for many years, a book fashioned from his *Nachlass* (leftovers) by his sister, entitled '*Will to Power*' and authorized only by her,[27] shaped Nietzsche's reception. Yet even after its authority was demolished, and her many forgeries exposed, this '~~Will to Power~~' went on distorting Nietzsche. Even Heidegger's great confrontation with him is rendered quixotic by his credulity in this phantom; his will-to-overcome required a Nietzsche he could lance, 'Caught you, you resenter.'[28] Lesser minds fare worse. In the Anglo-Saxon countries many interpreters of Nietzsche pay more attention to his leftovers than to his books or view his books in the light of his leftovers.[29] Reading Nietzsche this way is like reading Shakespeare with the names of the speakers cut, the pages shuffled, and both changes suppressed. Many in addition pay more attention to what someone lesser thought rather than Nietzsche.[30] Their leader is the playful, turgid, joyless '68 Communard Jacques Derrida, whose philosophy for the Last Man appeals to many Last Scholars.[31] Among the books one must ignore to do these things, none is more instructive than *Ecce Homo*, for it nowhere authorizes the reader to pay any attention to what Nietzsche did not publish. Part Three is not entitled 'Why I write such good *Nachlass*'. On the contrary, it pleads, 'Read my good books.'[32]

VII *Ecce Homo* as epilogue – Nietzsche's joy

For those who have read all of Nietzsche's books, studied them, and lived with them, especially *Zarathustra*, *Ecce Homo* is an epilogue. While reading *Zarathustra*, we see this man Zarathustra live with one thought and one thought only; we witness him announce it, evade it, face it, struggle with it, and finally embrace it in solitary dialogue and solitary song. But *Zarathustra* is a poem, and if we read it seriously, if we read it with its one thought in mind, we must wonder if any real human being could embrace what Zarathustra finally does. Can a human being embrace the thought of eternal return of the same? To be sure, that is one of Nietzsche's and Zarathustra's points; man so far has not even faced this challenging thought and only some being more than man, namely the *Übermensch*, could. Nevertheless, we wonder. In *Zarathustra II* Zarathustra himself accuses the poets of lying too much and then admits to being a poet. Perhaps there is too much lying in

Zarathustra. To this suspicion Zarathustra or Nietzsche might well reply with a smile: 'Yes, noble lying'. Indeed, by asking whether such an embrace of fate as *Zarathustra* makes is possible for a man, we are already coming under the ennobling or crushing spell of the question of eternal return. We are already measuring Nietzsche by the Nietzschean measure of measures. Thus we may no longer be asking 'Is it possible?' in a disinterested or hypothetical spirit, but in a personal spirit (even if we are not yet asking it by risking our lives).

So engaged by Nietzsche's question, it is natural for us to try to answer it by looking for someone who has tried. And if the author of *Zarathustra* has tried, that would give authority to his poetic representation of Zarathustra trying to. Indeed, it would be extraordinary if, having written *Zarathustra*, the drama of a man who first evades, then struggles with, and finally embraces the idea of the eternal return of the same, Nietzsche did not feel called to examine his own life from this point of view. Indeed, in the leftovers of the *Zarathustra* years, after a six-point sketch on the *Übermensch*, the following solitary remark appears:

> Ich will das leben nicht wieder. Wie habe ich's ertragen? Schaffend. Was macht mich den Anblick aushalten? Der Blick auf den Übermenschen, der das Leben bejaht. Ich habe versucht, es selber zu bejahen – Ach!
>
> (KGW VII 4[81])[33]

> [I do not want life *again*. How have I borne it? By creating. What has made me endure? The vision of the Surpassing Man who *affirms* life. I have tried to affirm life *myself* – but ah!]

After *Zarathustra* Nietzsche wrote several prose books, *Jenseits von Gut und Böse* (*Beyond Good and Evil*) is the best example, that aim to lead the contemporary reader away from various errors, whose history Nietzsche recounts, towards *Zarathustra*. In these books Nietzsche teaches those who are somewhat discontented with modernity to become more so, partly by making them realize how inedible its meals are, and partly by feeding them something better: *antipasto di Zarathustra*. In none of these books does Nietzsche himself face the idea of eternal recurrence. Meanwhile, he also worked on a project sometimes entitled 'Will to Power', which he thought of as either a philosophic expression of the insights of *Zarathustra* or perhaps a perfection of it. Both what Nietzsche wrote after *Zarathustra* and what he planned must be scrutinized from the point of view of *Zarathustra IV* where Zarathustra overcomes the temptation to teach the discontented but unliberated higher men. In what he published Nietzsche does not, it seems to me, give in to this temptation, for the reader is never handed the idea of the eternal return; instead, he is set on an arduous and risky path towards it. However, had Nietzsche expressed *Zarathustra* in a treatise it would certainly have been yielding to this temptation. It would also have been a colossal

evasion of the spiritual necessity of facing the idea of eternal return personally – in one's own life and vulnerable existence. For the author of *Zarathustra* to have published or written a treatise entitled 'Will to Power' would have
been a base stooping, a betrayal of one's own best hour, a forgetting of who
one is, and even a becoming of what one is not. And for the author of
Zarathustra not to have written *Ecce Homo* would have been spiritual cowardice. In August of 1881 Nietzsche discovered an idea; for the rest of his life
it discovered him. Up until he wrote *Ecce Homo*, he wondered if he had been
bitten by more than he could chew.

If so, then one cannot agree with Martin Heidegger, whose interpretation
of Nietzsche is the most serious and searching to appear. Because life and
work were so nearly seamless for Nietzsche, Heidegger is justified in attending
so carefully and thoughtfully to the leftovers and letters. Nevertheless, from
Nietzsche's point of view, Heidegger is not right when he misses the significance of *Zarathustra IV* for its author and when he ignores *Ecce Homo*
almost entirely. Nietzsche chose not to write a philosophic treatise; the part
of the 'Transvaluation' he did write, *Der Antichrist*, is a declaration of war on
Christianity, not a treatise. Heidegger regards Nietzsche's not doing so as a
'failure', thinks he knows the metaphysical reasons, and sets out to finish
what Nietzsche 'could not'. One wonders if Heidegger's failure to see that he
disagrees with Nietzsche does not rest upon his failure to appreciate the
ethical significance eternal return had from first to last for Nietzsche.

How then did Nietzsche face his life? Nietzsche began *Ecce Homo* on
October 15, 1888, his forty-fourth birthday. Most birthday celebrations hail
the birth of an individual in the light of an uncritical appreciation of his life
since birth. On our birthdays we feel we deserve a treat, of regarding ourselves without criticism, for example. At the party we indulge ourselves in the
sweets that quotidian guilt or good sense would forbid. Instead, Nietzsche
celebrated his birthday by launching a risky examination of his life and work,
every morning, every page; every headache, every thought; every meal, every
consequence; every evening and every solitude, all measured by the question:
Would you like these once more? After about twenty days, it was finished.
That he undertook it shows he was no spiritual coward; that he had the
courage to is almost victory itself. To know for sure, we must examine *Ecce
Homo* itself. Does it include such a confrontation? Has Nietzsche faced his
Devil?

Nietzsche says 'once more' to his life, first of all by saying 'once more' to
his body. Despite the sicknesses that he mentions, life has been great – not
good, but great. Nietzsche has enjoyed great health, though not good health.
Indeed, he could not, he affirms, have enjoyed great health without having
bad health. It is as his own best physician that he is responsible for such
health, and in *Ecce Homo* he celebrates the doctor more than the patient.
Illness is affirmed for the sake of the great health that is required to overcome
it. Thus Nietzsche affirms himself as willful physician, not an instance of

good φυσις. During his life he said 'I will be healthy'; now he celebrates his will's victory. (As we shall see 'great health' means the state *of* receptivity to Zarathustra; in *Ecce Homo* all roads of affirmation lead to *Zarathustra*.)

Nietzsche also says 'once more' to his life by the disposition he takes to other human beings (or would he like us to say 'towards human beings'?). Toward his parents, gratitude: towards his friends and enemies, praise for their virtues; and toward those he may have disappointedly loved, a gracious silence. About his parents he says the best that can be said without flattering. Being the son of his father meant growing up fatherless in a parson's house, but this atheist does not complain. Remarks on the 'idealism' of Naumburg cuisine are the closest Nietzsche comes to criticizing his mother (pretty close, I admit). Upon the accidents of climate, early education, and ancestry, Nietzsche looks cheerfully. What did not destroy one made one stronger. Meeting Wagner is treated as a great plus, even if his works are criticized, and Nietzsche's tremendous praise of *Zarathustra* does not make him blind to the merit of Peter Gast's music. Gay and savouring, Nietzsche looks out to dead friends like Pascal, Stendhal, and Montaigne. About whatever disappointment he felt over Lou von Salomé, Nietzsche is politely silent. Between the coming of the eternal return in August '81 and the birth of *Zarathustra I* in February '83, Lou appears only as the true author of the noble 'Hymn to Life'. The same graciousness and veiled affection is observed toward Cosima Wagner (Ariadne).

There is, however, one silence in *Ecce Homo* that is not so gracious. After sickness forced Nietzsche, not entirely reluctantly, to stop teaching at Basel, he lived on a pension from the university. He was on semi-permanent sabbatical. While not lavish, this pension allowed Nietzsche to range about Europe at leisure, and carefulness with it allowed him to partially finance the publication of his books (gifts from friends did the rest). It was Franz Overbeck who protected and maintained this pension. That none of this is mentioned – I do not mean proclaimed but courteously alluded to – in *Ecce Homo* seems dishonest, to the reader and perhaps also to himself. In a note intended for *Ecce Homo*, Nietzsche says Overbeck's good will toward him was really a means to poison him with self-doubt and calls Overbeck 'canaille'.[34] Perhaps there is some truth in this criticism: old friends who follow differing ways of life may find later meetings make them feel uneasy about the path they've chosen. Nietzsche was more gracious when Overbeck came to Turin to care for him; he embraced him warmly. Later Overbeck wondered if Nietzsche should not be shot; can one call a witless Nietzsche Nietzsche? 'Yes, die at the right time', the witty Nietzsche might have agreed. Overbeck is also to be praised for never turning over his correspondence to Elisabeth Nietzsche. Because of his loyalty and suspicion, her program of misrepresentation could never prevail entirely, or forever. Like living on a pension, dishonesty endangers one, by making one's life potentially weightless. Though no man deserved a pension more, perhaps Nietzsche would have been even better and deeper than he was if he had had to earn a living, say as a plumber. Certain it is that acknowledging this pension would have accorded better with honesty and graciousness.[35]

It is true that these silences are only objectionable if there is truth and we are meant to abide by it. From time to time, Nietzsche asked whether we should pursue truth, and if we find it, follow its maxims, obey its commands, and he even seems sometimes to question whether there is truth. I say 'seems' because he knew the proof 'there is no truth' is not only self-contradictory, but that it would require a complete investigation of the whole, which he certainly knew he had not conducted. Moreover, Nietzsche esteemed the virtue of honesty. Can you have honesty without truth? Not for long, and, I think, Nietzsche knew it all along. In the name of *Redlichkeit*, Nietzsche often objected to 'Die wahre Welt', but he could not escape the truth that *Redlichkeit braucht Wahrheit*.[36]

Another silence is ambiguous. In *Ecce Homo* Nietzsche has little to say about his mother and nothing to say about his sister. Apparently, this was deliberate, for in late December of '88, Nietzsche mailed a revision of 'Wise' 3, to his publisher, and in it he says the most profound objection to his most abysmal thought, the eternal return, has always been his mother and sister.[37] It seems to me that the silence in which he had, previous to this revision, left mother and sister was superior. That silence is conspicuous enough in contrast to the praise of his father. What of Nietzsche's double nature, as decadent and beginner? What does he owe to each parent? Is Nietzsche a decadent from his ghostly father and a beginner from his mother? Or, more likely, a decadent until his thirty-sixth year like his father and then by surviving that nadir year, a great beginner. Then it was that in his thinking and in his good books he really became 'untimely', 'ghostly', hyperborean, halcyon, dividing time, and for all times. Read closely, Nietzsche's account suggests he is only descended from his father and Elizabeth only descended from mother. The two versions are not as different as it first seems, and the first is noble in its silence. Still, considering what sister Elizabeth did to him later, by publishing a '~~Will to Power~~' 'book' from his *Nachlass* (leftovers), one wishes he had said something to forever keep her distant and arm his friends against her. Of course, writing a will and appointing a literary executor would have done the same, but I suppose the illusions of divinity that characterized Nietzsche's madness were not likely to have been preceded by so mortal a thought.

The fact that Nietzsche places such an emphasis on cuisine in his account of his wisdom draws attention, for those who agree with him, to something lacking in *Ecce Homo*, and in his work. There is not one good recipe in the whole of it. If Nietzsche had written a utopia or described an Eden, he would, according to the taste he espouses, have had to honor great chefs with busts; certainly the ice cream Nietzsche loved would have compelled him to honor the unknown discoverer of it with a Tomb of the Unknown Chef. Considering the relation between food and self-love, which Nietzsche tacitly acknowledges, we must agree with M. F. K. Fisher that one of the greatest tests of self-love is whether you can prepare a good five course dinner to eat by yourself alone. A bachelor such as Nietzsche ought to know how difficult that is. Yet, although Nietzsche says cuisine is important and recommends Piedmontese, he says no more. From the reports of visitors such as Zimmern, old friends such as Deussen and landlords such as Durish we doubt Nietzsche could have cooked himself a meal fit for a guest. The feast in *Zarathustra IV* is unspecified, probably a little honey from a pot and lamb roasted over a fire, neither requiring much preparation. No viand, sauce, or sweetie is named after Nietzsche. Celebration of the victory that turned back the Turks at the walls of Vienna gave us the *Sachertorte*. Neither Nietzsche's discovery of eternal return, Zarathustra's meeting it successfully, nor Nietzsche's doing the same, has given us the *Nietzsche-Torte*. Nietzsche liked good food, he lauded cooking as an art, but he was no cook. For that one would have to turn to the likes of Willa Cather.

According to Nietzsche food is no scrap on the plate of life, but it is also not the point. He would despise the vegetarian pacifists of today and all nutritionists, anybody who talks about calories at meals and lives from meal to meal thinking of meals, tourists of life. He had a jockey's view of food; up until the race you eat what keeps your weight down for the race; after winning come the desserts. Food is no scrap on the plate of life, yes, but for Nietzsche books are the dessert of life and his are all sweet victories, sweet discoveries, and sweet celebrations.

To affirm his life, Nietzsche had to reread all his books, Can you bear what you wrote? Do you stand by that? No changes needed there? Nothing to wince at, excuse, or forget? Can you love your old thoughts? Can you love yourself? Wholly? In 'Why I Write Such Good Books' Nietzsche answers with a series of prefaces in which he finds each book good and the whole very good. It is, however, as the author/receiver of *Zarathustra* that Nietzsche in *Ecce Homo* faces his life and says joyously 'once more' to it. Remove all reference to *Zarathustra* from *Ecce Homo* and few sections would be left undamaged; remove the eight sections on *Zarathustra* and the book's heart would beat no longer; without *Zarathustra* Nietzsche could not have affirmed his life.

Yet the affirmation of life that Nietzsche as the author/receiver of *Zarathustra* makes in *Ecce Homo* differs from Zarathustra's own affirmation. Both say 'once more' to their lives, but as their lives differ, so do their affirmations. For one thing, Zarathustra is not an author, either mundane or inspired. He writes nothing and publishes nothing; to the public, he makes only speeches, fewer and fewer of them. Moreover, nothing; except the abysmal thought of eternal return ever overtakes Zarathustra. There is no Zarathustra above Zarathustra; no place like Sils Maria, or Nizza or Aquila where he might go to await a visitation; to court his highest joy he has only to return home. After he left the University, Nietzsche went the opposite way; in *Ecce Homo* he sought a public. In *Zarathustra IV* Zarathustra refuses to teach higher men who seek him in distress. Zarathustra resists the temptation to pity them; he is courteous enough to give them a party, but prefers the solitary air outside his cave. In *Ecce Homo* Nietzsche addresses the same multitude in the city of the Motley Cow that Zarathustra learns to shun in *Zarathustra I*. In his writings after *Zarathustra* Nietzsche carries on skirmishes (*Götzen-Dämmerung*) and small wars (*Zur Genealogie der Moral*); and just before *Ecce Homo* he declares a big war (*Der Antichrist*). By comparison Zarathustra is almost a pacifist. Though he praises warriors (Za, 'Of War and Warriors') and criticizes priests, he declares no war. Proper names are almost absent from *Zarathustra*; the tarantula may be Rousseau (Za, 'Of the Tarantulas'); Wagner may be alluded to (Za, 'The Sorcerer'); only Christ is unmistakably referred to, though not by name. Zarathustra differs from Christ, but not by being a Caesar. Zarathustra does not rule; Nietzsche in *Ecce Homo* declares himself ready to. In *Zarathustra* we hear that, contra Plato and Christ, the best want to rule; we hear Zarathustra criticized for not wanting to rule; but at the end of *Zarathustra III* Zarathustra dwells in utter solitude. In *Zarathustra IV* Zarathustra is interested in who the Lords of the Earth shall be, but he himself dwells in his own mountain kingdom, without subjects or citizens, with just a talking eagle and a talking snake. The appearance of the birds and the affectionate lion at the end portend the nearness of Zarathustra's children, and perhaps the approach of his own free 'going under' or death. Nietzsche's *Ecce Homo* was a part of a campaign of self-presentation to the European public; as such it was also a bid for rulership: 'I am ready to rule Europe.'

Both Zarathustra's solitary *Seven Seals* and Nietzsche's forty-fourth birthday celebration, *Ecce Homo*, are preparations for death: Was that my life, then 'once more'. Both are prepared to leave life, but while Zarathustra stays around for the sake of his children, Nietzsche stays around for the sake of making himself public, waging war in various revaluations, and subsequent rule. Alas, Nietzsche stayed around for less than two months, but in his late autumn letters Nietzsche looks forward to an active spring, indeed a spring offensive; whatever Nietzsche's earlier plans for 'A Revaluation of all Values' were, the first of them, *Der Antichrist*, makes it clear that these are to be polemics, though with hearts of gold, like the middle of *Der Antichrist*; they were armies engaged in a war, which he thought would lead to rule; hence, the concluding section of *Ecce Homo* is entitled 'Why I Am a Destiny'. Nietzsche's speaking truth and loosing arrows will usher in a time of great wars and great politics. It is as a spiritual warrior that Nietzsche is a destiny dividing history into a before and after, a B. N. and A. N. Only in his mad, though witty, postcards did Nietzsche coarsen his claim to spiritual rulership with the delusion that he had the power to make men obey orders. In *Ecce Homo* he is still a teacher who respects the independent will of his students, knowing that all nobility is solitary. Coerced virtue is not virtue. (Though it might be a good habit: 'Eat your spinach.')

So while *Ecce Homo* has moments of strong advice, it issues no orders. No one is shot.[38]

VIII Joy and War

The solitary redemptive affirmation of Zarathustra is followed by no going down to men as teacher, let alone as ruler, and no offering of himself in these roles so that he might be slain, whereas Nietzsche's solitary redemptive affirmation is followed by an immediate going down to men as teacher and spiritual ruler. This difference is puzzling. It seems to put Nietzsche in a bad light. He seems so inferior, in solitude, self-mastery, repose and joy, to Zarathustra.[39] If it is your joy to look at life and the whole of life and affirm it with 'once more', why set about changing that whole by teaching or ruling? And, granted that it is desirable to face one's life at forty-four, why publish the record of the event? Indeed why undertake it with the intention of publishing? Zarathustra never repeats the 'Seven Seals' to another soul, why repeat your self-affirmation, your *amor fati* in public as *Ecce Homo*? Why, dear Nietzsche, do you expose yourself to the rabble? These innocent observations and prosecuting questions would convict Nietzsche of degrading and betraying his nobility if it were not for one consideration.

The peace of *amor fati* is not necessarily contradicted by the war of publication if the war is for the sake of peace, to protect it or secure it. If you love your life and life itself well enough to say 'once more' to it, you not only will eternity but by so doing declare yourself in favor of life for others who will live after you, including your children. Now if you do this, will you not want to defend life and its affirmation from everything that slanders and injures it? Will you not want to make war on all teachings that make war on life? Will you not want to attack the attackers of life? Nietzsche found that the foothills he had thrown up to help men up to *Zarathustra* were not enough. War on the plains was also needed. *Ecce Homo* was the first clash and *Der Antichrist* the second; he planned more such 'revaluations' for the spring. None of this is pitying or teaching the higher men; to fight such a spiritual war you need not expose your innermost high thought.

Nor do we have any reason to claim that such a thought as corresponds to Zarathustra's 'Seven Seals' with its courting of Woman Eternity is revealed in *Ecce Homo*, a mad January postcard, not *Ecce Homo* itself, is the only way we now know who Ariadne was. The premise of *Ecce Homo* is that the peace of *amor fati* and the war of publication are not only compatible but, in the case of a war to secure the possibility of *amor fati* for others living and yet to live, are required by each other. He who says 'once more' to life loves Eternity and for the sake of the children arising from his union with her will go to war against whatever teaching hinders his children from one day standing on the peak of themselves and rejoicing 'once more'. To subdue in yourself the spirit of revenge without then fighting a public war against it is, according to Nietzsche, to be a mere Christ; to fight a public war against a sect that spreads this spirit without first having subdued it in yourself is to be a mere Caesar. In *Ecce Homo* Nietzsche tried to be a Christ who lived on after his redemption to become a Caesar ready to fight a war for the earth and perish in it for the children of the earth.

The fact that Nietzsche was not able to carry on this spiritual war beyond January 1889, when he collapsed and disappeared in a cloud of witty-mad postcards, may not render his premise questionable. In writing *Ecce Homo* he prepared to perish. When else does it make sense to review your life, asking 'Do I want it once more?' except when you are about to die or enter some perilous battle? Two months into his war Nietzsche fell grievously wounded. The fact that he fell just around Christ's birthday,[40] that he embraced a flogged horse, and then played Wagner for hours suggests that the 'enemy' took him prisoner before it slowly annihilated him over the next decade. Excessive pity (for the horse, for a higher beast) as well as delusions of omni-personhood destroyed his loyalty to himself . . . to Nietzsche.

What sort of madness did Nietzsche suffer from? Was it Physical? Was it mental? Or something else? Soon after his breakdown in January of '89, two persons who knew him very well, Peter Gast and Franz Overbeck, and later Count Harry Kessler in 1895, thought that Nietzsche was faking madness. Certainly Nietzsche has much to say about madness in his works, and he even praises it, for example in *Dawn*, 14.[41] Moreover, it is to a Madman that he gives the first announcement of the 'death of God' (*Frolicsome Science*, 125). Why might Nietzsche himself fake madness? If a Madman says something fundamentally outrageous to a community, well, he's just a madman; by laughing at him, even licensing him as a Fool, or locking him up, the community can ignore his thought and dismiss his person. Did Nietzsche fake madness to protect himself from the revulsion his views, especially in *The Antichrist*, were likely to provoke, the revilement he was likely to receive, and perhaps also the loss of his pension? If he did, he overshot the mark, for as a result of his madness, faked or not, Sister Elizabeth got to suppress such writings as *The Antichrist* and *Ecce Homo* for a long while; she got to distort his leftover thoughts into '~~Will to Power~~' for even longer; and mad Nietzsche couldn't utter a word, or lift a finger, or write a line.

I can imagine an experience that would make all one's writings no more than straw, such that one fell silent unto death. I can imagine it with difficulty, but I can do so because Thomas Aquinas is reported to have had just such an experience. Not Nietzsche. And especially not the Nietzsche who had just written *Ecce Homo* about his writings and was all that fall much concerned with its publication. However, it seems to me not impossible that Nietzsche might come to think that only a complete indifference to publication accorded with the redeeming self-love he had achieved in *Ecce Homo*. After all, that is what Nietzsche's Zarathustra thinks. With the publication of his redeeming self-love Zarathustra is so little concerned that he does not write at all.

Another virtue Nietzsche often praises is solitude; in *Beyond Good and Evil* he makes it the replacement for moderation in the Platonic quartet of the virtues; and his abiding praise of Pascal is in the name of solitude. Nietzsche was mightily attracted to virtue, pure virtue. Perhaps he was attracted by this one. What could put one in a more solitary state than to go mad – or pretend to? So, maybe Nietzsche was pretending. One cannot, I think, dispel the suspicion that Nietzsche was faking. One must observe, however, that pretending to be mad might lead to madness. When your roommate says, 'For the next few weeks, I'm going to pretend to be mad' it would not be unwise to watch him carefully. Horatio should have watched antic Hamlet more carefully. Then again, pretending to be mad might be a very profound sign of it.

Solitude is dangerous. As Nietzsche says, whatever you take into solitude grows mightily in that rare atmosphere, like a plant in a hot house. Aristotle says, not accidentally in Book I of the *Politics*, that he who lives outside the polis must be either a beast or a god, for that man political and rational go together; it is hard to have the one without the other. In the fall of 1888, in *Twilight of the Idols*, Nietzsche adds, 'Leaving out a third case: one must be both – a philosopher.' True (and considering the end of the *Ethics*, where he urges us to become divine, a true reading of Aristotle), but by the time Nietzsche was signing postcards in the name of a god and then God, he would soon become a very dumb beast. There is a difference between being so reasonable that you have very few human beings to talk to and being so unreasonable that you cannot speak like one. Suffice it to say that the difference between Nietzsche writing and thinking and Nietzsche moaning and screaming, whether he was pretending or not, or got into true madness through feigned madness, is one of the most vivid instances of the difference between mind and mindlessness. Although he did not always praise reason, Nietzsche is one of the greatest instances of reason there could be; those who attack reason without reason or who celebrate the loss of reason might compare the state of witless confusion poor Nietzsche spent the last ten years of his life in with the ten years of thinking and writing it could have been.

Not the Nietzsche who wrote *Ecce Homo*, but the Nietzsche who could no longer write such a book was mad. For some, such as Strindberg, or the Elisabeth who displayed mad Nietzsche in white sheets, or lately legions of confused intellectuals, the madness of Nietzsche spreads a wonderful glow over what preceded it. All such adorers of madness should consider spending ten years as poor, mad Nietzsche did and then they might find out if madness is really as fun as they think. And the Deconstructionists among them, who do not like the high callings of Logos or the strict requirements that beautiful books make of readers, should not complain if they lose more reason than they have scornfully discarded or if their books are mistranslated, their views misunderstood, and pages from their wastebasket printed with their manuscript. Others, less frequent these days but still present, also see madness in the writings, but delight to cite these evidences as proof of the pernicious character of their fundamental thoughts and the character of the author formed by them. They should be asked whether catastrophe is always just. If Christians, they should be asked if the greatest failure of the greatest teacher – He offered the Kingdom and was rejected – means He deserved what He got? Those who admire philosophers might ask themselves whether Sokrates getting hemlocked means he deserved it? Of course, these are cavils. The proof that Nietzsche was not mad in *Ecce Homo* can only be established by showing the book makes sense, which is not quite the same as showing it is true.

By Nietzsche's own lights *Ecce Homo* is a success: in it he faces his life and affirms it, every illness, every page, and in it he begins to make war on those who slander the earth; he does so by making clear the polemical side of his earlier works and by naming himself 'Dionysus versus the Crucified'. Naming himself and not namely himself, for what Nietzsche says is 'Have I been understood? – *Dionysus versus the Crucified*' (EH, 'Why I am a Destiny' 9). Here he does not name himself Dionysus and in earlier saying he is a disciple of the philosopher Dionysus, he does not exclude the possibility he is also a disciple of the philosopher, or destiny, Christ. (There are even, as we mentioned earlier, reasons to think so.) If so, then he has somehow combined the wild and vengeful fury of Dionysus, the self-sacrificing destroyer of cities, with the vengeance-free redemption of Christ. Whether Nietzsche regards Christ as free of ressentiment is hard to tell, even after you study *Der Antichrist*. How Zarathustra and how Nietzsche stand towards vengeance and ressentiment is also hard. To behold Nietzsche, to understand him, to know what he was, requires study of all his books. This is the lesson of *Ecce Homo* that requires the reader to go beyond it.[42]

Although Nietzsche claims his life is a success, nevertheless, we may well ask: was it a success? Of systematic thinkers Nietzsche objected that they demand too much of both themselves and the whole; so far as we can now see, the whole is a deep night, perhaps deeper than thought can ever reach; he who aspires to make a system must falsify the whole and be false to himself. Is not Nietzsche in *Ecce Homo* open to the same objection? Does not his ideal of *amor fati* require too much of him? Granted that it is noble to live your life so that you can bless it as you leave it, need one bless every instant in it to bless it as a whole? Men like Nietzsche, who live solitarily in the midst of beautiful projects and inventive inquiries, are tempted to think so. He who writes books, even ones made up of aphorisms, writes in the shadow of the highest book, the book which is beautiful from every angle, satisfies a thousand different criteria and is supremely neat because it has nothing accidental about it. Nietzsche claims to have written or received such a book, *Zarathustra*. Can a life have the same neatness? Only, I think, in the case of the life of a God who was wholly responsible for his own being. We know of such a life, or alleged life: that of Christ. And in Plato's dialogues we see Sokrates' life made neat. This last example is telling. Zarathustra and Nietzsche are so unlike Sokrates, who, though he towered above other men, had conversations with them. Both Zarathustra and Nietzsche keep to solitude and the solitude of speeches. They do not meet much with other human beings. Or with chance. In *Ecce Homo* Nietzsche denies that there are for him any more accidents. Once there were things like birth, nation, parents, upbringing and parental cuisine, but not now. His will, or his love, have turned these accidents into changeless gold. As art his life has become perfect. Not to the aesthetic spectator but to the artistic inventor or maker is life justified.

Yet even for so isolated a life as Nietzsche's, with so few friends and so few mundane difficulties, is perfect art and perfect *amor fati* possible? Zarathustra himself never mentions his origins or parents – was he an 'author of himself'? Zarathustra doesn't notice his animals and Nietzsche doesn't mention his pension. Good fortune, mother, and Overbeck kept Nietzsche supplied with single rooms, railway fares, pots of honey, and ham sandwiches (his favorite). Bad fortune could have given him cholera, or crushed him in a train accident, scandal or calumny could have cost him his pension, and Lou accepting his proposal might have left him no tranquillity. To display his affirmation of his life, Nietzsche left out necessity and chance; to affirm his life he had, in this respect, to not know himself. His omission of an important material circumstance of his life and its connection to a friend or colleague might be insignificant if it were not entirely in accord with the dominant purpose of *Ecce Homo*. As such it reveals a great deal about his life and thought.

In *Ecce Homo* Nietzsche pretends to be a self, yet he should know he is a soul. What a splendid soul Nietzsche had, what delicacy, what nobility, what generosity, what strength, and what insight, yet Nietzsche did not make his soul. To be sure, his gifts would not have become his possessions, his seeds would not have bloomed and provided us with such fruits, without his deliberate, life-long, ardent, and suffering activity, but for those initial gifts he was not responsible. That he was born a man and not an elephant was not his decision. Who decided he would have a human soul? Nature? Nature's God? God? Who knows? It would take a very long inquiry to find out and still one might not. One thing is sure and Nietzsche must acknowledge it: Nietzsche did not create himself. Even his body, however well he kept it, was something given to him, by his procreative parents and theirs, and theirs, and by viviparous Life itself. There is gratitude in what Nietzsche says about his parents in *Ecce Homo*, even to the point of practicing monumental history, but one wonders if it is sufficient. Moreover, one doubts he paid proper gratitude to nature. Nietzsche was anti anti-nature, no question, but not sufficiently pro-nature. His many noes have a yes basis, but their number obscure it, even to him.[43]

There is also something insufficient about Nietzsche's account of sagacity. No experience in Nietzsche's whole life required, or even encouraged, him to attain sagacity (practical wisdom or prudence). He never had a job, never taught swimming at a summer camp, never ran a restaurant, never sat on a committee, never commanded soldiers, ran for office, or served as a minister. Until he was suddenly made full professor, without the Ph.D., his responsibilities were all solitary, or at most to a circle of friends. The prudence that Zarathustra talks of is what devices will protect one's solitude; the sagacity Nietzsche talks of in *Ecce Homo* has, in addition, to do with how to handle one's grumpy body. Nietzsche's sense of redemption is wholly personal, not political; even as world-redeemer he would be a personal re-creator god; and his sense of war is entirely spiritual. A Rommel, or a Lee, a Hannibal or a Fabius Maximus, he was not. It is possible to imagine Nietzsche as a Patton, leading a tank corps on a blitz or a rescue, but not winning other battles through deception, feint, retreat, counterattack, poise, measure, and understanding.[44] Still less had Nietzsche the sagacity of an Elisabeth, a Halifax, a Churchill, a De Gaulle, or a Lincoln. Though Nietzsche was a political thinker – always the center of his thought is the character of human life, both individual and earthwide – he did not recognize the statesman as a great type, nor the virtue that distinguishes him, practical wisdom, as a great and human virtue, as in truth a high form of loyalty to the earth. Nor did Nietzsche recognize the kinship of statesmanship and tragedy; how the statesman, like the artist Nietzsche so often praises, must often do 'evil' to serve good. The decisive event in World War II was Churchill's bombing of the French Fleet at Oran; this bloody destruction of a recent ally caused Churchill tears, tears, tears, and yet it and it alone convinced the United States to toil and sweat, and weep and bleed, along with Britain.[45] Judging from Nietzsche's general esteem of Thucydides, in which similar 'evil' deeds are portrayed, we might say that he understood this, but since he gives us no detailed examples of it, we must conclude he had no eyes for the statesman. Nietzsche's sense of rule was spiritual; he who could not have ruled a single country for a month aims to rule all for a thousand.[46]

Yet, we must acknowledge that Nietzsche has now ruled the world for a hundred years. Today, a century after he first put forward his abysmal thoughts in *Zarathustra*, they offer us the best modern account of our modern situation. Not Marx and not Freud, but Nietzsche forecast the terrible wars of our time. Today the long war for the world that began in 1914 proceeds, as he said it would, avowedly in the East, with reluctance in the West. Being wars for the world and coming in democratic times, such wars would be fought for ideas, they would be like civil wars, they would be more fiercely contested and followed by more savage peaces than other wars.

The wars of our century, for the whole earth, are but part of a greater war to master nature, which he also foresaw. In his time he knew people who advanced such mastery, especially over pain, and he knew the wish for greater mastery, so as to eliminate all weather from life, for example. Nietzsche foresaw that the balance between man and nature would shift enormously in the coming century. He also saw the ethical consequence: the possibility of what he calls 'weightlessness', the state in which you can't do much because you don't have anything to push against, in which everything has become too easy for man's own good. The conquest of nature will bring forth the Last Man. Big science and little men. Against this victory over nature, he thought no resistance could be mounted; precisely because none could be, he sought to educate the coming victors so that they would not be destroyed by the peace that would follow such a destructive conquest of nature.

Then, such victors will have to reinstitute nature; then the limitations and difficulties, such as pain, scarcity, fatigue, death, accident, weight, space, and time, which were once just there, will have to be willed and protected, in order to save man from becoming the Last Man. Once nature was a kind of mother, comforting and nourishing, limiting and punishing man. Now increasingly man will have to limit and punish himself. Where once nature was responsible for keeping man, now man will have to be. One may wonder whether those who are attracted by the conquest of nature, by the ease, speed, immortality, and freedom from pain it promises, are capable of such self-mastery. If offered the immortality Odysseus rejects again and again on his way home to Ithaka, would they have the same moderation?[47]

IX Nietzsche Once More

The world we live in was described by Nietzsche in the six books he wrote after *Zarathustra*. In these six he said 'Behold the world.' In the seventh 'Behold the man.' This seventh book was indeed a rest from looking at the modern world, which he did not find 'very good', but the ease Nietzsche enjoys in *Ecce Home* is no repose. It says, 'Look at man as he might one day be, a man worthy of world mastery and strong enough to preserve nature. Look at such a man. Look at me. Look at man himself. I am man become Man. Look at me.'

This is confirmed by the title. 'Ecce Homo' are the words of a Roman soldier, a servant of Caesar, and a representative of his authority. By speaking them, Nietzsche compares himself to a Roman, a servant of Caesar, his representative. However, these words, 'Ecce Homo', are also about Christ. So, by having these words point to himself, Nietzsche compares himself to Christ he claims to be another Christ or the man to whom these words are rightly addressed. Combining as his title does both subject and speaker, Nietzsche is, then, something of a 'Roman Caesar with the soul of Christ'. If so, then he amply fulfills the double claim of the title, *Ecce Homo*, which says both 'Behold the man' and 'Behold Man.'

I know of almost no one who has claimed such an authority. Only Sokrates, implicitly, and Christ, directly, if sometimes shyly, have claimed to have so become Man that all men should turn their way, hearken to their teachings, and imitate them. Well might we ask what evidence and what testimony might clinch such a claim. Both are to be found, if at all, in Nietzsche's books, which you will have to read and study in order to judge. To convince you to do so has been my purpose and it was also one of the purposes that compelled Nietzsche to write *Ecce Homo*.

There is an additional Nietzschean reason that might convince us. For Nietzsche the measure of life, what orders all ranks, is the quality and the strength of love. Do you love your life so much that you would like to repeat it eternally? There is an analogous form of this measure he did not think of, and yet he measures up to it too. A lot of people, many of whom never read his works, met Nietzsche. Many of them left accounts of these meetings. They have been collected and a portion translated into English recently. Almost all show Nietzsche to have been gracious, at once polite and yet helpful, courteous and nevertheless filled with thoughts. All who report such meetings are grateful. 'To see a great man close by during one's developing years is a gift of grace of immeasurable and indestructible value',[48] begins the recollection of one woman so privileged, Maria von Bradke. How many of us would trust our eternity, our reputation or our salvation, to the recollections of all those with whom we had walked a bit together? If the eternal return of the same preserves all that was great in the idea of eternity, the loss of which Nietzsche feared would destroy man, the measure of whether those who knew you would say of your life 'Yes, once more!' restores the measure of fame. The fame that Nietzsche sought, through publishing *Ecce Homo*, to win in the hearts of those of his readers who might never know him personally had already been won in the hearts of those who did meet him. Thus this book might unite all his conversants, living and dead, in one affirmation, 'Was that Nietzsche, why then once more.' Or, simply, 'Behold the Man.'

Notes

1. Work on this essay was begun with good students at Dartmouth, advanced with more at the University of Dallas, and at Heidelberg; its first version was written during a National Endowment for the Humanities summer seminar (and delivered to a panel at the American Political Science Association Convention); its revision was accomplished on an Alexander von Humboldt Fellowship, with several additions on an NEH fellowship, and later delivered to the Philosophy Department at Penn State. My thanks to all of these, and to my hosts at Penn State, the effervescent Stanley Rosen, the irreplaceable David Lachterman, and the steady Jim Wiley. And to *Nietzsche Studien* for publishing it (Band XXII). The present version includes some corrections and a few augmentations.

2. *Kritische Gesamtausgabe von Nietzsches Briefwechsel*, ed. Giorgio Colli and Mazzino Montinari (Berlin and New York: Walter de Gruyter, 1975–84), III (3), No. 581; Middleton's good selection of the letters, in English, gives this one an incorrect date. All quotations from Nietzsche are cited from the Giorgio Colli and Mazzino Montinari *Kritische Gesamtausgabe* (Berlin and New York: Walter de Gruyter, 1967–78), 30 vols., abbreviated KGW; the *Kritische Studienausgabe* (DTV/de Gruyter,

1980), by the same editors, follows the KGW and is abbreviated KSA; all translations are by Walter Kaufmann, some with slight changes; abbreviations for Nietzsche's books are the usual ones, e.g., *EH* for *Ecce Homo*.

3. Or released it in an impersonal book, as he did, in *Morgenröte*, No. 566.

4. See *The Minutes of the Vienna Psychoanalytic Society*, trans. M. Nunberg (New York: International Universities Press, 1974), Vol. II (meeting of 28 October 1908 on *Ecce Homo*), p. 32; for an excellent account of the relation of Freud to Nietzsche, see Lorin Anderson, 'Freud, Nietzsche', *Salmagundi* [Nos. 47–8, 1980] pp. 3–29; for the way the epigone Freud worked to bring about the worst fears of the master, the Last Man as Therapeutic Man, see Philip Rief's *Freud: Mind of a Moralist* and its sequel, *Therapeutic Man*. For Freud's low perspective read anything of his on something high, for example on Leonardo, or his patronizing remark on Sophocles' *Oedipus*. On fairy tales, whose authors he could have no access to, he was better, as E. H. Gombrich pointed out.

5. This remark appears in the *Nachlass* (leftovers) of the 1880s; see F. N., *Werke in Drei Bänden*, ed. Karl Schlecta (München: Hanser Verlag, 1956), III, p. 430.

6. *Götzen-Dämmerung* 'Streifzüge eines Unzeitgemässen,' No. 5.

7. There is some reason to believe that Nietzsche favors infanticide (*Frolicsome Science* 73), but not contraception or abortion (except on the pro-life basis, protecting the life of the mother). Admitting that Walter Kaufmann had good reason to translate 'Fröhliche' as 'Gay', but conceding that a polemical effort to narrow the semantic range of the word in English has succeeded, David Lachterman and I came up with 'Frolicsome', which has the virtue of being cognate with 'Fröhliche'. (May D.L. repose in frolicsome peace.)

8. Variations of the formula 'Behold . . .' are repeated as the narrative proceeds, by Pilate: 'Behold your king', and by Jesus on the Cross: 'Behold your son' and 'Behold your mother.'

9. KGW, 7:2, 289; this leftover (*Nachlass*) belongs to the period *Sommer–Herbst* 1884. Elizabeth Nietzsche put it in her arrangement of the leftovers, '~~The Will to Power~~', as No. 983. For reasons Walter Kaufmann stresses in his warning preface to his translation of '~~The Will to Power~~' (1967), and others mentioned below, I shall print the title to this non-book with strike-thru marks.

10. Nietzsche employed a four-part division in another book, *Fröliche Wissenschaft*, deliberately I think, since it ends with the appearance of the new god of wrath, beatitude, and love, Zarathustra. That he added a Book Five later accords with his assertion that Christ died too young and the fact that it was written after *Zarathustra*, who refuses to go down to the city and get killed, but instead remains in the mountains, eats a gay supper with students, and celebrates a comic festival. Not accidentally, *Zarathustra* too is in four books.

11. Several of these observations are indebted to Leon Craig's unpublished paper 'Nietzsche's "Apology": On Reading *Ecce Homo*'. What I say about the place of Christ in *Ecce Homo* will allow readers of Craig's interpretation to understand why I cannot entirely agree with his stunning conclusion. To others who have not read his paper, I can only say that Craig is the kind of reader Nietzsche talks about in *Ecce Homo*: 'a born adventurer and discoverer', whose careful 'deductions' lead to a stunning 'guess', and whose manly spirit and wit would please Nietzsche himself.

12. This numerical comparison is noticed by Hugh J. Silverman in 'The Autobiographical Textuality of Nietzsche's *Ecce Homo*', in *Why Nietzsche Now*, ed. Daniel O'Hara (Bloomington: Indiana U.P., 1985 [earlier as a special issue of *Boundary* 2]), pp. 141ff; the essay is limited to the first few pages of *Ecce Homo*, unfortunately. In the same volume, I found another contributor, Charles Altieri (pp. 389ff.), who has noticed Nietzsche's comparison of himself with Christ. In this volume there is also an

essay on *EH*, sort of, by Rodolphe Gasché; see also another 'sort of' by him in *Looking After Nietzsche*, ed. Laurence A. Rickels (Albany: SUNY Press, 1990).

13. In support of these various views, some, including many doctors, find an efficient physical cause of Nietzsche's subsequent madness. They, or rather one of them, may be right, but none have, I think, proved their case, and even if we exhumed Nietzsche's corpse, we might have a hard time distinguishing evidence of disease from evidence that Nietzsche, like many in the nineteenth century, took various concoctions that included things we now know to be poisonous; Nietzsche often wrote his own prescriptions; being a 'Dr.' and having a hard-to-decipher hand, they were filled. For some of those who find a bodily cause of Nietzsche's madness, e.g. Dr. Karl Jaspers, it saves the books of Nietzsche for thought, but for others finding such an efficient cause 'explains' the mad opinions in the books, which we need then pay no thoughtful attention to. For Jaspers, see his *Nietzsche* trans. Charles F. Wallraff and Fredrick J. Schmitz (Chicago: Regnery, 1969; original 1935); however, note his sympathetic account of Nietzsche's 'Friends and [his] Loneliness.'

14. This riddle, explicitly so called by Nietzsche, has been much attended to by Derrida (cited below) and his American train, but with no solutions provided, nor much attempt. It is true that explaining Hamlet's riddles to a Polonius would only make him all the more certain Hamlet is mad, but failure to try, once you've fussed with the matter, is no help. Considering the Freudianism of Derrida and his train, finding a reason in riddles is absolutely required. Not that Freud's paradoxical faith that there is more reason, order, plan in madness than in reason, including books, is other than a methodical madness. As to Nietzsche, it is almost always true that if you need something witty explained to you, it can't be.

15. Silverman (cited above) rightly observes that the second part of the title indicates this is a manual as well as an autobiography.

16. I think *klug* is better translated 'sagacious' and *klugheit* sagacity, than Kaufmann's clever and cleverness. Clever has a lower range, including 'tricky', 'corner-cutting', and even 'deceiving', 'cunning', and 'cruel', than *klug*, certainly as Nietzsche employs or means it. According to him, this virtue never includes either deception or cruelty. Nor is there any petty, commercial, or sensual purpose in it. When Nietzsche claimed he never coveted women, honor, or wealth, he seems to have been honest. Fame, recognition, power perhaps, but not these usual objects of merely clever men.

17. The theme of Alexander Nehamas' *Nietzsche: Life as Literature* (Cambridge: Harvard, 1985) is important and the author's disposition serious; unfortunately, his understanding of literature is not Nietzsche's; thus, on almost every page things from Nietzsche's *Nachlass* are mixed with sentences from his books, and these sentences are not understood in their context, either the passage, the section, or the book. The leftovers (*Nachlass*) of Nietzsche are more interesting than almost all books, but there is a world of difference between them and the beautiful books he wrote. Beautiful – that means with every word exactly where it should be, perfectly related to all others, splendid.

18. In the *Untimely Observation, Richard Wagner in Bayreuth* (Section 4), Nietzsche names as the three greatest sufferings for the individual, 'that men do not share all knowledge in common, that ultimate insight can never be certain, that abilities are divided unequally'.

19. *Fröhliche Wissenschaft*, 310.

20. For further interpretation, based on Nietzsche's other works see my 'Nature and *The* Order of Rank' *Journal of Value Inquiry*, Vol. XXII: 1988, pp. 147–65.

21. For more, see 'What Does Zarathustra Whisper in Life's Ear?', *Nietzsche-Studien*, Vol. XVII: 1988, pp. 179–94.

22. On the style of Nietzsche, especially in this book, see the citation-rich essay of Hans-Martin Gauger, 'Nietzsches Stil am Beispiel von *Ecce Homo*', *Nietzsche-Studien*, Vol. XIII (1984), pp. 332–55

23. If the seamless unity between life and work which Nietzsche claims he achieved in *Ecce Homo* justifies Heidegger in paying so much attention to letters and leftovers, it also criticizes him for not paying enough attention to Nietzsche's claims that *Zarathustra* is the peak of his life and, work – a life and work which in *Ecce Homo*, Nietzsche clearly, pace Heidegger, represents as perfect, even if not finished.

24. If so, *Zarathustra I* was a bit premature, since elephants gestate 22 months.

25. Without the name he does refer to the substance of its test of Zarathustra, in 'Wise', 4.

26. See *Fröhliche Wissenschaft*, 341.

27. Walter Kaufmann's reluctant translation (with R. J. Hollingdale) of '~~The Will to Power~~' (New York: Vintage, 1967) is prefaced by a good account of the effect of this non-book on Nietzsche's reputation and a sober warning about the status of the materials, to English-speaking Nietzsche scholars, who have largely ignored it. The editorial work of Giorgio Colli and Mazzino Montinari, especially their faithfully chronological edition of the *Nachlass*, has only added to the story and underlined the warning. Although Nietzsche considered writing a book with this title (twenty-five plans were found among his literary remains), he not only never published and never wrote one, he had definitely abandoned a project with this title by the first days of September 1888; in the months remaining to him, Nietzsche put together *Götzen-Dämmerung* and *Der Antichrist*, assembled *Nietzsche Contra Wagner*, and wrote *Ecce Homo* nearly from scratch; as Mazzino Montinari says. 'der Rest ist – Nachlass'. See Montinari's 'Nietzsches Nachlass von 1885 bis 1888 oder Textkritik und Wille zur Macht', in *Nietzsche Lesen* (Berlin: de Gruyter, 1982), pp. 92–119; Montinari's article appeared earlier, in 1975. For a judicious assessment of the philosophical consequences of Montinari's philological discoveries for Anglo-Saxon interpretation, see Bernd Magnus, 'The Use and Abuse of *The Will to Power*', in *Reading Nietzsche* ed. Robert C. Solomon and Kathleen M. Higgins (Oxford University Press, 1988), pp. 218–35. The article also relates some speculations, arrived at together with myself, about what Nietzsche's landlord at Sils Maria did with some of the *Nachlass*. That there is still (1992) no English translation of the Montinari/Colli arrangement of the *Nachlass* is the shame of English-speaking Nietzsche scholarship. Perhaps this is to be explained by its scandal: the number of prominent members who treat Nietzsche's *Nachlass* on a par with his books. Other shames are: no translation of the Janz biography; Löwith's book not translated; nor Eugen Fink's; nor Müller-Lauter's. [1997: the Löwith book is out, and a twenty-volume English translation of the whole Montinari/Colli text is underway, under the direction of Ernst Behler from Stanford Press; however, none of the eleven volumes that will translate the *Nachlass* into English for the first time are out.]

28. See my review of Martin Heidegger, *Nietzsche: Volume Four: Nihilism*, trans. by David F. Krell (Harper & Row, 1982) in *The Review of Metaphysics* (March 1984), pp. 637–9.

29. Consider the well known books by Danto and Schacht, the latter the current head of the North American Nietzsche Society, and the author of perhaps the longest tome on Nietzsche in any language; neither makes a distinction between what Nietzsche perfected for publication and what he had no chance to perfect or destroy. Although these scholars write books, they do not know what a book is; Nietzsche did know what a book is and requires readers who do, or who are willing to learn from him. To write a book on Nietzsche in a series on 'Arguments of the Philosophers' one has to ignore all Nietzsche said against systemizers. Danto's title *Nietzsche As Philosopher* is, as Lionel Trilling observed, cheeky. Danto as philosopher is not noticed by Nietzsche.

30. Recent favorites are Derrida, Foucault, and Lacan. One can have no *a priori* objection to a preference for another thinker than Nietzsche – one would even like a confrontation, provided Nietzsche gets his say in – but working Nietzsche over from the unexamined view of someone else is neither interpretation nor thinking. Since Gary Schipiro, 'How One Becomes What One Is Not', *Nietzchean Narratives* (Bloomington: Indiana U.P., 1989), pp. 142–67, is almost alone in confronting Montinari's philological work, I wish he had thought Nietzsche a greater authority than Lacan.

31. On *Ecce Homo*, more exactly evading it, see his *Otobiographies: L'enseignement de N. et la politique de nom propre* (Paris: Galilée, 1984); translation: *The Ear of the Other*, ed. Christie V. McDonald, trans. Peggy Kamuf (New York: Schocken Books, 1985); note Derrida's error in counting Nietzsche's years and in the discussion section, see the fine questions of Eugene Vance; for a good summary of Derrida on Nietzsche, see Ernst Behler, 'Nietzsche and Deconstruction', in *Nietzsche, Literature, and Values*, ed. Volker Dürr *et al.* (Madison: Univ. of Wisconsin Press, 1988); it is true, as Behler says, that Nietzsche anticipated Derrida. Indeed he did with nausea and with the defense that is *Ecce Homo*.

32. For a model of reading Nietzsche, confronting him with the thought of another, and thinking oneself, see Charles M. Natoli, *Nietzsche and Pascal on Christianity* (New York: Peter Lang, 1985).

33. Colli and Montinari's *Kritische Studienausgabe* (Vol. 10, p. 137) places this remark somewhere between November 1882 and February 1883, when Nietzsche wintered in Rapallo, began and finished *Zarathustra*. In it Nietzsche thinks of himself as creating something, the vision of the *Übermensch* (or Zarathustra?), while later in *Ecce Homo*, *Zarathustra* is treated as a gift and revelation as well as an invention. The usual 'Superman' and 'Overman' translate Nietzsche's *Übermensch* poorly, I think; the former because the Comic Book has vulgarized its nobility; the latter because it sounds high-minded, empty, and static. Since the *Übermensch* is over, above, and beyond man, man so far, only by being one who ever surpasses himself, I prefer the word 'surpassing'; it and its elided version 'passing' belong to the treasury of Shakespearian English: 'much surpassing the common praise it bears', 'passing fair', and 'passing strange' (*Winter's Tale*, 3.1.2; *Romeo and Juliet*, 1.1.234; *Othello* 1.3.160).

34. Printed by Walter Kaufmann in an appendix to his English translation (1967). Gast and Förster are included in the three German types so vilified. However, it should be reiterated that although Nietzsche attached some instructions for publication, he sent it all to Paraguay, not the publisher.

35. Zarathustra shows a similar failing in only belatedly appreciating his animals (*Zarathustra IV*) who were, I am certain, provided by the University of Basel. Like Nietzsche, Zarathustra is to believe that a philosopher can live outside the city, that one can be a man apart from other men.

36. Altieri (previously cited) thinks you can have truthfulness without truth and believes Nietzsche thought so.

37. The passage together with editorial information appears in Mazzino Montinari's 'Ein neuer Abschnitt in Nietzsches "Ecce Homo" ', in his *Nietzsche Lesen* (cited above). An excellent translation of this passage by David Krell appears in his 'Consultations with the Paternal Shadow', in *Nietzsche in Italy*, ed. Thomas Harrison (Stanford University: ANMA Libri, 1988), pp. 232–3; this volume also includes a translation of a few pages from Anacleto Verrecchia's *La catastrophe di Nietzsche a Torino* (Torino: Einaudi, 1978): the Harrison volume also contains several other essays on or around *Ecce Homo*, including the surpassing one by René Girard.

38. On the progress of Neitzsche into madness, see the pertinent parts of the KGA, Montinari's article on the shifting plans of Nietzsche in late 1888 (mentioned above), and the new material on Nietzsche's time in Turin in Anacleto Verrecchia, *Zarathustras Ende: Die Katastrophe Nietzsche in Turin* (H. Böhlau: Wien, 1986), a translation

from the author's Italian original of 1978 (Einaudi). Verrecchia's hostility to Nietzsche's thought, however reasonable, makes one wonder if there is bias in the account, since no great appreciation of what was lost in this catastrophe is evident. On the madness itself, was its cause organic or psychic? etc. see as a guide to the considerable literature, Horst Althaus, *Friedrich Nietzsche: Eine bürgerliche Tragödie* (München: Nymphenburger, 1985) and the judicious considerations of Daniel Breazeale, 'Ecce Psycho: Remarks on the Case of Nietzsche', *International Studies in Philosophy*, XXIII/2 (1992), pp. 19–33.

39. In one respect Nietzsche seems superior to Zarathustra; he acknowledges the contribution of more things in his past to his becoming who he is; he speaks of his parents, whereas Zarathustra never does.

40. That Nietzsche signed some of his last letters 'The Crucified' does not, I think, count as evidence of his 'succumbing to the enemy' since Christ is praised very highly *in Der Antichrist*. If 'The Crucified' means that Nietzsche now survives his own death and that his 'death' was gruesome and terrible, it might be evidence. However, the tone of his letters is agitated and joyous, not terrified, though the cause of justified concern in others.

41. The suspicion that Nietzsche chose madness is worked out in great detail by Claudia Crawford in her adventurous and ardent *To Nietzsche: Dionysus, I Love You, Ariadne* (Albany: SUNY Press, 1995); the case, which in its nature is hard to prove, since if true then the man tried to prevent us learning it, is harder still even to prove probable, because so many of the pertinent facts of Nietzsche's life are now so removed; nevertheless the case is made very plausible by Crawford. If Nietzsche faked madness, it was a grave fault. I can understand why a Brutus has to play mad, to deceive a tyrant, but I cannot think it necessary for Nietzsche. And to fail to write on, as he was so capable of, just in order to draw attention to oneself and one's writings is folly indeed. No gift-giving virtue there. No Nietzsche.

42. On these matters and much else, see the excellent remarks of René Girard, 'Dionysus versus the Crucified', *Modern Language Notes*, Vol. 99 (No. 4), (1984) pp. 816–35; also reprinted in *Nietzsche in Italy*. Although *The Bacchae* was for Nietzsche the paradigmatic tragedy and although he sometimes encourages vengeance, I must point out that he struggles with it and in *Zarathustra* celebrates its hero's overcoming of both vengeance and ressentiment.

43. See the middle section of my 'Nature and *The* Order of Rank', *Journal of Value Inquiry*, Vol. XXII: 1988, pp. 147–65.

44. See Charles de Gaulle's criticism of the fault of the German generals in World War I as Nietzschean, as lacking 'measure,' in his *La Discorde chez l'ennemi* (Plon: Paris, 1924).

45. For a further comparison of Nietzsche and Churchill, the only man since to confront the question of 'life once more,' see my 'Nietzsche, Churchill, and the End of the Human Species' when it appears.

46. It must be remarked that Nietzsche's way of writing and his disposition toward the whole requires and encourages an equivalent, in matters of thought, to practical wisdom, perhaps one should call it judgment. His enigmatic and sparkling remarks constantly teach the reader to judge according to circumstance, tone and context, to endure contradiction and uncertainty, and to suspect simplicity.

47. For further thoughts, see my 'Would Human Life Be Better Without Death?', *Soundings*, LXIII (3): Fall 1980, pp. 321–38.

48. See *Conversations with Nietzsche*, edited by Sander L. Gilman and translated by David J. Parent (New York: Oxford University Press, 1987), p. 188; for the originals, and more of them, see Sander Gilman, *Begegnung mit Nietzsche* (Bonn: Bolivar, 1981).

53

Suspicion, Deception, and Concealment*

Stanley Rosen

*Source: *Arion*, third series, vol. 1, no. 2, May 1991, pp. 112–27.

– une croyance presque instinctive chez moi c'est que tout homme puissant
ment quand il parle, et à plus forte raison quand il écrit.

(Stendhal)

I

The passage from Stendhal that serves as our motto is recorded by Nietzsche
in a notebook entry dating from 1887–88.[1] It expresses a theme that fascinates
Nietzsche at all stages of his productive life. The most powerful statement of
that theme occurs in paragraph 30 of *Beyond Good and Evil*, as part of the
climax of Nietzsche's account of the distance that separates the exceptional
human being from the multitude (par. 26–30):

> [O]ur highest insights must – and should – sound like follies, perhaps like
> crimes, when in an impermissible manner they reach ears which are not
> suited or predetermined for them. The exoteric and the esoteric, as the
> philosophers formerly distinguished them, among the Indians as among
> the Greeks, Persians, and Musulmen, in short, wherever one believes in
> rank-ordering and not in equality and equal rights –[2]

It is in this context that Nietzsche observes, ten paragraphs later: 'everything
that is deep loves the mask; the deepest things have a hatred for image and
likeness.'[3]

One may easily multiply references in Nietzsche to the superior being's
need for self-concealment. I restrict myself to two passages from the notebooks. First: 'the necessary *concealment* of the wise man: his consciousness,
to be unconditionally not understood.'[4] Second: 'What is noble? . . . always to
be disguised; the higher his nature, the more does a man require an incognito.

God, if there were one, would be required on grounds of decency to show himself in the world only as a human being.'[5] These texts suggest two reasons for the practice of esotericism by the higher man: prudence and the exercise of an aristocratic natural right. A detailed analysis of these motives would be of independent interest, especially in the contemporary Anglo-Saxon intellectual community. In this essay, however, I prefer to take my bearings by a more fundamental stratum in Nietzsche's thought. As is exemplified by the insights incorporated in the early Greek poets and thinkers, deception and concealment are intrinsic to existence itself. Esotericism is thus the inevitable consequence of our warranted suspicion of nature.

It would be only partially correct, and therefore misleading, to say that for Nietzsche, human existence is an illusion. We are put on the right track by the further statement that the dynamical structure of the illusion is intelligible. The key to Nietzsche's analysis is thus contained in his assertion that 'the true essence of things is a fiction of *des vorstellenden Seins.*'[6] The German expression may be translated as 'imaginative' or 'representational Being.' Scientific truth is for Nietzsche an artifact; like most modern philosophers, Nietzsche accepts the thesis that we know only what we make. Whereas Kant, for example, posits a transcendental process of world-constitution that is valid for all beings of our cognitive nature, Nietzsche substitutes a fanciful, random, intrinsically chaotic process of Becoming that expresses itself in a multiplicity of continuously shifting perspectives. Nietzsche traces this doctrine back to the earliest Greek thinkers: 'the Greeks taught us gradually *to organize chaos.*'[7] And again: 'To take possession of oneself, to organize the chaotic, to discard all fear of "formation" [*Bildung*] and to be honest: summons to *gnōthi sauton.*'[8]

Honesty here stands for philosophy as an existential requirement of the higher human type: a frank perception of the fanciful or invented status of natural order is the basis of concealment. To exist is to conceal chaos. And the higher man, who is alone capable of self-knowledge, *conceals this concealment.* Both levels of concealment underlie Nietzsche's famous invocation of art: 'Art and nothing but art. It is art that is the great rendering possible of life, the great seductress to life, the great stimulus to life.'[9] When Nietzsche asserts from his own experience 'that art is worth more than the truth,'[10] he is referring to the poeticizing reason which in man is the expression of the fanciful Being that produces what we perceive as order.[11] The 'will to power as knowledge' is accordingly 'not "knowing" but schematizing, a superimposing of enough regularity and form onto chaos as will satisfy our practical needs.'[12]

Whereas science is the result of 'a creative, formative constitutive power,' or the self-establishment of man within chaos,[13] so too is art. The higher value of art for life (and for the philosopher only as the legislator of a new type of human being) is that it encourages illusion and preserves the deception that is salutary for human existence. Science, on the other hand, tends to expose itself, the process of the dissipation of illusion, as the deepest of illusions. One must not infer from this that 'art' in the conventional sense of the term is for Nietzsche higher than philosophy – for the higher man. Nietzsche never deviates throughout his productive life from the view expressed in a letter to his sister, dating from his twenty-first year: 'in our researches, are we seeking tranquillity, peace, happiness? No; only the truth, even if it should be in the highest degree terrifying and hateful.'[14] At the peak of his creative powers, Nietzsche expresses the same thought in his notebooks as follows: 'we defend the artist and poet and whoever is a master, but as natures who are of the type higher than these who can only do something, than the merely "productive men," we do not confuse ourselves with them.'[15]

The fundamental stratum of Nietzsche's teaching, in all of its ramifications, may therefore be traced back to the insights of his youthful reflections as a classical philologist. The earliest Greek thinkers teach us to derive the cosmos from chaos.[16] But mankind as a whole lives in tranquillity, security and orderliness only when it forgets that truth is 'a moving army of metaphors, metonymies, anthropomorphisms,' when it forgets that the human being is an artist-creator.[17] We must distinguish here between two levels of truth in order to clarify Nietzsche's intention. Whereas the truth of the ordered cosmos is an artifact, the truth about cosmogony or fanciful Being is neither an illusion nor a perspective.

It is the latter truth about the artifactual nature of the former truth that necessitates dissimulation:

> The intellect, as a means to the preservation of the individual, develops its chief forces in dissimulation; for this is the means by which the weaker, less robust individuals preserve themselves, for which individuals the pursuit of a struggle for existence with horned creatures or the sharp bite of beasts of prey is excluded. This art of dissimulation reaches its peak in mankind. Here deception, flattery, lying and deluding, talking behind one's back, keeping up appearances, living within the concealed glance, masked existence, veiled convention, the stage-play before others and before oneself, in short, the continuous fluttering around the flame of vanity, is so much the rule and the law that it is almost inconceivable how an honest and pure drive for the truth could have arisen in human beings.[18]

In sum: human beings invent the distinction between truth and falsehood as a consequence of the emergence of language from society, which is itself a product of the need for peace.[19] But the entire process is precisely an invention of the fanciful Being or poeticizing reason. These in turn assume human shape and accommodate to human perspective, but the process of accommodation is not an artifact, not a perception. It is this which Nietzsche the philosopher describes in his analysis of dissimulation. The few conceal from the many what the many conceal from themselves. As reciprocal dissimulation, human activity exhibits rather than conceals the dynamic structure of Becoming. This concealment is extra-moral because, to employ a non-Nietzschean term, it is ontological. When Heidegger speaks of the presence of Being as self-concealment, he transforms into ontological abstractions Nietzsche's vivid analysis of the cosmogonic production of perspectives. What shows itself achieves presence or visibility as a falsification of the continuous inner excitation of chaos, or of what Hegel refers to as the terrible power of negativity. It is not simply that human beings conceal their thoughts from one another. Thinking is *as such* concealment: to be is to dissimulate.

Hegel represents the attempt of German philosophy to master Greek genesis by the structure of its own activity, or in other words, to interpret chaos as the formation process. This is in turn the result of an attempt to combine eternity with time, or what Kant calls the noumenal and the phenomenal. In Nietzsche, exactly the same attempt is visible, as may be indicated by a reference to the eternal return of the similar, Nietzsche's version of the Hegelian concept of totality. In Nietzsche, however, Hegel's synthesis of essence and appearance, or the identification of essence *as* what appears, is dissolved by the play of appearances themselves. We may describe the process of play, but as a metaphor or dissimulation, not as a quasi-mathematical or conceptually determinate structure. To conceptualize is for Nietzsche to suppress original dissimulation with an artifact or perspective. It is to dissimulate dissimulation, but it is also to produce a world, and thus to make life possible.

Nietzsche imitates the play of appearances in his texts, which are coherent but not 'systematic.' I am suggesting that the key to the play of appearances is the distinction between philosophical truth and the philosophical production or world-creation that this truth necessitates. The truth or cosmogonic process always reveals itself in a disguise, namely, as this or that cosmos, this or that perspective. The process is always the same, it is as it were the eternal return of the similar; and the accessibility of this sameness enables us to 'deconstruct' each manifestation as a dissimulation. For Nietzsche, however, there are only a finite number of fundamental cosmic dissimulations or human types, which thus serve as Platonic Ideas in the sense that they allow us to organize and understand the unending production of perspectives within those types.

Nietzsche's self-professed 'reversed Platonism' or replacement of the Ideas by 'life within illusion'[20] could be shown to be Platonic in more than one sense; I restrict myself here to noting the nonillusory perception of life *within* illusion. 'Within,' not 'as'; the distinction is crucial. From the standpoint of the esotericist, who sees from above downward, life is visible as within, and so as defined by, illusion, that is, by what I have called the cosmogonic process of dissimulation.

The question that interests me here is not so much whether Nietzsche's 'anti-Platonism' has been correctly understood, by himself or his disciples, but rather what evidence we can find in the pre-Socratic poets and thinkers to sustain Nietzsche's account of the schematizing of chaos. I propose to devote the balance of this essay to the gathering of such evidence, a gathering that is, of course, far from exhaustive but which is sufficient to justify the thesis that the root of Nietzsche's thought is Greek. Nietzsche is one of the many modern captains in Homer's army.[21]

II

The Greek *phainomenon* is a conjunction of presence and absence. Let us turn first to Pindar. In the Olympian Odes he speaks on numerous occasions of the truth as 'spotted,' 'stained,' or 'veiled' by lies, which are again compared to an obscure cloud that drags away the correct path of things from men's minds.[22] These images sustain the insight that falsehoods, the lies told by things and events themselves, are an intrinsic property of the truth, and not an extrinsic covering that may be easily removed.

The intrinsic stain of falsehood prevents us from knowing whether what happens is for the best. We can, of course, often judge the desirability of an event by its future consequences. But apart from the fact that the future may be as ambiguous as the past, we live and act in the present. In a single *moira* of time, differing winds change rapidly.[23] One wind is a blessing, the other is not: a mortal who knows the ways of truth should prosper while he can.[24]

Wisdom, in other words, consists in moderating one's desires and ambitions in the face of present ambiguity. Men's hopes rise and fall, borne on falsehoods that tumble in the wind. No mortal has ever succeeded in discovering a *piston symbolon* about coming events from a god.[25] One should not, for example, sacrifice the present attainment for a future wish; who knows what will happen a year from now?[26]

In sum: whereas the gods are not to be vilified, and are the source of all human excellence,[27] deception and concealment are intrinsic to divine action, that is to say, to the consequences for mortals of divine action. And human beings somehow resemble the gods.[28] It is against this background, of which I have provided a mere sketch, that I understand Pindar's statement *Nemean VII*:

> I even suspect that Odysseus' fame
> was greater than his worth, through the sweet words of Homer.
> For in his lies and in his winged devices
> there is an awesome power:
> wisdom is deceptive, seducing
> with its myths.[29]

This passage is not simply praise for poetry. Or rather it is praise for the wisdom of the poet, and hence of Pindar as well as of Homer, to respond to the greater power of the gods with the power of what Socrates will later call medicinal or noble lies, or in less shocking language, the seduction of myth. Human beings require to be seduced by the poets whose 'phantasms' (to employ another Platonic expression) accommodate the deceptions of the gods to the human perspective. Myths or phantasms speak, but in such a way as also to be silent: it is not better for every truth to show its face, as Pindar warns us; silence is often wiser.[30]

When the Muses tell Hesiod that 'we know how to tell many lies similar to the truth, but we also know how, when we wish, to proclaim the truth,'[31] they are making essentially the same point. The Muses convey to the poets the lies as well as the truths of the gods; that is to say, the wisdom of the poet is not a straightforward revelation of the truth. The origins are intrinsically ambiguous; poetic myth is from the outset an accommodation to or an interpretation of this ambiguity.

From our present standpoint, Hesiod, like Pindar, is a student of Homer. Let us therefore turn to the master, in our attempt to clarify the suggestion that the Greeks are distinguished by their recognition of what Nietzsche calls '*Wahrheit und Lüge im aussermoralischen Sinne.*' It is not simply the appearances that deceive: the divine causes of the human significance of the appearances are also deceivers. Once this is recognized, it is the part of the wise man to deceive his fellow mortals, not simply to conceal himself from their own duplicity, but also to protect them from the deception of the gods.

The symbolic representation of the aforementioned recognition is the transition from Achilles to Odysseus. There is a detailed analysis of the difference between the heroic ethos personified by Achilles in the *Iliad*, and the Ionian ethos of the *Odyssey*, as exemplified by Odysseus, in Wilhelm Luther's valuable study, '*Wahrheit' und 'Lüge' im ältesten Griechentum.*[32]

Luther shows that '*pseudos* contradicts the warrior Ideal of the *Iliad*' (84), in which lying is reserved for cowardly and incompetent mortals, whereas the Olympian gods regularly lie and deceive (85). The situation changes fundamentally in the *Odyssey*: 'the divine world of the *Iliad* in contrast inclines more to the human domain of the *Odyssey*' (95). Honesty, openness, absence of guile: these attributes of Achilles are no longer exemplified by Odysseus, who lies and deceives in common with beggars, merchants, and the lower orders, but who is no longer condemned for this behavior (87f.).

In the *Iliad*, Luther observes,

the behavior of the gods, in contrast to the heroic-aristocratic society of the warriors, is strikingly unheroic. Their attitude toward *pseudos, epiorkon, apatē, dolos*, and so on, is very close to that of the Ionians of the *Odyssey*, with the one difference that the gods behave in this respect much more arbitrarily than the mortals. On the other hand there is no essential deviation of the behavior of the gods in the *Iliad* from that in the *Odyssey*.

(117)

I restrict myself to one remark concerning Luther's own inferences from the evidence he assembles. Luther says that the ancient bards presented an idealized conception of primitive man in the *Iliad*, whereas their portrait of the gods coincides with that of contemporary Ionian man (117). But he does not attempt to explain why the bards leave us with two distinct portraits of human nature, or what the common behavior of the gods is intended to signify in contrast with the difference in human behavior, humans who are furthermore presented poetically as in chronological continuity. Luther does say, in contrasting Homer with Hesiod, that whereas in Hesiod the *pseudos*-phenomenon is presented explicitly and self-consciously as a problem, there is no reflection in Homer upon lying and deception as problematic (138).

In my opinion, Luther's conclusion does not do justice to his own evidence of Homer's subtlety. What Homer actually shows is that the lying and deception of the gods is a poetic representation of the intrinsic structure of human experience. This fact is directly evident to the lower orders, who must live by their wits as well as their physical labor, and who cannot afford to delude themselves about the nature of things.

In contrast, the earliest warrior-aristocrats, who are insulated by their class from the infinite labor of negativity (to repeat a Hegelian expression), may shape their lives, or more specifically the interpretation of their lives, in an aesthetic of nobility, one which extends to the sole negative activity of killing the enemy. Honesty, openness, and absence of guile thus constitute an inability to modify their conduct in the face of a reality which they reject as base and ugly, a reality which in due course will initiate the master–slave dialectic celebrated by Hegel. The heroes of the *Iliad*, and Achilles in particular, exhibit the simplicity of innocence. In Odysseus, as it were, we see the world-historical transformation or synthesis of aristocratic strength and bravery with the cunning and duplicity of the lower orders.

No doubt it is true that Homer does not comment on the significance of the transition from Achilles to Odysseus. One might infer that in this respect Hesiod represents a decline in aesthetic and psychological subtlety. Even if Hesiod is a necessary step in the emergence of philosophy from poetry, we pay a certain price in the form of a reification of sensibility. Truth acquires its inner merit from a contrast with falsehood, but it does not follow that the contrast gains in precision and flexibility, in the domain of practice, by being rendered fully explicit. And as we have just noted, Hesiod's explicitness reveals the similarity of falsehood to truth, or the dependence of their distinctness upon the wishes of the Muses.

One should not mistake the simplicity of Achilles for that of Homer. The distinction, attributed to Antisthenes by Dio Chrysostom, between what Homer appeared to say (*doksēi*) and what he said in truth (*alētheiai*), is not at all anachronistic.[33] In an any event, the difference between Achilles and Odysseus is unmistakable. This is already evident in the *Iliad*, in which Achilles says unequivocally of himself: 'Hateful to me as the gates of Hades is he who hides one thing in his mind and says another' (IX. 312). Odysseus' nature will be defined in the *Odyssey* by Nestor: 'no one could match himself against Odysseus in wisdom, because the divine Odysseus triumphed entirely in all *dolois*' (III. 120ff.).

It is to a radical or primordial version of this distinction that the Athenian Stranger refers in Plato's *Laws* (III. 679c4–7) when he says that the earliest mortals were good *dia tēn legomenēn euētheian*, by which he means that they were not wise enough, as are contemporary men, *pseudos hyponoein*, but believed that whatever they heard about gods as well as mortals was true. A similar point underlies Herodotus' account of the Persians, with whom the Greeks contrasted themselves sharply. The Persians hold it to be unlawful to speak of what it is forbidden to do, and 'they believe that the most shameful thing of all is to tell a lie' (I. 138).

This principle is illustrated, not contradicted, in the dialogue on the Persian revolution against the Medes, in which Darius is forced to introduce the need for deception:

> There are many things impossible to reveal in speech but possible in deed. Some things can be spoken, but no noble deed is engendered. . . . When it is necessary to lie, one must do so.
>
> (III. 72)

If space permitted, it would be interesting to analyze Xenophon's portrait of the education of the Persian gentleman in the *Cyropaideia* and to contrast it with Socrates' account of the philosopher-king in the *Republic*. Here I will merely summarize the Greek perception of the difference between themselves and the Persians by citing Aeschylus' *Persians*, lines 361ff., in which Darius is said not to have understood the *dolos* of a Greek gentleman nor the envy of the gods.

Throughout Plato's dialogues, one finds a continuous interest in falsehood, suspicion, deception, and concealment, an interest that is curiously unnoticed in the secondary literature. For an appreciation of this side of Plato, one must turn to Nietzsche, who is the first major thinker of my acquaintance to appreciate explicitly the connection between spiritual nobility and the mask.

The philosophical condemnation of the lie in the soul, or self-deception, is entirely compatible with the use of medicinal or noble lies.[34] Socrates' assertion that the worst lies are about gods and heroes, and his condemnation of the lying poets, in particular Homer and Hesiod,[35] must therefore mean that in the city under construction, the traditional falsehoods are not useful. In Book III, Socrates makes the interesting assertion that falsehood is not useful for the gods, whereas it is useful for mortals in the form of a medicine.[36] One must wonder whether divine falsehood would be sanctioned if it were indeed useful.

According to Homer and his followers, the gods are deceitful. This is to say that the origins are bad, or at the very least a mixture of the bad with the good. Hence the harshness of existence requires an accommodation on the part of nobility: the high must accommodate to the low, not for low motives, but in order to survive. The existence of nobility depends upon the practice of Odyssean *dolos*.

In the account of the gods presented in the *Republic*, Socrates seems to repudiate this commonsensical understanding of life. In fact, however, the situation is more complex. To begin with, the account of the origins in the *Republic* is clearly political and designed to assist in the concealment of the medicinal lies of the philosopher-kings. When Plato turns to a straightforward account of the origins of civilization, as in the *Laws*, he clearly regards these origins as bad.[37]

In the *Republic*, the defective nature of reality is easily inferred from the elaborate precautions that are required to preserve the best city from destruction, in particular from the passions, with *eros* prominent among them, but also by the *thumos* of the guardians which reminds us of the heroic and straightforward Achilles. *Thumos* must be regulated by the *dianoia*; one part of nature must regulate the other. Those natural qualities upon which political existence depends are the same qualities which, if left to themselves, would destroy the polis. This is what I called earlier the conjunction of presence and absence as the root of the relation between truth and falsehood.

The philosophical city is founded upon the *dolos* and *apatē* of the philosophers, and in the first instance by the *gennaion pseudos* of Socrates, the philosophical reincarnation of Odysseus. The city cannot be founded upon, or preserved by, the unmitigated truth because the 'goodness' of the Ideas, and so too of the god of the philosophers, has nothing to do with everyday human existence. In particular, it has no bearing upon political life. At bottom, Socrates' understanding of political life is no different from that of Homer.

The difference between the two lies in their understanding of the divine. According to Homer, the gods are jealous, vindictive liars and deceivers who walk among mortals in concealed forms for the purpose of satisfying their own desires, whether these bring happiness or misery to human beings. According to Socrates, the gods, for all practical purposes, do not exist. But the world of genesis behaves toward mankind exactly as though the tales of the poets, and of Homer in particular, were true.

Genesis is a magician, juggler, liar, deceiver, in a word, a sophist who continuously conceals himself under changing appearances. Let us assume here what is far from obvious, namely, that the philosopher is able to distinguish between the sophistical appearances of genesis and the theoretical vision of the true divinity of the Ideas. Whereas this may bring happiness to the soul of the philosopher, it changes nothing in the soul of the nonphilosopher. Political life in the comprehensive sense can be changed, if at all, only by the political *action* of the philosopher. And this action requires the philosopher to imitate the sophist, that is, the noble sophist Odysseus, by the use of *dolos* and concealment.

The least one can say is that the enactment of truth requires the mask of deception and concealment, almost exactly as we learn from the *Odyssey*. The one significant practical difference between Homer and Plato is that Odysseus wishes to return to the tranquil life of city and family, whereas the Socratic *eros* can be satisfied by neither. But the consequence of this difference is that Odysseus reveals his identity at the end of his adventures. There is, however, no end to the Socratic adventure, and as Nietzsche understood perfectly, the philosopher never relinquishes his masks.

As a final illustration of my thesis, I call attention to Plato's *Protagoras*, 316d3ff. The great sophist, in the presence of his assembled colleagues and students, reveals to Socrates and Hippocrates the surprising fact that the sophistic *technē* is very old, but that those who practiced it before him 'put forward a screen and concealed themselves, fearing the offensiveness of the *technē*.' Among the concealed sophists of the past, Protagoras cites poets, initiates in the mysteries and oracles, gymnasts and musicians, but no philosophers.

Protagoras goes on to say that he disagrees with his predecessors on the point of deception. They did not accomplish their intention, namely, to conceal themselves from those human beings who are capable of political action (*prattein*). Those few who are by nature political leaders will see through the screens. As to the many, 'they perceive nothing, so to speak.'[38] I cannot study here in detail the implications of Protagorean frankness. The following brief remarks must serve as a promissory note for a more exhaustive analysis.

According to Protagoras, those who practice concealment of their wisdom are transparent to the men of *praksis*. There are, then, two different degrees of intelligence, or as we may say, of participation in the Greek miracle. The sophists are private citizens who withdraw behind their masks for prudential reasons: they surpass Achilles but fall short of Odysseus. Only in the case of the poets could one discern an indirect political or pedagogical role.

Protagoras, on the contrary, seeks a direct political influence. He is too wise to attempt what is beyond his gifts, namely, to try to gain power in his own name. But he is also too ambitious to restrict himself to the private station of the poet. His *dolos* is to combine elements from Achilles and Odysseus in a new mask that contains an anticipatory element of Machiavellian frankness.

Protagoras accepts the wisdom of the rulers, who are thoroughly aware of the deception required by the sophistical nature of genesis. To this extent he is a member of the aforementioned army whose general is Homer.[39] There is on this teaching no eternal domain of goodness, openness, or pure illumination behind the mask of genesis. For Homer and his troops, in the case of genesis, the mask is the ultimate truth, and so too it is the ultimate falsehood. Plato allies Socrates with Parmenides and is the actual author of the speech by which Protagoras unmasks himself and his predecessors.

By writing this speech, Plato does not deny the Homeric understanding of genesis, that is to say, of its human consequences. Instead, his rejection of Homer's mask is the negative side of the positive construction in the *Republic* of the city of philosopher-kings by means of lies, deception, and concealment. Plato reconstitutes Greek origins in the light of a profound reinterpretation of the Odyssean perception of the conjunction of truth and falsehood in the structure of things.

So far as nonphilosophical life goes, Homer is correct and continues to be an authoritative text for Plato. As to the higher truth of the philosophical life, it has nothing intrinsic to do with political existence. If it is to be politically effective, it can only be so by means of the adoption of Odyssean practice. The essence of nonphilosophical life in Socrates' city is the same as the essence of nonphilosophical life in the actual Greek city. Plato thus repudiates Pythagorean frankness because he replaces the few who actually rule in the historical city by the few philosopher-kings.

More specifically, Pericles, as one could say, is replaced by Odysseus (the philosophers) and Achilles (the soldiers), but with Odysseus firmly in charge. This repudiation of Protagoras is thus at a deeper level a return to Homer. Protagoras is refuted or exposed, not because he is a disciple of Homer, but because he is a defective or renegade Homeric: a false philosopher.

Protagoras understands that Being is deceptive. This is not contested by Plato. The quarrel between Protagoras and Socrates is Plato's presentation of the quarrel between noble and base sophistry. And this, in passing, is why Socrates is amenable in the *Protagoras* to the identification of the good with the pleasant. The difference between the noble sophist and the philosopher is the vision of the Ideas, or in another vocabulary, it is the supplementation of poetry by mathematics. But this vision or supplementation is politically, if not irrelevant, secondary.

I have suggested that one cannot understand the Greek account of the origins apart from the perception of the conjunction of truth and falsehood, that is to say, of the presentation of the truth in and through falsehood, or as the Eleatic Stranger puts it in the *Sophist*, of the necessity of phantasms as an accommodation to human vision.[40] In the expression of the Athenian Stranger, the perception of truth is not the simple openness to divine revelation but the manifestation of suspicion toward stories about the gods.

I am certainly not suggesting that the Greeks were the first to notice the harshness of human destiny. What characterizes the peculiarly Greek understanding of this destiny is that suspicion, which should be joined to wonder as the source of wisdom, leads to the perception of concealment as not simply a practical requirement in the face of the hostility of genesis, but as the intrinsic structure of genesis itself, and so as the key to the enigma of truth. This is why, as Marcel Detienne puts it, the *maître de vérité* is also a master of deception.[41]

III

No more than a brief word of conclusion is required. The question of Nietzsche's anti-Platonism has tended in our time to have obscured his own origins as a classical philologist, more fundamentally, as a student whose philosophical nature was fecundated by the Greek understanding of genesis as dissimulation. Nietzsche's rhetoric of excess, which may be explained, following hints that he himself provides,[42] has tended to conceal that understanding.

We postmoderns, to vary a phrase of Nietzsche's, are no longer able to preserve the delicate interplay of frankness and dissimulation that Nietzsche exemplifies. The fanciful Being of art, and *a fortiori* of postphilosophy, has been sundered from the voice of science, and so of philology, with the net result that sobriety stands forth as ridiculous in the light of the patent richness of the texts of the masters. What we require is not anti-Platonism, and certainly not the Platonism of the philological academy, but the thoroughly Platonic *pharmakon* that consists of a mixture of sobriety and madness, in portions to be determined by the *esprit de finesse*. Only in this way will we be able to match the sinuosities of cosmogonic dissimulation.

Notes

1. XIII, p. 14: All citations from Nietzsche are from the *Kritische Studienausgabe*, edited by Giorgio Colli and Mazzino Montinari (Walter de Gruyter, DTV, Munich: 1980). Numbers designate volume and page; bracketed numbers contain the date and, where appropriate, the fragment or section number.

2. V, p. 48.

3. V, p. 57.

4. XI, p. 142 [1884; 25 (491)].

5. XI, p. 543 [1885; 35 (76)].

6. IX, p. 569 [1881; 11 (329)].

7. *Vom Nutzen und Nachteil Historie für das Leben*, I, p. 333 [1874; 10].

8. VII, p. 708 [1873].

9. XIII, p. 194 [1887/88; 11 (415)]; cf. *Götzen-Dämmerung*, VI, p. 127 [1889; Streifzüge 24].

10. XIII, p. 227 [1887/88; 14 (21)].

11. For a fuller discussion, see my 'Poetic Reason in Nietzsche: *Die dichtende Vernunft*' in *The Ancients and the Moderns: Rethinking Modernity* (Yale University Press, New Haven/London: 1989), pp. 209–34.

12. XIII, p. 333 [1888; 14 (152)].

13. IX, pp. 635f. [1881; 15 (7)].

14. *Sämtliche Brief*, KSA, ed. Colli and Montinari (Walter de Gruyter, DTV, Munich: 1986), II, p. 60 [11 June 1865].

15. XI, p. 544 [1885; 35 (76)].

16. Consider here *Die Philosophie im tragischen Zeitalter der Griechen*, in I, p. 864 [1873].

17. *Über Wahrheit und Lüge im aussermoralischen Sinne*, I, pp. 880, 883 [1873].

18. *Ibid.*, p. 876.
19. *Ibid.*, p. 877.
20. VII, p.199 [1870/71; 7 (156)].
21. Plato, *Theaetetus* 153a1–3.
22. I. 28; IV. 21f.; VII 23ff. (cf. V. 16–18); VII. 45–47 (the image of the cloud is replaced by that of the wind at 94f.).
23. *Olympian*, VII. 94f.
24. *Pythian*, III. 103ff.
25. *Olympian*, XII. 5ff.
26. *Pythian*, X. 61–66.
27. *Olympian*, IX. 35ff.; *Pythian*, I. 41; VII. 71ff.
28. *Nemean*, VI. 4ff.
29. *Nemean*, VII. 20ff.
30. *Nemean*, V. 17–19; cf. *Isthmian*, I. 63.
31. *Theogony*, 27f.
32. Verlag Robert Noske, Bern/Leipzig: 1935. Numbers in parentheses in the text will refer to pages in this edition until otherwise noted.
33. Cited from Marcel Detienne, *Homère, Hésiode et Pythagore* (Collection Latomus, vol. lvii, Bruxelles: 1962), p. 48.
34. *Republic*, III. 389b2ff., III. 414b9f., V. 459c2–d2.
35. II. 377d4ff.
36. *en pharmakou eidei*: III. 389b3–4.
37. III. 677c4ff.
38. 316e5–317b3.
39. *Theaetetus*, 151a1–3.
40. *Sophist*, 235c8ff.
41. *Les maîtres de vérité dans la grèce archaique* (Paris, Francis Maspero: 1973; deuxième édition), pp. 73, 77.
42. See my 'Nietzsche's Revolution' in the previously cited *The Ancients and the Moderns*, pp. 189–208.

54

Nietzsche*

Josiah Royce

*Source: *Atlantic Monthly*, vol. 119, March 1917, pp. 321–31.

[This essay on Nietzsche was recently found among the posthumous papers of Professor Royce. It will perhaps appear strange to many that the author of *The Duties of Americans in the Present War* and of *The Hope of the Great Community*, should have found so much, not merely of interest, but of sound doctrine – 'matter for the strengthening of hearts' – in the philosopher now claimed by modern Germany as its prophet and oracle. In reply it can only be said that modern Germany, and not Nietzsche, is at fault. Professor Royce's thesis is that only as a prophet of the soul, the portrayer of an ideal, is Nietzsche to be understood. The revolt which he preaches is not so much a revolt against others as against the self, against the narrow or commonplace or merely habitual self in the interests of ideal selfhood. And in a sense it may be said that the rigid *Weltpolitik* of modern Germany is the antithesis of the philosophy of Nietzsche. For all politics or statecraft is relative to a stereotyped world, and with such a world Nietzsche has nothing in common, – 'All this is poverty and a miserable ease,' – and the hour that he exalts is the hour 'in which not only your happiness but your reason and virtue as well become your loathing.' – W. Fergus Kernan.]

I

To many of his readers Nietzsche is simply a writer of aphorisms that express his passing moods. He is a skeptic from this point of view concerning all ultimate truths. On occasion, as his own words indicate, he doubts altogether the value of truth. Life is experience or activity. Man lives to express himself, not to conform to something not himself. As a fact, there are expressions of Nietzsche which are distinctly in this spirit. But to others of his readers and commentators Nietzsche is the expositor of a system. The difficulty of maintaining this thesis is the difficulty of extracting from his aphorisms any one consistent whole doctrine. Consequently, those who go to Nietzsche for positive teaching of permanent thought vary greatly in their interpretation of what is fundamental for his thought.

The freedom of the writer of aphorisms is not only dangerous in itself, but misleading to the reader who is in search of permanent instruction such as he can restate or apply. We in America have been trained more or less in dealing with precisely such problems as this by the cases of our own Emerson and of Walt Whitman. Emerson at one time influenced Nietzsche very deeply. With Walt Whitman he has not a few features of ideal and of doctrine in common. But in any case, like both Emerson and Walt Whitman, Nietzsche feels perfectly free to follow the dialectic of his own mental development, to contradict himself, or, as Walt Whitman said, 'to contain multitudes.'

On the other hand those misinterpret Nietzsche entirely who conceive the prime motive of his teaching as sensualism, or as the love of self-indulgence, or as pride, or as any form of merely self-centred narrowness. He is an individualist, without question. His ideal of life belongs among the many well-known forms of ethical Titanism. To judge him fairly you must bear in mind your Byron or your Goethe, or any other of the numerous writers who have expressed the purpose of life in terms of the conflict between the free individual and the world of convention, of tradition, or of destiny. Faust, Cain, Manfred, and the other heroes of individualism in the literature of ideals, must first come to mind, that one may see to what vast constellation this star of Nietzsche's belongs; although one would go wrong, and seriously wrong, if one identified the ideal or the problem of Nietzsche with those which these names suggest. The interest of the man lies just in the fact that he is not merely an individualist, but a very original one, adding to the well-known forms of the Titanic ideal a distinctly new one.

The central motive of Nietzsche seems to me to be this. It is clear to him that the moral problem concerns the perfection, not of society, not of the masses of men, but of the great individual. And so far he, indeed, stands where the standard of individualistic revolt has so often been raised. But Nietzsche differs from other individualists in that the great object toward which his struggle is directed is the discovery of what his own individuality itself means and is. A Titan of the type of Goethe's or Shelley's Prometheus proclaims his right to be free of Zeus and of all other powers. But by hypothesis Prometheus already knows who he is and what he wants. But the problem of Nietzsche is, above all, the problem, Who am I? and, What do I want? What is clear to him is the need of strenuous activity in pressing on toward the solution of this problem. His aristocratic consciousness is the sense that common men are in no wise capable of putting or of appreciating this question. His assertion of the right of the individual to be free from all external restraints is the ardent revolt of the strenuous seeker for selfhood against whatever hinders him in his task. He will not be interrupted by the base universe in the business – his life-business – of finding out what his own life is to mean for himself. He knows that his own will is, above all, what he calls the will for power. On occasion he does not hesitate to use this power to crush, at least in ideal, whoever shall hinder him in his work. But the problem over which he agonizes is the inner problem. What does this will that seeks power genuinely desire? What is the power that is worthy to be mine?

Nietzsche's contempt for popular morality is, therefore, only to be understood as a hatred for the spiritlessness, for the submissiveness, and, as he sometimes adds, for the treachery that seeks to avoid conflict, to escape from life's strenuous task, and to use the wiles of the morality of pity and human kindliness as a means for disarming the stronger and for leveling life to the commonplace. But it is unfair to interpret the austere, the unpitiful, the stern elements of Nietzsche's ethical doctrine, as themselves the expression of his central interest. If he is unpitiful he is so, most of all, toward himself. If he makes light of human suffering, it is above all of his own suffering that he has made light. In seeking self-expression, mastery, might, he is seeking something above all internal, perfectly consistent with the utmost sensitiveness to the pathos of life, and to the needs of humanity. If Nietzsche would sacrifice ordinary human interest and lives to the higher individuality, it is his first purpose to appeal to individual men as they are to sacrifice themselves to this higher selfhood. In the often-quoted introductory speech of Nietzsche's Zarathustra to the people, this view of the ideal is expressed in classic form.

> What is the greatest thing ye can experience? That is the hour of great contempt. The hour in which not only your happiness but your reason and virtue as well become your loathing. The hour in which ye say, What is my happiness worth? . . . The hour in which ye say, What is my reason worth? Longeth it for knowledge as a lion for its food? It is poverty and a miserable ease. The hour in which ye shall say, What is my virtue worth? It hath not yet lashed me into rage. How tired I am of my good and mine evil! All that is poverty and a miserable ease. The hour in which ye shall say, What is my justice worth? I do not see that I am flame and fuel. But the just one is flame and fuel. The hour in which ye shall say, What is my pity worth? Is pity not the cross to which he is being nailed who loveth men? But my pity is no crucifixion. Spake ye ever like that? Cried ye ever like that? Alas! Would that I had heard you cry like that! Not your sin, your moderation crieth unto heaven.

In this sense Nietzsche's doctrine is unquestionably not merely an individualism. Even against his will his doctrine, as soon as articulated, has the universality of a Kantian categorical imperative. Nothing is worthy of expression but the ideal individuality. Therefore the first task of every human being is indeed to revolt against tradition, but still more to revolt against his own narrowness and pettiness of sentiment, and to prepare for a sacrifice of what is dearest to his sentiment in order that he may thereby win through strenuous activity the discovery of what that higher ideal individual is to mean.

It is in the light of these considerations that we are able to get the most general perspective of Nietzsche's ethical doctrine. The values of life are internal values. In your heart are the issues of your own life. Whoever has inflicted upon you the law from without has degraded your moral individuality. If you have accepted this law merely as it came to you, and because it came to you, you are one of the slaves. You are the mere material to be used up in the process of humanity's higher growth. And the morality of Nietzsche treats you, in so far as you are contented with your lot, or are willing to remain the slave of your ethical destiny and of your religious tradition, with aristocratic contempt.

But does his appeal awaken you, then you are one of those who may take part in the task of aiming toward the higher individuality. You then become conscious that your will is the will for power. But the power that you desire is not mere earthly despotism. It is self-possession. You do not possess this power unless you are able to endure any degree of suffering and sacrifice of sentiment for the sake of discovering your meaning and your selfhood. Woe unto those that are at ease in this new Zion! Nietzsche's virtue has this at least in common with Christian charity, that it suffereth long, even if it appears rather unkind. Unsparing you are, but least of all do you spare what is commonplace about yourself. 'Ye have made your way from worm to man, and much within you is still worm. Once ye were apes; even now man is ape in a higher degree than any ape. Behold, I teach you beyond man.'

II

Of all Nietzsche's writings the book called *Thus Spake Zarathustra* is evidently the most frequently read, though also in some respects the most mysterious and the most in need of a commentary. Nietzsche's choice of a name for his ideal hero has nothing to do with an effort to paraphrase or to imitate the teachings or the personality of the Persian Zoroaster, whose name is thus employed. Zarathustra has in common with the Persian seer the tendency to think out his doctrine in solitude. The original Zoroaster notoriously made use of the fundamental contrast between a good and an evil principle. Nietzsche's Zoroaster is to overcome on a higher level the very oppositions on which the original doctrine of the Persian depended. These considerations, together with a good many oriental associations and the general desire to depict the career of the founder of a new faith, are responsible for the choice of the hero's name. Zarathustra is in part an idealized Nietzsche, in part the type of a hero whose existence must be conceived as a dim future possibility, for which the humanity of to-day is not worthily prepared. Long years of loneliness separate him from human kind. Communion with the secrets of nature, and with his own heart, has given him a higher wisdom. The negative part of this wisdom is summed up in the first article of his creed, namely, that God is dead; and that man has to live on the earth and under earthly conditions without any of the hope with which an older supernaturalism had surrounded his life. The positive aspect of this creed is summed up in the first place in the doctrine of the Superman.

The Superman is defined sometimes as an inevitably coming being, a product such as the doctrine of evolution requires us to anticipate. He will not come on earth as a result of any miracle. He will be related to man as man now is to the apes. The senselessness of our present human existence is justifiable only as a transition stage on the way to the Superman. 'Man,' says Zarathustra, 'is a something that shall be surpassed. What have ye done to surpass him?'

But Nietzsche has no means of giving a scientific proof that the Superman must come. Nor as a skeptic is he able at all permanently to maintain the theoretical probability of any one outcome of the evolutionary process rather than another. The Superman frequently appears simply as what he is, namely, an ideal, the vision of the individual that should be. That he will come to exist we know not. But our wills shall say, Let him come to existence. By this ideal we give sense to our life. And because the Superman is an ideal and not a definitely expected product of a nature process, the sense that this ideal gives to our lives comes through an imitation of this deliberately created concept of the perfect individual, but still more through a determination restlessly to labor upon the task of creating the concept.

The follower of Zarathustra has, therefore, no one fixed gospel preached to him. He must learn the dream and the interpretation thereof. Or, rather, he must learn, as it were, the art of heroic dreaming, and the art of living beyond every dream to a still higher ideal. Discontent is thus the constant accompaniment of Zarathustra's life and doctrine. But it is not a dreary discontent. Although it involves much suffering, it is a glorious, and, above all, a self-confident discontent. In the Heraclitean world of the higher individuality, where all is in flow, there appears at first to be nothing permanent but the law of the search.

Yet beyond all the seeking Zarathustra desires in the end, indeed, to define the law of life in terms that shall not be subject to the endless flow. Like Heraclitus, Zarathustra hopes to find what is permanent about this search for the higher individuality in the form of an absolute law to which all the apparently endless changes of the individual in the search for his ideal shall be subject. And the definition of this absolute law occurs to him in terms which had acquired a strange and decidedly fantastic significance in the mind of Nietzsche. There was an hypothesis with which Nietzsche evidently played for years and which also obviously had a somewhat pathological tendency to beset his imagination. This was the hypothesis, well known to human imagination ever since Pythagorean days, of the fatal tendency of the world to a precise repetition after long cycles of all its changes, of all its conflicts, ideals, evolutionary processes, and individual occurrences. The notion that countless times this precise thing has happened before, occurred to the Pythagoreans in ancient Greek thought, for reasons which probably had something to do with astronomical observations and astrological speculation. This notion became an important part of Nietzsche's own teaching, and of that of Zarathustra, because of its relations – relations not by any means superficial or insignificant – to his conception of the ethical problem. Seldom has a purely fantastic freak of the imagination stood in a more interesting relation to a profound problem of the formulation of an ethical ideal.

Zarathustra has at once to follow and to define the ideal. The ideal is that of the perfect individual. The perfect individual is to be self-contained, a law unto himself, no follower of God or of man, no recognizer of any rule that is imposed upon him from without. Yet the perfect individual is to be in no sense a seeker for self-indulgence, his existence is through and through strenuous. His every act is a transition. He cares not whether such act proves even to be a self-destruction, if only he may escape from lower ideals. The one thing that he cannot tolerate is commonplaceness, vulgarity, or mere content with convention, with tradition, with circumstance. Yet Nietzsche is equally conscious, and Zarathustra with him, that the higher life must be, not only a striving, but an experience; not only strenuousness, but an accomplishment; not only an endless spiritual agility, but an enjoyment of perfection; not only a heroism, but a self-possession. For were the higher life not all of these things, wherein would consist the meaning of the struggle, since neither heavenly joys nor the will of the gods, neither Nirvana nor the beatific vision, can be admitted into the doctrine to give purpose to life? If this infinite flow has not its meaning beyond itself, in heaven, or in that slavish service of mankind which Zarathustra condemns, and yet if at every stage of the process one finds nothing but a passing on to the next, what is the significance of the whole process?

The answer to this question is given in terms of the fantastic hypothesis of the eternal recurrence of every event in the world, and thus the hypothesis in detail asserts that life in its wholeness, with all its struggles expressed, with all its fate completely worked out, with all its individuality finally embodied, is present, not only once, but endlessly numerous times, in the course of infinite time. The idea thus suggested, mystical as it essentially is, is Nietzsche's equivalent in his closing period for what the religious consciousness had formerly sought in the conception of a divine plan of the universe. The conception is mystical because Nietzsche can grasp it only by intuition, and can give only the most insufficient reason for his belief. It appeals to him partly because it is unconventional, is no article of a traditional faith, and appears consistent with a purely naturalistic view of things, and with the existence of a world of rigid law. It is comforting to him as well as terrible. On the one hand, it comes to him with a pathological insistence and forms part of his suspicious attitude toward life. It is conceived as a blind necessity inflicting itself upon the world-order. On the other hand, the same thought long dwelt upon becomes at length pleasurable. One had feared it, because it seemed to make all endeavor vain. One accepts it in the end because it somehow assures us that all the problems of life are worked out and have been worked out endlessly often heretofore.

In the ceaseless change to which both experience and our self-criticism expose us, we look in vain for a final state for the sake of which life may exist and in the light of which it may be justified. Nietzsche's thought is that the justification of life must be the whole of life, for life is everywhere a passage from less to greater, or from problem to partial solution, or from the outworn to the new. In the whole circle of the world-life, granted only that the circle is a closed one, every possible transition from a lower to a higher, every possible facing of a problem, every possible transition from old to new must have been accomplished.

In the mysterious conversation with his own spirit which Zarathustra typifies as a meeting with a certain dwarf who personifies all his own weakness and temptation, Nietzsche's ideal hero thus narrates his view of the meaning of the eternal recurrence. The dwarf of the story, Zarathustra's baser self, scorning his aspiration, whispers, 'Thou stone of wisdom, thou throwest thyself high up, but every stone thrown must fall. Condemned unto thyself and thine own stoning, O Zarathustra, far thou threwest the stone indeed, but it will fall back upon thyself.' That is, in substance, this restless idealism, this search for the absolute individuality, is self-defeating. The task has to begin always afresh. One finds not the complete self. And in Zarathustra's world there is no God in whom the self should find its goal. The Sisyphus task of seeking the perfect is essentially vain. And thus the tempter dwarf expresses what is indeed the obvious problem of every untrammeled individualism.

'But,' Zarathustra tells us, 'a thing is within me – I call it courage. It hath hithero slain every evil mood of mine. This courage bade me at last stand still and say, "Dwarf, thou or I"; for courage is the best murderer, courage that attacketh. For in every attack there is the stirring music of battle. – "Halt, dwarf," said I, "I am the stronger of us two. Thou knowest not mine abyss-like thought. Thou couldst not endure that." Now there happened to be a gateway where we had to stop. "Look at this gateway, dwarf," I said. "It hath two faces; two roads meet here, the ends of which no one has ever reached. This long lane back, it stretcheth out for an eternity. And that long lane out there, it is another eternity. They contradict each other, these roads (the past and the future), and here at this gateway they meet. The name of the gateway standeth written above – Present Moment. But whoever would go along either of them and ever further and ever more remote, believest thou, dwarf, that these roads contradict each other eternally? –

From this gateway called Moment a long eternal lane runneth backward. Behind us lieth an eternity. Must not all that can run of things have run already through this lane? Must not what can happen of things have happened, have been done, have run past here already? And when everything has already existed, what dost thou, O dwarf, think of this moment? Must not this gateway already have been there? And are not all things so fast linked together that this moment draws after itself all coming things, and so does not it draw itself also after itself? For what can occur in this long way before us? It must once more occur. And this slow-moving spider that creeps in yonder moonlight, and this moonlight itself, and thou and I in the gateway whispering together about eternal things, must we not all have already existed? And must we not come again and run our course in that other lane, out there before us in that long-haunted lane?'

The thought thus expressed is ambiguously stated so far as concerns its significance for the speaker. The vision of the conversation with the dwarf is at once one of terror and of courage. In characteristic fashion Zarathustra opposes to the thought of the tempter, that all is vanity because nothing can be accomplished, the other thought that all which is possible has already been numberless times accomplished. But this thought, too, suggests vanity. The striving soul demands novelty. The individual shudders before this abyss of fate which yawns at his feet. Yet, as Nietzsche frequently says, it is the business of man to stand upon the edge of abysses and to learn not to fear them. The reaction from this terror at the haunted way of life comes when one remembers that the closed circle of eternal life is one of significant striving, and that therefore the very closing of the circle involves the completion of the striving. The wanderer in life's wilderness sees no shining light of an eternal city beyond him. His home is in wandering. He has not the romantic sentimentality, but he certainly has the deep restlessness of the hero of Schubert's *Wanderer's Song*. Nietzsche will have him learn courage and absolute endurance in his wandering. And the courage is to result from the very facing of this most abysmal thought, that the wandering as a whole is one completed expression of an endlessly restless, but still in each of its cycles perfectly self-expressed, life.

With this thought in mind Nietzsche thenceforth is able to speak of eternity as his delight and his goal. The deepest problem of life becomes the attainment of sufficient courage to endure the hardships of the world-cycle, knowing that by just this series of struggles the complete life has to be expressed. If this moment has its fixed place in the cycle that expresses the whole meaning of life, then one can return to a delight in the present for its own sake, which will reconcile the strenuousness of Nietzsche's ideal with the joyousness, with the naïveté in accepting experience, which is also one of his essential motives. The joy of life returns when one has become convinced that the goal of life is not something utterly undetermined, but absolutely predetermined.

The lesson of the experience has also for Nietzsche its general aspect. His constant teaching is, if you have any insistent horror, conquer it by facing it and thinking it out. If fate besets you, make what seems fate also appear to you as your own deed. If you have any evil thought, make it a part of your free self by expressing once for all its whole meaning. Do not suppress your weaknesses. Build your strength upon them. It is with the painful, as it is with the so-called evil element of your nature. It is to be won over to the service of perfection even by being fearlessly accepted, worked out, and thereby conquered.

III

The two doctrines, that of the Superman and that of the eternal recurrence, constitute the central contents of the creed of Zarathustra. You do not know what the concrete purpose in life of the Superman will be if ever he comes to exist, but you already begin to work his will in seeking for him. In attempting to define his purpose you raise the whole question, so fundamental in our actual life, of the meaning and purpose of individual existence. Nietzsche differs from traditionalism of all kinds, and agrees, I should say, with the loftiest idealism, when he declines to accept his ethical individual as something whose character is for us men now predetermined, or to be accepted ready made. Those who say that the ideal character has already been embodied, that what I am to be is predetermined by the example of some preceptor or master, find no support from Nietzsche. In this respect, I should say, Nietzsche is indeed at one with the very idealism whose philosophical expression, as it had been attempted in earlier German thought, he so vigorously rejected. Herein lies his highest value as a stimulating critic of life; and that value, as I must repeat, allies him to Emerson, to Walt Whitman, and to other apostles of a higher liberty and assailants of a stereotyped ideal. For Nietzsche there is no one way of salvation except the way of being different from every other individual and complete in yourself.

There is no doubt that, from the point of view of a more systematic idealism, Nietzsche appears as entirely failing to see the organic character of the true life of coöperating individuals. The great problem of reconciling the unique individual with the world-order is simply not Nietzsche's problem. One must not go to him for light upon that subject. Therein lies his perfectly obvious limitation. Yet there is no doubt, from the point of view of any deeper idealism, that this grave problem can be solved only upon the basis of the clearest knowledge, precisely that upon which Nietzsche insists – namely, the uniqueness of the life of every individual and the genuineness of the duty of every soul to seek its own type of salvation. That its own type of salvation will as a fact involve a higher coöperation with all other individuality, is indeed true, and it is a truth that you cannot learn from Nietzsche. But I do not object to the musician because he is unable to carve for me statues or to build me cathedrals. Nietzsche understands that the art of life is the struggle, the endeavor, the courage, and incidentally the delightfulness of experience which enables the free soul in its best moments to take delight in the very tasks that its skepticism and its self-criticism seem to make so endless, and in one aspect so hopeless. Be dissatisfied with yourself, and yet assert yourself. Believe nothing, and yet have courage in the midst of your very suspicions, and cultivate your intuitions even while suspecting them: these are some of Nietzsche's precepts. And whoever comprehends their problem of individuality will thank him for them.

In the light of this essentially fluent conception of the Superman much that is paradoxical in Nietzsche's expression becomes in general intelligible. He notoriously calls himself an immoralist. But by morality he means conventional morality. And his contention is in this respect not different in principle from the well-known contention of Kant, according to which what Kant calls heteronomy is ethically intolerable. What will can I follow but my own? The ethical problem is to find out what my will is. Nietzsche, indeed, rejects every statical concept of the content of the ideal. Any finished creed as to what an individual ought to be at once arouses his spiritual repugnance. He is up and away long before any such ideal can be sufficiently expressed to win even a fair hearing. What we have called the spiritual agility of the self as Nietzsche conceives it forbids the acceptance of any such static ideal.

> My brother, when thou hast a virtue, and it is thy virtue, thou hast it in common with nobody. To be sure, thou desirest to call it by name and to caress it and to amuse thyself with it. And lo! thereupon thou hast its name in common with the people. Thou hast become people and herd with thy virtue. Better were it if thou shouldst say, Unspeakable and nameless is that which maketh my soul's pain and sweetness, and that is mine inmost hunger. I desire it not as God's law. I desire it not as man's statute and necessity. It shall not point me the way to another world or paradise. It is an earthly virtue that I love. Once thou hadst passions and didst call them evil; now hast thou only thy virtues. They grew from thy passions. For by thee thine own highest ideal was instilled into these passions and thereupon they became thy virtues and thy delight; and though thou wert from the stock of the choleric, or of the voluptuous, or of the fanatical, or of the vindictive, at last all thy passions grew virtues, and all thy devils angels. . . . And from this time forth nothing evil groweth out of thee unless it be the evil that groweth out of the struggle of thy virtues.

In the *Zarathustra*, from which I quote these words, there now follows a characteristic passage concerning the struggles and the mutual jealousies of precisely the virtues that have been thus characterized. And the picture of triumph and of inner selfhood that has just been suggested is at once clouded by the observation that every such relative state of inner perfection is in us transient, dialectical, self-destructive. The immediate conclusion is, 'Man is something that must be surpassed. And therefore love thy virtues; for thou shalt perish from them.'

The other and fantastic thought of the eternal recurrence – that thought which we have just expounded – is, as one now sees, the almost inevitable counterpart and foil of this conception of the endless search for individuality. Rejecting every form of absoluteness except such as seems to him consistent with necessary laws of nature and with the endless flow of things, Nietzsche still needs the restful pole in the flight of phenomena of which Schiller speaks. He quite as much needs something eternal and dividing, to give significance to his struggle for individuality, as he would need if he were a devout believer in traditional creeds.

Nietzsche's fantastic thought is, however, much deeper than its mere appearance would suggest. As a fact, a concept of ethical individuality must be just to the endless pursuit of goals of which every strenuous life consists. It must also be just to our requirements that there shall be a finished ideal despite the fact that you cannot find anywhere in the series of life's facts the expression of this ideal in a static form. It must also be just to the consideration which so many religions have neglected, namely that the true goal of life is the whole of life and not any one point in it – the conquering of defects by their inclusion in a richer life, and not an excision of ills from life. The deepest question of an ethical idealism is the problem whether life in any sense constitutes a significant whole, and whether this wholeness has a determinate and individual character.

Now Nietzsche is well aware of this problem. It can be solved neither by the theory that there is, once for all, a substantial individual soul having its permanent static character which our ideal life merely portrays in successive deeds, nor yet by the doctrine that the moral law is something merely static or abstractly universal. The individual and significant wholeness of our life must depend upon something which is not now completely expressed, but which, on the other hand, is in no sense a static substance, but something now in the making. The whole meaning of life turns upon the question whether our life in its entirety constitutes one drama. And in Nietzsche's Godless world of natural necessity the concept of eternal recurrence is the sole means by which he can conceive this unity of life's plan. With this in mind he can become, as he says, eager for eternity.

> If I am fond of the sea and of all that is of the sea's kin; and if I am fondest of it when it contradicteth me angrily; if that seeking desire is within me that driveth the sails after what is yet undiscovered; if there is a sailor's joy in my joy; if my rejoicing hath ever cried, 'The shore has disappeared; now

the last chain hath fallen down from me. The limitless roareth around me. Far away time and space shine beyond me! Upwards and onward, my heart!' Oh, how could I fail to be eager for eternity and for the marriage ring of rings, the ring of the eternal recurrence?

IV

As we turn now to the less poetical productions, namely the *Genealogy of Morals*, and the *Beyond Good and Evil*, we reach works that are very easily misunderstood if one lays stress upon their more obvious and paradoxical expression. The *Genealogy of Morals* has been absurdly emphasized in some of the more popular and hostile criticisms passed upon Nietzsche. In the light of his fundamental interests in the problem of the genesis of the free individual, the paradoxes of this work become indeed comprehensive enough. Its purpose is to free men from the bondage of the merely conventional morality. This purpose is to be accomplished by means of a psychological interpretation of the history of the moral consciousness. Full of the whimsical and the paradoxical is this account. Yet the paradoxes in question are by no means novel in the history of thought. They are in part the well-known paradoxes of the Sophists in the Platonic dialogues. In part they are common to the assailants of sentimental religious faith generally.

Moral distinctions have, according to Nietzsche, a twofold origin in the history of the human mind. They are distinctions made by the noble, the strong, the consciously superior, the aristocratic. Or, on the other hand, they are the distinctions made by the weaklings, by the fearful, by the slaves. The distinctions of the first class are themselves in no wise static, infallible, or for Nietzsche necessarily acceptable. But their type as they appear in the history of thought is the higher of the two types. For the noble souls become self-conscious by virtue of their superiority. Life is everywhere the will to attain might. The strong know that what they want is good, and that they can attain that good, at least in some measure, by reason of their strength. Moreover, the desire to rise above the mass grows. For how shall the highest be attained, unless the higher themselves are ready to rise? And how should the good be won through the mere nourishing of the weaklings? The strong man may be, indeed, kindly and courteous and humane. But he is so because that is his strength and his choice, his way to embody his will in the world, and not because the weak desire him to do so. The stronger souls consequently make their distinction between the noble and the base, the good and the contemptible. Upon this basis arises the *Herren Moral*. Strongly opposed to this is the *Sklaven Moral*, whose historical monument is Christianity.

Nietzsche abounds in paradoxes when he discusses the faith that lies nearest to his own early training and that had obviously most deeply influenced much of his sensibility. The weaklings cannot express themselves by their own force. They have developed in the course of history the art of persuading the strong as well as themselves that weakness itself is a virtue, and that all that the weak need ought to be given them by the strong. The result of such morality has been the glorification of the commonplace, the stupid, the spiritless, and the broken-hearted.

The doctrine thus indicated in the briefest way occupies in Nietzsche's own mind a place that can be understood only in the light of the central and positive character of his individualism. There is here no historically accurate estimate of Christianity; and much of the onslaught upon its teachings involves many of the trivialities of negative liberalism – trivialities which only the brilliancy of Nietzsche's literary skill, and the actually wonderful insight of many of his psychological comments, can make tolerable to any one really accustomed to true liberality of thought.

As a fact, Nietzsche's own individualism has had its place in the history of Christian doctrine. There is no question of the shallowness of a great deal of what is called altruism, and of the dangerous tendency toward the commonplace which a conventional Christian morality has frequently involved. But there is that in the original Christian ideal which is not at all foreign to the spirit of Nietzsche's *Zarathustra*. Yet the value of this whole discussion, as well as of another work, the so-called *Anti-Christ*, which Nietzsche wrote just before his final collapse, lies not at all in its value as a fair historical estimate of anybody's faith, but only in its significance as a series of paradoxical illustrations of Nietzsche's central problem, the problem of the perfect individual selfhood.

The other, and in some respects the more highly organized and significant of his later expressions outside the *Zarathustra*, namely the *Beyond Good and Evil*, contains the following notable and deliberate statement of Nietzsche's view of virtue in general.

Our virtues? It is probable that we too (namely we so-called immoralists) still have our virtues. We Europeans of to-morrow, we firstlings of the twentieth century, with all our dangerous curiosity, our manysidedness, our art of disguising – we probably, *if* we still are to have our virtues, shall have only such as best agree with our most secret, our most heartfelt longing, with our most ardent needs. And so then let us seek for them in our own labyrinths, labyrinths wherein, as everybody knows, so much is lost and lost forever. And is there anything nobler than seeking for one's own virtues? And we too in our own way are men of duty. To be sure, sometimes we indeed dance in our chains – oftener, it is also true, we gnash our teeth in our bonds and are impatient because of all the secret painfulness of our fate. But, do what we will, the stupid and the look-of-things will agree in declaring that we are men who know no duties. We have always the stupid and the look-of-things against us.

It has been my effort in the foregoing to give some of the impressions of the sense in which these duties can exist for Nietzsche and of the reason why nevertheless he can appear as rebel against convention, as opponent of the faith, as immoralist, as teacher of paradoxes, as austere and self-asserting individualist. As a fact, it is not selfishness in its narrower sense; it is certainly not sensualism. It is still less any sort of supposably scientific outcome of Darwinism that characterizes Nietzsche. He is not a partisan of mere self-will. His ideal is not merely that of brute force.

Nor yet is it fair to say with Dr. Tille, his translator, that physiological perfection, or the power to survive, is in any sense for him the expression of the ideal. He proclaims the significance of health, but it is healthful vigor of will that he is thinking of, much more than athletic skill or any externally visible character. His paradoxes constantly insist upon the virtue of power and upon the possession of power as the sum of virtue, but the power of which he is thinking is inner power. He despises the commonplace virtues, but that is a whimsical way of expressing his love of absolute perfection. He cannot define what his absolute perfection is, but no one has better expressed in recent times than he the ideal of the search for a consciousness of perfection. He glorifies the aristocratic self; but the self of which he speaks turns out to be an invisible and ideal self, as unseen as is the risen and ascended Lord of the ancient faith; as much an object of service as was ever the God against whom Nietzsche revolted.

55

Christian Morality and *Ressentiment**

Max Scheler

*Source: Max Scheler, *Ressentiment*, trans. Lewis B. Coser and William W. Holdheim, Marquette University Press, 1994, pp. 63–89.

Friedrich Nietzsche characterizes the idea of Christian love as the most delicate flower of *ressentiment*. He believes that through this idea the *ressentiment* accumulated by an oppressed and at the same time vindictive nation, whose God was the 'God of revenge' even when it was still politically and socially independent, is justified before this nation's consciousness.[1]

If we fully appreciate the revolutionary character of the change which leads from the ancient to the Christian idea of love – Nietzsche himself has done this only vaguely and inexactly – this Nietzschean statement is much less paradoxical than would appear at first sight. Indeed, his discovery is one of the most profound which has ever been made on this question and is fully worthy of the most serious consideration. I stress this all the more because I consider his theory to be *completely mistaken*.

The Greek and Roman philosophers and poets have expressed the significance and value of love in ancient morality with admirable clarity. A brief summary, without reference to specific sources, will be sufficient here. First of all, logical form, law, justice – in short, the element of measure and equality in the distribution of goods and evils – are superior to love. Even though Plato, in the *Symposium* for example, establishes great differences in value between the various kinds of love, in Greek eyes the whole phenomenon of 'love' belongs to the domain of the senses. It is a form of 'desire,' of 'need,' etc., which is foreign to the most perfect kind of being. This view is the natural corollary of the extremely questionable ancient division of human nature into 'reason' and 'sensuality,' into a part that is formative and one that is formed. In the sphere of Christian morality, on the other hand, love is explicitly placed above the rational domain – love 'that makes more blessed than all reason' (Augustine). This comes out quite clearly in the parable of the prodigal son.[2] '*Agape*' and '*caritas*' are sharply and dualistically separated from '*eros*' and '*amor*,' whereas the Greeks and Romans – though they do acknowledge distinctions in value – rather see a continuity between these types of love. Christian love is a spiritual intentionality which transcends the natural sphere, defeating and superseding the psychological mechanism of the natural instincts (such as hatred against one's enemies, revenge, and desire for retaliation). It can place a man in a completely new state of life. But that is not essential here. The most important difference between the ancient and Christian views of love lies in the *direction of its movement*. All ancient philosophers, poets, and moralists agree that love is a striving, an aspiration of the 'lower' toward the 'higher,' the 'unformed' toward the 'formed,' the 'μὴ ὄν' towards the 'ὄν,' 'appearance' towards 'essence,' 'ignorance' towards 'knowledge,' a 'mean between fullness and privation,' as Plato says in the *Symposium*. Thus in all human love relations, such as marriage or friendship, a distinction must be made between a 'lover' and a 'beloved,' and the latter is always nobler and more perfect. He is the *model* for the lover's being, willing, and acting.[3] This conception, which grew from the relations of life in antiquity, finds its clearest expression in the numerous forms of Greek metaphysics. Already Plato says: 'We would not love if we were Gods.' For the most perfect form of being cannot know 'aspiration' or 'need.'[4] Here love is only a road to something else, a '*methodos.*' And according to Aristotle, in all things there is rooted an upward urge (an ὀρέγεσθαι and ἐφίεσθαι) towards the deity, the Νοῦς, the self-sufficient thinker who 'moves' the world as 'prime mover.' He does not move it as a being whose will and activity is directed toward the outside, but 'as the beloved moves the lover' (Aristotle)– as it were *attracting*, enticing, and tempting it. In this idea, with its unique sublimity, beauty, and ancient coolness, the essence of the ancient conception of love is raised into the absolute and boundless. The universe is a great chain of dynamic spiritual entities, of forms of being ranging from the 'prima materia' up to man – a chain in which the lower always strives for and is attracted by the higher, which never turns back but aspires upward in its turn. This process continues up to the deity, which itself does not love, but represents the eternally unmoving and unifying *goal* of all these aspirations of love. Too little attention has been given to the peculiar relation between this idea of love and the principle of the 'agon,' the ambitious contest for the goal, which dominated Greek life in all its aspects – from the Gymnasium and the games to dialectics and the political life of the Greek city states. Even the objects try to surpass each other in a race for victory, in a cosmic 'agon' for the deity. Here the prize that will crown the victor is extreme: it is a participation in the essence, knowledge, and abundance of 'being.' Love is only the dynamic principle, immanent in the universe, which sets in motion this great 'agon' of all things for the deity.

Let us compare this with the Christian conception. In that conception there takes place what might be called a *reversal in the movement of love*. The Christian view boldly denies the Greek axiom that love is an aspiration of the lower towards the higher. On the contrary, now the criterion of love is that the nobler stoops to the vulgar, the healthy to the sick, the rich to the poor, the handsome to the ugly, the good and saintly to the bad and common, the Messiah to the sinners and publicans. The Christian is not afraid, like the ancient, that he might lose something by doing so, that he might impair his own nobility. He acts in the peculiarly pious conviction that through this 'condescension,' through this self-abasement and 'self-renunciation,' he gains the highest good and becomes equal to God.[5] The change in the notion of God and his fundamental relation to man and the world is not the cause, but the *consequence* of this reversal in the movement of love. God is no longer the eternal unmoving goal – like a star – for the love of all things, moving the world as 'the beloved moves the lover.' Now the very *essence* of God is to love and serve. Creating, willing, and acting are derived from these original qualities. The eternal 'first mover' of the world is replaced by the 'creator' who created it 'out of love.'[6] An event that is monstrous for the man of antiquity, that is absolutely paradoxical according to his axioms, is supposed to have taken place in Galilee: God spontaneously 'descended' to man, became a servant, and died the bad servant's death on the cross! Now the precept of loving good and hating evil, loving one's friend and hating one's enemy, becomes meaningless. There is no longer any 'highest good' independent of and beyond the act and movement of love! Love itself is the highest of all goods! The *summum bonum* is no longer the value of a thing, but of an act, the value of love itself *as love* – not for its results and achievements. Indeed, the achievements of love are only symbols and proofs of its *presence in the person*. And thus God himself becomes a 'person' who has no 'idea of the good,' no 'form and order,' no logos above him, but only below him – through his deed of love. He becomes a God who loves – for the man of antiquity something like a square circle, an 'imperfect perfection.' How strongly did Neo-Platonic criticism stress that love is a form of 'need' and 'aspiration' which indicates 'imperfection,' and that it is false, presumptuous, and sinful to attribute it to the deity! But there is another great innovation: in the Christian view, love is a non-sensuous act of the *spirit* (not a mere state of feeling, as for the moderns), but it is nevertheless not a striving and desiring, and even less a need.[7] These acts consume themselves in the realization of the desired goal. Love, however, *grows* in its action. And there are no longer any rational principles, any rules or justice, higher than love, independent of it and preceding it, which should guide its action and its distribution among men according to their value. All are worthy of love – friends and enemies, the good and the evil, the noble and the common.[8] Whenever I see badness in another, I must feel partly guilty, for I must say to myself: 'Would that man be bad if you had loved him enough?'[9] In the Christian view, *sensuous* sympathy – together with its root in our most powerful impulse – is not the source, but the partial *blockage* of love.[10] Therefore not only positive wrongdoing, but even the failure to love is 'guilt.' Indeed, it is *the* guilt at the bottom of all guiltiness.

Thus the picture has shifted immensely. This is no longer a band of men and things that surpass each other in striving up to the deity. It is a band in which every member looks back toward those who are further removed from God and comes to resemble the deity by helping and serving them – for this great urge to love, to serve, to bend down, is God's own essence.

I do not here analyze the constructive forms which this emotional reversal has taken in dogma, theology, and religious worship, though the task is tempting – especially in the cases of Paul and Augustine. Confining myself to the essential, I ask: whence this reversal? Is *ressentiment* really its mainspring?

The more I reflected on this question, the more clearly I realized that the root of Christian love is entirely *free* of *ressentiment*, but that *ressentiment* can very easily use it for its own purposes by simulating an emotion which corresponds to this idea. This simulation is often so perfect that even the sharpest observer can no longer distinguish real love from *ressentiment* which poses as love.[11]

There are two fundamentally different ways for the strong to bend down to the weak, for the rich to help the poor, for the more perfect life to help the 'less perfect.' This action can be motivated by a powerful feeling of security, strength, and inner salvation, of the invincible fullness of one's own life and existence. All this unites into the clear awareness that one is *rich enough* to share one's being and possessions. Love, sacrifice, help, the descent to the small and the weak, here spring from a spontaneous overflow of force, accompanied by bliss and deep inner calm. Compared to this natural readiness for love and sacrifice, all specific 'egoism,' the concern for oneself and one's interest, and even the instinct of 'self-preservation' are signs of a blocked and weakened life. Life is essentially expansion, development, growth in plenitude, and not 'self-preservation,' as a false doctrine has it. Development, expansion, and growth are not epiphenomena of mere preservative forces and cannot be reduced to the preservation of the 'better adapted.' We do believe that life itself can be sacrificed for values higher than life, but this does not mean that all sacrifice runs counter to life and its advancement.[12] There is a form of sacrifice which is a free renunciation of one's own vital abundance, a beautiful and natural overflow of one's forces. Every living being has a natural instinct of sympathy for other living beings, which increases with their proximity and similarity to himself. Thus we sacrifice ourselves for beings with whom we feel united and solidary, in contrast to everything 'dead.' This sacrificial impulse is by no means a later acquisition of life, derived from originally egoistic urges. It is an *original* component of life and *precedes* all those particular 'aims' and 'goals' which calculation, intelligence, and reflection impose upon it later. *We have an urge to sacrifice* before we ever know why, for what, and for whom! Jesus' view of nature and life, which sometimes shines through his speeches and parables in fragments and hidden allusions, shows quite clearly that he understood this fact. When he tells us not to worry about eating and drinking, it is not because he is indifferent to life and its preservation, but because he sees also a *vital* weakness in all 'worrying' about the next day, in all concentration on one's own physical well-being. The ravens with neither storehouse nor barn, the lilies which do not toil and spin and which God still arrays more gloriously than Solomon (Luke 12:24 and 27) – they are symbols of that profound total impression he has of life: all voluntary concentration on one's own bodily well-being, all worry and anxiety, hampers rather than furthers the creative force which instinctively and beneficently governs all life. 'And which of you with taking thought can add to his stature one cubit?' (Luke 12:25). This kind of indifference to the external *means* of life (food, clothing, etc.) is not a sign of indifference to life and its value, but rather of a profound and secret confidence in life's own *vigor* and of an inner security from the mechanical accidents which may befall it. A gay, light, bold, knightly indifference to external circumstances, drawn from the depth of life itself – that is the feeling which inspires these words! Egoism and fear of death are signs of a declining, sick, and broken life. Let us remember that the fear of death was so wide-spread in antiquity that some schools of philosophy, that of the Epicureans among others, see the aim of philosophy in freeing man from it.[13] The periods of greatest vitality were indifferent to life and its end. Such indifference is itself a state of mind which has vital value.

This kind of love and sacrifice for the weaker, the sick, and the small springs from inner security and vital plenitude. In addition to this vital secur-ity, there is that other feeling of bliss and security, that awareness of safety in the fortress of ultimate being itself (Jesus calls it 'kingdom of God'). The deeper and more central it is, the more man *can* and *may* be almost playfully 'indifferent' to his 'fate' in the peripheral zones of his existence – indifferent to whatever is still accessible to 'happiness' and 'suffering,' 'pleasure' and 'dis-pleasure,' 'joy' and 'pain.'[14]

When a person's spontaneous impulse of love and sacrifice finds a specific goal, an opportunity for applying itself, he does not welcome it as a chance to plunge into such phenomena as poverty, sickness, or ugliness. He does not help this struggling life because of those negative values, but *despite* them – he helps in order to develop whatever may still be sound and positive. He does not love such life *because* it is sick, poor, small, and ugly, and he does not passively dwell upon these attributes. The positive vital values (and even more, of course, the spiritual personal values of that individual) are com-pletely *independent* of these defects and lie much deeper. Therefore his own fullness of life can (and therefore 'should') overcome his natural reaction of fearing and fleeing them, and his love should helpfully develop whatever is positive in the poor or sick man. He does not love sickness and poverty, but what is *behind* them, and his help is directed *against* these evils. When Francis of Assisi kisses festering wounds and does not even kill the bugs that bite him, but leaves his body to them as a hospitable home, these acts (if seen from the outside) could be signs of perverted instincts and of a perverted valu-ation. But that is not actually the case. It is not a lack of nausea or a delight in the pus which makes St. Francis act in this way. He has overcome his nausea through a deeper feeling of life and vigor! This attitude is completely different from that of recent modern realism in art and literature, the exposure of social misery, the description of little people, the wallowing in the morbid – a typical *ressentiment* phenomenon. Those people saw something bug-like in everything that lives, whereas Francis sees the holiness of 'life' even in bug.[15]

In the ancient notion of love, on the other hand, there is an element of *anxiety*. The noble fears the descent to the less noble, is afraid of being infected and pulled down. The 'sage' of antiquity does not have the same firmness, the same inner certainty of himself and his own value, as the genius and hero of Christian love.

A further characteristic: Love in Jesus' sense helps energetically. But it *does not consist* in the desire to help, or even in 'benevolence.' Such love is, as it were, immersed in positive value, and helping and benevolence are only its consequences. The fake love of *ressentiment* man offers no real help, since for his perverted sense of values, evils like 'sickness' and 'poverty' have become goods. He believes, after all, that 'God giveth grace to the humble' (I Peter, 5:5), so that raising the small or curing the sick would mean *removing* them from their salvation.[16] But this does not mean that the value of love in the genuine Christian sense lies in the usefulness of its helping deed. The useful-ness may be great with little love or none at all, and it may be small while love is great. The widow's mites (Mark 12:42–44) are more to God than the gifts of the rich – not because they are only 'mites' or because the giver is only a 'poor widow,' but because her action reveals *more love*. Thus the increase in value originally always lies on the side of him who loves, *not* on the side of him who is helped. Love is no spiritual 'institution of charity' and is not in contrast to one's own bliss. In the very act of self-renunciation, the person eternally wins himself. He is blissful in loving and giving, for 'it is more blessed to give than to receive' (Acts 20:35). Love is not valuable and does not bestow distinction on the lover because it is just one of the countless forces which further human or social welfare. No, the value is love *itself*, its penetra-tion of the whole person – the higher, firmer, and richer life and existence of which its movement is the sign and the gem. The important thing is not the amount of welfare, it is that there should be a *maximum of love* among men. The act of helping is the direct and adequate *expression* of love, not its meaning or 'purpose.' Its meaning lies in itself, in its illumination of the soul, in the nobility of the loving soul in the act of love. Therefore nothing can be further removed from this genuine concept of Christian love than all kinds of 'socialism,' 'social feeling,' 'altruism,' and other subaltern modern things. When the rich youth is told to divest himself of his riches and give them to the poor, it is really not in order to help the 'poor' and to effect a better distribution of property in the interest of general welfare. Nor is it because poverty as such is supposed to be better than wealth. The order is given because the *act* of giving away, and the spiritual freedom and abundance of love which manifest themselves in this act, ennoble the youth and make him even 'richer' than he is.

This element is also present in the metaphysico-religious conceptions of man's relation to God. The old covenant between God and man, which is the root of all 'legality,' is replaced by the love between God and his children. And even the love 'for God' is not to be founded on his works alone, in gratitude for his constant gifts, his care and maintenance. All these experiences of God's actions and works are only means to make us look up to 'eternal love' and to the infinite abundance of value of which these works are but the proof. They should be admired and loved only because they are works of love! This conception was still very strong among the best medieval Christians. Thus Hugo de Saint Victor, in his *Soliloquy on the Earnest Money of the Soul* (*Soliloquium de arrha animae*), refers to a love which is founded only on God's works and good deeds as 'a love like a whore'! But already in Solomon's proverb 'When I have you, I do not ask for heaven or earth' we find this strict opposition to the idea of the covenant – an idea which contains the germs of that love based on gratitude which typifies all average religiosity. We should not love God because of his heaven and earth: we should love heaven and earth because they are God's, and because they adumbrate eternal love by means of sensible *expression* rather than as a purposive idea.[17] The same is true for the concept of God. Antiquity believed that the forces of love in the universe were limited. Therefore they were to be used sparingly, and everyone was to be loved only according to his value. The idea that love has its origin in God himself, the infinite Being, that he himself is infinite love and mercy, naturally entails the precept of loving both the good and the bad, the just and the sinners, one's friends and one's enemies. Genuine love, transcending the natural sphere, is manifested most clearly when we love our enemy. The ancient precept of loving the good and the just, and of hating the evil and the unjust, is now rejected as 'pharisaism.' Indeed, in a wider metaphysical context, God is not only the 'creator' (instead of a mere ideal, a perfect being, the goal of the world's upward movement), but even the 'creator out of love.' His creation, the 'world' itself is nothing but the momentary coagulation of an infinitely flowing gesture of love. The deity of Greek metaphysics is the ideal of the 'sage' in its absolute form: a logical egoist, a being closed in itself, self-observing and self-thinking νόησις νοήσεως), who cares little about the course of earthly events and is not truly responsible for the world.[18] The Christian deity is a *personal* God who created the 'world' out of an infinite overflow of love – not because he wanted to help anyone or anything, for 'nothing' existed before, but only to express his superabundance of love. This new notion of the deity is the conceptual theological expression of the changed attitude toward life.

There is not a trace of *ressentiment* in all this. Nothing but a blissful ability to stoop, born from an abundance of force and nobility!

But there is a completely different way of stooping to the small, the lowly, and the common, even though it may seem almost the same. Here love does not spring from an abundance of vital power, from firmness and security. Here it is only a euphemism for *escape*, for the inability to 'remain at home' with oneself (*chez soi*). Turning toward others is but the secondary consequence of this urge to flee from oneself. One cannot love anybody without turning away from oneself. However, the crucial question is whether this movement is prompted by the desire to turn toward a positive value, or whether the intention is a radical escape from oneself. 'Love' of the second variety is inspired by self-hatred, by hatred of one's own weakness and misery. The mind is always on the point of departing for distant places. Afraid of seeing itself and its inferiority, it is driven to give itself to the other – not because of his worth, but merely for the sake of his 'otherness.' Modern philosophical jargon has found a revealing term for this phenomenon, one of the many modern substitutes for love: 'altruism.' This love is not directed at a previously discovered positive value, nor does any such value flash up in the act of loving: there is nothing but the urge to turn away from oneself and to lose oneself in other people's business. We all know a certain type of man frequently found among socialists, suffragettes, and all people with an ever-ready 'social conscience' – the kind of person whose social activity is quite clearly prompted by inability to keep his attention focused on himself, on his own tasks and problems.[19] Looking away from oneself is here mistaken for love! Isn't it abundantly clear that 'altruism,' the interest in 'others' and their lives, has nothing at all to do with love? The malicious or envious person also forgets his own interest, even his 'preservation.' He only thinks about the other man's feelings, about the harm and the suffering he inflicts on him.[20] Conversely, there is a form of genuine 'self-love' which has nothing at all to do with 'egoism.'[21] It is precisely the essential feature of egoism that it does not apprehend the full value of the isolated self. The egoist sees himself only with regard to the others, as a member of society who wishes to possess and acquire *more* than the others.[22] Self-directedness or other-directedness have no essential bearing on the specific quality of love or hatred. These acts are different *in themselves*, quite independently of their direction.

Thus the 'altruistic' urge is really a form of hatred, of self-hatred, *posing* as its opposite ('Love') in the false perspective of consciousness. In the same way, in *ressentiment* morality, love for the 'small,' the 'poor,' the 'weak,' and the 'oppressed' is really disguised hatred, repressed envy, an impulse to detract, etc., directed against the opposite phenomena: 'wealth,' 'strength,' 'power,' '*largesse*.' When hatred does not dare to come out into the open, it can be easily expressed in the form of ostensible love – love for something which has features that are the opposite of those of the hated object. This can happen in such a way that the hatred remains secret. When we hear that falsely pious, unctuous tone (it is the tone of a certain 'socially-minded' type of priest), sermonizing that love for the 'small' is our first duty, love for the 'humble' in spirit, since God gives 'grace' to them, then it is often only hatred posing as Christian love. We clearly feel how the sight of these phenomena fills the mind with secret 'satisfaction' and how they themselves are loved, not the higher values which may lie behind them. Nor can the helping deed be the important thing in this perspective, since it would make the 'small' less agreeable to God and would therefore be an expression of hatred. The whole value lies in dwelling upon these phenomena. And when we are told, in the same tone, that these people will be rewarded in 'heaven' for their distress, and that 'heaven' is the exact reverse of the earthly order ('the first shall be last'), we distinctly feel how the *ressentiment*-laden man transfers to God the vengeance he himself cannot wreak on the great. In this way, he can satisfy his revenge at least in imagination, with the aid of an other-worldly mechanism of rewards and punishments. The core of the *ressentiment* Christian's idea of God is still the avenging Jehovah. The only difference is that revenge is now masked as sham love for the 'small.' There is no longer any organic and experienced bond between the 'kingdom of God' and the visible realm, so that the values and laws of retaliation of the former have ceased to be simply a purer and more perfect expression of those which already appear in life. The 'kingdom of God' has become the 'other world,' which stands mechanically beside 'this world' – an opposition unknown to the strongest periods of Christianity. It is merely a plane of being where the shadows of the people and events we experienced carry on a dance led by *ressentiment*, according to a rhythm which is simply opposite to that of the earth.

It is true that Jesus is mainly interested in the poor, the sick, the wretched and oppressed, the publicans, and shows a mysteriously strange affection for the sinners (cf. the 'adulteress,' the sinful woman anointing Jesus, the parable of the 'prodigal son'). He cannot refer to the 'good and the just' without some irony. Statements like 'They that are whole, have no need of the physician, but they that are sick: I came not to call the righteous, but sinners to repentance' (Mark 2:17) do not explain these tendencies – let us remember that he rejects the epithet 'good' even for himself ('Why callest thou me good? None is good save one, *that* is God.' Luke 18:19). Yet all this cannot make me believe in *ressentiment* on his part. His statements, so it seems to me, do not mean that salvation is dependent on those negative qualities, as *ressentiment* would have it. Their true meaning lies in the paradoxical form in which the highest and ultimate *personality values* are declared to be *independent* of contrasts like rich and poor, healthy and sick, etc. The world had become accustomed to considering the social hierarchy, based on status, wealth, vital strength, and power, as an exact image of the ultimate values of morality and personality. The only way to disclose the discovery of a new and higher *sphere* of being and life, of the 'kingdom of God' whose order is independent of that worldly and vital hierarchy, was to stress the vanity of the old values in this higher order. There are only certain passages, chiefly in the Gospel of Luke, which may go beyond this interpretation, for they seem to represent the kingdom of God as the reverse of the earthly realm. Thus the Beatitudes in Luke

6:20–22, 24–26: 'Blessed be ye poor: for yours is the kingdom of God. Blessed are ye that hunger now: for ye shall be filled. Blessed are ye that weep now, for ye shall laugh. Blessed are ye when men shall hate you, and when they shall separate you *from their company*, and shall reproach you, and cast out your name as evil, for the Son of man's sake. . . .' And further: 'But woe unto you that are rich: for ye have received your consolation. Woe unto you that are full: for ye shall hunger. Woe unto you that laugh now: for ye shall mourn and weep. Woe unto you when all men shall speak well of you: for so did their fathers to the false Prophets.'

Another example is the blunt assertion (in Luke 18:25) that 'it is easier for a camel to go through a needle's eye, than for a rich man to enter into the kingdom of God,' though it is considerably softened by the preceding passage: 'How hardly shall they that have riches, enter into the kingdom of God'–and also by the subsequent statement that God can lead even the rich into the kingdom of God. Here indeed it seems to me that the author's form of presentation cannot be absolved of *ressentiment*. Yet this trend is confined to Luke, and even there it is a personal coloring in the *presentation* of ideas which are by no means rooted in *ressentiment*.

Even the precepts 'Love your enemies, do good to them which hate you, bless them that curse you, and pray for them which despitefully use you. And unto him that smiteth thee on the one cheek, offer also the other: and him that taketh away thy cloak, forbid not to take thy coat also' (Luke 6:27–29) do not demand a passivity which is only 'justified' by the inability to seek revenge (as Nietzsche wrongly thought). Nor do they seek to shame the enemy in secret vengefulness, or indicate a hidden self-torment which satisfies itself through paradoxical behavior. These precepts demand an extreme activity against the natural instincts which push us in the opposite direction. They are born from the Gospel's profound spirit of individualism, which refuses to let one's own actions and conduct depend in any way on somebody else's acts. The Christian refuses to let his acts be mere *reactions* – such conduct would lower him to the level of his enemy. The act is to grow organically from the person, 'as the fruit from the tree.' 'A good man out of the good treasure of his heart, bringeth forth good things: and an evil man out of the evil treasure, bringeth forth evil things.' 'For out of the abundance of the heart the mouth speaketh' (Matthew 12:34 and 35). What the Gospel demands is not a reaction which is the reverse of the natural reaction, as if it said: 'Because he strikes you on the cheek, tend the other' – but a rejection of all reactive activity, of any participation in common and average ways of acting and standards of judgment.

I spoke of Jesus' 'mysterious' affection for the sinners, which is closely related to his ever-ready militancy against the scribes and pharisees, against every kind of social respectability. Is this an element of *ressentiment*? Certainly this attitude contains a kind of awareness that the great transformation of life, the radical change in outlook he demands of man (in Christian parlance it is called 'rebirth'), is more accessible to the sinner than to the 'just,' who tries to approach the ideal of the law step by step and day by day. In the 'sinner' there is the powerful movement of life and, as it were, the great possibility! We must add that Jesus is deeply skeptical toward all those who can feign the good man's blissful existence through the simple lack of strong instincts and vitality. But all this does not suffice to explain this mysterious affection. In it there is something which can scarcely be expressed and must be felt. When the noblest men are in the company of the 'good' – even of the truly 'good,' not only of the pharisees – they are often overcome by a sudden impetuous yearning to go to the sinners, to suffer and struggle at their side and to share their grievous, gloomy lives. This is truly no temptation by the pleasures of sin, nor a demoniacal love for its 'sweetness,' nor the attraction of the forbidden or the lure of novel experiences. It is an outburst of tem-pestuous love and tempestuous compassion for *all* men who are felt as one, indeed for the universe as a whole; a love which makes it seem frightful that only some should be 'good,' while the others are 'bad' and reprobate. In such moments, love and a deep *sense of solidarity* are repelled by the thought that we alone should be 'good,' together with some others. This fills us with a kind of loathing for those who can accept this privilege, and we have an urge to move away from them.

Expressed in sober concepts, this is only a consequence of the new Chris-tian idea that the act of love as such is the *summum bonum*, as 'abundant love' (Luther), independent of the value of its object. In the view of the ancients, love for the bad is bad itself, while here the value of the *act* of loving stands out even more distinctly when the sinner is its object.

Another element must be added. The notorious 'sinner' is also one who *acknowledges* the evil in his soul. I am not only thinking of verbal confession, as before a tribunal, but also of admission before oneself or through the deed in which the sinful desire has issued. Let what he acknowledges be evil and sinful: the fact *that* he does it is not evil; it is good! In this way he purges his soul and prevents the spreading of the poison. But if he represses his evil impulses, the poison will penetrate more and more deeply, and at the same time it will become ever more hidden from his knowledge and conscience. Finally even the 'beam in one's own eye' will no longer be felt – but the 'mote in one's brother's eye' all the more! Therefore the sinful deed which is fol-lowed by remorse – and does not remorse begin with the very deed insofar as it is a confession? – is better in Jesus' eyes than the repression of the sinful impulse and the consequent poisoning of a man's inner core, which can easily go with the conviction of being good and just before the law. That is why 'joy shall be in heaven over one sinner that repenteth, more than over ninety and nine just persons' (Luke 15:7). That is why we read: 'To whom little is for-given, the same loveth little' (Luke 7:47). Jesus, who in his Sermon on the Mount sees adultery in the very act of 'looking on a woman to lust after her' (Matt. 5:28), must judge like this to be consistent. Also Luther's much-abused dictum 'peccare fortiter' is only the stormy outburst of a man who has lived in constant fear of the law, who consumed himself in unceasing efforts and tormenting, humiliating experiences of 'relapse,' and who despaired at last of finding 'justification' in this way.[23] Criminals have often described the deep satisfaction, the peace and liberation which they felt shortly after committing a deed on which they had pondered for months, again and again repressing their impulses while their minds became progressively more poisoned, peaceless, and 'evil.'

In this respect as well, the Gospel's morality preserves its severely individualistic character. The *salvation* and the *being* of the soul is its primary concern. If indeed we follow the criterion of social utility, we must judge and feel differently. Then the inner state of the individual soul, especially of its unconscious layers, is unimportant: the main thing is to keep the sinful impulse from harming the common interest. Indeed an impulse is only 'sinful' if it could lead to such harm. Jesus judges differently: the sinner who sins is better than the sinner who does not sin, but whose sinful impulse turns inward and poisons his soul – even if the community is harmed by the former and not by the latter. Thence his basic distrust, drawn from deep self-knowledge – distrust not merely of the pharisee who only looks at his morally well-trimmed social image, or of the Stoic who wants to be able to 'respect himself' and therefore does not look at his being, but at his image as it appears in his self-judgment, but distrust even of him who decides only after 'conscientious self-scrutiny' that he is 'good' and 'just.' Even he may well bear the germs of sin within him, so that only the added sin of insufficient lucidity with respect to his own motives distinguishes him from the sinner who knows himself to be a sinner. In this context, St. Paul (I Cor. 4:3 and 4) sharply condemns not only all false 'heteronomy' but also all Stoic and Kantian 'autonomy' and all 'self-judgment': 'But with me it is a very small thing that I should be judged of you, or of man's judgment: yea, I judge not mine own self. [Indeed I could say] I know nothing by my self, yet I am not hereby justified: but he that judgeth me is the Lord.' In this affection for the sinners we can find no *ressentiment*.[24]

Just as there are *two* ways of stooping lovingly to the weak, we can distinguish (among others) *two* sources of *ascetic* actions and value judgments. The ascetic ideal of life may be founded on an estrangement from one's body which can actually turn into hatred. I already indicated that this attitude is frequently the consequence of repressed impulses of hatred and revenge. This state of mind is often expressed in reflections such as 'the body is the prison of the soul,' and it can lead to diverse forms of bodily self-torture. Here again, the primary motive is not *love* of one's *spiritual* self and the wish to perfect and hallow it by disciplining the body. What is primary is *hatred of the body*, and the concern for 'salvation of the soul' is a pretense which is often added only later. Another outgrowth of *ressentiment* are those forms of the ascetic ideal and its practice which are to justify one's impotence to acquire certain things – as when inability to do lucrative work leads to the imperative of poverty, erotic and sexual impotence to the precept of chastity, lack of self-discipline to obedience, etc. Nietzsche believes that the core of Christian asceticism can also be interpreted in this way.[25] In the ascetic ideal he sees the value reflex of a declining and exhausted life which secretly seeks death, even if its conscious will is different. Such life turns to ascetic values because they serve its hidden purpose. For Nietzsche, Christian asceticism as well falls under the rules and valuations which spring from *ressentiment*. Even virtues like the 'toleration' of pain and misfortunes, and forgiveness and humility in the intercourse with others, are supposed to be due to *ressentiment*.[26]

But asceticism can have completely different origins and an entirely different meaning. It may simply serve the purpose of educating the citizens for certain fixed national goals, such as war or hunting. An example would be the strongly 'ascetic' education in Sparta. This type of asceticism is entirely foreign to our context. There is a much higher and nobler form, which springs from vital plenitude, strength, and unity and derives meaning and value from life itself, from its glorification and greatest advancement, not from any transcendent goal. If this form of asceticism is to have any theoretical foundation, life must be viewed as an *autonomous* and *primary* agent, not reducible to mental phenomena (feelings, sensations), physical mechanisms, or a combination of both. Then inorganic matter and its mechanism is merely a medium for the representation and actualization of life, which is an organized structure of forms and functions. If we adopt this premise, then life also contains its own *values* which can never be reduced to utilitarian, hedonistic, or technical values.[27] Then the strongest life is not that which functions with a *maximum* of natural or artificially created mechanisms which are adapted to the surroundings, but a life which is still able to exist, grow, and even advance with a *minimum* of such mechanisms. In this case ascetic morality is the *expression* of *strong* life, and its rules are destined in turn to exercise and develop the purely vital functions with decreasing use of the necessary mechanisms.[28]

But when a hypothesis has the profundity of Nietzsche's speculation about the origin of Christian morality, it is not enough to reject it as false. We must also show how Nietzsche was led to his error and how it could gain for him such a high degree of probability.

There are two reasons. One is his *misjudgment* of the *essence of* Christian morality, notably of the Christian idea of love, in conjunction with the false standards by which he judges it (this last error is not historical and religious, but philosophical). The second reason lies in the factual *deformations* which Christian morality, starting with its early history, has undergone through reciprocal interchanges with values which have sprung from an entirely different historical background. These deformations often remained decisive for its future history.

There can be no doubt that the Christian ethos is inseparable from the

Christian's *religious* conception of God and the world. It is meaningless without this foundation. There have been well-meaning attempts to invest it with a secular meaning which is separable from its religious significance, to discover in it the principles of a 'humanistic' morality without religious premises. Such attempts, whether they are made by friends or foes of Christian religion, are fundamentally mistaken. At the very least, Christian morality must be tied to Christian religion by the assumption of a spiritual realm whose objects, contents, and values transcend not only the sensory sphere, but the whole sphere of *life*. This is precisely what Jesus calls the 'kingdom of God.' The precept of love is addressed to man as a *member* of the kingdom of God, where all are solidary. Even the feeling of unity and community, insofar as it does exist in the Christian world, refers to the kingdom of God or is at least founded in it.[29] However love, and the communion based on it, may work out in the secular forms of community, however much it may further our material welfare, free us from pain and create pleasure – all this is of value only if these communities, and the forces of love which cement them, have their living roots in the 'kingdom of God' and refer back to it. This affirmation does not say to what degree the 'kingdom of God' is represented either as 'transcendent,' 'other-worldly,' or as 'immanent' and active in this world – to what degree it is represented as beginning after death or as always 'present' and accessible to the pious. In any case it is conceived as a level of being – independent of the order, laws, and values of life – in which all the others are rooted and in which man finds the ultimate meaning and value of his existence.

If we fail to recognize this, then the Christian values – and all imperatives which spring from them – must be referred to a standard which, if valid, would indeed make them appear as values of decadence in the biological sense: the standard of what is most conducive to life. This is Nietzsche's interpretation. However, for the Christian, life – even in its highest form: human life – is never the 'greatest good.' Life, and therefore human society and history, is only important because it is the *stage* on which the 'kingdom of God' must emerge. Whenever the preservation and advancement of life conflict with the realization of the values which exist in the kingdom of God, life becomes futile and is to be rejected, however valuable it may seem in itself. The body is not the 'prison of the soul,' as in Plato's dualism: it is the 'temple of the holy Ghost' (I Cor. 6:19). Yet it is only a 'temple' and does not constitute the ultimate value. Therefore it is said: 'If thine eye offend thee, pluck it out. . .' (Mark 9:47).

Love is not seen as a spiritual activity which *serves* life, nor as life's 'strongest and deepest concentration' (Guyau). It is the activity and movement of love which embues life with its *highest meaning and value*. Therefore we can very well be asked to renounce life – and not only to sacrifice individual life for collective life, one's own life for somebody else's, or lower forms for higher forms of life: we can be asked to sacrifice life as such, in its very essence, if such an act would further the values of the kingdom of God, whose mystic bond and whose spiritual source of strength is love.[30] Nietzsche interprets Christianity from the outset as a mere 'morality' with a religious 'justification,' not primarily as a 'religion,' and he applies to Christian values a standard which they themselves refuse consciously: the standard of the maximum quantity of life. Naturally he must conclude that the very postulation of a level of being and value which transcends life and is not relative to it must be the sign of a morality of decadence. This procedure, however, is completely arbitrary, philosophically wrong, and strictly refutable. The idea of goodness cannot be reduced to a biological value, just as little as the idea of truth. We must take this for granted here – the proof would lead too far.[31]

For the same reason, Nietzsche necessarily erred in another respect. If the Christian precepts and imperatives, especially those which refer to love, are detached from the kingdom of God and from man's spiritual personality by which he participates in this kingdom (not to be mistaken for his 'soul,' which is natural), there is another serious consequence: those postulates must enter in *constitutive* (not only accidental) conflict with all the laws which govern the development, growth, and expansion of life.

I insist that love for one's neighbor, in the Christian sense, is not originally meant to be a biological, political, or social principle.[32] It is directed – at least primarily–at *man's spiritual core*, his individual personality, through which alone he participates directly in the kingdom of God. Therefore Jesus is far removed from founding a new political order or a new economic distribution of property. He accepts the emperor's rule, the social distinction between master and slave, and all those natural instincts which cause *hostility* between men in public and private life. There is no idea of 'general brotherhood,' no demand for a leveling of national distinctions through the creation of a 'universal community,' corresponding to the Stoic ideal of a 'universal state' ('cosmopolites') and a universal law of reason and nature. Nor is there any tendency to establish an independent Jewish state or to realize any social and political utopia. The immanence of the kingdom of God in man is not bound to any particular structure of state and society.

The forces and laws which rule the evolution of life and the formation and development of political and social communities, even wars[33] between nations, class struggle, and the passions they entail – all those are taken for granted by Jesus as permanent factors of existence. He does not want to replace them by love or anything else. Such demands as universal peace or the termination of the social power struggle are entirely foreign to his religious and moral sermon. The 'peace on earth' for which he asks is a profound state of blissful quietude which is to permeate, as from above, the historical process of struggle and conflict which governs the evolution of life and of human associations. It is a sacred region of peace, love, and forgiveness, existing in the depth of man's soul in the midst of all struggle and preventing him from believing that the goals of the conflict are ultimate and definitive. Jesus does not mean that the struggle should cease and that the instincts which cause it should wither away. Therefore the paradoxical precept that one should love one's enemy is by no means equivalent to the modern shunning of all conflict. Nor is it meant as a praise of those whose instincts are too weak for enmity (Nietzsche speaks of the 'tamed modern gregarious animal')! On the contrary: the precept of loving one's enemy presupposes the existence of hostility, it accepts the fact that there are constitutive forces in human nature which sometimes necessarily lead to hostile relations and cannot be historically modified. It only demands that even the true and genuine enemy – he whom I know to be my enemy and whom I am justified in combating with all means at my disposal – should be my 'brother in the kingdom of God.' In the midst of the struggle, *hatred* should be absent, especially that *ultimate* hatred which is directed against the salvation of his soul.[34] There is no value in the disappearance or moderation of revenge, power, mastery, and subjugation, which are acknowledged as belonging to a complete living being. The virtue lies in the free sacrifice of these impulses, and of the actions expressing them, in favor of the more valuable act of 'forgiveness' and 'toleration.' Indeed one *cannot* 'forgive' if one feels no revenge, nor can one 'tolerate' if one is merely insensitive.[35]

Thus the greatest mistake would be to interpret the Christian movement on the basis of dim analogies with certain forms of the modern social and democratic movement. Jesus is *not* a kind of 'popular hero' and 'social politician,' a man who knows what ails the poor and the oppressed, an 'enemy of Mammon' in the sense that he opposes capitalism as a form of social existence. Yet Friedrich Nietzsche's own conception of Christianity is strongly influenced by this widespread Jesus picture, which was propagated by Christian and non-Christian socialists. Therefore he thinks that the motives and arguments which set him against modern Socialism and Communism also apply to Christian morality and its genius. But Nietzsche's attack touches Jesus and the core of Christianity as little as the praise of those 'socialists,' since both share the same mistaken premise. Christianity does not contain the germ of modern socialist and democratic tendencies and value judgments. Nor did it ever affirm the 'equality of souls before God,' to which Nietzsche always points as the root of democracy – except in the sense that God's judgment on men is preceded by an elimination of the value delusions which are due to human situations, to human narrow-mindedness, blindness, and self-interest. But the notion that all men are equivalent 'in God's eyes,' that all value distinctions and the whole value aristocracy of human existence are merely based on anthropomorphic prejudice, one-sidedness, and weakness, is reminiscent of Spinoza and entirely foreign to Christianity. It is in radical contradiction with ideas such as 'heaven,' 'purgatory,' 'hell,' and with the whole internally and externally *aristocratic* structure of Christian-ecclesiastic society – a structure which is continued and culminates in the invisible kingdom of God. The autochthonous Christian notion would rather be the opposite: that God sees an immeasurable abundance of differences and value distinctions where our eyes, fixed on outward appearances, see nothing but a seeming uniformity in the values of men, races, groups, and individuals. According to Pascal, even the human 'spirit' is characterized by the ability to grasp the inner difference between men below their uniform appearance.

The communist organization of the original Christian communities does not prove any inner bond between Christian morality and the economic communism which is derived from democratic eudaemonism. This community of property was only the outward expression of the unity 'of heart and soul' described in the Acts of the Apostles. Each individual was free to sell his houses and lands and to turn the proceeds over to the apostles, but there was no artificial and coercive expropriation, carried out by the state with the conscious purpose of guarantying general welfare. Nor was it believed that man's moral constitution could in any way be changed by the establishment of new property relations. Peter does not blame Ananias (cf. Acts 5:3 and 4) because he failed to turn over the full proceeds of his sale, but because he was 'insincere' in pretending that the amount he brought to the apostle was the full amount. His property rights are explicitly acknowledged: 'While it (i.e., the good) remained, was it not thine own? and after it was sold, was it not in thine own power?' This communism was founded on *voluntary* gifts, whose religious and moral value lay in the act of sacrificing and 'giving.' It was only an incidental phenomenon – due to the fact that all individuals happened to acknowledge the value of such behavior of their own free will. Moreover, the communism of these small early Christian circles applied to the fulfillment of needs, but not to the forms of production. Though they were surrounded by non-communist communities, they never indulged in any agitation which was to propagate their way of living or to extend it over the whole state. Therefore even this 'social' twist given to the Christian idea of love, which was later called 'caritas,' everywhere presupposes the individualistic system of property.

We cannot fail to recognize this, except if we take the identity of the name for the identity of the thing. No Christian who was really inspired by the spirit of the Gospel has ever called for communism either for the sake of a 'just' distribution of property, or as the natural and necessary result of a progressive interlocking of interests. Wherever Christian communism does appear, as in the forms of life of the monasteries, it is exclusively based on *free* acts of love and sacrifice. The value of these acts lies in themselves alone and in the testimony they bear to the spiritual and religious freedom and elevation of the sacrificers as persons. Christian love and sacrifice *begins* where the demands of 'justice' and the dictates of positive legislation end. Many modern philosophers[36] believe that the increase of legally justified demands makes voluntary love and sacrifice ever more superfluous. Such a view is diametrically opposed to Christian morality. Even when the law regulates a branch of social relief which used to be dependent on voluntary charity – as in the case of poor relief, which the state took over from the Churches and private individuals, or in modern German social legislation – this merely means that the Christian's love should turn to *wider*, *higher*, and *more spiritual* goals. It can never mean that love has become 'superfluous' and is replaced by law and justice.

Christian love becomes visible in its purity where the mere interlocking of interests, which makes an action which is useful for A equally useful for B and C, *ceases* to function in favor of general welfare. Christian love is tied to the idea of a *definitive* 'sacrifice,' not a provisional one which ultimately enhances the quantity of pleasure in society.

Some philosophers, such as Herbert Spencer, believe that the 'altruistic urge' (which they put in the place of love) will expand and 'develop' through the increasing community of interests, and they posit an 'ideal' goal[37] of development in which all kinds of 'sacrifice' are eliminated. This urge, growing with the community of interests, has nothing at all to do with genuine 'love.'

Notes

1. Cf. *Genealogy of Morals*, part 1, section 8.

2. It has been rightly said that the father's attitude toward his two sons is a blow against the ancient idea of justice.

3. The terminology is different only in the case of an erotic attachment of a man to a boy. Then the φιλόμενος is younger and less perfect, the ἐρασθής older and more perfect. But even here there is an equality of values between the two.

4. This prejudice is completely unfounded. Cf. *The Nature of Sympathy*.

5. We find a particularly clear expression of this view in the sections on love of Thomas à Kempis' *Imitatio Christi*.

6. The later theological thesis according to which God has created the world 'for his glorification' is foreign to the spirit of the Gospel. It is an element of ancient philosophy which has entered Christian theology. Only the thesis that God glorifies himself in his creation of love corresponds to the evangelical spirit.

7. Therefore the most profound contentment is not connected with the achievements of love (taken as an act of aspiration): it lies in love itself. 'Thus God's joy in bestowing his gifts is greater than our joy in receiving them' (cf. François de Sales, *Treatise on the Love of God*, vol. I, ch. IX).

Quite objectively, the ancients were fundamentally mistaken in defining love as an 'aspiration' and a 'need.' Love may entail intense striving and yearning for the beloved, but in its essence it is an entirely different act. In the act of love, we rest contentedly in a value, regardless of whether this value has already been realized or if it is an object of aspiration. Cf. *The Nature of Sympathy*.

8. In his *Nicomachean Ethics*, Aristotle examines in detail how much love should 'justly' be bestowed upon the various groups of men (such as parents, friends, children, strangers), depending on their degree of closeness to us. In the Christian perspective, this would be meaningful for benevolence and benefaction – but both are mere consequences of love. This approach is meaningless if applied to love as such, since the value of the human beings themselves is partly determined by the value of each act of love. Whenever the idea of justice transcends its purely rational factor (which

demands that the same should be given to equals) – wherever it has somehow determined just *what* should be given to each – it presupposes love. In the rational sense, a man would be 'just' even if he always equally harmed, hampered, or killed equals – and yet he would have no claim to the moral virtue designated as 'justice.'

9. Either him or a third person, 'x,' who knew him. [On the extension of the principle of solidarity, cf. *Formalismus*, section VI B.]

10. The basic question is whether the act of love is only a refinement, a shift or sublimation of original *sensory impulses* – instincts such as vital sympathy and, in the strongest form, the sexual urge – or whether it is an *originally spiritual* act. The latter assumption underlies the Christian idea of love. It implies that the act of love, with the laws that govern it, is *independent* of the physical and sensuous constitution. It merely combines with the urges and feelings of the affective sphere, in such a way that the affects come to determine the *selection* according to which (and the *intensity* with which) we factually apprehend the object of the intentionality of love. This is the conviction which underlies the Christian idea of love. Its objective justification has been discussed in detail in my book on sympathy, in the chapter 'Love and Instinct.' Here I only want to say this: if this view is correct, then the affective and vital sympathy (with its strict gradation according to similarity, etc.) cannot be considered as the *source* of love, but only as a *force that restricts and distributes it* – a force that makes it serve the vital goals. This does not make love a result and product of vital development.

11. As an example of a personality propelled by *ressentiment* we named the Church Father Tertullian. Already Nietzsche quotes a passage in which Tertullian declares heavenly bliss to be based on the sight of the torments of the damned. We may add his famous 'Credo quia absurdum, credo quia ineptum' and his whole immoderate attitude toward ancient civilization and religion. All this shows that often he only *uses* the Christian values in order to satisfy his hatred of the ancient values. The development of a *ressentiment* Christian is excellently described in Conrad Ferdinand Meyer's short story 'The Saint.'

12. We purposely confine our exposition to this vital aspect, ignoring the fact that the purely spiritual acts and the laws that govern them – as well as their objects and the interrelations of these objects – cannot be understood by any philosophy based on 'life.' These are whole series of values and valuable acts which are *independent* of vital acts and values. The Christian's 'security' is primarily a state of security in a world which is essentially *above* life and its vicissitudes. But this assertion cannot be our premise here, since Nietzsche – who formulated the thesis that *ressentiment* is the source of the Christian idea of love – rejects it and wants to subsume even the idea of truth under the 'vital values.' It is sufficient to show that his view is mistaken even if we accept his own premise, according to which the maximum of life is the highest value. Concerning the true place of the 'vital values' in the hierarchy of values, cf. my detailed discussion in *Formalismus*, part II [Section V 5].

13. Cf. my book *Der Tod und die Seele*, to be published shortly. [The author never published this book. In *Formalismus*, part II (1916), the projected study was several times announced under the title *Der Tod und das Fortleben*. After about 1916, the plan was extended, and the projected study was to bear the title *Vom Sinn des Todes*. A part of the notes was published in 1933 in the previously mentioned *Nachlassband*, under the title 'Tod und Fortleben' (written about 1912/13).]

14. The characteristic of 'bliss' in the Christian sense is that it rests securely and immutably in the core of the soul, in the midst of the variations and changes of those emotions. The experience of bliss contains the conviction that it cannot be destroyed from the outside. [On 'bliss' as the deepest layer of feeling, and on the other layers of feeling, cf. *Formalismus*, section V 9.]

15. According to the *Fioretti* (ch. 10), Francis – when asked why he among all was chosen to guide men towards true life by his preaching – replied as follows: '. . . His holy eyes saw none among the sinners who was more miserable than I, none more incompetent, none who was a greater sinner. In order to accomplish the miraculous work he planned, he found no creature on earth that was more miserable. Therefore he chose me, for he wished to shame the world with its nobility, with its pride, its strength, beauty, and wisdom. . .' In this way we may be tempted to see *ressentiment*. However, when he refers to 'nobility, pride, strength, beauty, wisdom of the world' and speaks about putting them to 'shame,' Francis only means that these values are subordinate to those of the kingdom of God. But the kingdom of God by no means derives its own value from its *contrast* to the 'world': it bears its value in itself, *independently* of the 'values of the world.'

16. Therefore the emotion which Schopenhauer calls 'pity' also springs from *ressentiment*. For Schopenhauer, its significance does not lie in the fact that it is an expression of love – quite on the contrary, he traces love to pity. Nor does he see in pity a factor leading to benevolence and benefaction. To him, pity is the supposed recognition that the will, which suffers from itself, is metaphysically identical in all individuals. All benevolence and benefaction based on it can only *detract* from this metaphysical knowledge, ensnaring us again in the world of individuation. Thus when his friends lament their miseries and misfortunes, Schopenhauer can only answer one thing over and over again: 'See how true my philosophy is!' Cf. Schopenhauer's letters to Frauenstädt.

17. Cf. the conclusion of the verses of St. Theresa:

For even if I hoped not as I hope,
I still would love as I love.

(Cf. also Franz Brentano, *Vom Ursprung sittlicher Erkenntnis*, Leipzig, 1889, Notes). Or the passage in the prayer of St. Gertrude where she expresses the wish that Jesus were as small and poor as she and that she were all-powerful and omniscient as God– so that she could divest herself of what she had and come down to Jesus (cf. *Preces Gertrudianae*). Or the wish of Meister Eckhart 'that he would rather be in hell with Jesus than in heaven without him.' Such references could be multiplied at will. They show how *completely unfounded* is the assertion of Immanuel Kant and many others that all moral activity which has any reference to God is eudaemonistic and egoistic, since it is guided by concern with reward and punishment. 'Nothing is sweet that does not lead me to God: may the Lord take away all he desires to give me, and give to me *only himself*' (Augustinus, *Enarrationes* 2). Cf. the author's previously cited books, *The Nature of Sympathy* and *Formalismus*, part II. [Cf. the criticism of eudaemonistic ethics in *Formalismus*, section V, especially chapters 9 and 10.]

18. As we know, it is a matter of dispute whether the God of Aristotle even knows about the world and its contents. The latest theory is Franz Brentano's [cf. his work on Aristotle in the book *Grosse Denker*, edited by E. Von Aster, vol. I, 1911, section VI, p. 166], who concludes that God, by knowing himself, at the same time knows the world in himself. But this is based on the assumption that Aristotle taught the evident superiority of inner observation – an affirmation which seems questionable to me.

19. It goes without saying that by 'attention' we do not mean self-analysis, but the interest in (and care for) one's own salvation.

20. Cf. my typology of the delusions of sympathy in *The Nature of Sympathy*, part I.

21. No one has shown this more clearly than Aristotle in his *Nicomachean Ethics*. Cf. the chapter 'Self-Love' in Book IX: by sacrificing his life and possessions to his

friend, man accomplishes the highest act of 'self-love.' For leaving the lower goods to his friend, by his act of sacrifice he covers himself with the 'glory of the noble action, i.e., the higher good.'

22. [On egoism, egotism and self-love, cf. *Formalismus*, Cf. index of 4th ed., 1954.]

23. This is not to justify the dictum in question, only to understand it.

24. Malebranche cites Paul's passage in support of his doctrine of the 'sens interne,' which he sets up against his teacher Descartes, in whose opinion introspection is evidently superior to external observation. Cf. *De la recherche de la vérité*, I.

25. Nietzsche ignores that Christian morality does not *value* poverty, chastity, and obedience as such, but only the autonomous *act of freely renouncing* property, marriage, and self-will, whose existence is presupposed and which are considered as *positive goods*. Therefore J.H. Newman says that 'genuine' asceticism is to admire the earthly things by renouncing them. Cf. Nietzsche's treatise 'What is the Meaning of Ascetic Ideals?' It is entirely based on this misinterpretation.

26. Cf. the author's essay 'Zur Rehabilitierung der Tugend' in *Vom Umsturz der Werte*, notably the conclusion of the section on humility.

27. I have shown this in detail in *Formalismus*.

28. An example would be the respiration exercises etc. of Indian Yogis.

29. Cf. the essay 'Die christliche Liebesidee und die gegenwärtige Welt' in *Vom Ewigen im Menschen*.

30. Thus in the Pauline interpretation, Jesus himself dies on the cross out of love, spurred on by the urge of one who is secure in God to sacrifice himself for mankind.

31. In part II of *Formalismus*, the author has established this point in detail, refuting any 'biological' ethics which makes all values relative to life. [Section V 5]. Cf. also the author's article 'Ethik' in the *Jahrbush für Philosophie*, Jahrgang II, ed. By Max Frischeisen-Köhler, Berlin 1914.

32. Cf. also Ernst Troeltsch's pertinent discussions in his works *Politische Ethik und Christentum* (Göttingen, 1904) and *Dis Soziallehren der christlichen Kirchen und Gruppen*, vol. I (Tübingen, 1912; in English: *The Social Teaching of the Christian Churches*, tr. by Olive Wyon, New York, 1931).

33. In my book, *Der Genius des Krieges und der deutsche Krieg* (Leipzig, 1915), I exhaustively proved that martial and Christian morality can form a unity of style.

34. Richard Rothe says perceptively and strikingly: 'Christians fight – as if they did not fight.'

35. 'Forgiving' is a *positive* act which consists in freely sacrificing the positive value of expiation. Thus it presupposes the impulse of revenge instead of being based on its absence. In the same way, 'toleration' (of an insult, for example) is not, as Nietzsche thinks, mere passive acceptance: it is a peculiar *positive* attitude of the person toward an impulse which does not want to be obstructed, a positive curbing of this impulse. This is why Christian morality opposes anaesthesia or the autosuggestive modification of pain by means of a judgment – such as the Stoic doctrine that 'pain is no evil.' Christian morality only indicates a new way to guide pain 'correctly.' Cf. my essay 'Vom Sinn des Leides' in *Krieg und Aufbau* (Leipzig, 1916). [This essay was republished by the author, in a considerably extended form, in *Moralia* (1923). vol. I of the *Schriften zur Soziologie und Weltanschauungslehre*.]

36. Herbert Spencer, for example, construes the whole historical development of moral life in accordance with this principle. On the fallacy of the genetic view that the feeling of love and sympathy are mere epiphenomena of a growing solidarity of interests, cf. *The Nature of Sympathy*, part II, ch. VI.

37. The state of 'social equilibrium.'

56

The Morality of Nobility*

Georg Simmel

*Source: Georg Simmel, *Schopenhauer and Nietzsche*, trans. Helmut Loiskandl, Deena Weinstein, and Michael Weinstein, University of Massachusetts Press, 1986, pp. 161–81.

Nietzsche's life has been described as: a repetition of Greek sophism, which already had evinced a radical opposition against all historically established and recognized morality; a general acceptance of nature as the guide to conduct; preference for individual spontaneity over objective norms; and an affirmation of the right of the strong to override equality under the law, which was taken to be a groundless protection for the weak. But this analogy inverts the actual relation. Sophism's essence is to substitute the value of the subject for the objective value and meaning of being and conduct, whereas for Nietzsche the subject gains importance only by virtue of its objective value; sophism measures objectivity on a subjective scale, whereas Nietzsche does just the reverse. For Nietzsche, however, objectivity does not inhere in some palpable work or in some overtly successful conduct, but in the degree to which the quality of a human type realizes an evolutionary advance. Nietzsche clearly does not subsume the worth of the person under any utilitarian category: the person remains the definitive bearer of goals and values, but his being and conduct are significant in terms of his specific subjectivity. Nietzsche's method of arriving at values presupposes an acute and subtle conceptual distinction. He does not define humanity apart from individuals in the way that sociologists sometimes define society, but holds that individuals exist in humanity, which yet is made the standard of their value. In sophism, the subject finds only himself through an inward look, but, for Nietzsche, the subject discerns himself in the advance or decline of humanity and is determined by the value criteria of human evolution. Thus, the definition of the subject is fully objective whether or not there is agreement on what contents are progressive and on how those contents should be graded. Here we grasp the distance between Nietzsche and Max Stirner, which cannot be bridged despite superficial indications of the sort that made Nietzsche appear to ally with the sophists. As did the sophists, Stirner holds that all objective standards and values are imaginary and inessential, ghostly shadows confronting subjective reality. Stirner would find it meaningless to claim that the ego referred to anything beyond itself or that it should be graded according to a scale of values. He represents the renaissance of sophism, whereas Nietzsche writes: 'We find abominable any decadent spirit who says: "Everything only to me!"'

Nietzsche's difference from Stirner gives his doctrine a certain aura of nobility. In the realm of the spirit, there is unanimous agreement that objectivity means nobility: the hallmark of a noble spirit is to treat an opponent's opinion objectively, to argue fairly, and not be drawn into the tempests of subjective passion. Therefore, nobility must be described, and we will examine this more closely below, as a formal conduct which characteristically unites a resolute personality and a lucid objectivity. As an approach to the quality of personal value, nobility denotes the acknowledgment of the individual's objective value. A genuine aristocratic sentiment demands severity toward oneself and the measurement of the value of one's existence by the dignity of one's life as a whole, and not according to the accidents of one's position or the harvest of gifts and pleasures one has accumulated: the noble person has 'dignity.' Dignity is an inherently relational concept: one is worthy of something according to an objective criterion, whether or not one receives his due. One gives the impression of being worthy and of having dignity by demanding no more and no less than is due to him for his being and conduct in terms of an objective standard. An aristocrat may believe that human beings and things should serve him, but he is to be distinguished from those who are guided by egoistic illusions and carry with them a secret insecurity. The aristocrat has the firm conviction that he deserves service on the basis of objective justice, his personal quality, and the conduct that follows from this quality. His duty, which is the consequence of his right, is directed first upon himself and not upon some task: his duty is to form and conserve his being so that it remains the source of his rights. Both the system of ranking that is so obvious in Nietzsche's thought, and his interpretation of the value of the individual in terms of the development of humanity, stem from the sentiment of nobility.

It is but a consequence of the structure of the ideal of nobility that rank is not determined by overt deeds but by the closed and inward dimension of the individual. A valuable person will evidently act in a worthy manner, but emphasis should not be placed on success–which is always conditioned by the impact of being on circumstance and by the powers of the environing world, and which involves a step from the interior to the exterior. Nietzsche calls those actions which are judged by their results 'epidermal.' What counts for him is the superiority of the person; all else is accidental. Action may be one of the means assisting humanity in its ascent, but it is not growth itself, which is only evinced in humanity through its highest representatives. Thus, Nietzsche attacks those who oppose hero worship and who beg the question by comparing deeds of great men to those of the masses. The equation of the essential value of a great man with his overt effects involves, for Nietzsche, a profound misunderstanding: 'But the higher nature of a great man resides in his being different and in his distance in rank, not in any impact he makes, even if it were to move the world.' Here Nietzsche's unmitigated opposition to any social interpretation again becomes obvious. Society is only interested in what an individual does, and his being is of concern only as a guarantee that his conduct will always be directed along specific lines. If society nurtures pure morality and the ethical power of self-transcendence, it does so merely to prevent adverse external consequences. The social principle, which is the influence of each on the others, defines individuals solely through their effects. Society leaves the inner dimension, what the individual is in himself, what his quality is, to each one, and is indifferent to any ranking other than that based on external consequences. For Nietzsche, social morality is merely the residue of the old teleology that has fundamentally been overcome: though man is no longer the meaning of the world, he is still retained as the meaning of others. Even the most sublime form of moral action, in which all value resides in the 'good will,' overlooks the most profound and purely human dimension. Though the ethics of intention admit that the moral value of a personality cannot be predicated on the degree of success of a conduct, whether it influences real life or is blocked by the forces of reality, this view still presupposes that the effects emanating from the personality are the essence of value. The soul remains centrifugal here, even if the point at which value is assessed is no longer external to the active individual and placed in the social world, but is fixed within the person. If, as for Schopenhauer, the total human being is not identified with his will, then, despite the impossibility of making distinctions based on overt acts, there will be a profound decision in value experience: individual value is determined either by the pure quality of being or by its exterior impact on practical relations.

Thus, to use Schiller's expression, aristocratic natures pay with what they are, and lower natures with what they do. Aristocratic morality raises the individual quality of being – which is subjective for a social interest and for a morality of the will – to the status of objective value. But we are now faced with the most grave and consequential question: Where do individual human qualities gain their objective legitimation as values? As I have shown up to this point, Nietzsche's response is that natural breeding generates specific human qualities. Through the occurrence and growth of these qualities, humanity has reached the level it presently occupies, which constitutes a criterion that is independent of any subjective and merely personal evaluation. But this conclusion, though it may seem to be compelling, is logically faulty. The evolution of our species has actually produced not only beauty and purity, greatness of conviction and honesty, and value and power, but also their opposites. The degree to which one of the two series has prevailed over the other cannot be determined empirically and is irrelevant to the nature of value. Thus, it is necessary first to define those traits contained in factual historical evolution that are the core of human value, because they are the imperatives for our actions and the proof of our value itself. Natural evolution cannot decide the value of our essential qualities through an objective standard. Indeed, the basis for any selection of high and low qualities from the evolutionary process must be based on prior ranking, even if evolution is defined normatively. It had seemed that a concept of life given new meaning by evolution could provide what everyone wanted, that is, a logical deduction of the content and meaning of the 'ought' from a given and verifiable reality. The great difficulty of every doctrine of ethics and values has been that within the realm of the verifiable and real, taken in an inclusive and not in a crudely materialistic sense, what is valuable and morally necessary could not be deduced. The sphere of value had to be ceded, it seemed, to the nonrational individual will, which was left to decide according to strictly personal convictions. Most metaphysics attempted to elude these consequences by a mystification that transposed the good and the 'ought' into the realm of the most eminent reality. By positing the concept of life as an all-inclusive form that includes everything essential to man, and by assuming that life is constituted by the urge to grow intensively and extensively and to become more noble, Nietzsche could view the life-process as one of increasing value. Thus, the creation of ideals could be interpreted as proceeding along the innermost direction of human reality, which might not always be observable but was ever present. But now the lack of relation between the evolutionary process and progress toward ideals has been revealed: real evolution produces the negative with the same disinterested necessity as it generates the positive. Put another way, not only noble exalted qualities help individuals to gain power, open up their lives, and develop all of their potentials; innumerable victories in life's struggle are also won by people who lack honesty and conscience, and who are motivated by lust for property and by crass practical materialism. Thus, the selection of the elements that Nietzsche recognizes as values in concrete existence is not predetermined by the structure of life, but must arise from a sense of value that is independent of this structure. Only an optimistic and enthusiastic belief in life that, similar to Schopenhauer's pessimism, can be neither verified nor falsified can regard values constituted by other sources as forming the nerve center of life and of its actual development. Nietzsche, therefore, is finally unable to develop a scale of qualitative individual values from a principle of value based on the increase of life. This is why there must be a split in his account between the principles and forms of human values and qualities as they appear within real contexts.

The objectivity of values in Nietzsche's thought does not follow from their origin or cause, but, as has just been explained, from the ideal of nobility. The existence of certain people and human qualities is valuable not because of their relations to other people or their effects, but by virtue of a 'higher law' that makes their existence an end-in-itself. This end-in-itself is not a subjective and specific sense of life or an intrinsic pleasure, but is objective: the totality of things is more meaningful, distinguished, and valuable the more such noble existences are found in it. The objective essence of the values of nobility entails that the price that must be paid for their realization in individual life – subjective suffering, sacrifice of energy, and subjugation–is completely without importance. A noble person does not ask after the price. Therefore, the style of aristocratic life is diametrically opposed to that of the money economy where the value of things tends increasingly to be so identified. Taine observes that the aristocracy of the *ancien regime*, which enjoyed great luxury, regarded it as a mark of nobility not to take money into account at all. This is clearly the opposite of the luxury of conspicuous consumption, which is based on extreme esteem for money. Nietzsche's deep aversion to all of the specific phenomena of the money economy must be traced to his fundamental value commitment to nobility: in the money economy one weighs benefits and sacrifices, and regards something as a value when it is not purchased at great expense; whereas, for Nietzsche, one dissolves the relation between value and price by remaining indifferent to expense. The principle of nobility is brought to its extreme in the assumption that the objective value of humanity is represented only by its most advanced individuals and that the suffering, oppression, and retardation of the masses do not matter because they are but the price of ascent. Nietzsche's law of history and philosophy is that the human being could not develop to his greatest power and sublimity without the most severe process of selection and trials, and without much recklessness and cruelty. Although it appears to be paradoxical and seems to be plausible only if the basic and elementary ethical forms are purified and intellectually freed from all sentiments related to their contents, it is just by such purification that Nietzsche transforms Kant's basic sentiment from an individual morality into an ethics of the species. For Kant, morality is only intelligible as the overcoming of the lower and sensual parts of our essence. In his view, the human being is naturally sensual and lustful, and is not good by nature, but rationality fights an ongoing struggle for liberation against the earthly elements that weigh it down: spoliation of the lower man by the higher man is not possible without pain. This is one of the fundamental themes of the history of the human soul: the essential elevation of our being is effected through pain, and the basic differences in world views are related to how this fact is viewed and understood. Kant has condensed the connection between pain and overcoming in the extreme point of subjectivity so that the value of a person is acknowledged only in self-sacrifice. Nietzsche transfers this connection beyond the individual to mankind: only discipline attended by great pain has brought forth 'all elevation of humanity.' Thus, it becomes possible to dissolve the self-evident identity of the one who ascends and the one who suffers pain: the pain, oppression, and sacrifice of innumerable people create in one person the conditions for the power, productivity, and potential of the soul whereby humanity conquers a new plateau on the evolutionary path. The Kantian value of the individual soul is expanded to include the totality of historical society, and the tension between value and suffering is no longer centered in the individual soul but in a diversity of subjects who are contained in the unity of humanity.

It is, indeed, peculiar to base the formation of values solely on their object-ive existence and simultaneously to claim that these values are realized in an absolutely personal way in the individual existence of the soul, so that only the height of evolution matters, regardless of its cost in terms of sacrifices and subjective conditions. But this is just the counterpart of the afore-mentioned indifference to the effects of the worthy individual. The value of the individual's being is as independent of its conditions of origin as it is irrelevant to its consequences. The value of great men is not determined by what others receive from their eminence or by the benefits they them-selves derive from it. Therefore, the personalism of an objective formation of values is not at all common egoism or hedonism. The representation of being in subjective sentiments of pleasure and pain is quite different from the value of being, whether one refers to oneself or to someone else. I shall quote some important passages, because Nietzsche has been more seriously misunderstood on this point than on any other:

> 'Do I ask for happiness?' Zarathustra queries. 'I ask for my work. . . . Freedom means becoming more indifferent to stress, hard work, depriva-tion, and life itself; having the masculine instincts, such as the instinct for happiness. Liberated man tramples on the despicable kind of well-being dreamed of by merchants, Christians, cows, women, Englishmen, and democrats. . . . One should not wish to enjoy when one has not given. And, one should not wish to enjoy. . . . My deep indifference toward myself, I do not wish for any advantage from my insights and I do not avoid the dis-advantages that stem from them. If one wants happiness then one must join the company of the poor in spirit. . . . Be it hedonism, pessimism, or utilitarianism, each way of calculating the value of things according to pleasure and pain, according to circumstances and external things, is naive and fixated on the foreground: everyone who understands creative forces will view them with both derision and compassion.'

The struggle of the church against sensuality and the joy of life is intelligible and justified in relative terms, only on the understanding that the church deals with degenerates who 'are too weak-willed to impose on themselves a limit to their concupiscence.' Thus, 'lust is only a sweet poison for the weak-ling, but for those who will with a lion's heart it is the reverently reserved wine of wines.' And Nietzsche judges the disposition to 'love thy neighbor' to be a poorly disguised expression of the impulse to love oneself: 'Higher than love of one's neighbor is love for those farthest away and still in the future – those who are far away must pay for your "love thy neighbor."' But let me add that love for those who are distant could denote an extension of a more clear-sighted means for the Christian love for the neighbor. There is no more severe judge of everything anarchic, undisciplined, and soft than Nietzsche, who finds the reason for the engulfing contemporary decadence in the disappearance of strict discipline, piety, and authority in the face of the ignoble tendency toward equalization and universal happiness. Certainly he preaches selfishness, but his exhortations to the elevated and select, the leaders, to retain themselves are meant to save the permanent values, from which they derive their eminence, from momentary impulses that would spoil them and soften their hearts. Thus, he requires an inner distance from the lowly so that the great man will not exteriorize himself and be dragged down to their level, and, thus, destroy the highest values. But none of this is a matter of illogical will or the quest for pleasure. As he says, the noble man must accept 'his privileges and their exercise as a duty,' and, therefore, he would not 'lower his duties to make them everyone's duties.' The meaning of what is called Nietzsche's selfishness is the preservation of the highest personal values. Thus, he must demand unbending severity toward himself and others: 'The prime will always be sacrificed and we are this prime. But that is what our species wants, and I love those who do not try to preserve themselves.' Certainly Nietzsche preaches recklessness, harshness, and even cruelty, but only because these seem to him to be the only school and discipline through which strength – which is endangered by the reduction of our ideals and our reality to the interests of the average and general public – can once again grow: 'There will be ever greater hardship and duress for you, because only in this way can man ascend, where lightning strikes him and breaks him into pieces: Upward to lightning!' One of the strangest mistakes in the history of morals is that Nietzsche's doctrine could have been understood as a frivolous egoism and as a sanctification of Epicurean laxity. This error was essentially possible because the new synthesis in which Nietzsche united the elements that form value was nor understood. Old associations were still operative and these were joined to single elements of Nietzsche's synthesis. Nietzsche made personalism into an objective ideal, placing it definitively apart from strict egoism, which always returns to the subject. Egoism aspires to have something, personalism to be something. Thus, personalism posits itself beyond the opposition of hedonism and moralism, and thereby subsumes the Kantian morality under itself. Hedonism asks, What can I get from this world? Moralism queries, What can I do for this world? For Nietzsche even the question of what to give is excluded. Although he is concerned with a quality of being naturally evinced in actions and in 'giving virtue,' for him, value does not depend on phenomena and consequences, but is immediately given with the quality of being, to the degree that it represents a specifically higher level in the evolution of humanity. Similarly, the quality of being may contribute to subjective happiness, but unless happiness reflects depth of growth and animation of existence, the accent of value is placed on being itself, which is the basis for what is expressed in sentiments of pleasure and pain, and not in its emotional consequences.

Thus, Nietzsche continually stresses that life becomes more disciplined and severe the more it ascends. Nobody would have been more disturbed than Nietzsche by the abuse of his concept of the overman, which transforms the liberation from democratic-altruistic morality and concern into a justification for libertinism, rather than into the duty to move onward to an objectively higher level of humanity. From the standpoint of Nietzschian duty, the poorly masked and subjectivistic hedonism of the so-called Nietzschians is only a reversion to a lower level, to the laxity of pessimism, and to a barren use of power, inasmuch as a life that follows the subjective conditions of pleasure and pain must run into a dead end. Thus, the hedonism of the Nietzschians is decadence and declining life, which transfers its objects from the lower elements of society to the baser elements of the subject.

Nietzsche's synthesis of the factors of value into the ideal of nobility should have made it clear that the specificity of his ideals is indivisibly linked to an essential and necessary mood of responsibility. Every proper aristocracy is saved from the pure enjoyment of its prerogatives by acknowledgment of its self-responsibility, not of its responsibility to others or to an external law. Nietzsche's interpretation of this responsibility, which springs from the depth of one's own being, is in terms of the concept of a humanity which achieves the height of evolution through its most progressive individuals. The existing aristocracy appears to him to be false and decadent, not ideal at all. It seems to me that the sense of responsibility that resides in a morality of nobility is the ultimate theme of one of Nietzsche's most peculiar doctrines, that of the eternal recurrence. If, as he teaches, the cosmic process occurs in infinite time and within an infinite mass of forces and matter, then all resultant combinations of elements will occur within finite time, no matter how long this time lasts. After that finite time is over, the game must begin anew and, in light of causality, the previous combinations must be repeated in the same way, and so on *ad infinitum*: given the continuity of the cosmic event, every moment can be viewed as a point at which one cosmic period ends and another begins. Thus, the content of every moment and of the entire life of each human being has already appeared an infinite number of times in exactly the same sequence. The real meaning of this doctrine is evident in its first expression:

What will happen if one day a demon follows you to your most secluded solitude and says: This life that you are living now and that you have been living you will have to live again, innumerable times again, and there will not be anything new in it, but all the unspeakably small issues and great issues of your life will have to be faced by you again, and all of them in the same order and sequence. The eternal hourglass of existence will be turned around and around, and you will be turned with it from dust to dust. If this thought won power over you it would change the you who now exists and perhaps it would crush you under the grave weight of questioning at each time and in each situation: Do you want this once again and for innumerable times? How good to yourself and to life would you have to be in order not to ask for anything else than for this final and eternal confirmation and seal!

Thus, for Nietzsche, the endless repetition of our conduct becomes a criterion for conscious decision about its worth. A momentary action that normally seems to be inessential and easily banished from consciousness with the feeling that 'whatever has passed away has passed away' takes on a formidable weight and can no longer be brushed aside when one knows that it will be infinitely repeated. Eternal recurrence means that every existence is eternal. If there is infinite repetition, then the duration of an existence is synonymous with its eternal continuation. We are responsible for our conduct in a new way, or at least we understand our responsibility differently, if we know that no moment of our life is ever over once and for all, but that we and humanity must experience it innumerable times just as we shape it now.

Thus, one of Kant's basic themes is transported into a new dimension by Nietzsche. Kant finds the ground for an action done according to duty in the possibility that the acting person could wish the principle that guides his action to be a universally valid law. The temptation to lie, to steal, to be adamant against the needy, or not to develop one's own personal potential can be countered on the moral basis that nobody would want a human world in which such temptations held sway as laws of nature: such a world would destroy itself by inner contradiction. The very egoistic interest of the person would declare against such actions being generalized, because they would also be directed against himself. Indeed, the character of an unethical conduct is not altered by its incessant repetition, but in light of such repetition, as under a microscope meanings become visible that are overlooked in a fleeting world of the only-once. But this is the practical meaning of the Kantian norm. The expansion of our actions into a general law does not lend any significance to them that is not already present in each of them taken singly. But the specific quality of our mental apperception is such that an isolated action is frequently not judged according to its full weight: its consequences are blended with the innumerable cross-cutting strands of social life, and its pure effects are distorted in their emphasis. The real import of an action stands out only if the practical milieu is attuned to it, if there are no contrary actions or effects overshadowing it, and, in sum, if it is not an accidental singular case within a chaos of other cases, but a norm without exception, a general law. Kant places action into the dimension of infinite repetition in the one-alongside-the-other of society, whereas Nietzsche has action repeat itself in the infinite one-after-the-other of the same person. Here Kant is consistent with his emphasis on the consequences of an action, and Nietzsche with his stress on the immediately manifest being of a subject. Both multiplications of action serve the same goal of getting beyond the accidentality that colors representation in their only-now and only-here. The inner value of an action, or that for which we are responsible, is in itself beyond time and number, where and how often; but we are chained to these categories and can only be impressed with the real weight of an action by appeal to them.

Fichte's development of the Kantian formula already comes close to the transposition into formal time that is accomplished in the doctrine of eternal recurrence. 'The empirical ego,' as Fichte puts it, 'has to be tuned in the way in which it could be tuned forever. Thus, I would express the principle of morality in the following formula: Act so that the rule of your will could be imagined as an eternal law for you.' The extension of the moral criterion into the dimension of time rather than into that of society makes the individual the basis of that criterion, just as for Nietzsche individual duration is decisive and not the multiplication of individuals. But in Kant, Fichte, and Nietzsche, the same proclivity is shown for gaining a reasonable basis for the values to which we are responsible in terms of their realization.

If the doctrine of eternal recurrence had only the importance expressed in the previous quotation of showing tangibly the infinite responsibility of individuals for what they do, then we would not have to broach the question of objective truth. That doctrine would be a symbol, similar to Kant's categorical imperative, which would function as an idea but not as a reality. But insofar as Nietzsche does not stop at that point and insists instead on the reality of eternal recurrence, we cannot be silent about the difficulties of his thesis. Even if we agree that the cosmic process occurs among finite elements in infinite time, there is no proof forthcoming that any configuration of elements must be repeated at any time or even in infinite time. Such repetition might occur, but a combination of cosmic elements which were not repetitive can be imagined.[1] But this argument can be left aside, because reality can add nothing to the importance of the eternal recurrence as a regulative idea of ethics. The deep emotion and devotion with which Nietzsche sometimes speaks of his doctrine can be explained, in my opinion, only in terms of his imprecise logical conceptualization. From a logical viewpoint, there is no inherent importance to repetition, because no synthesis is possible of successive repetitions. If an experience is repeated within my existence, this repetition can be of enormous importance for me, but only because I remember the first instance and only if I have already been altered by it. But if we assume the empirically impossible case in which the second instance finds me in exactly the same state as I was when the first instance occurred, then my reaction the second time would be the same as it was initially and, therefore, the repetition would have no importance for me. The importance of repetition depends upon the persistence of the ego, which finds a new meaning and new consequences in the first instance in light of the reappearance of the same contents a second time. And the case is no different when it is the whole of existence that returns. The second instance would only have significance if it were compounded by the first one, that is, if the same ego were present in both. But in reality I do not return, but a phenomenon appears which is identical with me in all of its traits and experiences. If the qualitative reality of the second instance referred to the first one and thereby acknowledged itself to be second, then it would not be an exact repetition of the first, just by the virtue of that acknowledgment. I think that Nietzsche has been tempted by an imprecise concept of the ego to see a resurrection of the previous ego when there is only a recapitulation of the same phenomenon. Therefore, he grants significance to the successive egos, none of which is the first ego and each of which is merely qualitatively of the same type as the others. In light of the foregoing discussion, it is clear that not even the first ego has the importance ascribed to it in Nietzsche's doctrine. If many absolutely identical worlds exist in space, but there is no communication among them, then the content of my ego would be repeated identically in each of them. Yet I would not be entitled to say that I live in each of these worlds. And it is obvious that these identical persons living alongside one another would behave in the same way as persons living successively, as they do according to the doctrine of eternal recurrence. The eternal recurrence only has import for someone who watches, reflects on, and unites the many returns in his consciousness; it is nothing as an external reality. The ethical-psychological import of the doctrine lies in referring to it at specific moments in given cosmic epochs. But the reality of recurrence does not add a thing to the imaginative function of the idea.

I do not believe, however, that it is sound to argue that the ideas of eternal recurrence and of the overman are opposed to one another. Both of them are norms of and challenges to our conduct. The overman is just the crystallized thought that man can and ought to develop beyond his present state. Why should man stop on the way that has led him from a low animal form to humanity? Just as the present form is above the animal, so the future form will be above man. The overman is a task that grows with the progress of humanity: once the task posed by a particular present is fulfilled, a new one posed by the ideals of this present arises immediately. As long as man is a being who can evolve, the task that is inherent to the concept of the overman can never be definitively fulfilled. This task dogs the steps of mankind as a demand which remains unsatisfied by any of the attempts to fulfil it and as an expression of the fact that, in every moment of his empirical existence and even at the highest imaginable levels, man is still a path and a bridge. There appears to be a contradiction between the ideas of eternal recurrence and of the overman only insofar as the infinity of the overman's task cannot be reconciled with the finitude of cosmic periods: within each period, humanity could be vested with only a limited number of forms of evolution, which could be constantly repeated, whereas the ideal of the overman demands a straight line of evolution heading toward the infinite. But in reality there is no contradiction if the overman is understood not as a rigid structure with an absolutely determined content, but as a functional ideal indicating the human form that is superior to the present real one. It is quite irrelevant that humanity might not be able to transcend a level of evolution that had been reached in a certain cosmic configuration. Whichever the ideal might indicate, whether something high or low, something that could really be improved or something that could not, something singular or some recurrence, that ideal would be transcendent over every moment of reality and would be independent of all of the limits typical of reality. We can formulate this point in terms of one of Kant's categories: thus we shall live in every moment, regardless of the character of its reality, as if we wished to develop toward a goal which transcends our present reality in an ideal projection of evolution; that is, we should live in such a way that we would will to live that way forever, as if there was an eternal recurrence.

The importance of the idea of recurrence is rather questionable on the level of reality. But on the level of ethical regulation that has already been discussed, and on the metaphysical level, it has a significance that makes up for its defects. Through the thought of recurrence Nietzsche has brought together into a strange union two fundamental and opposed themes of the soul: the need for the finite, for concrete limits, for definite forms in everything given, and the need to lose oneself in the limitless. In the realm of logic these needs might seem to be contradictory and negate each other. But in psychological reality they are found side by side, working together and replacing one another. This peculiar coexistence, which transcends pure logic, is reflected in the structures of metaphysics. For metaphysics, concepts and images appear in such a way that the question of truth cannot be posed in a concrete and logical sense, because these objects are so distant from individual phenomena and on such a high and abstract level that they lose the sharp contours that are so necessary for practice, logic, and science. Thus, the objects of metaphysics are as differentiated from those of other studies as are the objects of art from those of science or action. Metaphysics has its own requirements and norms which cannot reasonably be expected to meet the demands of other scientific approaches. The 'unity' of many elements achieved by metaphysics does not result from the application of the norms of all of the other studies, but is often the objectivization or conceptual expression of the spiritual unity in which we experience the diversity of logically disparate elements and melt them into one. Thus, the idea of the eternal recurrence is the synthesis of the need for the infinite and the need for the finite. It teaches that finite contents and phenomena that are limited in form and number take on the form of an infinite through endless succession. It is not a matter here of the accidental conjunction of determinations, but of the same causality which is at the root of concrete and finite facts, and which pushes these facts beyond themselves and finally leads them back, through the exhaustion of possible combinations, to their starting point. Thus, there is infinite repetition, because the only-once retains a finite form that is limited by new configurations. The most meaningful symbolization for this idea is that of a ring with an infinite circumference which allows infinite and limitless movement within itself, and progress from sector to sector and yet continual return. There is the firmest of statements in Nietzsche's unedited papers: 'Acumen of meditation: the eternal return of everything is the closest approach of the world of becoming to the world of being.' Here is the justification for my interpretation of the doctrine of recurrence as a synthesis of the need for finitude and the need for infinity on the highest metaphysical level. Ever since the dispute occurred between Heraclitus and the Eleatics, the metaphysical process has been lodged between being and becoming. The whole of Greek philosophy is a history of attempts to unite into a noncontradictory picture of reality the substantial rigidity and closure of being – which allows the soul to find peace, realization, and finality – and flux and change, the diversity and vitality that are found in both soul and world. Being and becoming are the most general, formal, and inclusive formulations of the basic dualism that patterns all human beings: all great philosophy is engaged in founding a new reconciliation between them, or a new way of giving decisive primacy to one over the other. Nietzsche's eternal recurrence also has the function of mediating between being and becoming, and in this concept the two poles move toward each other simultaneously. On one side, the empirical chain of finite and individual events forms an uninterrupted becoming that ebbs and flows ceaselessly. Here, in the river of Heraclitus, everything that seems to be substantial is dissolved. But, through their infinite return these events gain being and inevitable continuity: everything finite becomes a fixed point through which the river of becoming passes endlessly. All content is thereby liberated and removed from the flux: finitude wraps itself into the form of the infinite, and becoming into the form of being. On the other side, within the doctrine of recurrence it is just being which seems to be finite, defined by a form, and concrete. The contents of being only gain infinity through the causality of becoming. What we are is limited at any moment; our real action can be inspected, and our need for finite limitation is satisfied by the real content of our existence. But by placing the contents of being under the causal principle of becoming, which necessitates all possible combinations and, therefore, their infinite repetition, the infinity of becoming integrates the finitude of being: the need for boundlessness and measureless transcendence quenches its thirst in the river of becoming. Certainly, only abstract concepts such as finitude and infinity, and being and becoming, can be extended to form diverse combinations that sparkle with different meanings. But metaphysics thrives on just this constitution of concepts. Here our task is only to show how these concepts are related in the idea of eternal recurrence. The infinite repetition of a being that is limited by finitude, and the causality through which phenomena that surge up and then disappear like waves in a continuous river win a durability and an eternity of being – which was stolen from them by their temporal destiny – make the eternal recurrence into a synthesis or, as Nietzsche would say, into an 'approximation' between being and becoming. This approximation is expressed in an ambiguous relation among concepts: they transform the finitude of becoming into the infinity of being, or the finitude of being into an infinity of becoming. It does not matter from which point the line that connects the metaphysical poles is drawn, so long as the idea of recurrence is retained. And if one looks back to the historico-philosophical basis for the doctrine of the eternal return, which Nietzsche's thought shares with Schopenhauer's, but which also contains their differences, we find that this doctrine negates an absolute goal of being. And we also find here a hidden and profound reason, which is not otherwise easily detected, why Nietzsche felt that recurrence was an absolutely essential and central element in all of his thinking. Nietzsche replaces a final goal with an evolutionary process that contains diverse goals and values: instead of one absolute level that is intended by the cosmic process, any level that supersedes the actual one gains significance. But the evolutionary process still contains the disquiet of boundlessness and fosters an insecurity based on the impossibility of any overview of the whole. In the notion of eternal recurrence, however, Nietzsche retains any perspective and any conclusion that being can still exhibit after an absolute goal has been eliminated, because, although each cosmic period is limited, there is still a regulative idea demanding the growth of values toward the limitless. The thought of recurrence includes infinity through the way that the finite appears in installments: endless becoming achieves form and secure boundaries through contents that are formed by definite combinations of numbers and types. For most people the thought that life returns endlessly and changelessly would be abhorrent and chilling, but Nietzsche finds it comforting and beneficial. The infinite drifting that results from the restlessness of his nature and his negation of a cosmic goal are placed within the limits of the circumference of the 'ring.'

Among all of Nietzsche's doctrines, that of eternal recurrence has the greatest metaphysical import, even though its moral intention is evident in his emphasis on the enormous responsibility of man in light of the eternalization of action by its continuous repetition. Despite his self-proclaimed immoralism, his thought is far more ethically oriented than that of Schopenhauer, who incessantly asserts that morality is the fundamental value of life and the meaning of all meaning. Nietzschian morality is a morality of the base which does not grow to the summit, as do the doctrines of Plato, Spinoza, Kant, and Schopenhauer, which infuse transcendent being into human volition. The ideal of nobility, which through the theme of responsibility places recurrence in its service, has an earthly and empirical nature: it is the final point of a deeply rooted evolutionary process, which lacking a sacred atmosphere does not encounter the difficulties of values and norms that originate from above in a transempirical sphere. This is, perhaps, the reason why nobility has not been recognized until the present time as a special value-quality of the soul. It is to Nietzsche's credit that he was the first one to teach the specificity of this ideal unambiguously and through rich applications, though not abstractly and systematically. Indeed, the idea of nobility cannot be subsumed under the traditionally fundamental categories of value, even though it touches the aesthetic as well as the ethical dimension. The metaphysical tones that resonate beauty and morality are clearly missing here and, thus, indicate a disjunction. The limits of morality might be drawn as naturalistically and empirically as they could be, but any thought that is more profound than is Nietzsche's meets a boundary of interpretation beyond which extends the empire of mysticism, religion, metaphysics, and even skepticism. The transition across this boundary is often barely perceptible. In the same way, the interpretation of aesthetic pleasure extends its roots and branches into this same empire, though in a different direction. As a consequence of its lack of relation to the transcendental, the content of the idea of nobility, though not its bearers, is deprived of genuine depth. Despite all of the human values they evince, the infinite and profound significance and meaning of human beings in the religious paintings of Rembrandt or in the novels of Dostoevsky lack nobility, just because these values somehow spring from transcendence or grow into it. The essence of nobility is the logical cope-stone of Nietzsche's entire doctrine of values, because it postulates the exclusion of the majority, the rejection of all comparison, and the seclusion of essences in opposition to the continuity of sharing. What counts in the Nietzschian image of human value is not quantity but the qualitative level of evolution that has been achieved. The specific nature of nobility resides in the fact that the noble being in his own lonely existence is an absolutely valid representation of the meaning of evolution. The idea of nobility has a biological character: the noble man is a product of breeding, just as are the historico-social aristocracies. Nietzsche's passionate desire to liberate morality from transcendence is consistent with this biological tendency of his morality. His demand for the infinite growth of all given empirical and earthly qualities of value is counterbalanced by his understanding that this growth should only occur on an empirical and historical ground, and that infinite increase must remain in touch with this ground.

It has frequently been stressed that Nietzsche's doctrine is in opposition to his personality: a rude, warlike, and yet bacchantic cry erupts from an extremely sensitive, quiet, introspective, and lovable man. Certainly this does not constitute an argument against the doctrine's validity. Often a philosopher expresses in his doctrine the opposite of what he is, supplementing his shortcomings in a personal dialectic and compensating for the desires he has never realized, thereby striving for full humanity. But nobility is the point at which the ideal Nietzsche teaches and the reality of his nature meet: it is the high-water mark of his personal being from which he floats into the empire of human desire.

Many misunderstandings of the overman result from overlooking the absolutely earthly nature of this ideal, which is fundamental to the opposition between the doctrine of Nietzsche and that of Schopenhauer. Nietzsche dogmatically proclaims the absolute and indisputable value of life. The life-process itself, this mysterious form in which the cosmic elements appear, has exercised an evident intoxicating and overpowering influence on Nietzsche. It appeared absurd and completely contradictory to him that there could be an imperative against life and an order of value inimical to it: a judgment against life could only be a symptom, he contends, of a specific mode of life, and the right to make such a judgment could only proceed from beyond life. But life *is* the empirical, the historical phenomenon. Even if the soul and its contents, life's mysterious blossoms, have an import beyond their earthly limits, life remains an absolute captive of the earth, its child; the ideal of nobility is but the most sublime of the sublimations achieved by the life-process through evolution, selection, and breeding. With an unerring instinct, Nietzsche, who finds value only in life, turns his love toward the idea of nobility, because it is the only ideal element of the soul that does not force life to go beyond itself into the transcendent realm or, at least, to take account of that realm. Thus, his doctrine rests on the dogmatic imperative: Life shall be! And here we find the reason why Nietzsche ultimately regards Schopenhauer as his real philosophical opponent, an invincible opponent, because he negates Nietzsche's presupposition and replaces it with the antithesis: Life shall not be! By arguing from the position that life is and shall be valuable, which was self-evident to him, Nietzsche declared victory over Schopenhauer on the basis that pessimism destroys life. But one can probably say that Nietzsche did not understand Schopenhauer's profound metaphysical dimension, because for Schopenhauer the negation of life and all that that implies is a demonstration of truth and not, as Nietzsche had it, the grounds for refutation.

We meet here the limits of the logical understanding. Nietzsche did not realize that he was trying to refute Schopenhauer on the basis of a dogmatic value-presupposition which was exactly the presupposition that his opponent rejected. This indicates an opposition of being which cannot be bridged by the intellect, just as one cannot reach a point on a line that is parallel to another one by staying on the latter. To search for peace between these two adversaries is the same as any other meritless venture: it is worse than useless because it falsifies the meaning of their opposition and, thus, the meaning of each one of them. On one hand, we have the conviction that life is valueless, which is based on selecting from all of the diverse and nonobservable meanings only monotony, the preponderance of suffering, and failure. On the other hand, we have the belief that life is value and that every deficiency is but a step toward a new attainment, every monotony but an interplay of infinite vitality, and every pain inconsequential in light of the surge of values in the process of realization in being and action. Such convictions are not theoretical knowledge but the expressions of fundamental states of the soul. They cannot be reconciled in a 'higher unity,' because there is no identity between them. The value of what might be called their synthesis consists precisely in the fact that humanity has developed such a magnitude of tensions in life-experience and sentiment that it can include both of them. There can be no unification based on objective content, but only one achieved by a subject who can regard both positions. By sensing the reverberations of spiritual existence in the distance opened up by these opposites, the soul grows, despite, indeed, because of, the fact that it does not decide in favor of one of the parties. It finally embraces both the desperation and the jubilation of life as the poles of its own expansion, its own power, its own plenitude of forms. And it enjoys that embrace.

Notes

1. I refer to the proof of the problematicity of eternal recurrence outside the text itself, because it is a specialized concern. I will argue here in terms of the most simple case of a system consisting of only three elements. Imagine three wheels of equal size rotating around the same axle. There is one point marked on each one of them so that the three points are aligned on a straight line at a certain moment, which may be indicated by a thread straightened across the wheels. Now the wheels start to rotate, the second wheel at twice the speed of the first one. The two marked points on the wheels will be aligned under the thread when the first wheel has finished one revolution and the second wheel has completed two revolutions. They will be aligned again after the second revolution of the first wheel and the fourth revolution the second wheel, and so on. In short, both wheels return to their starting positions after n revolutions of the first one and 2n revolutions of the second. Now let us suppose that the speed of revolution of the third wheel is $1/\pi$ of that of the first wheel. Then the 1, 2, 3, . . . , n rotations of the first wheel are expressed by $1/\pi$, $2/\pi$, $3/\pi$, . . . , n/π rotations of the third wheel. According to the nature of the number π, none of these fractions can be a whole number. This means that the third wheel will never have finished a whole number of rotations when the first wheel has completed a whole number of rotations. But because the instantaneous position of alignment, under the thread, of the points marked on the first and the second wheels will occur only after the first wheel has made a whole rotation, the marked point on the third wheel never can pass under the thread at the same moment that the marked points of the two other wheels pass under it. In consequence, the starting position of the three wheels cannot be repeated through eternity. So, if there exist anywhere in the world three motions that are identical to the motion-relation of these three wheels, the relative positions taken by them could never return to their original relations. The finitude of the number of elements in the system, even if one grants infinite time for their motions, does not, therefore, necessitate the repetition of any specific momentary relation. Of course, things might not be as I have described them. Cosmic motions could be structured in such a way that they passed again and again through a recurring cycle of combinations. But the possibility just sketched is sufficient by itself to render this so-called proof for the eternal recurrence an illusion.

57

A More Severe Morality: Nietzsche's Affirmative Ethics*

Robert C. Solomon

*Source: *Journal of the British Society for Phenomenology*, vol. 16, no. 3, October 1995, pp. 250–67.

> She told me herself that she had no morality, – and I thought she had, like myself, a more severe morality than anyone.
>
> (Nietzsche, in a letter to Paul Rée, 1882)

A mad dog, foaming at the moustache and snarling at the world; that is how the American artist David Levine portrays Friedrich Nietzsche in his well-known caricature in *The New York Review of Books*. It is not so different in its malicious intent, nor further wrong in its interpretation of Nietzsche, than a good number of scholarly works. This is indeed the traditional portrait, – the unconsummated consummate immoralist, the personally gentle, even timid, arch-destroyer. Of course, Nietzsche himself made adolescent comments about his own destructiveness not infrequently – throughout the whole of *Ecce Homo*, for example. Nevertheless, these give a false impression of his intentions as well as of the good philosophical sense to be made of his works.

In recent years, we have been treated to a rather systematic whitewashing of Nietzsche. Gone is the foam and the snarl; indeed, what has come to replace the 'revaluation of all values' has become so tame that, a certain impatience for scholarship aside, one of these new Nietzsches (perhaps not the French one) would find himself very much at home on most university campuses. This new Nietzsche, founded by Walter Kaufmann and now promoted by Richard Schacht, is the champion of honesty against the forces of hypocrisy.[1] Or, more recently, he is Harold Alderman's benign Californish guru, urging us simply to 'be ourselves,' preferably by reading Heidegger.[2] This picture is no less false than the first, but it has the undeniable virtue of welcoming Nietzsche, belatedly, back to the fold of professional philosophers. Better respectable than rabid, one might suppose, though I would guess Nietzsche himself would opt for the latter.

The new French Nietzsche, on the other hand, enjoys the *philosophe* at the extremes, almost beyond the limits of the imaginable, an adolescent implosion of forces dancing on the edge of nothingness. He is, accordingly, a thoroughly playful Nietzsche. He is the 'anti-Oedipe' as well as the 'anti-Christ,' a deconstructionist, a Derridaidian, a Dada-idian, before his time. He does not destroy but rather revels in the destruction we have already inflicted upon ourselves. He is a burst of energy rather than a philosopher, an explosion instead of a visionary. Most of all, he plays, and he reminds us of the importance of dancing and the unimportance of serious scholarship and Truth. And, we are assured (for example, by David Allison in his introduction to 'The New Nietzsche'), he is wholly outside of that somber and intellectually fraudulent onto-theological tradition that he so playfully attacks, but in which we less imaginative and playless scholarly souls are still enmired.[3]

Perhaps. But of all the authors in German history, Nietzsche must surely be the most historical and even 'timely,' as well as one of the most solemn (as opposed to bourgeois 'serious'). He was, from all evidence, incapable of even the uptight version of dancing propounded by his Zarathustra. His playfulness seemed largely limited to the scholarly joke. Lou Andreas Salomé once described him (in 1882):

> . . . a light laugh, a quiet way of speaking, and a cautious, pensive way of walking . . . He took pleasure in the refined forms of social intercourse . . . But in it all lay a penchant for disguise . . . I recall that when I first spoke with him his formal manner shocked and deceived me. But I was not deceived for long by this lonesome man who only wore his mask as unalterably as someone coming from the desert and mountains wears the cloak of the wordly-wise . . .[4]

Playful, indeed. And as for 'the tradition,' as it has come to be called, Nietzsche as philosopher can be understood only within it, despite his unselfcritical megalomania about his own 'untimely' and wholly novel importance.

It was decidedly *within* that somber philosophical tradition, typically traced in misleading linear fashion back to Socrates, that I want to try to understand Nietzsche's ethics. His reputation as arch-destroyer and philosophical outlaw has so enveloped Nietzsche's notorious 'reputation,' largely at his own bidding, that the kernel of his moral philosophy – and I do insist on calling it that – has been lost. There is in Nietzsche, unmistakably, an ethics that is considerably more than nihilism or academic good fellowship or playfulness, an ethics that is very much part of 'the tradition.' It is, however, a brand of ethics that had and has been all but abandoned in the wake of Kant and the anal compulsiveness of what is now called rationality in ethics. It is this other brand of ethics, for which Nietzsche quite properly failed to find a name, that I would like to indicate in this essay.

Nietzsche's Nihilism, and Morality

Nietzsche's novelty is to be found, in part, in his energetic descriptions of what he calls 'nihilism.' It is, first of all, a cultural experience, a profound sense of disappointment not only, as some ethicists would have it, in the failure of philosophy to justify moral principles, but in the fabric of life as such, the 'widespread sensibility of our age' more sympathetically described by Camus a half century later. It is also, Nietzsche keeps reminding us, a stance to be taken up as well as a phenomenon to be described. Zarathustra, in one of his more belligerent moments, urges us to 'push what is falling' and, in his notes, Nietzsche urges us to promote 'a complete nihilism' in place of the incomplete nihilism in which we now live (*WP* 28).[5] Here again we note Nietzsche's self-conscious 'timelessness,' and his devotion to a tradition dedicated to completeness in ethics.

'Nihilism,' obvious etymology aside, does not mean 'accepting nothing.' Like most philosophical terms, subsequently raised to an isolated and artificial level of abstraction, this one does its work in particular contexts, in specific perspectives, often as a kind of accusation. Some traditional but much-in-the-news Christians use the term as a more or less crude synonym for 'secular humanism,' on the (false) assumption that a man without God must be a man without Christian values as well. (The dubious argument by Ivan Karamazov: 'if there is no God, then everything is permitted.') But note that I say 'Christian' values, for the accuser might well allow, indeed insist, that the nihilist does have values, – subjective, self-serving and secularly narrow-minded though they be. (Brother Mitya, perhaps: hardly a paragon of virtue.) Similarly, an orthodox Jewish friend of mine refers as 'nihilists' to any people without a self-conscious if not obsessive sense of tradition, assuming that others must lack in their experience what he finds so essential in his own. Marxists use the term (sometimes but not always along with 'bourgeois individualism') to indict those who do not share their class-conscious values. Aesthetes use it to knock the Philistines, and my academic colleagues use it to chastise anyone with 'looser' standards and higher grade averages than themselves. Stanley Rosen attacks it at book length without ever saying exactly what's wrong with it, except that it falls far short of his own rather pretentious search for Hegelian absolute truth.[6]

If Nietzsche made us aware of anything in ethics, it is the importance of *perspectives*, the need to see all concepts and values *in context*. How odd, then, that the key concepts of Nietzsche's own ethics have been so routinely blown up to absolute – that is nonperspectival – proportions. Nihilism is an accusation, in context. Outside of all contexts, it is nothing (which, of course, leads to some quaint and cute Parmenidean wordplay.) As Blanchot has written, nihilism is a particular achievement of a particular sort of society.[7] It becomes a world-hypothesis only at the expense of losing what is most urgent and cleansing in Nietzsche, the attack on the transcendental pretension of understanding the world 'in itself' on the basis of our own limited and limiting moral experience.

Nietzsche's nihilism is an accusation *within* the context of traditional ethics (what other kind of ethics could there be?). It points to a tragic or at any rate damnable hollowness in 'the moral point of view,' which we might anticipate by asking why moral philosophers ever became compelled to talk in such a peculiar fashion. Indeed, it is part and parcel of the whole history of ethics that morality is emphatically *not* just 'a point of view'; it is necessary and obligatory. Such talk already betrays a fatal compromise; 'perspectivism' and Morality are warring enemies, not complementary theses. What is morality, that it has been forced and has been able to hide behind a veneer of pluralism, to search for 'reasons' for its own necessity which – successful or not – leave the acceptance of morality unchallenged?

What is morality? This, perhaps more than any other question, guided Nietzsche's ethics. It is the concept of morals that intrigues Nietzsche: how morals ever became reduced to Morality, how the virtues ever got melted together into the shapeless form of Virtue. But, as I shall argue shortly, there are many meanings of 'morality' just as there are many different sorts of morals. It is the terms themselves – but not just the terms – that are most in question here. The definition of 'morality' that preoccupies Nietzsche, and which I shall be employing here, is the definition provided by Kant – of morality as a set of universal, categorical principles of practical reason. 'Morals,' on the other hand, is a term much less precise, and I shall be using that term much as Hume used it in his *Enquiry*: morals are those generally agreeable or acceptable traits that characterize a good person – leaving quite open the all-important nonconceptual question what is to count (in what context) as a good person. Ethics, finally, I take to be the overall arena in which morality and morals and other questions concerning the good life and how to live it are debated. Morality in its Kantian guise may not be at all essential to ethics; indeed, one might formulate Nietzsche's concern by asking how the subject of ethics has so easily been converted into Moral Philosophy, that is, the philosophical analysis of Morality *á la* Kant rather than the somewhat pagan celebration of the virtues *á la* Hume, which is not to say that Nietzsche would have felt very much at home with the Scotsman either, whatever their philosophical affinities.

In his recent book, *After Virtue*,[8] Alasdair MacIntyre has attacked Nietzsche and nihilism together, as symptoms of our general decay ('decadence' would be too fashionable and thus too positive a term for our moral wretchedness). But in doing so, he has also rendered Nietzsche's own thesis in admirably contemporary form; morality is undone, hollow, an empty sham for which philosophers busily manufacture 'reasons' and tinker with grand principles if only to convince themselves that something might still be there. What philosophers defensively call 'the moral point of view' is a camouflaged retreat. It serves only to hide the vacuousness of the moral prejudices they serve. Morality is no longer a 'tablet of virtues' but a *tabula rasa*, for which we are poorly compensated by the insistence that it is itself necessary. Or, in Hume's terms, morality is the repository of those 'monkish' virtues whose degrading, humiliating effects are disguised by the defenses of reason.[9] For Hume as for Nietzsche, 'some passions are merely stupid, dragging us down with them.' And this will be the area where an adequate understanding of morals will emerge, in the realm of passion rather than reason. The good person will emphatically not be the one who is expertly consistent in universalizing maxims according to the principles of practical reason.

Nietzsche, Kant and Aristotle

Nihilism is not a thesis; it is a reaction. It is not a romantic 'Nay-saying' so much as it is a feature of good old enlightenment criticism in the form of a critical phenomenology or a diagnostic hermeneutics. Indeed, in Germany romanticism and *Aufklärung* were never very clearly distinguished, except in rhetoric, and so too, beneath the bluster of nihilism a much more profound and, dare I say, reasonable Nietzsche can be discerned. In fact, I want to argue that Nietzsche might best be understood, perhaps ironically, in the company of that more optimistic decadent of ancient times, Aristotle, and in close contrast to the most powerful moral philosopher of modern times, – Immanuel Kant. They were hardly nihilists; indeed they remain even today the two paradigms of morality, the two great proponents of all-encompassing ethical world views. Next to them, the contemporary fiddling with so-called 'utilitarianism' seems, as Hegel complained in the *Phenomenology*, rather petty and devoid of anything deserving the honorific name 'morality.'[10]

It has always seemed to me perverse to read Aristotle and Kant as engaged in the same intellectual exercise, that is, to present and promote a *theory* of morality. They were, without question, both moralists; that is, they had the 'moral prejudices' that Nietzsche discovers beneath every philosophical theory. This, of course, would not bother them (except perhaps the word 'prejudices'). They were both also, Nietzsche would be the first to argue, *reactionaries*, trying to prop up with an ethics an *ethos* – an established way of life – that was already collapsing. To do so, both ethicists appealed to an overriding (if not absolute) *telos* of reason and rationality, the suspicious status of which Nietzsche deftly displays vis-a-vis Socrates in *Twilight of the Idols*.[11] Both philosophers too saw themselves as defenders of 'civilized' virtues in the face of the nihilists of their time, though Aristotle displays ample affinity with Protagoras and Kant had no hesitation about supporting Robespierre. But, nevertheless, there is a profound difference between these two great thinkers that too easily gets lost in the need to sustain the linear tradition that supposedly begins with Socrates, ignoring the dialectical conflict that is to be found even within Socrates himself. Aristotle and Kant represent not just two opposed ethical theories, 'teleological' and 'deonto-logical' respectively, synthesized by the *telos* of rationality. They represent two opposed ways of life.

Aristotle may be a long way from the Greece described by Homer, but the form of his ethics is still very much involved with the Homeric warrior trad-ition. The virtue of courage still deserves first mention in the list of excel-lences, and pride is still a virtue rather than a vice. It is an ethics for the privileged few, though Aristotle, unlike Nietzsche, had no need to announce this in a preface. But most important of all, it is an ethics that is not primarily concerned with rules and principles, much less *universal* rules and principles, categorical imperatives. Indeed, Aristotle's much-heralded discussion of the so-called 'practical syllogism' in Book VI of the *Nicomachean Ethics*, in which something akin to principles universal in form (and as ethically invigorating as 'eating dry foods is healthy') is quite modest, hardly the cornerstone of his ethics, as some recent scholars have made it out to be.[12] Aristotle's ethics is not an ethics of principles, categorical or otherwise. It is an ethics of *practice*, a description of an actual ethos rather than an abstract attempt to define or create one. Ethos is by its very nature bound to a culture; Kantian ethics, by its pure rational nature but much to its peril, seems not to be. Of course, any philosopher can show how a practice is *really* a rule-governed activity, and then proceed to formulate, examine and criticize the rules.[13] Indeed, one might even show that children playing with their food follow certain rules, but to do so clearly is to misdescribe if not also misunderstand their activity.[14] But what is critical to an ethics of practice is not the absence of rules; it is rather the overriding importance of the concept of *excellence* or virtue (*aretē*). What Aristotle describes is the ideal citizen, the excellent individual who is already (before he studies ethics and learns to articulate principles of any kind) proud of himself and the pride of his family and community. He is surrounded by friends; he is the model of strength, if not only the physical prowess that was singularly important to Achilles (who was far from ideal in other virtues). He may have been a bit too 'civilized' already for Nietzsche's Homeric fantasies, but he represents a moral type distinctively different from that described by Kant, 2000 years later. His ethics are his virtues; his excel-lence is his pride.

Kant, on the other hand, is the outstanding moralist in a very different tradition. The warrior plays no role and presents us with no ideal; individual talents and the good fortune of having been 'brought up well,' which Aristo-tle simply presupposes, are ruled out of the moral realm from page one.[15] Kant's ethics is the ethics of the categorical imperative, the ethics of universal rational principles, the ethics of obedient virtue instead of the cultivation of the virtues. It is an ethics that minimizes differences and begins by assuming that we all share a common category of 'humanity' and a common moral faculty of reason. The good man is the man who resists his 'inclinations' and acts for the sake of duty and duty alone. This extreme criterion is qualified in a number of entertaining ways, for example, by suggesting that the rule that one should cultivate one's talents is itself an example of the categorical imperative and that one has a peculiar duty to pursue one's own happiness, if only so that one is thereby better disposed to fulfill one's duties to others.[16]

What I want to argue here should be, in part at least, transparent. Nietzsche may talk about 'creating new values,' but – as he himself often says, it is something of a return to an old and neglected set of values – the values of masterly virtue – that most concerns him. There are complications. We do not have the ethos of *The Iliad*, nor even the tamer *ethe* of Homer or Aristotle, nor for that matter even the bourgeois complacency of Kantian Königsberg with its definitive set of practices in which the very idea of an unconditional imperative is alone plausible. There is no context, in other words, within which the new virtues we are to 'create' are to be virtues, for a virtue without a practice is of no more value than a word without a language, a gesture without a context. When Nietzsche insists on 'creating new values,' in other words, he is urging us on in a desperate state of affairs. He is rejecting the mediocre banality of an abstract ethics of principles, but he has no practice upon which to depend in advancing his renewed ethics of virtue. No practice, that is, except for the somewhat pretentious and sometimes absurd self-glorification of nineteenth-century German romanticism, which Nietzsche rebukes even as he adopts it as his only available context.[17] This is no small point: Nietzsche is not nearly so isolated nor so unique as he needs to think of himself. Dionysus, like 'the Crucified,' is an ideal only within a context, even if, in *Der Fall Nietzsche*, it seems to be a context defined primarily by rejection.

Nietzsche's nihilism is a reaction against a quite particular *conception* of morality, summarized in modern times in the ethics of Kant. Quite predictably, much of Judeo-Christian morality – or what is often called 'Judeo-Christian morality' – shares this conception. It too is for the many, not just a few. It too treats all souls as the same, whether rational or not. It too dwells on abstractions, whether such categorical imperatives as 'the Golden Rule' or the universal love called *agapē*, which applies to everyone and therefore to no one in particular. Hegel was not entirely wrong when, in an early essay, he had Jesus on the Mount deliver a sermon taken straight from *The Critique of Practical Reason*.[18] Nor was Kant deceiving himself when he looked with pride on his moral philosophy as the heart of Christian ethics, interpreting the commandment to love as well as the desire to be happy as nothing more nor less than instantiations of the categorical imperative, functions of practical reason rather than expressions of individual virtues and exuberance for life.[19]

Aristotle and Achilles versus Kant and Christianity. It is not a perfect match, but it allows us to explain Nietzsche's aims and Nietzsche's problems far better than the over-reaching nonsense about 'the transvaluation of *all* values' and 'Dionysus versus the Crucified.' On the other hand, it is not as if Kant and Nietzsche are completely opposed. It is Kant who sets up the philosophical conditions for the Nietzschean reaction, not only by so clearly codifying the central theses to be attacked but also by conceptually undermining the traditional supports of morality. The (*Aufklärung*) attack on authority ('heteronomy') and the emphasis on 'autonomy' by Kant is a necessary precondition for Nietzsche's moral moves, however much the latter presents himself as providing a conception of morality which precedes, rather than presupposes, this Kantian move. It is Kant, of course, who so stresses the importance of the Will, which is further dramatized (to put it mildly) by Schopenhauer and which, again, Nietzsche attacks only by way of taking for granted its primary features. (Nietzsche's attacks only on 'the Will,' especially 'free will,' deserve some special attention in this regard. 'Character' and 'will to power' are not the same as 'will power.') It is Kant who rejects the support of morality by appeal to religion, arguing instead a dependency of the inverse kind, and though Nietzsche's now-tiresome 'God is dead' hypothesis may be aimed primarily at the traditional thesis, the bulk of his moral arguments rather presuppose the Kantian inversion, religion as a rationalization of, not the precondition of, moral thinking.

Meanings of morality

It was Kant too, perhaps, who best exemplified the philosophical temptation to suppose that 'morality' refers to a single phenomenon, faculty, or feature of certain, if not all, societies. Moral theories and some specific rules may vary, according to this monolithic position, but Morality is that one single set of basic moral rules which all theories of morality must accept as a given. This is stated outright by Kant, at the beginning of his second *Critique* and his *Grounding of the Metaphysics of Morals*.[20] Every society, one might reasonably suppose, has some 'trump' set of rules and regulations which prohibit certain kinds of actions and are considered to be absolute, 'categorical.' Philosophers might argue whether there is a single rationale behind the variety of rules (a 'utility principle' or some principle of authority). Others might challenge the alleged universality and disinterestedness of such principles, but morality everywhere is assumed to be the same, in form if not in content, or in at least intent, nevertheless. Indeed even Nietzsche, in his later works, is tempted by the monolithic image; his pluralistic view of a 'tablet of virtues hanging over every people' is explained by his familiar exuberant account: 'it is the expression of their Will to Power!' In his repeated 'campaign against morality,' he too makes it seem too much as if morality is a monolith rather than a complex set of phenomena whose differences may be as striking as their similarities.

What is in question and what ethics is about, according to moral philosophers since Kant, is the *justification* of moral principles, and along with this quest for justification comes the search for a single *ultimate* principle, a *summum bonum*, through which all disagreements and conflicts can be resolved. The question 'what is morality?' gets solved in a few opening pages; the search for an adequate answer to the more troublesome challenge, 'why be moral?' becomes the main order of business. The question, however, is not entirely serious. 'But there is no reason for worry,' Nietzsche assures us (*BGE* 228);[21] 'Things still stand today as they have always stood: I see nobody in Europe who has (let alone *promotes*) any awareness that thinking about morality could become dangerous, captious, seductive – that there might be any *calamity* involved' (Ibid.). Thus today we find a nearly total moral skepticism (nihilism?) defended in such centers of Moral Standards as Oxford and Yale, under such non-provocative titles as 'prescriptivism' and 'emotivism.' But, whatever the analysis, these folks still keep their promises and restrain themselves to their fair share of the High Table pie. The quest for justification is not a challenge to the monolith; it is only an exercise.

In fact, it is the phenomenon of morality itself that is in question. More than half a century before Nietzsche issued his challenge to Kant, a more sympathetic post-Kantian, Hegel, attacked the Kantian conception of 'morality' in terms that would have been agreeable to Nietzsche, had he been a bit more receptive to the German *Geist*. Hegel too treated the Kantian conception of morality as a monolith, but he also saw that it was surrounded by other conceptions that might also be called 'moral' which were, in the *telos* of human development, both superior and more 'primitive.' One of these was *Sittlichkeit*, or the morality of customs (*Sitten*).[22] It is what we earlier called a morality of *practice*, as opposed to a morality of principles. Hegel proposed not just a different way of interpreting and justifying moral rules (though this would be entailed as well); he rather defended a conception of morals that did not depend upon rules at all, in which the activity of justification, in fact, became something of a philosophical irrelevancy, at best. The need to justify moral rules betrays an emptiness in those rules themselves, a lack of conviction, a lack of support. Since then, Hegel has mistakenly been viewed as lacking in his concern for the basic ethical question, leading several noted ethical commentators (Popper, Walsh)[23] to accuse him of a gross amorality, conducive to if not openly inviting authoritarianism. It is as if rejecting the Kantian conception of morality and refusing to indulge in the academic justification game were tantamount to abandoning ethics – both the practice and the theory – altogether.

If we are to understand Nietzsche's attack on Morality, we must appreciate not so much the breadth of his attack and the all-out nihilism celebrated by some of his more enthusiastic defenders but rather the more limited and precise conception of Morality that falls under his hollow-seeking Hammer. We can then appreciate what some have called the 'affirmative' side of Nietzsche's moral thinking, the sense in which he sees himself as having 'a more severe morality than anybody.' In *BGE* he boasts, 'WE IMMORALISTS! – . . . We have been spun into a severe yarn and shirt of duties and CANNOT get out of that – and in this we are "men of duty," we too ... the dolts and appearances speak against us, saying, "These are men *without* duty." We always have the dolts and appearances against us' (*BGE* 226). To write about Nietzsche as a literal 'immoralist' and the destroyer of morality is to read him badly, or it is to confuse the appearance with the personality. Or, he would say, it is to be a 'dolt.'

For Nietzsche as for Hegel and as for Aristotle, morality does not consist of principles but of practices. It is *doing* not willing that is of moral significance, an expression of character rather than a display of practical reason. A practice has local significance; it requires – and sets up – a context; it is not a matter of universal rule, in fact, universality is sometimes argued to show that something is *not* a practice. (For example, sociobiologists have argued that incest and certain other sexual preferences are not sex practices because – on the basis of their alleged universality – they can be shown to be genetically inherited traits.[24]) Some practices are based upon principles, of course, but not all are; and principles help define a practice, though they rarely if ever do so alone. Hegel and Aristotle, of course, emphasize *collective* social practices, in which laws may be much in evidence. Nietzsche is particularly interested in the 'genealogy' of social practices in which principles play a central if also devious role, but he too quickly concludes that there is but one such 'moral type' and one alternative 'type,' which he designates 'slave' ('herd') and 'master' moralities, respectively. In fact, there are as many moral 'types' as one is willing to distinguish, and to designate as 'master morality' the entire historical and anthropological gamut of relatively law-less (as opposed to lawless) societies is most unhistorical as well as confusing philosophically.

The monolithic image of morality, divorced from particular peoples and practices, gives rise to the disastrous disjunction – common to Kant and Nietzsche at least – it is either Morality or *nothing*. If Nietzsche often seems to come up empty-handed and obscurely calls for 'the creation of new values,' it is because he finds himself rejecting principles without a set of practices to fall back on. If only he had his own non-nihilistic world – something more than his friends and his study and his images of nobility – where he could say, 'here is where we can prove ourselves!' But what he finds instead is the hardly heroic world of 19th-century democratic socialism. In reaction, he celebrates self-assertion and 'life.' This is poor stuff from which to reconstruct Nietzsche's 'affirmative philosophy.' Add a synthetic notion, 'the will to power,' and Nietzsche's ethics is reduced to a combination of aggressive banality and energetic self-indulgence. (Would it be unfair to mention Leopold and Loeb here? They were not the least literate of Nietzsche's students.) What we find in appearances, accordingly, is not an 'affirmative' philosophy at all. Having given us his polemical typology of morals, the rejection of Morality – misinterpreted as a broad-based rejection of *all* morality (for example, by Philippa Foot, who is one of Nietzsche's more sensitive

Anglo-American readers) – seems to lead us to nothing substantial at all.[25] The banality of Zarathustra.

'What is morality?' The very question invites a simple if not simple-minded answer. But 'morality' is itself a morally loaded term which can be used to designate and applaud any number of different *ethe* and their justificatory contexts. Nietzsche famously insisted that 'there are no moral phenomena, only moral interpretations of phenomena.' I would add that there are only moral interpretations of 'morality' too. Indeed, I would even suggest that Nietzsche might mean the very opposite of what his aphorism says, that there are *only* moral phenomena, in precisely the sense that Kant denied, especially regarding the supposedly neutral word 'Morality' itself.

Areteic Ethics: Nietzsche and Aristotle

In *After Virtue*, Alasdair MacIntyre gives us a choice, *inter-alia* Nietzsche *or* Aristotle.[26] There is, he explicitly warns us, no third alternative. MacIntyre sees Nietzsche's philosophy as purely destructive, despite the fact that he praises the arch-destroyer for his insight into the collapse of morals that had been increasingly evident since the Enlightenment. MacIntyre chooses Aristotle as the positive alternative. Aristotle had an *ETHOS*; Nietzsche leaves us with nothing. But Nietzsche is nevertheless the culmination of that whole tradition – which we still refer to as 'moral philosophy' or 'ethics' – which is based on a tragic and possibly irreversible error in both theory and practice. The error is the rejection of ethos as the foundation of morality with a compensating insistence on the rational justification of morality. Without a presupposed ethos, no justification is possible. Within an ethos, none is necessary. (Nietzsche: 'not to *need* to impose values . . .') And so after centuries of degeneration, internal inconsistencies and failures in the Enlightenment project of transcending mere custom and justifying moral rules once and for all, the structures of morality have collapsed, leaving only incoherent fragments. 'Ethics' is the futile effort to make sense of the fragments and 'justify' them, from the Scot's appeal to sentiments and Kant's appeal to practical reason to the contemporary vacuity of 'meta-ethical' theory. Here is the rubble that Nietzsche's Zarathustra urges us to clear away. Here is the vacuum in which Nietzsche urges us to become 'legislators' and 'create new values.' But out of what are we to do this? What would it be, 'to create a new value'?

Macintyre, by opposing Nietzsche and Aristotle, closes off to us the basis upon which we could best reconceive morality: a reconsideration of Aristotle through Nietzschean eyes. Nietzsche, of course, encourages the antagonistic interpretation. But the opposition is ill-conceived, and the interpretation is misleading. MacIntyre, like Philippa Foot, takes Nietzsche too literally to be attacking *all* morality. But quite the contrary of rejecting the ethics of Aristotle, I see Nietzsche as harking back to Aristotle and the still warrior-bound aristocratic tradition he was (retrospectively) cataloging in his *Nicomachean* (Neo-McKeon) *Ethics*. Whatever the differences between Greece of *The Iliad* and Aristotle's Athens, there was a far vaster gulf – and not only in centuries – between the elitist ethics of Aristotle and the egalitarian, bourgeois, Pietist ethics of Kant. Nietzsche may have envisioned himself as Dionysus versus the Crucified; he is better understood as a modern-day Sophist versus Kant, a defender of the virtues against the categorical imperative.

When I was in graduate school an embarrassing number of years ago, my professor Julius Moravcsik began his lectures on Aristotle with a comparison with Nietzsche. They were two of a kind, he said, both functionalists, naturalists, 'teleologists,' standing very much opposed to the utilitarian and Kantian temperaments. Moravcsik never followed this through, to my knowledge, but his casual seminar remark has stuck with me for all of these years, and the more I read and lecture on both authors, so different in times and tempers, the more I find the comparison illuminating. Nietzsche was indeed, like Aristotle, a self-proclaimed functionalist, naturalist, teleologist, and, I would add, an elitist, though on both men's views this would follow from the rest. Nietzsche's functionalism is most evident in his constant insistence that we *evaluate* values, see what they are *for*, what role they play in the survival and life of a people. He never tires of telling us about his 'naturalism,' of course, from his flatly false declaration that he is the first philosopher who was also a psychologist (MacIntyre here substitutes sociology) to his refreshing emphasis on psychological explanation in place of rationalizing justification. Nietzsche often states this in terms of the 'this-worldly' as opposed to the 'other-worldly' visions of Christianity, but I think that this is not the contrast of importance. Indeed, today it is the very 'this-worldly' activity of some Christian power blocs that is a major ethical concern, and there is much more to naturalism (as opposed, for example, to Kant's rationalism) than the rejection of Heaven and Hell as the end of ethics. (Kant, of course, would agree with that too.)

Nietzsche's teleology is at times as cosmic as Aristotle's, especially where the grand *telos* becomes 'the will to power.' But on the strictly human (if not all-too-human) level, Nietzsche's ethics like Aristotle's can best be classified in introductory ethics readers as an ethics of 'self-realization.' 'Become who you are' is the slogan in the middle writings; the *telos* of the *Übermensch* serves from *Thus Spake Zarathustra* on. Indeed, who is the *Übermensch* if not Aristotle's *megalopsychos*, 'the great-souled man' from whom Nietzsche even borrows much of his 'master-type' terminology? He is the ideal who 'deserves and claims great things.' He is the man driven by what Goethe (the most frequent candidate for *Übermensch* status) called his 'daemon' (the association with Aristotle's '*eu-daimonia*' is not incidental).

Aristotle's teleology begins modestly, with the *telos* of the craftsman, the physician, the farmer. Each has his purpose, his own criteria for excellence, his own 'good.' But such modest goods and goals are hardly the stuff of ethics, and Aristotle quickly turns to 'the good for man,' by which he means the ideal man, and the 'function of man,' by which he means man at his best.[27] There is no point to discussing what we banally call today 'the good person,' who breaks no rules or laws, offends no one and interests no one except certain moral philosophers. There is no reason to discuss *hoi-polloi*, who serve their city-state well and honor their superiors appropriately. It is the superiors themselves who deserve description, for they are the models from whom the vision of humanity is conceived. What sort of insanity, we hear Aristotle and Nietzsche asking in unison, can explain the idea that all people are of equal value, that everyone and anyone can serve as an ideal, as a model for what is best in us? With leaders like Pericles, who needs the categorical imperative? ('What are morals to us sons of God?') With leaders like our own, no wonder we are suffocating with laws.

To reject egalitarian ethics and dismiss the banal notion of 'the good person' as no ethical interest is not to become an 'immoralist.' It does not mean breaking all the rules. It does not result in such inability as suffered by Richard Hare, a temporary incapacity to morally censure Hitler for any rational reasons.[28] Or, if we want an 'immoralist,' he might be at worst the sort of person that André Gide created in his short novel of that name, a man who senses his own mortality and luxuriates in his own bodily sensations, amused and fascinated by the foibles of people around him.[29] This is not, of course, the man whom Aristotle has in mind. The Stagirite was concerned with statesmen, philosopher-kings, the flesh and blood *Übermenschen* who actually exist, not just in novels and philosophical fantasies and Zarathustra's pronouncements. But Nietzsche too, when it comes down to cases, is concerned not with a phantom but with real life heroes, the 'great men' who justify (I use the word advisedly) the existence of the society that created them – and which they in turn created. But though he may shock us with his military language, the *Übermenschen* more near to his heart are for the most part his artistic comrades, 'philosophers, saints and arists.'[30] The rejection of bourgeois morality does not dictate cruelty but rather an emphasis on excellence. The will to power is not *Reich* but *Macht* and not supremacy but superiority. Nietzsche urges us to create values, but I believe that it is the value of creating as such – and having the strength and the *telos* to do so – that he most valued. The unspoken but always present thesis is this: it is only in the romantic practice of artistic creativity that modern excellence can be achieved.

Elitism is not itself an ethics. Indeed, I think both Aristotle and Nietzsche might well object to it as such. It is rather the presupposition that people's talents and abilities differ. It is beginning with what is the case. (Cf. John Rawls: 'It is upon a correct choice of a basic structure of society ... that justice ... depends.'[31]) The purpose of an ethics is to maximize people's potential, to encourage the most and the best from all of them, but more by far from the best of them. It is also the recognition that any universal rule – however ingeniously formulated and equally applied – will be disadvantageous to someone, coupled with the insistence that it is an enormous waste as well as unfair (both authors worry more about the former than the latter) for the strong to be limited by the weak, the productive limited by the unproductive, the creative limited by the uncreative. It will not do to mask the point by saying that elitism does not treat people unequally, only differently. It presumes inequality from the outset, and defends it by appeal to the larger picture, Aristotle by appeal to the well-being of the city-state and the natural order of things, Nietzsche by a more abstract but very modern romantic appeal to human creativity. Of course, Nietzsche refuses to be so Kantian as to appeal to 'humanity' as such, and so he appeals to a step beyond humanity – *über*-humanity. But what is the *Übermensch* but a projection of what is best in us, what Kant called 'dignity' but Nietzsche insists is 'nobility'? The difference, of course, is that Kant thought that dignity was inherent in every one of us; Nietzsche recognizes nobility in only the very few.

What is essential to this view of ethics – let us not call it elitist ethics but rather an ethics of virtue, *areteic* ethics – is that the emphasis is wholly on excellence, a teleological conception. What counts for much less is obedience of rules, laws and principles, for one can be wholly obedient and also dull, unproductive and useless. This does not mean that the 'immoralist' – as Nietzsche misleadingly calls him – will kill innocents, steal from the elderly and betray the community, nor even, indeed, run a car or a chariot through a red light. The *Übermensch* character is perfectly willing to act 'in accordance with morality,' even, in a qualified way, 'for the sake of duty,' that is, if it is a duty that fits his character and his *telos*. In a much-debated passage, Nietzsche even insists that the strong have a 'duty' to help the weak, a statement that is utterly confusing on the nihilist interpretation of Nietzsche's ethics.[32] What the *Übermensch*-aspirant does not recognize are *categorical* imperatives, commands made impersonally and universally, without respect for rank or abilities. As a system of hypothetical imperatives useful to his purposes, however, the *Übermensch* might be as moral as anyone else. (Why Philippa loves Friedrich, and how the spirit of Sils Maria finally came to Oxford.)

MacIntyre's diagnosis of our tragic fate turns on his recognition that the singular ethos upon which a unified and coherent ethics might be based has fragmented. We no longer have a culture with customs and an agreed upon system of morals; we instead have pluralism. Our insistence on tolerance and our emphasis on rules and laws are a poor substitute, more symptoms of our malaise rather than possible cures. But Nietzsche is something more than the pathologist of a dead or dying morality. He is also the champion of that sense of integrity that MacIntyre claims we have lost. The question is, how is integrity possible in a society without an ethos or, in more positive terms, in a 'pluralist' society with many *ethe*, some of them admittedly dubious? Does it make sense in such a society to still speak of 'excellence,' or should we just award 'achievement' and recognize limited accomplishments in cautiously defined sub-groups and professions? Or should we rather express the atavistic urge to excellence with an intentionally obscure phrase – 'will to power'?

Nietzsche's Problem

In Aristotle, two convening ideals made possible his powerful teleological vision: the unity of his community and the projected vision of the *telos* of man, which not incidentally coincided with the best images of his community. We no longer have that unified community – although those are not the grounds on which Nietzsche rejects bourgeois morality. (Indeed, sometimes it is the small-mindedness of small communities that he most violently reacts against.) It is not difficult to see Nietzsche's provocative ethics as precisely the expression of a rather distinctive if ill-circumscribed community, namely the community of disaffected academics and intellectuals, but this in not an ethos that Nietzsche could recognize as the basis for his rather extravagant claims for a new ethics. Nevertheless, Nietzsche, like Aristotle, held onto the vision of an overriding human *telos*, an enormous sense of human *potential*, a hunger for excellence that is ill-expressed by his monolithic expression, 'will to power.'

Depending on one's views of Aristotle (some rather priggish Oxford ethicists have called him a 'prig'), this view of Nietzsche may or may not be considered another case of Anglo-American whitewash. After all, Aristotle may have retained some of the warrior virtues, but most of his virtues are distinctively those of the good citizen, concerned with justice and friendship and getting along together. There is little of the fire and ice that Nietzsche talks about, certainly no emphasis on cruelty and suffering. Aristotle was hardly the lonely wanderer in the mountains and desert whom Nietzsche sometimes resembled and celebrated in *Zarathustra*. However aristocratic they may be, Aristotle's virtues seem too genteel, too much in the spirit of party life to be comparable to Nietzsche's severe moral strictures (cf. Zarathustra's 'party' in Part IV). It would be an unforgivable historical mistake to call Aristotle's virtues 'bourgeois,' but, nevertheless, they surely lack the cutting edge of Nietzsche's pronouncements.

The problem, however, is that Nietzsche's affirmative instructions are often without substantial content. It is all well and good to talk about the glories of solitude, but Nietzsche's own letters and friendships show us that he himself lived by his friends, defined himself in terms of them. Zarathustra, Biblical bluster aside, spends most of his time looking for friends. 'Who would want to live without them?' asked Aristotle rhetorically in his *Ethics*. Surely not Nietzsche. And he was, by all accounts, a good friend, an enthusiastic friend. And if he remained lonely, that is a matter for psychiatric, not ontological diagnosis. As for the warrior spirit, the cutting edge of cruelty, the fire and ice, there is little evidence that we have that Nietzsche either displayed or admired them, Lou's description of the glint in his eyes notwithstanding. His own list of virtues included such Aristotelean traits as honesty, courage, generosity and courtesy (*Dawn* 556).[33] And, at the end, didn't he collapse while saving a horse from a beating?

One needn't ask whether Aristotle lived up to his own virtues. But Nietzsche leaves so much unsaid, and gives us so much hyperbolically, that an *ad hominem* hint is not beside the point. One can grasp the struggle with morality that is going on in the man, so readily expressed in the murderous language of adolescence, without confusing the rhetoric with the ideals. There are different warriors for different times. Achilles suited *The Iliad*. Our warrior today is Gandhi.

Nietzsche's problem is that he sees himself as a destroyer, not a reformer or a revisionist. ('On the improvers of Mankind' in *Twilight of the Idols*, for example.[34]) He sees the Judeo-Christian tradition and the Morality that goes with it as a single historical entity, against which there is no clearly conceived alternative. Consequently, he gives us two very different prescriptions for our fate, which includes the moral collapse that has been so systematically described by MacIntyre. First, he urges us to recapture a sense of 'master' morality – which I take to mean a morality of nobility, insofar as this is possible, given two thousand intervening years of Christianity (which Nietzsche by no means sees as wholly a debilitating influence). But, as Rousseau also insisted, 'we can't go back.' The Polis Nietzsche so much admired – indeed, the war-torn pre-polis of *The Iliad* – is gone and, in the world of modern nation states, inconceivable. Democracy and socialism have rendered the aristocratic virtues unacceptable – even where these coincide exactly with the good bourgeois virtues (courtesy, for instance). The foundation is gone; equality has become an *a priori* (i.e. unchallengeable) truth. If 'Christianity is Platonism for the masses,' then democratic socialism is Christianity for the middle class.

That is on the one side – an impossible nostalgia, not unlike the American (and European) fantasy about the American West, 'where men were men' (but in fact unwashed and hungry refugees eking out a difficult living). But if there is no warrior ethos to which we can return, then what? 'The creation of values!' Nietzsche says. But what is it to 'create a value'? Not even Nietzsche suggests one – not even *one*! What he does is to remind us, again and again, of old and established values which can be used as an ethical Archimedean point, to topple the professions of a too abstract, too banal, morality that fails to promote the virtues of character. He appeals to weakness of will (not by that name) and resentment – what could be more Christian vices? He charges us with hypocrisy – the tribute that even 'immoralists' pay to virtue. He points out the cruelty of Tertullian and other Christian moralists. He chastises the Stoics for emulating wasteful nature. He attacks Spinoza for being too in love with 'his own wisdom.' He attacks Christianity as a whole as a 'slave' morality, a 'herd instinct' detrimental to the progress of the species as a whole. New values?

Ethics is an expression of an ethos. There is no such thing as 'creating new values' in Nietzsche's sense. It is not like declaring clam shells as currency and it is not, as in MacIntyre's good example, Kamehameha II of Hawaii declaring invalid 'taboos' whose function had long ago been forgotten. Nietzsche does not reject morals, only one version of Morality, which has as its instrument the universalizable principles formalized by Kant whose ancestry goes all the way back to the Bible. But, as Scheler says in defense of Christianity, the diagnosis is not complete. Indeed, it would not be wrong (as Lou Salomé observed) to see Nietzsche as an old-fashioned moralist, disgusted with the world around him but unable to provide a satisfactory account of an alternative and unable to find a context in which an alternative could be properly cultivated.

None of this is to deny that Nietzsche is, as Kaufmann calls him, a moral revolutionary, or that he has an affirmative ethics. He is indeed after something new and important, even if it is also very old and something less than the creation of new values. He is, as MacIntyre puns, after virtues, even if he would prefer to think of them in Homeric rather than Aristotelean form. And in his writings and his letters, the focus of that alternative is as discernible as the larger concept of Morality he attacks. It is Aristotle's ethics of virtue, an ethics of practice instead of an ethics of principle, an ethics in which *character*, not duty or abstract poses of universal love, plays the primary role. 'To give style to one's character. A rare art.'[35] in that one sentence, Nietzsche sums up his own ethics far better than in whole books of abuse.

One more word against Kant as a *Moralist*. A virtue must be *Our Own* invention, *Our* most necessary self-expression and self-defense; any other kind of virtue is a danger . . . 'Virtue,' 'duty,' the 'good in itself,' the good which is impersonal and universally valid – chimeras and expressions of decline, of the final exhaustion of life, of the Chinese phase of Königsberg. The fundamental laws of self-preservation and growth demand the opposite – that everyone invent *his own* virtue, his *own* categorical imperative. A people perishes when it confuses *Its* duty with duty in general . . . ANTI-Nature as instinct, German decadence as philosophy – *THAT IS KANT.*

(A11)[36]
University of Texas at Austin

Notes

1. Walter Kaufmann, *Nietzsche: Philosopher, Psychologist, Antichrist,* 4th ed., Princeton: Princeton University Press, 1974.

2. Richard Schacht, *Neitzsche*, London: Routledge and Kegan Paul, 1983.

3. David Allison, ed. *The New Nietzsche*, Columbus: Ohio University Press, 1980.

4. Lou Salomé (1882) quoted in Karl Jasper's *Nietzsche*, Tucson: University of Arizona Press, 1965, pp. 37–8 and in R. C. Solomon, ed. *Nietzsche*, New York: Doubleday, 1963, p. 8.

5. Nietzsche, *The Will to Power*, trans. and ed. by Walter Kaufmann, New York: Random House, 1968. All references are to paragraph numbers.

6. Stanley Rosen, *Nihilism*, cf. his more recent *G. W. F. Hegel: An Introduction to his Science of Wisdom*, New Haven: Yale University Press, 1974.

7. Maurice Blanchot, 'The Limits of Experience: Nihilism,' *L'Entretien infini*, reprinted in Allison, op. cit., pp. 121–8.

8. Alasdair MacIntyre, *After Virtue*, Notre Dame, IN: University of Notre Dame Press, 1981.

9. David Hume, *A Treatise of Human Nature*, Oxford: Oxford University Press, 1978. Book II, esp. pp. 297ff.

10. G. W. F. Hegel, *The Phenomenology of Spirit*, trans. A. V. Miller, Oxford: Oxford University Press, 1977. See esp. paras. 559–62 and Hegel's attack on the Enlightenment emphasis on 'the Useful' ('an abomination' and 'utterly detestable').

11. Nietzsche, *Twilight of the Idols*, trans. Kaufmann in *The Viking Portable Nietzsche*, New York: Viking, 1954, pp. 473–9 and 479–84.

12. See, for example, G. E. M. Anscombe in *Intention*, Oxford: Oxford University Press, 1957, esp. pp. 58–66, and John Cooper's rebuttal in his *Aristotle*.

13. E.g. William Frankena, *Ethics*, 2nd ed., Englewood Cliffs, N.J.: Prentice-Hall, 1973, 62–7.

14. The delightful use of this example is in MacIntyre, op. cit., contrasting descriptive reports of practices with prescriptive rules.

15. Immanuel Kant, *Grounding for the Metaphysics of Morals*, Indianapolis: Hackett, 1983, part 1, p. 7.

16. Ibid, p.12.

17. E.g.

At first, I approached the modern world . . . *hopefully*. I understood . . . the philosophical pessimism of the nineteenth century as if it were the symptom of a greater strength of thought, of more daring courage, and of a more triumphant *fullness* of life . . . What is romanticism? Every art and every philosophy may be considered a remedy and aid in the service of growing and struggling life, but there are two kinds of sufferers: first those who suffer from an *overfullness of life* . . . and then there are those who suffer from the *impoverishment of life* . . . To this dual need of the *latter* corresponds all romanticism . . .

The will to *eternalize* also requires a dual interpretation. First, it can come from gratitude and love . . . But it can also be that tyrannic will (i.e. *ressentiment*) of one who is seriously ailing, struggling, and tortured . . .

(*Gay Science*, 370)

Cf. Novalis: 'The world must be made more romantic. Then once more we shall discover its original meaning. To make something romantic . . . the lower self becomes identified with the higher self.'

18. G. W. F. Hegel, *The Life of Jesus* (1975), trans. by Peter Fuss, Notre Dame: University of Notre Dame Press, 1984.

19. Kant, op. cit., p. 12.

20. Kant, op. cit. and the second *Critique*, trans. L. W. Beck, Indianapolis: Bobbs-Merrill, 1956.

21. Nietzsche, *Beyond Good and Evil*, trans. Kaufmann, New York: Random House, 1966. All references are to paragraph numbers.

22. Hegel, *System der Sittlichkeit* (1802) and *The Phenomenology*, Part C (AA), Chapter VI ('Spirit'), esp. paras. 439–50.

23. Karl Popper, *The Open Society and its Enemies*, London: Routledge and Kegan Paul, 1954. W. H. Walsh, *Hegal's Ethics*, New York: St. Martin's, 1969.

24. Edward O. Wilson toys with this argument, for example, in the infamous 27th chapter of his *Sociobiology*, Cambridge: Harvard University Press, 1978.

25. Philippa Foot, 'Nietzsche: The Revaluation of Values,' in Solomon, ed. op. cit., pp. 156–68.

26. MacIntyre, op. cit., pp. 103ff.

27. Aristotle, *Nicomachean Ethics*, trans. H. Rackham, Cambridge, Mass.: Harvard University Press, 1946, Bk. I, Ch. ii.

28. Richard Hare, *Freedom and Reason*, Oxford: Clarendon, 1963, e.g., p. 172.

29. André Gide, *The Immoralist*, New York: Vintage, 1954.

30. Alexander Nehamas has completed one long-needed bit of empirical research in this regard: in *Beyond Good and Evil*, he has found that better than three quarters of the candidates for *Übermensch* are writers. See his forthcoming *Nietzsche: Life as Literature*, Harvard University Press (unpublished at the time of this writing).

31. John Rawls, *A Theory of Justice*, Cambridge: Harvard University Press, 1971.

32. 'When the exceptional human being treats the mediocre more tenderly than himself and his peers, this is not mere courtesy of the heart – it is simply his duty.' Nietzsche, *The Antichrist*, trans. Walter Kaufmann in *The Viking Portable Nietzsche*, New York: Viking, 1954, para. 57.

33. Nietzsche, *Dawn*, trans. Cambridge: Cambridge University Press, 1983. References are to paragraph numbers.

34. Nietzsche, *Twilight of the Idols*, trans. Kaufmann in *The Viking Portable Nietzsche*, op. cit.

35. Nietzsche, *The Gay Science*, trans. Kaufmann, New York: Random House. 1974, para. 290.

36. *The Antichrist*, op. cit.

58

Nietzsche and Heidegger*

Gianni Vattimo

Translated by Thomas Harrison

*Source: Thomas Harrison (ed.) *Nietzsche in Italy*, Anma Libri, 1988, pp. 19–29.

To raise once more the question of the relationship between Heidegger and Nietzsche is not to engage in philological analysis of a topic already amply investigated by both Nietzscheans and Heideggerians. Rather, it is to discuss a problem which, at least in continental European philosophy, constitutes a central theme or – in my opinion – *the* central theme of contemporary philosophical debate.

One could start with an uncontroversial fact: a great part of continental philosophy of the last twenty-five years – to select a chronological limit – has developed in relation to two issues: the meaning of Nietzsche's thought, the study and philological investigation of which is renewed around the beginning of the Sixties,[1] and the philosophy of the 'second' Heidegger, which also becomes an important issue toward the end of the Fifties.[2] The fortune of the second Heidegger and the Nietzsche renaissance are two philosophical events that coincide more than chronologically. It is well-known that a dominant factor of the Nietzsche renaissance was precisely the publication of Heidegger's two volumes on Nietzsche, collections of his university courses and other writings of the years 1935–46.[3] Heidegger's interest in Nietzsche is not simply one aspect among others in his recollection of the history of metaphysics. Nietzsche is for him a counter comparable in importance only to the Presocratics or maybe Hölderlin. Although the Nietzsche renaissance is also related to philological studies independent of the interpretive issues raised by Heidegger (the work of Colli and Montinari in the critical edition remains extrinsic to Heideggerian discussions, even where it confronts the task of a philosophical 'commentary' on Nietzsche's works), it is largely interwoven with the fortune of the philosophy of the second Heidegger. Whoever reads Nietzsche cannot help coming to terms with Heidegger's interpretation and thus encounters (it happened even to me, precisely at the beginning of the Sixties) the necessity of retracing his entire philosophical itinerary; for Nietzsche is not, as it was once thought, just a historiographical 'theme' of marginal concern to Heidegger.

At the same time Heidegger scholars find themselves going back to Nietzsche's texts precisely on account of the decisive importance that Heidegger assigns to them in the history of metaphysics. There thus develops in much recent European philosophy a to and fro movement between Heidegger and Nietzsche which – and this will be my thesis – is not limited, as one might expect, to understanding Nietzsche by means of the interpretive work of Heidegger. There is also an opposite movement: far beyond the explicit theses proposed by Heidegger in his interpretation of Nietzsche, the significance of Heidegger's philosophy itself tends to be approached through Nietzsche. One may thus speak not only of Heidegger as an interpreter of Nietzsche but also of Nietzsche as an interpreter of Heidegger. In the status of interpreter and not only of interpreted text, Nietzsche does not at all coincide with the image of him proposed by Heidegger's work. Thus arises a paradoxical, though very diffused, situation, especially in Italy and France. Many Heideggerians read Nietzsche in a Heideggerian perspective, but in one which does not accept, or only partially accepts, the explicit claims of Heidegger about Nietzsche. I would like to show that this is not the consequence of an incomplete or fragmented knowledge of Heidegger on the part of his interpreters, but rather this: that, to be faithful to Heidegger's most authentic intentions, one must to some extent 'betray' his reading of Nietzsche.

Testimony to this thesis is the fact – which I do not intend to document here analytically – that in much contemporary Heideggerianism the name of Nietzsche does not stand as one of the authors of the metaphysical tradition which we must try to overcome (as would be the case with Descartes and Hegel). The name rather indicates a thinker who, like Heidegger, is already on a philosophical path that has left metaphysics behind it. It is obvious that this 'privileged' position of Nietzsche is partially predicted by Heidegger himself, who, seeing his predecessor as the last metaphysical thinker, the one in whom the oblivion of being reaches its culmination, locates him also at a turning point: 'Where danger grows,' in Hölderlin's verse so often cited by Heidegger, 'there also grows the saving power.' Yet without doubt Heidegger considers Nietzsche to be very distant from himself in the degree to which Nietzsche still belongs to the history of metaphysics and theorizes being as will to power. Now, it is precisely this distance between Heidegger and Nietzsche which tends to disappear in much contemporary Heideggerian thinking.

This is the case even with an author like Hans-Georg Gadamer, in whose work the Heideggerian thematic of overcoming metaphysics nevertheless has a very limited development. In a subtle and central passage of *Truth and Method*[4] dealing with the significance of the Heideggerian renovation of the question of being, Gadamer speaks of Nietzsche as a precursor of Heidegger, in preference to Dilthey and Husserl. Remaining within the context of 'classical' interpreters of Heidegger – those of the first Heideggerian generation – one may reasonably hypothesize that even Karl Löwith thinks of Heidegger and Nietzsche as substantially parallel, or as moved by the same intentions. It is notable that Löwith interprets the Heideggerian *Kehre*, or turn, of the Thirties as an essentially political concession without real theoretical reasons. But when he describes Nietzsche as one who tries to recuperate a Greek vision of being at the apex of modernity, and who fails in the attempt, is he not also describing, in theoretical and not merely political terms, Heidegger's effort to overcome metaphysics, an effort which strikes Löwith as unsuccessful? Löwith's position is quite particular and does not completely enter the frame of our discourse, for one cannot really describe him as a Heideggerian – even if, in light of the hypothesis I have proposed, one might rethink this issue too. It is nevertheless true that the closeness of Heidegger and Nietzsche is more or less presupposed by all contemporary hermeneutics, that is, by that philosophy which presents itself as a development of Heidegger's thought and which, on this specific issue of the interpretation of Nietzsche, removes itself from many of its master's conclusions.

I do not want to discuss here whether, and to what extent, authors like Foucault, Derrida, and Rorty enter this hermeneutic frame. But in all of them, more or less explicitly, one can trace a vision of Nietzsche in which he is interpreted as essentially continuous with Heidegger, much more so than Heidegger was disposed to admit. In fact, one could describe Foucault's thinking as a culmination or 'synthesis' of Nietzsche and Heidegger, realized from a prevalently Nietzschean point of view, which nevertheless leaves too little space to the ontological intentions of Heidegger. To a certain extent one can say the same of the image of Nietzsche and Heidegger in the work of Derrida and his disciples (Sarah Kofman and Bernard Pautrat), and even earlier in Deleuze. The separation between Heidegger and Nietzsche is never accentuated. Both, in different ways and degrees, are counted among the thinkers who indicated a path of thought beyond metaphysics.

Even the return to Nietzsche in Italian philosophy in the last decades has occurred in relation to Heidegger. The problem of technology has a central bearing here. Even and above all as 'thinkers of technology,' Nietzsche and Heidegger have appeared to be in substantial agreement (I am thinking of the work of Massimo Cacciari, but also of Emanuele Severino, even if it is in polemic with Heidegger, considering as it does – with good reasons, as we will see further on – both Nietzsche and Heidegger to belong to the same nihilistic perpective).

The thinkers I have referred to here are examples of a fact which seems to be generally visible in continental thought of recent years. This thought develops on the basis of a privileged reference to Nietzsche and Heidegger. And even when it presents itself as a development of Heidegger's philosophy, it does not 'take seriously' all the implications of the Heideggerian interpretation of Nietzsche. Rather, it sees between Heidegger and Nietzsche a continuity that contrasts with the explicit interpretation of Nietzsche given by the works of Heidegger. I propose to consider this paradox as a significant theoretical problem, and will attempt to clarify why one may (and in my opinion must) be Heideggerian without following Heidegger's interpretation of Nietzsche. On the contrary, I will conclude that one can follow the deepest intentions of Heidegger's thought only by describing his relation with Nietzsche in terms that are different from the ones in which he himself described it.

The shift that Heidegger effected on interpretations of Nietzsche, especially with his ample studies published in 1961, consisted in the proposal to read Nietzsche in relation to Aristotle – that is, as a thinker whose central theme was being, a metaphysical thinker and not simply a moralist, 'psychologist,' or 'critic of culture.'[5] On the basis of this interpretive decision Heidegger gave preferential treatment to Nietzsche's later writings, especially to the notes which were initially to serve for the *Will to Power*, and tended to leave aside much of Nietzsche's more 'essayistic' production: works like *Human, All Too Human, Daybreak*, and *The Gay Science*. These, together with aphoristic works of the late period such as *Beyond Good and Evil* and Zarathustra's 'poem,' were the ones which had determined the prevailing conception of Nietzsche during the first decades of the century, that conception which Dilthey in his brief *Essence of Philosophy* (1907) summarized by placing Nietzsche next to 'philosophical writers' like Carlyle, Emerson, Ruskin, Tolstoy, and Maeterlinck. Dilthey saw these figures as emblematic of a situation in which philosophy, once the great epoch of metaphysics was over, tended to become *Lebensphilosophie* – not in that sense of 'vitalistic metaphysics' which the word now has for us, but in the sense of a reflection on existence which no longer aims at demonstrative cogency but rather assumes the characteristics of subjective expression, of poetry and literature.[6]

Dilthey's description of Nietzsche is on many counts radically opposed to Heidegger's. But on one fundamental point the two readers agree. Both Dilthey and Heidegger consider the character of Nietzsche's philosophy to be determined by its place at the end of metaphysics. For Dilthey, then, this 'final' or epigonic position translates into the fact that what becomes dominant in Nietzsche is a literary – though more amply we might say 'essayistic' or 'cultural-critical' – approach to philosophical problems. For Heidegger, on the other hand, to see Nietzsche in relation to the history of metaphysics means to seek his work above all for theses and statements on the great themes of traditional metaphysics – being, God, freedom, the subject, and so on. Here Dilthey appears to be more radical and coherent than Heidegger. If Nietzsche is at the end of metaphysics, this means not only that he sees being and other metaphysical 'objects' in a different way than Plato and Descartes but also that the *shape* of his thought is different. In other words, Dilthey sees more clearly than Heidegger that Nietzsche's 'metaphysics' must be sought precisely in those pages which seemed to be most characteristic and meaningful to his earliest readers, in his 'psychological' and 'cultural-critical' pages.

Although this reading does not at all contradict Heideggerian theses, Heidegger did not develop it. In him there ever remains a hiatus between the truly metaphysical themes of Nietzsche – nihilism, will to power, eternal return, the overman, justice, according to the list of *Leitworte* which he traces in Nietzsche's work – and Nietzsche's critique of morality, religion, the individual, etc.

Why does Heidegger not unify these two aspects of the final thinker of metaphysics? A plausible motive might be sought in the diffidence that Heidegger felt, with good reason, for the 'philosophy of culture' of neo-Kantian vein (such as that of Cassirer or Dilthey himself) and for the Hegelian-Marxist 'critique of ideology.' But it is hard to remain satisfied with this explanation, especially if one considers that, at least in a certain sense, what Dilthey says about Nietzsche can be perfectly well applied to Heidegger's own style of thought. The closeness of philosophy and literature, the articulation of philosophical discourse in a rhythm more 'edifying' than demonstrated or scientific, and the identification of philosophy with a reflection on the history of culture (which Heidegger equates with the history and destiny of being) are all traits which Heidegger shares with Nietzsche. They are those that Dilthey describes as belonging to *Lebensphilosophie* – even if he considers this to involve a subjectivist and impressionist thinking, in so far as Dilthey continues to cultivate the dream of a 'rigorous' philosophy as the heritage of the 'critical,' Kantian form of metaphysics, conceived as a 'transcendental psychology' or a typology of *Weltanschauungen*. But once this metaphysical dream is removed, as it is in Heidegger, Nietzsche's *Lebensphilosophie* is not so distant from the 'thought of being' which Heidegger takes upon himself.

I mean to say that if we consider the different way in which the description of Nietzsche as the final thinker of metaphysics is articulated in Dilthey and Heidegger we find that Heidegger tends not to see the tie between Nietzsche the metaphysician and Nietzsche the 'culture critic,' for this tie, once recognized, would oblige him to recognize his own closeness to Nietzsche. This closeness is what contemporary Heideggerianism perceives at length, even if it has not turned it into an explicit theme of discussion.

What, indeed, does it mean that Nietzsche's ontology is inextricably tied to his genealogical reconsideration of the history of morals, religion, and the European conscience, that is, with his 'archaeology of knowledge'? This archaeology has nothing to do with a 'critique of ideology,' that is, with a thinking that presumes to unmask the 'human, all too human' lies of metaphysics – of systems of values, institutions, and artistic practices – in order finally to lead them back to an authentic foundation. Facing the erring of past culture and its metaphysical pretensions, Nietzsche does not practice this still metaphysical unmasking precisely insofar as he also unmasks the idea of truth, of a 'foundation' on which one may finally 'stand.' Nietzsche's archaeology celebrates instead, in the face of metaphysics, 'festivals of memory,'[7] retracing the history of such erring as the 'history of being.' From *Human,*

All Too Human on,[8] Nietzsche is aware that to unveil the 'becoming' and the interests that lie at the bottom of whatever is presented as truth, value, and 'eternal' beauty does not mean to abolish these things but to discover once and for all that they are the only 'substance' available to us, the only contexts within which our experience of the world can acquire significance. This is what he calls the 'necessity of error,' and which aphorism #54 of *The Gay Science* defines as 'the universality of dreaming and the mutual comprehension of all dreamers . . . thus also *the continuation of the dream.*' The being of which metaphysics has always spoken is an 'error'; but error – the symbolic forms produced by cultures in the course of time – is the only being there is, and we *are* only insofar as we exist in relation to all this.

Is the Heidegger who conceived of post-metaphysical thinking as *An-denken*, as rememoration and metaphysical retracing, so distant from this Nietzsche of the 'festivals of memory'? The two thinkers are actually quite similar, linked by their conception of being not as structure and *Grund* but as *event*. If Heidegger is unaware of this closeness it is because he refuses to accept and articulate explicitly the nihilistic implications of the meaning of being. As for Nietzsche, for him, too, thinking is *An-denken*, and not representation or foundation, for *there is no other being* than the historico-destinational clearings in which types of historical human beings experience the world. And the fact that these historico-destinational clearings are not manifestations of an eternal structure but events does not condemn them to abolition; on the contrary, it confers on them the dignity that metaphysics conferred on stable and eternal being, as in Nietzsche's 'festivals of memory.'

Between the two thinkers is thus established an intricate relationship, not on the level of philosophical historiography understood in the *historisch* sense, but on the level of a *geschichtlich* reply to their appeal. Heidegger is determinant in attributing meaning to Nietzsche's thought – a meaning which philosophical historiography, precisely on the *historisch* level of the reconstruction of texts and their connections, has difficulty determining, especially if one considers the almost irresolvable contradictions arising around concepts like the eternal return, will to power, *Übermensch*, active and reactive nihilism, and so on. Heidegger does not furnish instruments for reconciling these contradictions, either on a logical level or on the 'psychological' level sometimes preferred by Nietzsche criticism (Nietzsche's 'madness'). However, he does furnish a frame within which all these concepts acquire significance as aspects of the history of being in the epoch of the end of metaphysics.

To give just one example: the almost unthinkable concept of the eternal return of the same becomes much less inconceivable if one sees it as a description of the 'ahistorical' temporality of the technical world, of the *Ge-stell* in which metaphysics accomplishes itself as a total organization of the world, excluding historicity as unplanned and undominated novelty. Whatever philological problems remain still open and perhaps insoluble for the historiographical reconstruction of Nietzsche's thought, the fact is that they become significant for us, that is, capable of speaking productively in the actual philosophical situation, only – or almost only – thanks to Heidegger. Concepts like will to power, eternal return, and *Übermensch* acquire significance as *ways in which being is given* at the end of metaphysics, whereas they appear full of insoluble contradictions if one considers them to be metaphysical descriptions of a being given 'out there.' On this level of a still metaphysical descriptivity remains that interpretation of Nietzsche limited to seeing his philosophy as an 'unveiling' of the *fact* that being is will to power and consequently proposing a morality of power and strife (the 'fascist' reading of Nietzsche, though there are traces of a similar interpretation in Foucault).

While Heidegger lends significance to Nietzsche as a philosopher of the end of metaphysics, the analogy between the Nietzschean 'festivals of memory' and the Heideggerian *An-denken* also alerts us to the fact that Nietzsche himself lends Heideggerian 'being' its authentic meaning. What, indeed, does it mean when Heidegger says that being (if one can speak of it) is eventual? Does it perhaps mean no more than what Reiner Schürmann calls the 'principle of anarchy'?[9] According to Schürmann this expression defines the outcome of Heidegger's destruction of the history of metaphysics, in which he reveals that everything which has presented itself in the history of thought as *archē*, *Grund*, or foundation supporting and dominating a culture (we may also think of Foucault's *epistemai*) is nothing but 'position' and event. What, however, is the result of this thesis? It might be the pure and simple recognition that every *archē* is merely the result of a play of forces, only will to power, in which case we return to the 'unmasking' Nietzsche that Heidegger would be taking literally. If we try to avoid this conclusion, however, as Schürmann seems to do, then the risk is one of thinking that, once we have discovered that *archai* are events, what becomes possible is another and alternative access to being than that which has been practiced by metaphysics. However, in this case, the overcoming of the metaphysical conception of *archai* would lead to a type of negative or mystical theology deluding itself with the possibility of somehow gathering being in its difference and irreducibility with respect to the principles and foundations imagined by past philosophy. The risk is not entirely absent from Schürmann's work, seeming as it does to oscillate between a Foucaultian outcome (the *epistemai* as pure effects of a play of forces) and a 'mystical' outcome. Of course, the latter is largely authorized by Heidegger himself, in the degree to which, next to the 'description' of being in terms of event, in his texts there is also always an aspiration to a situation in which being might once more speak to us 'in person.'[10] Nevertheless, what is hidden here is a possible self-misunderstanding on Heidegger's part. If, going *beyond* its events (the *archai* which have dominated metaphysics time and again, *je und je*), we are supposed to accede in some way to being, even if not foundationally – then the enterprise of overcoming metaphysics ends in a new metaphysics, in a new 'representation' or conception (*Begriff*) of being.

But the *An-denken* to which Heidegger has called our attention cannot be conceived as a rememoration which 'recuperates' being as something we can encounter face to face. Rememoration remembers being as that which it can *only* remember and never re-present. This is to say, as Heidegger often does, that the event *of* being is to be understood not only in the subjective sense of the genitive (the *archai* and epochs as events belonging to being, and not only as occurrences of entities), but also, inseparably, in the objective sense (being as nothing more than its events). This means that being is never thinkable as some stable structure which metaphysics has simply forgotten and which we must rediscover. This, thought through to the end, is what I think must be called Heidegger's 'nihilism.' The overcoming of metaphysics can be realized only in the degree to which, as Heidegger writes of Nietzschean nihilism, 'nothing is left of being as such.'[11] *The overcoming of metaphysics is not the overturning of the metaphysical oblivion of being; it is this very oblivion (nihilism) taken to its extreme consequences.* If he does not want to find himself thinking being as *archē*, *Grund*, or stable structure, Heidegger cannot escape this conclusion.

If Heidegger confers meaning on Nietzsche by demonstrating that the will to power is 'the destiny of being' (and not a pure play of forces unmasked through a critique of ideology), Nietzsche gives meaning to Heidegger by clarifying that the destiny of being (thought unmetaphysically) is nihilism. That is, being takes leave of its metaphysical configuration not (simply) by revealing the *archai* as masks, or events, but by *giving itself* in the form of that which *is not* but *has* (always already) *been*, and which holds sway only as memory, in a faded and weakened form. To this destiny of the weakening of being – which dissolves the authoritative and essentially violent form in which the 'foundation' has always presented itself – belongs the nexus, so important in the first and second Heidegger, between the event of being and human mortality. The historico-destination clearings in which things come to being are epochal and not 'eternal,') simply because the generations or 'Daseins' through which and for which they come to light are not eternal. To it belongs also the process of dissolution which Nietzsche describes in *Twilight of the Idols* in the chapter entitled 'How the Real World at Last Became a Fable' – the dissolution, that is, of the *archai* and the presumed objectivities characteristic of the development of Western philosophy. This being which 'evaporates,' as Nietzsche writes in a passage often quoted by Heidegger, is not only a false image of being which should be substituted by a more solid and truer one. It is precisely that being which, after Nietzsche, in post-metaphysical thinking, can 'unveil itself' as not identifiable with the object, the *archē*, or foundation – but with the 'mittance' to which thought corresponds *An-denken* and 'festivals of memory.'

Notes

1. These are the years in which the Colli and Montinari edition of Nietzsche's works begins to be published, first in Italian (Milan: Adelphi, 1963ff.).

2. *Holzwege* was published in 1950 (Frankfurt am Main: Klostermann), *Vorträge und Aufsätze* in 1954 (Pfullingen: Neske), *Unterwegs zur Sprache* in 1959 (Pfullingen: Neske).

3. Martin Heidegger, *Nietzsche*, 2 vols. (Pfullingen: Neske, 1961). The English edition, translated by David Farell Krell and published by Harper & Row, New York, is organized as follows: *Nietzsche 1: The Will to Power as Art* (1979), *Nietzsche 4: Nihilism* (1982), *Nietzsche 2: The Eternal Recurrence of the Same* (1984), *Nietzsche 3: Will to Power as Knowledge and as Metaphysics* (1987).

4. Hans-Georg Gadamer, *Truth and Method*, tr. Garrett Barden and John Cumming (New York: Continuum, 1975) 228.

5. Martin Heidegger, *Nietzsche 1: The Will to Power as Art* 65ff.

6. See, for instance, the chapter entitled 'The Connecting Links Between Philosophy and Religion, Prose and Poetry,' in Wilhelm Dilthey, *The Essence of Philosophy*, tr. Stephen A. Emery and William T. Emery (Chapel Hill: University of North Carolina Press, 1954) 27–33.

7. Friedrich Nietzsche, *Human, All Too Human: A Book for Free Spirits*, tr. Marion Faber (Lincoln: University of Nebraska Press, 1984), aphorism 223.

8. See the whole first section of *Human, All Too Human*, especially the concluding aphorism 34.

9. Reiner Schürmann, *Le Principe d'anarchie: Heidegger et la question de l'agir* (Paris: Seuil, 1982).

10. I am thinking of the concluding pages of the lecture, 'Time and Being,' in Martin Heidegger, *On Time and Being*, tr. Joan Stambaugh (New York: Harper & Row, 1972) 1–24.

11. *Nietzsche 4: Nihilism* 200.